Once Upon the Permafrost

Critical Green Engagements

Investigating the Green Economy and Its Alternatives

Jim Igoe, Melissa Checker, Molly Doane, Tracey Heatherington, José E. Martínez-Reyes, and Mary Mostafanezhad
SERIES EDITORS

Once Upon the
Permafrost

Knowing Culture and
Climate Change
in Siberia

Susan Alexandra Crate

THE UNIVERSITY OF
ARIZONA PRESS
TUCSON

The University of Arizona Press
www.uapress.arizona.edu

We respectfully acknowledge the University of Arizona is on the land and territories of Indigenous peoples. Today, Arizona is home to twenty-two federally recognized tribes, with Tucson being home to the O'odham and the Yaqui. Committed to diversity and inclusion, the University strives to build sustainable relationships with sovereign Native Nations and Indigenous communities through education offerings, partnerships, and community service.

ISBN-13: 978-0-8165-4155-3 (hardcover)
ISBN-13: 978-0-8165-4154-6 (paperback)

Cover design by Leigh McDonald
Cover art: A 2018 refrigerator magnet featuring *Jyl Oghuha*. Photo by author.
Typeset by Sara Thaxton in 10/14 Warnock Pro with Baskerville URW and Trade Gothic Next LT

Publication of this book is made possible in part by the proceeds of a permanent endowment created with the assistance of a Challenge Grant from the National Endowment for the Humanities, a federal agency.

Library of Congress Cataloging-in-Publication Data are available at the Library of Congress.

Printed in the United States of America
♾ This paper meets the requirements of ANSI/NISO Z39.48-1992 (Permanence of Paper).

for Tuyaara

Contents

Illustrations

Maps

Notes on Transliteration and Transcription

Throughout this text, Sakha words are transliterated and in *italics* and Russian words are transliterated and are *italicized and underlined*. Both are transliterated according to a modified version of the American Library Association–Library of Congress (ALA-LC) system for Cyrillic. Ties are not used over these letters: ц (t͡s) = "ts"; ю (i͡u) = "iu"; я (i͡a) = "ia." Glyphs are not written over й (ĭ) but written "i" or over ė, which is the transliteration of э, so it is written "e." Further, in personal names and at the beginning of words ю (iu) is written "yu" and я (ia) is written "ya." Additionally, inhabitants' and collaborators' names discussed in the text and cited for their quotes are spelled phonetically for readability.

Additionally, the seven letters of the Sakha language not present in Russian are written accordingly:

Ҕ = gh; Дь = j; Ҥ = ng; Нь = n'; Ɵ = ö; Һ = h; Ү = ü

I realize that the combination Дь is often transliterated as "d'" as in *D'yl Oghuha*. However, considering that the Sakha language was first written using the Latin alphabet and that Дь was the cyrillization of Sakha's letter "J," I have taken the liberty of using "J" to express the original intended sound.

In cases where a word is used extensively in Western sources in a spelling other than Library of Congress, I use the established English spelling; for example, I use Yakutsk rather than Iakutsk. This applies to both Sakha and Russian place-names, which follow the transcription of the US Board of Geographic Names with the addition of Sakha letters as needed. I include eleven maps in the text. The first, map 1, is a close-up of the study area with named locations demarcated. Map 2 is of the entire Sakha Republic and includes the major and minor settlements mentioned in the text and the location of the study area. Additionally, people's names are transliterated according to ALA-LC but with elements retained to preserve pronunciation, for example, Зоя Еремеева, is transliterated as Zoya Yeremeyeva and not Zoia Eremeeva. I include a glossary of all foreign words in the back matter. I define each foreign word the first time it appears in the text in parentheses. All translations are mine, and the more complex meanings have been verified by linguist extraordinaire Prokopii Mitrofanovich Yegorov. In transcriptions, I use three spaced dots (. . .) to indicate a pause.

Preface

I was looking out the plane window at the flat-as-a-pancake landscape below me that continued in every direction. Two hours before, I had taken off from Ulan Ude, capital of the Buryat Republic in southern Siberia. It was a crystal-clear morning, and as the plane ascended to head north, I had a spectacular view of Lake Baikal, nestled between the Primorsky range to the west and the Baikalsky mountains to the north. Lake Baikal was what first drew me to Siberia in 1989. Who wouldn't be drawn to the oldest, deepest lake in the world, holding one-fifth of the planet's fresh free-flowing water? Once I got to Baikal, I discovered the dramatic mountains and steppe landscapes surrounding the mighty lake. I spent the three summers, from 1989 to 1991, studying Buryat, Mongolian, and Tuvan folklore and interpreting for environmental projects in and around Baikal. With this flight north, I suddenly found myself in terra incognita, the flatlands of Siberia. My only consolation was I knew I'd be back in the Baikal mountains in two weeks. I was headed to Yakutsk, capital of the Sakha Republic, to attend the 1991 International Jew's Harp Conference. Honestly, I was hesitant when I received the tele-grammed invitation to the conference a month earlier. I had heard the Jew's harp played at North Carolina fiddlers' conventions. The idea of a week of listening to them was disconcerting. But I decided to have an open mind. Now I was on my way.

It turned out that the Jew's harp conference was actually quite amazing. The instrument is in the "plucked idiophone" family, classified as those that make a sound without the use of strings, membranes, or being blown into. Plucked idiophones are found in more countries than any other family of musical instruments. A lot of varieties of the Jew's harp were on display that week. Three women from Japan played bamboo harps, participants from Tuva made melodies on two-inch-long harps, and most breathtaking for me, a woman from Karakalpakstan, an autonomous region in Uzbekistan, played a half-inch-long harp, first in front of her mouth and then inside her mouth hands free. Midweek was the time of the *yhyakh* (Sakha's summer festival). Conference participants were flown to different regions to take part. I was sent to Viliuisk. I learned that the festival was held around the summer solstice, just before hay cutting and primarily to make a request to the sky deities for the best summer conditions to produce good harvests. The festival was transformative. Despite Soviet-period atheism, *yhyakh* had retained a lot of its sacred spiritual aspects. I had attended multiple festivals in Buryatia, Tuva, and Mongolia, all of which had been reduced to sports gatherings and lacked sacred elements of any form. The most powerful part of *yhyakh* for me was *ohuokhai*, Sakha's circle dance fueled by improvisatory call-and-response singing. I joined the circle and spent hours immersed in the language and dance. I was hypnotized. Something otherworldly was going on. Despite not knowing the Sakha language, I felt the power of the lead singers' words. I wanted to know more. Before leaving Yakutsk, I proposed to study the *yhyakh* for my master's thesis in folklore. I left with an invitation from the minister of culture to return in 1992. That same summer, and a short three weeks after I arrived back in the States, the Soviet coup happened, the end of the USSR. In and amid all the resulting changes, the *yhyakh* took on new meanings of identity and ethnic solidarity for Sakha.

In March 1992, I returned to Yakutsk to conduct archival research, interview festival specialists, and plan my summer field research trip. The latter came together unexpectedly. As part of immersing myself in all things *yhyakh*, I attended a *kylyhakh* (Sakha throat singing) demonstration for culture workers from different regions of the republic, led by the renowned actor Afanasii Semenovich Fedorov. Midway through the class, Afanasii announced that there was an American folklorist present who wanted to study the *yhyakh* in the Suntaar region and would anyone volunteer to host her. A hand immediately shot up, "*Min yngyrabyn, min yngyrabyn!*" (I will invite, I will invite). A young, willowy woman, perhaps twenty-five at the most, had volunteered. We spoke after the class. She lived in Elgeeii, just north of the Suntaar regional center on the Viliui River. We exchanged contact information and I was set.

I arrived at Elgeeii in early May in a *tramvai*, a river boat seating about thirty passengers that transited daily between the regional centers of Nyurba and Suntaar. It was dark and raining. The head of the village met me on the shore and led me to a house just a hundred feet away from the *tramvai* stop, where I met Elvira a second time, along with her grandmother, *Ebe* Marina, her cousin Galina, her husband, Anatoli, and son Toli. *Ebe* Marina was blind but nonetheless greeted me with a warm hearty handshake, then went to get bread for our meal, singing, "*Sarsyn, sarsyn, sarsyarda*," ("Tomorrow" but literally "Tomorrow, tomorrow, [in the] morning") a classic *toiuk* (improvised song) by the renowned Sergei Zverov.

In the weeks leading up to the festival, Elvira arranged interviews with people knowledgeable about the *yhyakh* and helped me make a plan for attending the event in both large and small settlements. I was quickly regarded as "The American," with some commenting that the last time an Anglophone did research in the Viliui regions was Kate Marsden, a British missionary who came to find a cure for Viliusk encephalomyelitis in the late 1800s. The interviews took us all across the western part of the Suntaar *uluus* (region). One trip I remember distinctly was traveling to Kutana. At that time, in 1992, roads were still the "old-fashioned" kind, meaning they were not built up and fortified to withstand spring floods and other seasonal predicaments. Halfway to Kutana, we came to an impassable puddle in the road. We tried to go around it with no luck. An hour later we heard a distant rumbling sound growing louder and louder. It was our Kutana host driving a Soviet-period tractor, the kind with tank treads, moving ever so slowly toward us. It continued through the puddle, with water almost reaching the driver's cabin in the deepest part. Without hesitation, Elvira climbed on the back, pulled me up, and off we went. This was just one of many out-of-the-ordinary adventures I have in my memory. All in all, that summer I interviewed some seventy people and attended five *yhyakh* festivals, thanks to Elvira and countless others who helped me. At the Elgeeii *yhyakh* I won the stick pull and arm-wrestling contest and won a calf.

I went home with more than sufficient material to show how *yhyakh* began, how it changed over time, and how it had transformed after the fall of the USSR. I also went home with a new objective. I needed to learn Sakha. In the field that summer my lingua franca was Russian. But most of the elders

Figure 1 *Ebe* Marina with Toli and my prize calf,
Chyychaakh (little bird). 1992. Photo by author.

I interviewed about the *yhyakh* did not know Russian. Wherever we went, I had a translator to assist me, usually the Russian or English teacher of the immediate village where I was interviewing. However, too many times I was told, "It does not translate into Russian." Although it was frustrating, it also made sense. The *yhyakh*, and for that matter the Sakha people, had been around for centuries before the seventeenth-century Russian colonization of Siberia. *Yhyakh* was founded upon Sakha's worldview and cosmology. Sometimes a single word in Sakha requires an entire sentence in Russian to define. I craved to know the language. I wanted to understand my interviews and the *ohuokhai* singing in their full richness (luckily, I had recorded both). I wanted to be able to cognize interactions and events myself.

Something else hits me when I now contemplate my thirst for the language at the time. Just as *yhyakh* had retained its spiritual aspects as compared to southern Siberian festivals, Sakha also had maintained their language. Many Sakha spoke their native language in their daily lives. When working in southern Siberia, I never heard Buryat, Tuvan, or Mongolian, except when people sang their ethnic songs. I knew that Sakha's persistence in continuing both to use their vernacular language and to enact the sacred aspects of their *yhyakh* signaled a cultural resolve that I found both compelling and mysterious. At the time, my first step into that mystique was knowing the language, a form of currency that not only opens a culture up to the learner but also opens the learner up to a culture.

I returned in September 1993 with a nine-month grant to learn Sakha. My plan was to study for six weeks in the city followed by six weeks in the village then back to the city. However, when I went to the village that first time, I never left. Yes, people spoke Sakha in Yakutsk, but there was still a large Russian population there, and I had to switch back and forth too much. In the village I could be immersed; I heard, saw, and lived the language. The village also presented challenges at first. After decades of being told their language was backward and a sign of illiteracy, many local inhabitants instantly spoke Russian to me. They were indoctrinated to speak the "great" Russian language when they saw someone with a European face. But by and by, people grew used to me and were even delighted that I spoke Sakha, however crudely at the time.

Winter in Sakha was my next terra incognita after the pancake lands. I thought I had prepared for the −60 degrees Celsius temperatures and for the relative darkness in winter. I brought "the best" insulated boots, a heavy down coat, and an all-spectrum light bulb. However, my feet froze at the first temperatures below −20 degrees Celsius. I promptly took everyone's advice and got *unty*, boots made of the leg hides of reindeer, the densest fur on the animal. I also hung up my down coat to don a multilayer wool coat complete with red fox hat and muff. The all-spectrum bulb to stave off seasonal affective disorder stayed in its box. Yes, it was crazy in the deepest winter when the sun rose at 10 a.m. and set at 4 p.m., appearing above the trees, moving along their tops for a few hours, and sinking back behind them. But the significant change in sunlight immediately following the winter solstice, in both the length of daylight (from shortest day, six hours, to longest day, twenty-three hours) and the light's quality of brilliance and whiteness, energized me.

I shared many of my experiences with family and friends back home. In one letter, which is pinned to my office wall to this day, I detailed the various layers I needed to venture out into the −60 degrees Celsius winter and illustrated it with a picture of myself dressed like a bundle, with only my eyes, nose, and mouth showing. I also shared some of my Sakha language progress. I reported how the village immersion was giving me a constant exposure and I was able to pick up the language fairly quickly. To give people a taste for how different Sakha was from Russian or English, I cited the longest word in Sakha, *kydamalahynnarbaghakhtaryttan*. I explained that it was based on the word *kydama*, which is the name of the longest pitchfork, and meant "They would not let me help with the final stacking of the hay stack." Indeed, I was in a place so very "out there" and different from anything I had yet experienced. After language training, I continued to pursue other avenues of interest, initiating research projects on the environmental issues of the Viliui regions, conducting my dissertation research, and, since 2005, focusing on issues surrounding climate change. In 1995 I married Prokopii Mitrofanovich Yegorov, a local linguist, jewelry maker, and resident of Elgeeii. My sense of truly putting down roots in these distant flatlands grew stronger with the birth of our daughter, Kathryn Tuyaara. She took her first trip there at six months, and we have maintained warm relationships with her six aunts, three uncles, thirty-plus cousins, and many nieces and nephews. Not only were we embracing our new family and community, we were being embraced by them. Shortly after Tuyaara's birth the Suntaar regional paper's front-page headline read, *"'Amerikanka Kiiiippit Kyys Ogholommut'—Deheller Suntaar Olokhtookhtoro"* ("Our American daughter-in-law had a baby girl"—Suntaar residents are saying).

Flash forward to 2020 and I am still in those flatlands. Call it destiny or fate, upon reflection I understand it as a journey of the heart. Despite any anthropologist's sincerest attempts at "objectivity" in ethnography, I argue that the only way to fully grasp another culture's world is by fully living it. The personal and professional often lose a clear boundary. Feelings are ever present in social worlds and often provide some of the most grounded understandings of events taking place. More importantly, opening to our shared humanity with research collaborators keeps us honest and cultivates the trust needed to do our work based in the soundest of ethical principles.

Over the last thirty years I have made many friends and also built some deeper relationships. Among them all, my friendship with Elvira Samoilevna Eremeeva is unique. Our relationship reminds me of the bond I have with several people I have known since childhood. No matter what happens, when we get together, we have a primordial connection. I met Elvira when I was brand-new to Sakha language and culture. The depth of our history hit me in 2018 at Elvira and Vasya's twenty-fifth anniversary celebration. I was catapulted back to the willowy young woman who, without hesitation, shot her hand up to take me home with her. We were both so young (she much more than I), and we were both single. Knowing only Russian and no Sakha except for *üchügei* (good), I depended on her for everything. Even so, I still found myself lost sometimes. Whenever Elvira was heading out, she explained she was going to *yalga*. For the longest time I thought she had some sort of relationship with a man named "Yalga," only to later realize that it was Sakha for "to a household." Today I am near fluent in Sakha. We both have grown children who are pursuing their passions in the world, and we both have developed professions that bring us great satisfaction. Over the course of the last decades, Elvira has assisted me in my various projects and provided me with critical insights to life in this now not-so-faraway place.

Another relationship that has given me a sense of grounding in Sakha is with Alexander Nikolayevich Fyodorov. I met him in 2005 while looking for a natural scientist in Yakutsk to work with after hearing elders' testimonies of how the *Jyl Oghuha* (the Bull of Winter) was gone. I needed an expert to help me understand

Figure 2 Me with Elvira at her and Vasya's twenty-fifth anniversary celebration. Elgeeii, summer 2018. Photo by author.

the physical effects of climate change in the Viliui regions and to potentially collaborate with. I met with several scientists in the city center, but they all lost interest in a partnership when they learned I was an anthropologist. Disciplinary silos were strong. I almost gave up. But I decided to trek out to the Melnikov Permafrost Institute, in the city's border regions, for a final meeting. It turned out to be pivotal. When I introduced myself as an anthropologist working in the Viliui regions, Alexander Nikolayevich lit up with excitement. He instantly got it. He understood the importance of "figuring out the humans" in climate change research. We exchanged materials and continued to communicate as I developed a research proposal focused on an interdisciplinary investigation of Viliui Sakha's local perceptions, understandings, and responses to climate change. I later learned that he grew up in Nyurba, the region bordering Suntaar. This gave him a deeper level of insight into what the changes meant for households and communities. When I proposed we conduct "knowledge exchanges" (see chapter 6) to bring his scientific experience and local inhabitants' expertise together to build understanding, he heartily agreed. He organized the logistics for our 2010 knowledge exchanges, and we spent two weeks working in eight settlements. The longer I work on issues of permafrost thaw with Alexander, the stronger my

Figure 3 Me with Alexander (Sasha), during a work session. Notice the permafrost map gracing the wall. Summer 2018. Photo by an office worker.

sense of responsibility to do what I can to communicate and remediate the situation, however that could be done, grows.

Over these decades something else has also happened. When I look at the letter on my office wall that I sent home during my first winter, I realize that a place that was so far away, so unknown, so otherworldly then is now not only familiar to me but like a second home. I feel consoled and assured when I arrive in Yakutsk and also when I get to Elgeeii and Kutana. I spend time visiting to catch up with people's lives and tell them about mine. I have also known loss in these places over this time, most poignantly of elders. During my dissertation research I interviewed elders to understand the recent past. I originally planned to interview five male and five female elders. However, in 1999 there were still elders who were born "by the *alaas*," on the home-steads scattered across the landscape prior to collectivization. Their depictions, both verbal and schematic (they drew what they remembered of their homestead), enthralled my imagination and showed how much change they had seen over the course of their lives. They were born in a time when everything was done by either animal or human power; they witnessed the introduction of mechanization, electricity, automobiles, televisions, telephones, refrigerators, freezers, public schools, and health services. By the year 2010 I could add that they had witnessed the introduction of the Internet and cell phones. But it was their stories of life back before all these new phenomena that held my attention. I ended up interviewing fifty-five elders for my 1999 research. By 2019 only three were still with us.

The elders' oral histories personalized, with a richness and context, the changes over the last century. But none rivaled what I learned from my mother-in-law, Matryona Naumovna Yegorova (*Ebee*). I witnessed her daily life for a total of sixty-nine months between 1993 and 2018. She taught me what it was to be Sakha. She chose her words carefully. She did everything by hand and wasted nothing. She worked hard and loved napping in the sun, under the larch trees. *Ebee* taught me to make *suorat* (yogurt), *kymys* (fermented mare's milk), *küörchekh* (whipped cream), *leppueske* (flatbread), *belimien* (dumplings), and *bereski* (pies); to feed the spirit of the home hearth, and to sew anything that was needed out of found materials. When Kathryn Tuyaara was born, she was the best grandmother this world has known.

I also had the opportunity to hear her stories as she remembered them, often at meals when I shared what I had learned from talking with elders that day. Once I told how an elder remarked that in their youth, they took their shoes off after the snow melted in May and would not put them on until the first snow fell in September. They did so, not because it was warm, but because they didn't have shoes! *Ebee* commented how, especially in the cooler mornings of spring, they would stand in the fresh cow manure and urine to warm their feet. There were no rubber boots, and if they wore their *eterbes* (handmade cowhide shoes), they would ruin them. *Eterbes* could only be worn when it was dry. They barely wore them anyway because they were simple suede

Figure 4 *Ebee* (Matryona Naumovna Yegorova) and Tuyaara, summer 2018. Photo by author.

boots and needed to be saved. Usually everyone had only one pair, made from the hide of the one cow households were allowed during the collective times. *Ebee* made *eterbes* for her eleven children, borrowing leather from others who had fewer feet to cover. Another day at tea I mentioned that, when visiting one old homestead, we had eaten *kiihile* (sorrel)—a plant with bitter, zesty tasting leaves. *Ebee* told how during the *achchyk jyl* (starvation year 1942), *kiihile* and *dölühüön* (rose hips) were all they ate sometimes for days. After sharing her memories, she said it brought about a longing for some *kiihile*. The next day I biked to a field and picked her a bag. She ate a few leaves every day for weeks. What I would give to know the memories that flooded her mind with the taste of each leaf.

Over my years in Sakha, the change due to global climate change is unequivocal. In the winter of 2015, I traveled with my daughter and her dad to visit our relatives in Yakutsk, Elgeeii, and adjacent villages. Tuyaara had lived

Figure 5 *Jyl Oghuha*. Artist: Vasili Kirillin.

in Elgeeii for a Sakha winter during my year of dissertation research when she was four years old. She knew it was cold. She saw pictures of herself bundled up to the point that all you could see were her eyes. But she wanted the experience of Sakha winter *now* that she was older and cognizant. Given the warming, I wondered if she would. The winter of 2015, like most winters in the decade before it, was not "cold" in the sense that local people knew. How I wished I could give Tuyaara an experience of the real Sakha winter, to know *Jyl Oghuha*, and her Sakha heritage.

My next plan is to get there and show her the ancestral *alaas* of her *Ebee* in Töbÿrÿön and her *Ehee* in Kuchakanga. Let's hope the permafrost holds out long enough to do that.

Acknowledgments

This book spans my work of thirty years, since 1991 when I first came to the Sakha Republic. Over those years, many people provided insights, ideas, and their personal stories. Many of them are represented in this book. I have endeavored to represent their stories to the best of my ability. I acknowledge and thank each of them. I also acknowledge those not directly mentioned but who have nonetheless worked with me along this path. First and foremost, I owe deep heartfelt thanks to the inhabitants, both past and present, of the Elgeeii and Kutana villages. I extend a special thanks to those who opened their homes to me, especially those who worked as consultants on research and most gratefully to the several hundred who participated in interviews and focus groups over the years. I also acknowledge the inhabitants of Kÿÿkei, Khoro, Suntaar, and of the other villages in the Suntaar, Nyurba, Verkhnyviliuisk, Viliuisk, and Mirnyi *uluus* that I have had the opportunity to work in since 1991. Several people were key on my path to this work, including Eduard Alekseev, who telegrammed me an invitation to the Jew's Harp conference in 1991; Andre Borisov, who provided my official invitation to return in 1992 to study *yhyakh*; and Elvira Samoilevna Eremeeva, who enthusiastically hosted me in Elgeeii during that 1992 master's research—thank you, Elvira!

During all subsequent visits I stayed with my Yegorov kin. A special thanks to Olga Mitrofanovna Yegorova in Yakutsk; Shura Mitrofanovna Yegorova, Tanya Mitrofanovna Yegorova, and Kiesha Mitrofanovich Yegorov in Suntaar;

and in Elgeeii, until 2019 with the late Matryona Naumovna Yegorova, and now with Prokopii Mitrofanovich Yegorov. In Kutana I am grateful to my hosts since 2014, Izabella and Yegor Tretiyakov. Before that time, I was hosted by Lena Mitrofanovna Yegorova in both Kutana and Tumul, where I lived and worked with her and Olga Naumovna Trofimova (Edjay). I am grateful for all their support and hospitality over the decades.

For their participation in my 2018–19 research that this book is founded upon, I thank all inhabitants of Elgeeii and Kutana villages who took part, and specifically participants of the life history accounts (chapter 5): Valerian Yegorovich Afanaseyev, Sardana Mikhailovna Gerasimova, Anatoli Petrovich Fyodorov, Tatiyana Constantinovna Zhanova, Osip Dmitriyevich Andreyev, Margarita Ilyinichna Zabolotzkaya, Vladimir Nikolayevich Semyonov, Olympiyada Nikanderovna Kirilina, Ksenya Prokopiyevna Semyonova, Mariya Leekenovna Ivanova, Yegor Yegorovich Tretiyakov, Izabella Nikolayevna Tretiyakova, and Matryona Nikolayevna Pavlova; and participants of the household interviews quoted in the book: Nadyezhda Yegorovna Savvinova, Vasili Mikhailovich Lvov, Svetlana Gavrilovna Martinova, Rozaliya Semyonovna Nikolayeva, Arian Andreyevich Kondratyev, Zoya Alekseyevna Novogitzina, Marfa Koninovna Ivanova, Afanasee Ivanovich Trofimov, Mariya Pavlovna Afanaseyeva, Semyon Petrovich Yegorov, Spartak Ivanovich Spiridonov, Oksana Petrovna Sofronova, Fyodorova Ira Prokopiyevna, Nikolai Makarovich Semyonov, Zakharova Paulina Ivanovna, Nadyezhda Ivanovna Zakharova, Viktor Yegorovich Vasiliyev, Alexander Nikolayevich Semyonov, Arkadi Nikolayevich Semyonov, Ludmilla Nikolayevna Pavlova, Daria Ivanovna Grigoriyevna; and inhabitants of Khatilii and Siirdaakh: Yevdokiya Fyodorovna Olisova, Lidiya Nikolayevna Fillipova, Valeri Ivanovich Danilov, and Nikita Nikolayevich Novgorodin.

For the main scientific and interdisciplinary focus of this book, I extend thanks to Dr. Alexander Nikolayevich Fyodorov (Sasha), permafrost scientist of the Melnikov Permafrost Institute. I could not have gained the knowledge I have about permafrost and *alaas* without his generous and ready assistance. I would like to believe that he too has gotten a lot from our collaboration also, telling me on several occasions that my request to collaborate with him back in 2006 was a perfect segue into doing work that he felt was critical: that is, bringing what he has learned as a scientist to the people most affected and in need of information about the dangers of permafrost degradation and what actions they can take to protect themselves and the permafrost beneath their feet. It is a win-win situation. Every academic knows that interdisciplinary collaborations are critical to address the monumental challenges of the twenty-first century. However, finding partners with whom you have synergy and work well is key. Thank you, Sasha! I also thank Sardana Boyakova, Viktoriya Fillipova, and Ekaterina Romanova at the Institute of Humanitarian Research, Yakutsk, for their research consultations. I acknowledge the family of Anastasia Varlamova and especially her daughter, Galina Borisova, for granting me permission to include my English translation of the song "Agham Alaaha." Similarly, I am grateful to Pavel Semenov (Baibal) for letting me use his song, "Törööbüt Doidum," as an example. For their assistance in getting permission to include important figures in the book, a special thank you to Sargilana Maksimova, Aitalina Stepanova, Inge Unte, Liutsia Popova, Emma Stockton and Chris Burn, Lena Yegorova, A. Ignatiev, Vladimir Semyonov, Vladimir Tretiyakov, Pavel (Baibal) Semenov, Vladimir Romanovsky, and Alexander Fedorov. A heartfelt thanks also to Nadia Dasheiva, ethnologist at the Culture Institute in Ulan Ude, for our early collaborations in Tuva, Mongolia, and Buriatia that bolstered and supported my work in Sakha. And I am grateful for the research assistance of Prokopii Mitrofanovich Yegorov for refining my translation from English to Sakha and for his insights to Sakha culture throughout the book.

I have many to thank for their support and constructive insights as this book took shape, especially my PhD adviser, Bruce Winterhalder, Professor Emeritus UC Davis, for his careful reading of drafts all along; Pey-Yi Chu, Associate Professor of History Pomona College, for her expertise in the history of permafrost; Vladimir Romanovsky, Professor at the University of Alaska, Fairbanks, for adding substantially to my permafrost knowledge; and William Fitzhugh and Daniel Temple for their extensive input in prehistory and archaeology. For reading draft chapters and offering invaluable constructive critique, I thank Inge Bolin, Valerie Chaussonnet, Julie Cruikshank, Gail Fondahl, Grete Holvesrud, Beth Marino, and Kathryn Tuyaara Yegorov-Crate. I express a special thanks to Prokopii Mitrofanovich Yegorov for all his help over the decades learning Sakha and for giving me a unique understanding of Sakha's world. I thank Olaf Jensen for engaging me in the Mongolia project and Dr. Bud Mendsaikhan (Mendee) for her expert field assistance and guidance in Mongola. For support and being there in all other ways, I thank Craig Campbell, Judy Carter, Virginia Chambers, Linda Connor, Carole Crumley, Molly Dias, Gina Drew, Jenanne Ferguson, Shirley

Fiske, Bruce Forbes, Andrei Golovnev, Kathryn Graber, Otto Habeck, Patricia Hammer, Sherilee Harper, Anna Jarrett, Olaf Jensen, Glenn Juday, Simon Kerr, Seth Kramer, Jack and Marge Kruse, Sharon LaPalme, Eric Lassiter, Gail McCormick, Jean MacGregor, Freya Mathews, Liz McLachlan, Bud Mendsaikhan (Mendee), Daniel Miller, Monica Minnegal, Joe Newberry, Jeremy Newburger, Mark Nuttall, Ben Orlove, Vera Osadchaya, Laura Packer, Christine Parker, Donna Reinsel, Susie Stockton-Link, Olga Rubel, Cathy Tucker, Cindy Raxter, and Rick Wilk.

I also want to express my gratitude for the financial support I have received for my work and research on the Viliui. Funding for the time and resources to focus specifically on this book project (eighteen months in 2018–19) came from a Royal Anthropological Institute/British Museum Urgent Anthropology Fellowship. Thanks to David Shankland, RAI director, and staff for all their coordination. I also extend a special thanks to Amber Lincoln, who worked with me at the British Museum during my research time there. Major funding for my initial projects focusing on climate change were 2007–10 National Science Foundation (NSF), Office of Polar Programs (OPP), Arctic Social Science Program grant 0710935; and 2009–13 NSF, OPP, Arctic Systems Science grant 0710935. I thank NSF and especially Anna Kerttula de Echave, my program officer extraordinaire. Regarding funding prior to 2007, I express my gratitude to all those enumerated in my 2006 monograph (Crate 2006a). Lastly, I thank George Mason University, where I have had the honor of teaching and doing research and service since 2004.

I thank the managing editor, Tracey Heatherington, and the editorial group at the University of Arizona Press, including Allyson Carter, Jim Igoe, Ruth Melville, Mary Mostafanezhad, and two anonymous reviewers, all of whom helped me to shape the manuscript to best serve its purpose. Also, thanks to Kathryn Conrad, Scott de Herrera, Savannah Grace Hicks, Amanda Krause, and Leigh McDonald at UAP for answering multiple questions.

Finally, for her constant and daily support and reminder of the blessing of being able to pass along my legacy, I thank my daughter, Kathryn Tuyaara Yegorov-Crate.

S.A.C.

Once Upon the Permafrost

Introduction

Golden autumn, summer's end
One mysterious feeling from the season changing
Fills my spirit with longing
I miss my homeland more strongly everyday
> My father's *alaas*
> At the Lebiie lake
> In the shadow of the great birch tree
> I see it and rejoice
On the *alaas* edge there is a birch grove
By the camp tent and the fire pit
Scythes tapping, tobacco smoking
And slowly we gather the *buguls* [small hay piles]
> My father's *alaas*
> At the Lebiie lake
> In the shadow of the great birch tree
> I see it and rejoice
For as many as we are, we grow up and go our way
With our own fates, becoming people of our own
Nevertheless, in my spirit, in my heart it is always there
The unforgettable memory of my father's *alaas*.
> My father's *alaas*
> At the Lebiie lake

In the shadow of the great birch tree
I see it and rejoice

Anastasia Varlamova (b. 1948) of the Baatara village in the Menge-Khangalas *uluus* wrote "Agham Alaaha" (My Father's *Alaas*) in the early 1980s in honor of her uncle and his birth *alaas*, Lebiie. Varlamova is of a certain generation of lyricists who wrote about their birth *alaas*, reflecting a youth immersed in their village life and engaged in the summer work of haying, herding, gardening, berrying, hunting, and fishing.

Sakha songs like "Agham Alaaha" evoke powerful emotions for Sakha to this day. I distinctly remember waiting backstage to perform a Sakha song at the 2018 Suntaar *yhyakh* and listening to the Elgeeii men's choir sing "Agham Alaaha." As the choir exited the stage, I went to congratulate them on their beautiful rendition of the song. They all nodded, without making eye contact, their eyes filled with tears.

I have long pondered what it is about *alaas* that musters such power for Sakha. When I contemplate the meaning of *alaas*, so much has come to me in retrospect. I reflect on my own experiences and soon find a plethora of examples, some apparent and others more elusive.

I walked out into the entry room at daybreak and found Lena turning the old separator by hand, a bucket catching the skim milk stood on the floor and a pint of *süögei* [crème fraîche] under the spout. "The electricity went out in the middle of the night for repairs. It's better isn't it? I mean, it doesn't make any noise like the electric one does so you could sleep." "Thank you!" Honestly, I didn't want to sleep in. I had come to Tumul to experience what it takes to keep cows for Sakha and I had already missed helping with the morning milking. Lena looked up from her work, "Edjay[1] is out cutting hay in the fields just beyond the neighbor's house. We can have tea and go rake where she cut two days ago if you want." "Yes!" As I headed to the outhouse, I took a slight detour to catch a glimpse of Edjay. I could barely make out her scant figure in the distance, engaged in the slow rhythmical movement of scything. The morning mist rising as she went made it almost eerie. I wondered where Edjay found her strength. At 77 years old and measuring 4 feet and 10 inches tall and maybe 90 pounds, she would work all day and into the night keeping her herd of 16 cows. (Journal entry, May 2000)

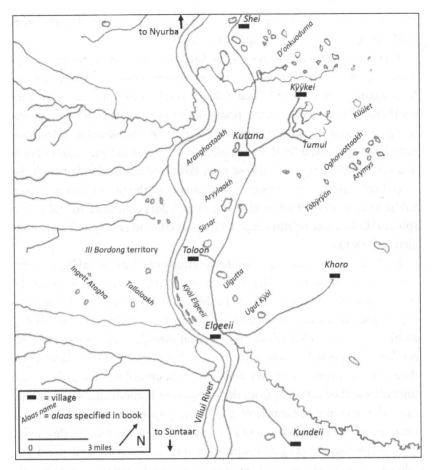

Map 1 Map of the two main research villages, Elgeeii and Kutana, with the outlying settlements and *alaas* locations mentioned in this book. Map by author.

Decades later, I understand what I was seeing; today the pieces fit. Insights like this come to me one after another when I ponder the multiple meanings of *alaas* for Sakha. An *alaas* is a physical phenomenon, but more and more I understand it as a cultural concept and symbol of Sakha's core identity. My many memories in Tumul, working with Lena and Edjay, witnessing Edjay's daily rhythms, her rituals and seasonal practices that all revolved around her commitment to *alaas*, clarify how Edjay lived for her *alaas*. Born in 1931 by the Töbürüön[2] *alaas* (map 1), ten kilometers from Tumul, Edjay learned the knowledge of and hard work involved in living "by the *alaas*." She was relocated to Tumul in the mid-Soviet period and continued to live the practical and spiritual ethic of living "by the *alaas*."

Etymologically, *alaas* is an endemic Sakha word originally understood as a wide-open area that includes hayfields, pasture, a lake, and nearby forests for foraging. From the time that Sakha's Turkic ancestors migrated from southern Siberia to make their home in the north, they settled on *alaas*, using its abundant resources for their horse and cattle subsistence. In colloquial language, Sakha lived "by the *alaas*," with *alaas* as their locus of horse and cattle subsistence and also of their cosmological world. Although the forced collectivization into dense settlements of the Soviet period moved Sakha away from their physical *alaas*, most Sakha continued to maintain a spiritual link. These relationships with *alaas* continue today and are entangled in daily life.

I reflect and see other clues to the centrality of *alaas* for Sakha. I understand why, in 1991, the Sakha minister of culture insisted on walking the entire circumference of the lake of his birth *alaas* before boarding the helicopter back to Viliuisk. I remember the moment, six months later doing archival research on Sakha's summer festival *yhyakh*, when I learned of their pre-Soviet dispersed settlement pattern of living "by the *alaas*." *Yhyakh* was their annual request to the sky deities for a bountiful harvest and the one time of year they gathered from their dispersed homesteads. Another clue came that summer at Ugut Kyöl, the Elgeeii *yhyakh* area three kilometers from the village center (see map 1). Out of nowhere, four swans flew overhead as the *ohuokhai* began. People looked up in reverence and awe. I was told later that the swans came because they were the totem spirit ancestors of the pre-Soviet *agha uuha* (patrilineal clan) who inhabited the Ugut Küöl *alaas* for centuries before (map 6*b*).

The Sakha meaning of *alaas* comes more fully to me when reflecting on my 1999–2000 oral history interviews. Fifty-five Elgeeii and Kutana elders detailed their childhood and youth living on one of many *alaas* in the outlying areas of their present village. They carefully articulated memories of the *alaas*, casting it as an almost magical place imbued with a lush and vibrant nature. Yes, *alaas* is a physical place, but it is also so much more. It is an idea, a sacred vow with the ancestors, an entangled, interdependent set of relationships between human and nonhuman animals, plants, lakes, glades, and spirits. A promise of life and abundance. Sakha's identity is founded upon their intimate human-environment relationship with *alaas*.

The Polish ethnographer E. K. Pekarski, who wrote Sakha's first dictionary, gave this definition of *alaas*: "a meadow or spacious field, surrounded by woods; a piedmont valley; a long, clear glade among the forest; a field or meadow, surrounded by forest" (Pekarski 1958: 67). Pekarski knew the Sakha meaning of *alaas* because he lived for a long time with Sakha and learned their vernacular language. He referred to the areas where Sakha lived with the term Sakha used for those areas, *alaas*. Other non-Sakha of the early colonial period who came for geographical, ethnographical, or other study did not use the term *alaas* in their landscape descriptions but rather used the terms they had in their vocabulary: valley, glade, lake edge, and so on.[3]

This dissonance between how Sakha used and non-Sakha did not use the term *alaas* became even more pronounced with the advent of the scientific study of *alaas*, an effort critical to the twentieth-century Soviet project to expand infrastructure and initiate industrial mining. To the extent that these activities were proposed on *alaas* landscapes, those landscapes needed to be studied, and the scientific knowledge of *alaas* advanced. At first the definition was a broader conception, not unlike how Sakha defined their physical *alaas*. However, soon it changed to refer to a very specific type of permafrost ecosystem. Scientifically defined *alaas* had exact geophysical characteristics, distinguished by large areas of subsided ground surface resulting from the thawing of ice-rich permafrost (Solovyev 1973). These newly defined *alaas* were found only in a fraction of the areas where Sakha knew *alaas* to be and where they historically used to live "by the *alaas*." This began the tension between how Sakha understood *alaas* and how scientific knowledge defined *alaas*.

These two understandings differ based on physical characteristics and because Sakha imbue *alaas* with the inherent spiritual qualities that historically animate their living and nonliving worlds. *Alaas* permeate Sakha historical narratives, belief system, and present world understandings. Contemporary rural inhabitants wax poetically about the deeper cultural meanings of *alaas*. One of many testimonies to this comes from Agrafina Vasiliyevna Nazarova, resident of Elgeeii village in the Suntaar *uluus*,

> Our ancestors lived by the *alaas* . . . the round fields with forests shaped like
> an *alaaji* [small round pancake] with a lake. . . . The Sakha person is born on
> the *alaas* and lives on the *alaas* and makes their life there and from there . . .
> it is the birthland, the *alaas* . . . our birth soil . . . where you are born and
> raised and connected . . . you can keep animals and all the rest you need to

live is there . . . a small world in and of itself, the lake has fish and there is pasture and hay for the animals and the forest has berries and hunting animals. (Interview, July 2, 2018)

This is not just an understanding held by rural Sakha. *Alaas* are equally important to urban Sakha, many of whom have no physical contact with their ancestral *alaas*. I could stop any Sakha in the capital city Yakutsk and ask them what the concept of *alaas* means. Ninety percent of them would describe *alaas* along the lines of the quotation above, reifying the cultural meaning of *alaas*. In the urban environment *alaas* are alive in multiple cultural depictions, from visual art to theatrical performances to music and dance. Most strikingly, contemporary Sakha songs are woven through with sensory depictions of *alaas*. These songs of nostalgia for their birth *alaas* are written not only by Sakha of Varlamova's generation but also by the next generation of songwriters, even though they spend their lives in the regional and urban centers without the same span of time spent by their birth *alaas*. Longtime Yakutsk resident Pavel Semenov or Baibal, born in 1974 in the Timpii village of the Viliuisk region, weaves images and other sensory qualities of his birth *alaas* into his songs:

The green field spreads out before me
A cool, light wind brushes my face
The stillness of my birth *alaas*
Makes my thoughts learn to fly.
    It's true, it's certain
    The memory does not leave
    Does not fade away, does not cool
    To you, my life's loves
    To my birthland, my mother, my father
    To all my people.
The scent of new larch needles fills the air
I wait in excitement for it every spring
And for the sun's bright, radiant rays
That spread across grandmother lake's surface
    It's true, it's certain
    The memory does not leave
    Does not fade away, does not cool

> To you, my life's loves
> To my birthland, my mother, my father
> To all my people.
>
> In the crowded city among other people
> Trying to get used to the shallow existence
> I can't sleep day or night
> Constantly thinking of my birth *alaas*.
>
> It's true, it's certain
> The memory does not leave
> Does not fade away, does not cool
> · To you, my life's loves
> To my birthland, my mother, my father
> To all my people.
>
> ("Törööbüt Doidum")

Be it in the contemporary songs that echo in urban and rural areas alike, or in inhabitants' individual testimonies, *alaas* continue to be a central source of cultural grounding and spiritual sustenance for Sakha.

Over the last thirty years I have heard countless descriptions from both young and old Sakha of *alaas* and its meaning. In recent years I have begun to hear depictions that are qualitatively different: "In almost all the *alaas* areas, where *ötökh* [places of old homesteads] were always very flat, the land surface is now rolling and wavy . . . this is because the permafrost is thawing . . . we Sakha have started to call it *abaahy üngküüleebit* [evil spirits danced]" (Yegor Yegorovich Tretiyakov, interview, May 22, 2019).

Today Sakha watch their *alaas* transform before their eyes. They *know* that this rapid change is happening based on their expert knowledge of place, informed by annual pilgrimages to their birth *alaas* and haying and other foraging activities in the outlying *alaas* areas. Nevertheless, even in the face of the rapid physical change of *alaas*, the deeper cultural identification with *alaas* remains: "Even if the *alaas* disappear they will not change. *Alaas* . . . it is the most important and dear connection that Sakha have to nature . . . it is connected with everything. . . . *Alaas* are like our mother and that connection will never change" (Nadyezhda Yegorovna Savvinova, interview, June 12, 2018). These changes in the landscape are being studied by scientists in Sakha. They are studying permafrost thaw, largely due to anthropogenic climate change, but only in the areas within the scientifically defined *alaas*.

The conflicting understandings of *alaas*, as a cultural and spiritual land-scape used by a people for centuries versus a technically defined landscape, reflect two very different ways of knowing *alaas*. These two knowledge systems assign importance to different aspects of the *alaas*. One knowledge system is rich in cultural history, depth, and meaning, while the other is focused on specific physical technicalities. I have cobbled together Sakha's understanding of *alaas* in the process of long-term ethnography complemented by the analysis of archival documents, peer-reviewed publications, and the popular press. In contrast, information about scientifically defined *alaas* is more easily accessed and also prominent in Sakha's contemporary parlance of climate change and permafrost science. Granted there exists a diversity of nation-based scientific entities worldwide, many of which use their craft as a tool of the subaltern to articulate alternative visions. It is critical to understand that "science is not a heartless pursuit of objective information. It is a creative human activity, its geniuses acting more as artists than as information processors" (Gould 1979: 201). Nonetheless, at a global scale, there exists a scientific knowledge hegemony that takes precedence and determines how we think about and make decisions for the rest of the world. By doing so, it perpetuates the neoliberal agenda. Our understanding of the world would be less hegemonic and more pluralistic if we took to heart the idea that "all knowledge is 'local' and culturally/socially contextual, which means that scientific knowledge is situated (cultural) practice" (Goldman et al. 2011: 14).

This tenet of hegemony is illustrated further by an experience I had serving as lead author for the Intergovernmental Panel on Climate Change's (IPCC) Special Report on Oceans and Cryosphere in a Changing Climate (SROCC) from 2017 to 2019. I had known of the IPCC's work since 1990 when they began generating Assessment Reports (AR) to gauge the complex planetary changes due to anthropogenic climate change. I knew that IPCC reports were the result of a lengthy and highly vetted process that involved over two hundred international scientists collectively writing a report over the course of two years. The special report I worked on was one of three written between the fifth and sixth AR, specifically to focus on global systems that needed more in-depth analysis than the AR could provide space for. We met for week-long intensive writing workshops four times over the two years. I collaborated on chapter 1, the framing for the rest of the report. Within chapter 1, I took on the task of framing other knowledge systems, specifically Indigenous knowledge and local knowledge.[4] I was excited to contribute my expertise and to collaborate with others in this area.

But my heart sank during our chapter team's first meeting. We began by sharing our expertise around the table. After several others had explained their work in oceanography or satellite data or cryosphere science, I introduced myself as an anthropologist who conducted longitudinal ethnographic research in northeastern Siberia. The faces around the table went blank. I began to worry. With a few more introductions my worry abated. One person on the team worked on community health issues with Indigenous populations in the Arctic and another on socioenvironmental issues with communities in South Asia. The three of us huddled together during the first coffee break to share ideas and strategies to educate the rest of our chapter team on Indigenous knowledge and local knowledge. Over the course of the week, we each proposed to the group different ways to bring the relevance of knowledge systems other than science into the report's framing. It was a hard sell. Many of our colleagues were polite. Others were outspoken, doubting that our contribution was necessary. Nevertheless, by the end of the week we had gotten a place in the chapter outline, "Knowledge Systems for Understanding and Responding to Change." Now we had to draft it.

By the time we met again, something amazing had happened. It was like night and day. Our interactions with our chapter colleagues during that second team meeting were qualitatively different compared to the first week. Everyone on the chapter team had bought into our section. Perhaps it was the group work on the Googledoc over the interim six-month period and the process of group editing and feedback throughout. Instead of considering a knowledge systems section at arm's length, many engaged directly in our discussions, commenting on how they were seeing the importance of knowledge systems for their own work and for the report overall. We knew we had made our case when the one scientist who had expressed the most hesitancy in our first meeting actually vouched for the importance of including knowledge systems in the report during a larger plenary session.

Nevertheless, the two-year process continued to challenge our three-person team. We had to repeatedly make the case for the knowledge systems section to the lead authors of the report's other five chapters. But the time given also enabled us to include holders of Indigenous knowledge and local knowledge as contributing authors. That the IPCC had yet to invite holders of Indigenous knowledge and local knowledge as lead authors was and remains a major oversight. We did our best to crack that door open by engaging them as much as we could. They reviewed and made recommendations on the knowledge section over the process of our writing, collaborated in creating definitions for both systems, and contributed written sections to the report detailing their opinions of how IPCC could best utilize Indigenous knowledge and local knowledge in the AR (Abram et al. 2019, sec. 1.8.2).

Perhaps the biggest challenge was how to name these knowledge systems. The term "scientific knowledge" was first up for critique. Our contributing authors, Indigenous knowledge holders, objected to referring to what we know as "science" with the term "scientific knowledge," arguing, "Our Indigenous knowledge has developed over generations, is time tested and empirical. It is also science." They explored with us different ways to name scientific knowledge—"Western scientific knowledge" or "elite scientific knowledge"—but both failed to make an accurate differentiation. In the end, we settled on using the term "scientific knowledge" with the clear disclaimer that the other knowledge systems were also empirically derived.

Our next decision was how to label the other knowledge systems. Here we found ourselves in acronym soup! Interest in knowledge systems spans the academic disciplines of ethnoecology, anthropology, geography, biodiversity, development studies, and so on, and the applied areas of NGO and policy work. In total there exists a range of terms to signify these systems, including traditional knowledge (TK), ecological knowledge (EK), traditional ecological knowledge (TEK), Indigenous knowledge (IK), local knowledge (LK). In the process of streamlining this milieu of terminology to formally frame knowledge systems for SROCC, we decided that the main qualitative difference was best represented by differentiating Indigenous knowledge and local knowledge, using the following definitions:

Indigenous knowledge (IK) refers to the understandings, skills and philosophies developed by societies with long histories of interaction with their natural surroundings. It is passed on from generation to generation, flexible and adaptive in changing conditions and increasingly challenged in the context of contemporary climate change. Local knowledge (LK) is what non-Indigenous communities, both rural and urban, use on a daily and lifelong basis. It is multi-generational, embedded in community practices and cultures, and adaptive to changing conditions. (Glossary, IPCC 2019: 689, 690)

Our knowledge systems work also involved a cross-chapter box in which we drew examples from each of the chapters to highlight how Indigenous knowledge and local knowledge were relevant. This included a visual depiction of our main argument: the importance of engaging all relevant knowledge systems in a given context. Early feedback suggested we depict Indigenous knowledge and local knowledge as complementing scientific knowledge. We rejected this idea, explaining that each knowledge system had standing in its own right. The task is not to quantify other ontologies to fit into prescribed scientific categories to make generalizable arguments (Gearheard et al. 2010), but rather to let each contribute its unique elements. In turn, this process renders many of the prescribed technocratic frameworks of climate science (e.g., adaptation, resilience, and vulnerability, or ARV) useless (Goldman et al. 2018). But that is the point here. Including the diversity of ways to understand and act in the world cannot be understood by scientifically determined frameworks. How could an ARV frame account for the cosmological and spiritual importance of *alaas* and its central place in Sakha cultural identification? We need new inclusive frames of reference. In the end, we represented the three knowledge systems—Indigenous knowledge, local knowledge, and scientific knowledge—as equals, each along their individual trajectories of development and change over time, and each coming into contact to intermingle with the others in specific contexts (Abram et al. 2019: CB4.1 p. 104).

Despite the rocky beginnings of our IPCC work, we achieved our goal to frame the knowledge systems, to present each as empirically derived, and to emphasize the use of all available knowledge systems as critical to comprehensive understanding and policy approaches. In the process, we substantiated Indigenous knowledge and local knowledge in this and all proceeding IPCC reports and also brought knowledge holders closer to being fully involved in the IPCC process.

Clearly, Indigenous knowledge (cf. Nunn and Reid 2016; Green and Tapim 2010) and local knowledge (cf. Lee et al. 2015; O'Neill and Graham 2016) deliver depth and place-specific cultural context to understandings of change. Acknowledging a plurality of knowledge systems means reprioritizing whose opinion counts. It means assigning priority status to affected communities' understandings of vulnerability and risk to avoid perpetuating the colonial project, "moving people out of the way of environmental risks as they are conceived within colonial traditions, while moving them into the way of risks as conceived through the eyes of remote Indigenous communities" (Veland et al. 2013: 314). It also entails accommodating the holistic context of the knowledge system to account for "a deeper understanding of the epistemology of knowledge within a culture" (Walshe and Argumedo 2016: 166). Otherwise, research and policy directives will continue to glean only what is "(arte)factual" evidence (Briggs 2005: 7).

These vernacular knowledge systems matter within the contemporary context of global change and development research because Indigenous knowledge and local knowledge "can supply the nonlinear and pluralistic perspectives that increasingly are being called for to provide a socially relevant context" (Klubnikin et al. 2000: 1304). Anthropology may not be the best interlocuter with knowledge holders in areas of biology or other natural sciences, but anthropologists can bring to light "the more inclusive cultural contexts of our local teachers and values ways of translating Indigenous knowledge that reflect the symbolic and institutional contexts in which the knowledge is generated" (Scott 1996: 71). Inasmuch as vernacular knowledge systems are gateways to understanding how a culture perceives, understands, responds, and adapts to change (Gómez-Baggethun et al. 2013; Pretty 2011; Reyes-Garcia 2010; Tengö et al. 2014; Sillitoe 2007; Cash et al. 2003), they are critical inroads to a culture's specific perceptions of, interactions with, and responses to climate change (Huntington 2000; Maldonado et al. 2016).

Some are taking up the important dialogical exercise of forefronting Indigenous knowledge and local knowledge, including integrating Indigenous mitigation and adaptation strategies into policy-led adaptation responses (Nyong et al. 2007; Egeru 2012; Hiwasaki et al. 2015; Orlove et al. 2020); adapting frameworks to integrate Indigenous narratives with global assessments (Alexander et al. 2011); engaging the rich and fine-grained knowledge on the ground to ground truth climate models (Reyes-Garcia et al. 2016); and demonstrating the efficacy of Indigenous knowledge and local knowledge in global assessments (Ford et al. 2016; IPCC 2019: 99–105). In the end, the fact that Indigenous peoples have a long, often millennial history of responding to a changing climate makes these efforts to bring Indigenous knowledge and local knowledge into climate science seem inverted. It should be the other way around. *They* are the experts that scientists need to listen to. My argument is not that scientific knowledge is irrelevant, but that, at present, it dominates and fails to provide a complete understanding of global change. Indigenous knowledge and local knowledge offer the balance via their capacity to ground truth and provide cultural context for global change. Critical to leveling this playing field is to challenge the sanctity of scientific knowledge and to repatriate the status of Indigenous knowledge and local knowledge. This book is one effort in this larger process.

Which brings me to my title. I initially chose the phrase "Once Upon the Permafrost" to convey that something most of us thought was eternal was not only rapidly thawing but threatening the centuries-old adaptation of a culture and ending their "story" in that place. In the context of our discussion so far, the title juxtaposes a classic fairy tale motif with a scientific term. Both are misunderstood, with one slighted as being the stuff of frivolous adolescent childhood, and the other as an absolute truth.

Fairy tales have long been used to teach and perpetuate knowledge, ethics, and mores. Their origins date back thousands of years (Da Silva and Tehrani 2016). Most feature an archetypal protagonist, whose journey illustrates some existential truth. Cinderella represents the persecuted heroine, one of many universal archetypes found throughout the world's diversity of oral heritages. Also, in concert with those other traditions, fairy tales play on the extraordinary to reframe what is ordinary, thereby providing insight to life's deeper meanings (Tatar 2017). This mirrors our species' propensity toward artistic expression overall, our need to focus "our attention away from the given to a world of shared, humanly created possibility" (Boyd 2009: 125). The Enlightenment, the advent of printing, rise of literacy, and acculturating forces of globalization either erased or transformed these oral modalities. Those that survived were coded into written texts. What was once a diversity of oral traditions that not only shaped and framed cultural worlds but also were dynamic and adapted to change over time were transferred ex situ, in static enshrinements of the written word.

In sharp contrast to these comprehensive narratives, Western science is made up of bytes of information (data: temperature, weight, etc.). It tells a story, but one that is thinly constructed and one-dimensional. Considered without the benefit of Indigenous knowledge and local knowledge, it leaves the listener with the question, "And so?" How do we bring these assembled bytes into our lives and act upon them in purposeful and meaningful ways? It's like trying to tell the tale of "One Thousand and One Nights" by simply saying that the main protagonist told narratives night after night. The listener is left with a dangling statement void of context, color, emotion, and that fails to evoke insight or present a moral truth.

In this context, consider the scientific term, "permafrost." In Russian, *vechnaia merzlota* (eternal frost), in Sakha *irbet tong* (nonthawing frozen-ness), and in English, *permafrost* (permanent frost), the word communicates a state of permanence and implies nothing close to the phenomenon's true nature. Permafrost is not eternal but, technically speaking, only needs to be frozen for two years to be classified as permafrost. Furthermore, climate science today tells us unequivocally that not only has it changed in range and depth over the course of its million-plus year history on the planet but that it is thawing and losing coverage today at a pace unknown over that historical period.

Once Upon the Permafrost juxtaposes the tenacity of human archetypal structures over the course of human history with the deficiency of science, by itself, to meet our present climate crisis. You may be curious why I chose a Western trope and not one from a nonhegemonic culture. I consciously did so to capture the attention of students, educators, and a general population whom I define broadly as those reliant upon the very consumer culture that has landed us in our climate change predicament. In short, with this book I endeavor to get the attention of those who most need to hear and act upon my story.

Science shows us the "big picture" of how our planetary system is chang-ing unprecedentedly. But it is just one of many "big pictures." It is just one cultural way to understand this monumental change. Permafrost supports the livelihoods of multiple cultural ways of being. Our best defense against per-mafrost thaw is to engage that diversity of understandings of and responses to permafrost change. Bringing to the fore the multiplicity of ways of know-ing involved in a given context is not only about *knowledge-making* (episte-mology) but also about *world-making* (ontology) practices, which radically work within the "plurality of existing worlds" (Goldman et al. 2018: 3).

This book focuses on one culture's *world-making* within the hegemony of science to uncover "how scientific understandings of the environment are packaged, stabilized and circulated . . . and with what effects" (Goldman et al. 2011: 5). In the process, it underscores the issues associated with that hegemony and questions of expertise by showing how there exist "multiple, sometimes incommensurable, ways of knowing the environment" (Nadasdy 2011: 130). By substantiating Sakha's expertise of their environment and their perceptions and accommodations of the changes in their world, I make the case for the importance of engaging multiple worlds and knowledge systems in understanding culture and climate change across the global context.

Bridging Global Change to the Local and Back Again

I was taken aback when I heard Father Segundo Leon's statement to our documentary film team while on a shoot in the Peruvian Andes. To me, his words were too profound to be coming from any Catholic priest I had yet to meet: "This thaw, it is something that can be proven. The idea of assuming that the earth will end is inside oneself. In the spiritual, in Christianity, everything always changes. It transforms. It's a message, a call to the conscience to be able to take on these challenges, challenges that will come, and could come, and will come" (Feast of the Assumption in San Miguel de Aco, Peru, August 15, 2012). But then I realized that he lives among affected communities who are witnessing profound change. He also is part of that affected community. He could be guiding his community with Christian dogma about God's will, eschatology, and the end of the world. This was the narrative of Catholic priests and evangelists in Kiribati, an area where communities are challenged by sea-level rise and where we also shot footage for the documentary film, *The Anthropologist* (Kramer et al., 2015). Instead, Father Segundo was listening and responding with empathy and insight. I felt hopeful that there is a growing awareness within such a powerful institution, and that "business as usual" potentially could, in fact, change.

The human species today is challenged by a kind of change that, played out into the future, will far outpace the changes of the Industrial Revolution, colonialism, world wars, economic depressions, and more recent changes including mass extinction events, the decline and exhaustion of ecosystems' integrity, plastic and toxin contamination, and extreme economic disparity. The change to our planet's atmospheric concentration of heat-trapping gases has set in motion systemic changes that will be extremely difficult to reverse. We first need a historic gaze: "How did we get to this point of staring cataclysmic changes in the face? How can we move effectively toward the long-delayed imperatives that lie ahead? The first step is to examine the past and draw the lessons from it to guide our way to a hopeful future" (Schneider 2009: 8). Assessing the past shows how the causes of climate change are

ultimately about cultures increasingly reliant on consumption and nonre-
newables. We have the technology we need to transition to a regenerative
food, fiber, and energy system (cf. The Solutions Project 2020). What we fal-
ter with is summoning the cultural changes needed to realize that transition,
or how we talk about it as a major issue.

Climate change is communicated to the public using scientific explanations that are, for most people, far too abstract. Humans use tacit knowledge
in daily life and best understand phenomena like climate change within that
frame. Public knowledge of climate change, whether that "public" is an inhabitant of an affected area or of an urban center, depends on the translation of
climate science into the vernacular (Rudiak-Gould 2012). We need to talk
about climate change in ways that reach people on a personal and emotional
level so they understand and are motivated to act and behave differently
(Dannevig and Hovelsrud 2016). To appeal to the heart and motivate people
toward change we need new narratives, ones that engage the vernacular but
also break down old stereotypes of ourselves as independent individuals to
meet the realities of a profoundly changing world (Rose et al. 2012). In lieu of
that, there will remain disconnect for most participants of consumer society
who live relatively buffered from the direct daily effects of climate change, a
phenomenon John Meyer terms as a *resonance* problem (2015).

Another hurdle to motivating action is the complexity of how the earth
system is changing in response to the warming of the atmosphere. There are
multiple feedbacks within global, regional, and local climate systems, and
within sociocultural systems. Because of this, impactful responses and reme-
diations require action across those multiple scales. "To successfully address
climate change in the long run, the day-to-day activities of individuals, families, firms, communities, and governments at multiple levels . . . particularly
those in the more developed world . . . will need to change substantially.
Encouraging simultaneous actions at multiple scales is an important strategy
to address this problem" (Ostrom 2010).

Life in the twenty-first century is challenging, and prospects for a sustainable future appear dim. Running and hiding from this reality or living with
a fixed vision of the future leaves us with no options. The only way to get to
our future is by engaging what we each know, individually and collectively,
across disciplines and differences to make "oddkin" and aspire to "stay with
the trouble" (Haraway 2016). For researchers, this involves engaging an inter-
disciplinarity that works to bring to light the multiple issues of climate and

other twenty-first-century change (Palsson et al. 2013) and to expand notions of "appropriate solutions" and "relevant evidence" (Castree et al. 2014: 763).

Climate Ethnography

I practice climate ethnography, a critical, collaborative, multi-sited approach conducted in concert with affected communities that engages the diversity of knowledge systems necessary to understand and respond to change (Marino 2015; Crate 2011a). My method is inductive and based on principles of grounded theory to discern what I see, hear, and "know" from fieldwork. I elicit narratives to understand how people's stories shape and are shaped by cultural perceptions of change over time. I recognize how "research is story-catching. Stories are data with a soul and no methodology honors that more than grounded theory. The mandate of grounded theory is to develop theories based on people's lived experiences rather than proving or disproving existing theories" (Brown 2020). I capture narratives and build theories or "systematic view(s) of phenomena by specifying relations among variables, with the purpose of explaining and predicting the phenomena" (Kerlinger 1977: 5). Developing theories via a grounded inductive approach is a messy process largely because it engages qualitative material that interdicts precoded ways of studying our social world (Plows 2018). Despite its messiness, the process of using grounded theory, based in the elicitation and analysis of cultural narratives, is the best way I have found to capture the depth and breadth of a people's experience, in this case of unprecedented climate change.

My authority to understand and speak about *alaas* is based on "being there," conducting ethnography with Sakha communities over extended periods to allow "for a slower accumulation of evidence and understanding and for key insights to arise unexpectedly, during experiences that allow glimpses of how the world is perceived and experienced by local peoples" (Roncoli et al. 2009: 88). I understand change over time based on participant observation, the elicitation and analyzing of narratives to contextualize *what people say* within a cognitive frame and within the knowledge system(s) with which that specific culture shapes, understands, gives meaning to, and references their world (Agrawal 1995; Escobar 2001). I unpack and interpret tacit knowledge, "a portfolio of intertwined knowledge systems . . . used ephemerally, contingent to the task at hand" (Bremer et al. 2017: 673).

My approach also involves attention to the more visceral experiences in the field: The moment I looked up inside a cow barn and saw a *salama* (braided horsehair rope with gifts for the cow deity), what I thought was a long-forgotten Sakha practice, only to learn that many contemporary cow keepers continued to use them and practice this belief. Or the day in 2000, after an oral history interview, in which an elder eloquently described the old ways of skidding hay and gathering wood that transported me to that before-time, when I left their house and was jerked back to the present by two teenagers walking past, brandishing pierced navels and orange hair. Or the witnessing of one cow keeper's sacred relationship with her cow herd when hearing her assure a steer headed to slaughter that this was his next step to the upper sky world to join the cow deity. Or the time after tea in Tumul when, starting toward the fields to rake, Lena veered us off the main path and to the lake's edge where she laid nine *alaaji* on the shore. As we stood there in silence with the mist burning off the water, Lena began speaking softly, asking the spirit of the lake to accept the presence of this visitor from America in Tumul.

By engaging these methods and approaches, this book is my contribution to the nascent field of climate ethnography. Beth Marino (2015) pioneered the effort in her monograph *Fierce Climate, Sacred Ground*, the careful analysis of one Inupiaq settlement's confrontation with the multiple disasters that climate change has ushered in. She uses a vulnerability framework, forefronting Inupiaq understandings of change, to unpack how unprecedented flooding and erosion present a physical threat and a potential loss of sacred homeland for the Shishmaref community. Using a multi-sited approach, her analysis also reveals how the failures of policy, funding, and organizational response are intimately entangled in the community's future. My approach is to challenge the hegemony of scientific knowledge and neoliberal "solutions" to climate change by bringing to light the importance of the depth and breadth of one culture's knowledge system that is part of the multitude of ways of knowing on the planet, and the need to engage them all to move forward toward solutions.

Organization of the Chapters

This book is organized inductively to mirror the grounded theory approach of my research, but here to replicate the historical process of how knowledge systems came to be. This chronology of "knowing" reveals how the under-standings of change in contemporary time are rooted in history and are translated into different cultural, community, and individual realities. I first present how the specific knowledge systems of permafrost (chapter 1) and of *alaas* (chapter 2) developed and coevolved. Sakha's Indigenous knowl-edge of both is the basis of local understandings and adaptations across a deep time scale. It is also founded on Sakha's animistic belief that assigns sentience to the living and nonliving world. Scientific knowledge of perma-frost and of *alaas* is, by contrast, relatively recent. Chapter 3 intertwines contemporary ethnography with historical documentation to illustrate how universal Soviet and post-Soviet policy changes interfaced with local con-texts, affecting Viliui Sakha's physical relation with *alaas* but unable to break their spiritual connection.

Chapters 4 and 5 focus on the "complexity of change," the suite of changes, including intergenerational, economic, and environmental, that entangle the lives of contemporary inhabi-tants. Figure 6, of the entry door to a long-abandoned *buluus* (under-ground permafrost storage) against the backdrop of the modern Kutana school building, visually depicts the complexity of change for Viliui Sakha. The *buluus* are obsolete not only because they are flooded from thawing permafrost but also because of the convenience of elec-tric freezers, an overall move toward modernity and, more saliently, away from physically living "by the *alaas*."

I weave testimonies of the com-plexity of change at the community level (chapter 4) and via individ-ual life histories (chapter 5), both which detail how change comes into daily life and the constancy of the concept of and Sakha's identifi-cation with *alaas*. These chapters

Figure 6 The juxtaposition of a long-abandoned *buluus* entry door against the backdrop of the modern Kutana school building visually captures the complexity of change.

also clarify how the quickened pace of change due to climate change can be tracked as an intergenerational phenomenon. In 2002, Igor Krupnik and Dyanna Jolly edited the seminal volume *The Earth Is Faster Now*, focused on Indigenous elders' narratives of change. In the two decades since its publication, researchers in the Arctic find that elders are no longer the sole witnesses of local climate change. Rather, it is now common knowledge across the generations. In chapter 6 I place Viliui Sakha's negotiation of their historically based human-environment relationship in the context of twenty-first-century unprecedented change, updating how both permafrost and *alaas* knowledge are developing in the Anthropocene. The contemporary change in permafrost threatens *alaas* in its physical form, but Sakha's cultural identity with *alaas* remains. This highlights the tenacity of *alaas* for Sakha and how *alaas*, as a largely cultural and spiritual entity in contemporary times, functions and serves Sakha, rooting their identity even as *alaas* transform before their eyes.

In chapter 7 I show how the Sakha and *alaas* case is relevant to other contexts where communities are similarly dependent on permafrost, both directly and indirectly. My overarching goal is to bring my readers close in to understand one culture's long history in a specific ecosystem that today is threatened because of climate and other change, and to show how their experience is both unique and shared by many others: the persistence of their essential relationship through a continued cultural identification with and perpetuation of the concept of *alaas*; how that relationship to *alaas* is intimately and intrinsically known via their vernacular knowledge system; that a similar human-environment relationship and relevant knowledge system exists in the myriad of cultures across the planet who also depend on ice and permafrost landscapes; and how this matters not just to those living on permafrost landscapes but to all of Earth's inhabitants. Permafrost provides one of the main structural foundations for Arctic ecosystems, which, in turn, work with the planet's other ecosystems to maintain planetary balance. Metaphorically speaking, *we all live on permafrost.*

Chapter 1

"Knowing" Permafrost

My first "hands-on" encounter with permafrost was during hay cutting in 1992. After lunch, our host disappeared to put the butter and *süögei* somewhere behind the trees. I was curious about where he went with them. Instead of explaining, he took me there and invited me to put my hand under a raised tussock of grass. I can, to this day, still feel the sharp contrast between the scorching summer heat and the cool of the underground cavity.

Inhabitants of permafrost areas know permafrost, but not in the way that modern science "knows," via instrumental measuring and modeling, by defining its properties and temperature regimes and developing classifications for the diversity of permafrost types. Inhabitants of permafrost areas know permafrost via their utilitarian ways of living with it, by knowing the lifecycles of the plants and animals they depend upon, the properties of water they need, and the ecosystem characteristics of the myriad of other resources needed to survive.

Two examples immediately come to mind that illustrate how human and nonhumans alike know permafrost. The first is how Marusa responded about the difference in winter temperatures when I asked her how the seasons had changed over her lifetime.

MLI: We knew how cold it was before because the cold made a sound.

SAC: What do you mean that the cold made a sound?

MLI: We didn't have thermometers back then. In the morning we would go outside and blow out of our mouth and if it "made a sound," we knew it was −50 or −60.

SAC: What did it sound like?

MLI: It went "Shuruushuruu."

SAC: Did you hear it this year?

MLI: NOOOO it does not go below −40 now! When you breathe out now your breath just goes out . . . it does not fall.

(Mariya Leekenovna Ivanova, interview, June 26, 2018)

The second is exemplified in the adaptation of one of the "others"[1] in Sakha's midst, that of Dahurian larch,

The adaptations of the Dahurian larch tell us a lot about what it takes to survive in this extreme "home."

Dahurian larch (*Larix gmelinii* [Rupr.] syn *Larix dahurica*) is a coniferous, deciduous tree, the most permafrost-tolerant of boreal species. It survives on top of solid frozen ground by sending its roots out laterally through the thin layer of moss covering the forest floor. *L. gmelinii* is very tolerant of low-nutrient, high stress environments and a range of soil conditions, but it is very intolerant of shade, with a reputation as the most light-demanding tree of boreal Eurasia (Nikolov and Helmisaari 1992). This has not been a problem since *L. gmelinii* lacks competition during colonization in the severe climate. It is usually found in pure even-aged stands (Dylis 1961). (Crate 2006a: 13)

Like the Dahurian larch, Sakha have been able to "make a living" in their extreme continental climate. Unlike the larch, they did so by developing a specific knowledge system. Being relative newcomers to the north, they based this knowledge, in part, on how other, more ancient cultures had adapted: "Archeological data from ancient arctic sites show that the populations of Yakutia [contemporary Sakha Republic] contributed to world culture by mastering the natural and climatic zone of the Far North and developing adaptation standards for survival in future generations under extreme natural conditions" (Argunov and Pestereva 2018: 34). The mastery referred to here includes that of the permafrost, a major underlying constraint of the ecosystem that challenges human adaptation and development.[2] Permafrost has persisted as part of the earth system for some 700,000 years (Froese et al. 2008). The range of permafrost on the planet is extensive and dynamic, changing in range over global temperature fluctuations. In the Last Glacial Maximum (LGM, around 21,000 years ago) permafrost extended much farther south than it does today (Lindgren at al. 2018).

The Deep Time Knowing of Permafrost

Humans have lived in permafrost ecosystems for millennia. Archaeological findings, though sometimes debated and even contested, can nevertheless give some sense of the long trajectory of human inhabitance on permafrost. In the Arctic,[3] an area with a more or less constant permafrost presence,[4] there were coastal communities in the Scandinavian countries as far back as 9,000 years Before Present (BP) and on the Bering Sea and Greenland from 5,000 BP. In western Russian, the earliest inhabitants date to approximately 40,000 BP at two principal sites, Kostenki (Holliday et al. 2007) and Mamontovaya Kurya (Pavlov et al. 2001).[5]

In northeastern Eurasia, archaeological evidence verifies the existence of the Duiktai culture some 40,000–35,000 BP (Mochanov 1977), who inhabited much of the coastal, riverine and delta environments, including parts of the contemporary Sakha Republic (Ricaut et al. 2005; Mochanov 1969; Fedoseeva 1999).[6] This Paleolithic group likely represents the first establishment of permanent occupation.

Other scientists question Mochanov's claims: "The unreasonably high dating of the so-called Duiktai culture, allegedly beginning 35,000 years ago and continuing without particular changes up to 10,000 years ago (Mochanov 1977: 223–40), is justifiably a subject of criticism" (Dikov 2004: 11). Dikov explains the improbability that any culture would "stagnantly" exist for some 25,000 years and proposes instead "the progressive character of the Paleolithic in Northeast Asia." Beyond charting a progressive evolution of cultures across time, the possibility remains of colonization at an even earlier point by highly fragmented populations that did not leave descendants. This is suggested, for example, by a recent finding of a mammoth in eastern Siberia, whose skeletal remains show signs of human hunting dated 50,000 years ago (Pitulko et al. 2016; 2017).

The archaeological record shows how the significant changes in the global climate regime with the onset of the Holocene (approx. 10.5 thousand years

Figure 7 The process of working in the cryolithozone at the multilayered site Belk-achi I. (Bel'kachinsk culture, 5.2–4.1 thousand years BP), 1967. Source: Mochanov and Fedoseeva 2013.

BP) brought successive change in human inhabitance. A new culture, the Sumnaginsk, began replacing the Duiktai throughout their cultural range (Boyakova 2001). Duiktai hunted mammoth, bison, and other large mammals with large stone tips resembling those found in the Americas, suggesting that they followed the mammoths over the Bering Strait around that time (Argunov and Pestereva 2018). Five thousand years later, the Syalakhsk culture, with their new technologies, including bone harpoon tips, bows and arrows, grinding tools, and earthenware containers, either assimilated or forced away Sumnaginsk (Boyakova 2001). Accordingly, cultures with more successful technologies replaced the Syalakhsk, including Bel'kachinsk (5.2–4.1 thousand years BP), Ymyiakhtakhsk (4.1–3.3 thousand years BP), Ust-Milsk culture of the Bronze Age (3.3–2.4 thousand years BP), and cultural complexes of the early iron era (2.4–0.5 thousand years BP) (Argunov and Pestereva 2018).

The main subsistence of these early cultures was inland hunting and fishing. The first archaeological evidence of sea mammal hunting dates to 2000–3000 BP. Reindeer herding evidence appears only after 2000 BP, with archaeological evidence tracing its beginnings to southern Russia and Mongolia and spreading north from there (Levin and Cheboksarov 1955).

Critical to the adaptive success of these early cultures was the flexibility to move between subsistence practices in response to climatic fluctuations (Krupnik 2014).

Archaeological evidence suggests the utilitarian knowledge of ecosystems and also a culture's "knowing" via their cosmology, their understanding that they were one of many sentient (spirit-filled) entities. Robert McGhee eloquently describes this spiritual aspect while explaining Palaeo-Eskimo tool manufacturing practices:

> The Palaeo-Eskimos did not limit their manufacturing skills to the production of economically useful tools and weapons . . . they transmuted many of their ideas about the spiritual world into material objects. Tiny carvings in ivory or wood portray spirit animals, the faces of human-like beings, creatures suggesting human-animal transformations. . . . These "fossilized ideas" allow archaeologists an unusual insight into the spiritual life of the first peoples of the Arctic. (McGhee 2001: 10)

Findings excavated at the Yana RHS site dating back to 28,000 BP include ornamented and symbolic objects carved from mammoth tusk with anthropomorphic designs that echo the hunting practices and shamanistic images of the early twentieth-century Yukaghir (Pitulko et al. 2012).

Much later evidence supports a vernacular "knowing" of an ecosystem alive in physical and spiritual parameters, in this case of the sentience of permafrost. A description by E. Ysbrants Ides, a Danish diplomat who traveled to China in 1692 via Russia and parts of Siberia, documented how the local people on the Ket River understood the origins of mammoth teeth and body parts found there:

> Concerning this animal, there are very different reports. The Heathens of Yakut [Sakha], Tungus and Ostiak say that they continually, or at least by reason of the very hard frosts, mostly live underground, where they go backwards and forwards; to confirm what they tell us, that they have often felt the Earth heaved up when one of these Beasts was on the march, and after he was past the place, sink in, and thereby make a deep pit. They further believe that if their animal comes so near to the surface of the frozen Earth as to smell or discern the air, he immediately dies, which they say is the reason that several of them are found dead, on the high banks of the river where

they unawares came out of the ground. This is the opinion of the infidels concerning these beasts, which are never seen. (Ides 1706: 24)

Other testimonies further support the idea of permafrost's sentient quality. Academic K. Baer noted that the word "mammoth" was from Finno-Ugric *maa muut* or "earth rat." *Maa muut* lived underground and caused the ground to move (permafrost heaving); they were never found alive because upon surfacing, they would die instantly from the sun's rays (Protopopov et al. 2018).

Sakha's relatively recent arrival in the north and their adaptation of a southern horse and cattle breeding subsistence practice to an extreme continental climate give an explicit understanding of how a culture negotiated its adaptation to a new climatic regime and continued to adapt to the unprecedented change of contemporary times. It also means that Sakha's ways of "knowing" their new permafrost environment are more accessible. Sakha's permafrost knowledge is reflected in how they have adapted to their specific permafrost place, both physically and spiritually, and how they have used this "cold resource" (Suleymanov 2018) to their utmost advantage. The development of that knowledge system began with their migration north.

Sakha as Newcomers in the North

Sakha's historical narrative of Omoghoi and Ellei explains the how and the why of their Turkic ancestors' migration north.

At the foot of the Ural Mountains lived a man named Khonn'os-Khiyyppar. He had four sons. One day he went hunting. With his arrow he shot a bird with beautiful multi-colored plumage. While plucking the bird he cut off the two wings and the tail. He gave two of his sons each a wing and another the tail. The last son was offended and angry and said crying, "He gave to his favorite sons but he didn't give me anything." From that time, he held a grudge against his parents and held it in his mind to run away from them to a distant land. Khonn'os-Khiyyppar was a Tatar.[7] He had a friend named Khongkhor-Saara. One day he told his friend, "to the northeast of us, in all likelihood, is a beautiful country where those same beautifully plumed birds spend summer and get very fat." The fourth son heard this and, without saying a word to his parents, disappeared with his wife. He was called Omoghoi and was about 70 years old. He found the headwaters of the Lena and, sitting on a floating tree, came downstream.[8]

One day Khongkhor-Saara was again with his friend. Khonn'os-Khiyyppar was crying, and told about how his son had disappeared, "When I told that day about the northeast country, the son listened with special interest. More than likely he ran to that empty place where there are no people and no herds. Because of that there is no news of him." When Khongkhor-Saara got to his home he told his family about the escape of his friend's son. He also had a few sons of which one was named Ellei, whom his parents didn't love. Ellei, hearing his parents' telling of the escape of Omoghoi to the mysterious northeast edge, also decided to run there. He reached the Lena headwaters and discovered foam from a fallen larch and the traces of a fire, and guessed that another person had recently been there. All along his journey downriver he found the same traces of fallen trees and fires. Finally, he reached the Lena valley and met with Omoghoi there who already had horses and horned herds and a few daughters. Ellei asked, "How did you start herds without bringing them with you?" to which Omoghoi answered, "I found them here. Being here without herds made me very sad and I cried. I prayed to my gods to give me horses and horned herds so that I had something to eat and exist from. And one day, walking about the place behind *Ytyk Khaia* [sacred mountain], I found a pair of colts, one male and one female. They grew and multiplied and I had mares. Then at the north of *Ytyk Khaia* I found a pair of calves, also one male and one female. That is how I got herds." Omoghoi had 2 sons and a daughter. Ellei liked Omoghoi very much and stayed to live and work with him (Ksenofontov 1975: 55–56).[9]

Not long after Ellei began to work for Omoghoi the two begin to disagree and fight. When Omoghoi learned that Ellei had married his only daughter, his anger exploded. To spite the newlyweds, Omoghoi gave them only a hunchbacked piebald horse and a one-horned cow as a dowry. Ellei and his wife decide to build their home like the houses of the Indigenous Tungus and far away from Omoghoi. They created the first Sakha *uraha* [the summer dwelling, a birchbark tent with a round configuration of postholes]. Ellei next burns the first *tüpte* [dung burned to ward off insects]. Omoghoi's herds gather at Ellei's *tüpte* and he and his wife steal the mare's milk in the night and make a great amount of *kymys* [fermented mare's milk]. Next Ellei takes the birch bark from the trees, brings it to his wife who makes the first great *saar yaghas* [a huge ceremonial birch bark container] and many smaller birch bark containers. Ellei fashions the first horse hair ropes to tie the newborn colts, and carves the first *choroon* [wooden chalice made from birch wood]. After all these preparations, he organizes the first *yhyakh* in these new northern lands. (Alekseev et al. 1995)

The Ellei and Omoghoi narrative explains Sakhas' southern ancestry and their horse and cattle agropastoralism in the subarctic. Shifting to another Sakha historical narrative, we find an explanation of the origins of the Viliui Sakha, Sakha who inhabitant areas along the Viliui River:

In ancient times the Tumat inhabited the Viliui regions. They practiced hunting, fishing and reindeer herding. In one of the encounters with Tungus, many Tumat were killed. One girl by the name of Dzhardakh survived. She sat on a raft and floated down the Viliui. At the mouth of this river it met the Lena where the girl found a small boat and decided that somewhere up that river there were people living. She got in that boat and went up the river to find the place Saisari, where Tygyn lived at that time. He took her as his younger wife and had 5 sons with her. Tygyn loved Dzhardakh and their 5 sons more than his older wife and sons. Out of jealousy and envy, the older wife agreed with her sons to murder Dzhardakh's sons. Dzhardakh, having learned of the plan, took her sons and hijacked the livestock that were on the summer pasture up along the left bank of the Lena. Tygyn sent a posse for the runaways, chasing them westward, believing that Dzhardakh would be returning to the Viliui. Many days passed and the posse returned but the runaways had arrived by the middle of August to a place called *"üchügei alaas,"* or very good *alaas*. It was in the present-day Olyokminsk valley and this is where they wintered.

Finding out that Dzhardakh had gone up the Lena, Tygyn sent another posse in the spring. As the result of the first battle with the fugitives the posse had run out of arrows, and they went back. After that Dzhardakh told her people, "I know very well Tygyn's revengeful character. He will either send an army for us or he will come himself. We need to go even farther. My homeland is a good place. There are fields and wild animals in abundance. My land is north of here and if we leave now, we will get there in time for the hay cutting." The runaways arrived on the Viliui (river) above Suntaar. Here they met with Tungus and offered this idea: Why should we kill each other for the land, which is plentiful for all? Let your man go into battle with our bold man. If yours kills ours, we will leave and if ours kills yours, you leave.

The plan was accepted. Birkinga Bootur represented Dzhardakh's side and from the Tumat side, they sent their main shaman, a great conjurer. Birkinga Bootur was the victor and the Tumat left for a distant place. Dzhardakh's people settled as such: Iria Tirilik and Boskhon Bialgiati in Khocho, Toiuk Bulgudakh, Suordaaii Biargian and Dzhardakh herself in Suntaar, and by the Nyurba lake Birkinga Bootur. Later Tygyn sent people to the Viliui regions for Dzhardakh and her sons, but no one came back: they all remained to live on the Viliui. (Mikhaleva-Saia et al. 2013: 288)

These origin narratives are perpetuated from generation to generation within Sakha culture to make sense of their world, of how they came to be in the extreme north, and the foundations of their sacred practices, most notably *yhyakh*.

OTHERS' ACCOUNTS OF SAKHA ORIGINS

Another source of historical narrative documenting Sakha's southern origins and settlement in the north are the accounts of explorers, academics, and political prisoners of the Imperial Russia era,[10] and the investigations by academics and government researchers in the twentieth century.[11] These are interwoven with archaeological and historical findings to produce a main narrative that establishes how, in the context of the *longue durée* of human inhabitance in northeastern Eurasia, Sakha are relative newcomers. Their Turkic ancestors migrated from Central Asia to the Lake Baikal area of southern Siberia in approximately 900 BP, then migrated north in the Genghis Khan period, arriving on the middle Lena in the fourteenth and fifteenth centuries (Ksenofontov 1992).[12] They represented two Turkic components, the Kurykan and Kipchak (Gogolev 2000). The Sakha language is Turkic with many Mongol linguistic elements from their several century sojourn in the Baikal regions and also Tungus aspects from their new northern homeland (Boyakova 2001). Sakha's unique ethnic economy, culture, physical appearance, and language came fully into being in their new northern homeland in the processes of their human-environment and human-cultural interactions (Gogolev 2000).

The development of this narrative is rooted in early accounts and has evolved over time. During the Jessup expedition to north Asia (1897–1902), Waldemar Jochelson wrote that Sakha had come north from the Buryat-Mongol area in the time of Genghis Khan and spoke a language of the Turko-Tatar tribes from the south. He further noted that outsiders used the Tungus word "Yakut," for them, but that they called themselves "Sakha" 'person' (Jochelson 1895: 6–7). Both Sakha's southern origin and their Turkic roots are evidenced by the archaeological analysis of *uraha* and *balaghan* (typically the winter dwelling, a wooden structure with a rectangular footprint) in both northern Sakha and southern Kurykan (a Turkic culture of Baikal) sites (Gogolev 2015b: 66).

The twentieth-century academic Gavriil Ksenofontov traced Sakha's ancestors' migrations from southern Siberia along the Lena River north. His work shows how they used several different routes, including one path along the Chona River to bring them to the Viliui River regions (Ksenofontov 1992: 6–10). At the time, the Viliui regions were inhabited by reindeer-herding, hunting, and fishing Tungus (Evenk and Even) (Mikhaleva-Saia et al. 2013: 135). As Sakha began settling the Viliui, Tungus either fled to adjacent mountainous areas, assimilated into Sakha culture, or were plundered (ibid). A 1676 census map shows Sakha populating the central regions with scattered settlement in the Viliui regions, which were held predominantly by Tungus. By 1897 a similar census map shows Tungus only in the more remote areas of the Viliui, with the predominant population Sakha (Mainov 1927). Early Soviet accounts reference the displacement, assimilation, or plunder of the Tungus and also the changes to the land that Sakha introduced.

> The Yakuts [Sakha] . . . came from the south . . . being cattle raisers . . . first occupied pastures and valleys [which] began their inroads into the heart of the Lena-Viliui plateau. In the process of time the former inhabitants, the Tunguses, were gradually driven out of the country and a complete change in the occupation of the inhabitants ensued: the breeding of cattle being substituted for the chase [hunting]. This change was accompanied by the destruction of the primeval forest, which was resorted to by man to increase the area of pastures and meadows . . . on such tracks appear rich grass meadows, occasionally assuming the character of peculiar meadow-steppes. (Abolin 1929: 338)

The author is describing how the horse and cattle breeding Sakha managed existing pastures and also made new ones in order to expand their herding capacity. Despite substantial evidence, some continued to question how and why Sakha landed in the north: "Of all who have considered this situation, the question remains of exactly when, by whom, and how cattle and horses got here. And along with those questions, the firm conviction that such a cold and completely forested region could not become a birthplace for an independently appearing pastoralist culture" (S. I. Nikolaev 1976: 111).

Perhaps the exact how and why of Sakha's northern migration can only be left to speculation. It is certain that Sakha's historical narratives and the archaeological and linguistic evidence to date show how Sakha's Turkic ancestors migrated from the south to the north in the 1300s or 1400s and represent a unique horse- and cattle-breeding culture on the permafrost (Gogolev 1993, 1992; Ksenofontov 1992; Okladnikov 1970; S. I. Nikolaev 1995).

Sakha's Indigenous Knowledge of Permafrost

> As it fits the conquerors of the pole of cold, Yakut [Sakha] are always ready to use the freeze like their partner in daily life. (S. I. Nikolaev 2009a: 25)

Northern cultures adapt physically and culturally to be successful in their environment. They have done so historically (cf. Redman 1999) and in contemporary contexts (cf. Krupnik and Jolly 2002). Sakha use the cold to not just survive but to thrive. Their adaptations reflect a way of knowing, in this case, of knowing permafrost and the ecosystem it supports, that can be extrapolated from their historical narratives, linguistic heritage, forecasting and prediction practices, innovations within their specific ecosystem, and food systems.

Historical Narratives. For all of human history, humans have used narratives to explain their origins and to teach the next generation (Cruikshank 1997; Lawrence and Paige 2016). Sakha's *Taal Taal Emeekhsin* (Old Woman Taal Taal) narrative teaches about Sakha's adaptation to the extreme north and how that adaptation is intertwined with their understanding of the sentience of all living and nonliving beings. Old Woman Taal Taal is an elderly woman who ventures out on the river ice one day to get water. She slips and falls and is not able to get up because the ice is holding her down. She begs the ice to release her, but when nothing happens, she beckons the sun to help her by shining brightly to melt the ice. The sun shines but is quickly covered by a cloud, who claims itself superior to the sun. Taal Taal then appeals to the wind to blow the cloud away, but as it begins to blow, a mountain blocks the wind. The mountain begins to claim its supreme power over all, when a mouse begins to burrow through the mountain. Next, a dog arrives and swiftly bats the mouse away. A human then commands the dog to obey, displaying human superiority. Seeing this, Taal Taal challenges the human to confront the *abaahy* (devil), who soon arrives and scares away the human. Next the *oiuun* (shaman) arrives to confront and banish the *abaahy* by beating their drum and making incantations. Curious about the *oiuun's* supreme power, Taal Taal challenges the *oiuun* to jump into the fire. The *oiuun* admits fire's superiority, when suddenly water jumps up to put out fire. But as water continues to flow away from where the fire was, Mother Earth soaks up the water. Taal Taal asks Mother Earth if there is anyone stronger than her. Mother Earth answers no, there is no one or no thing that is stronger than her. Then Taal Taal knows who is the strongest and who she needs to ask for help. Then Mother Earth frees Taal Taal from the ice. Taal Taal bows to her and gives her gifts. The narrative of "Old Woman Taal Taal" teaches that Sakha live within a world of sentient beings and that they are in a subservient relationship to Mother Earth.

Narratives also explain cultural understandings of how seasons came to be. One explains the length of seasons. Creating the world, the Gods asked humans, "Do you want winter to be longer or summer?" The humans answered, "Ask our friends . . . the horse and bull." The horse wanted summer longer because in winter its legs and hooves felt very cold. But the bull wanted winter longer because in the summer heat its nose got wet. Then the Gods made winter longer and summer shorter. Having gotten angry, the horse kicked the bull in the nose and knocked out its upper teeth. The bull butted the horse in its side and pierced through its bile. Since that time horses have no bile and horned cattle no upper teeth (Sivtsev 1996: 131). Although this explanatory narrative leaves the listener a bit perplexed about its deeper meaning (horses have no gallbladder but they still produce bile; horned cattle *do* have upper teeth), it does explain the long winters and short summers.

A narrative that explains the winter's unique climatic conditions, specifically the extreme dry, cold three-month period of Sakha's subarctic area, is *Jyl Oghuha* (the Bull of Winter) (Ergis 1974: 123–24; Kulakovskii 1979: 45–46; Seroshevskii 1993: 26). *Jyl Oghuha* is a white bull with blue spots, huge horns, and frosty breath. Historically, the first snows fall in September but stop in mid-December when *Jyl Oghuha* arrives from the Arctic

Figure 8 *Jyl Oghuha* represented on a 1997 calendar, showing *Akhsynn'y* (December) when he arrives, *Tokhsunn'u* (January) when he loses one horn as temperatures lift, and *Olunn'u* (February) when the other horn and his head come off and he leaves as spring shows it first signs. Source: Bichik-Poligrafist wall calendar. Photo configuration by Kathryn Tuyaara Yegorov-Crate.

Ocean, thanks to excessive cold and dryness. *Jyl Oghuha* holds temperatures at their coldest (−60 to −65 degrees Celsius; −76 to −85 degrees Fahrenheit) through January. In early February, as temperatures begin to break, one of the bull's horns falls off. In another few weeks, with more warming, the second horn falls. Finally, in another few weeks, the bull's head falls off, the snows fall once again, and spring is sure to have arrived.

Sakha's Linguistic Heritage

A second way to discern a people's vernacular knowledge is via their linguistic heritage (Harrison and Raimy 2007). Language is a definitive entry point into how a culture perceives, makes sense of, uses or interacts with, and positions itself in its world (Kempton 2001; D'Andrade 1995).

Perhaps the most compelling linguistic evidence of Sakha's permafrost knowledge is their unique terminology for permafrost's different forms. Although many Sakha words for landscape features come directly from southern pastoralist practices (IHRISNA 1962: 2), Sakha are credited with developing the words that describe the cyclical progression of their permafrost system and its surface qualities. *Byllar* (*bylar*) are high-centered polygons (ice wedges). They are often found in concert with *ieie* (*ie*) thermokarst[13] depressions (areas of erosion), which have water between the high-centered polygons. The next formation is *jüöje* (*diuedia*) a thawing lake. *Tyympy* is a *jüöje* that is full of water. *Bulgunn'akh* (*bulguniakh*) is a domelike hill that is founded on an underground ice core. Lastly, *bayjaraakh* (*baidarakh*) are formations that resemble earth mounds as thawing progresses further. Sakha developed this specific knowledge of changing permafrost conditions to succeed in their pasture-making activities in the new northern climate. I include the Russian words to show how they are derivatives of the Sakha terms and represent a language acquisition pattern that contradicts the normal flow of words from Russian into Sakha. The accuracy of the terms in designating the cycles of permafrost conditions is verified by the fact that these words are the lingua franca of contemporary international permafrost science (Efimov and Grave 1940; Solovyev 1959: 10–12; Czudek and Demek 1970; Troeva et al. 2010).

Sakha names for seasonal cycles and months reflect how seasonal changes and climatic conditions interface their subsistence practices. Sakha divide the subsistence year into two: winter and summer, not unlike other southern pastoralist cultures of Asia and Europe (Gogolev 2015a: 18). Sakha orient their annual cycle to both the four directions and the times of day. The new year is morning and begins in the east, the direction of the origin of all life. Spring is considered daytime and comes from the south where the bright *Ürüng Aiyy Toion* (Great Lord Deity) lives. Autumn comes from the west and is the evening of the year. Winter, when the sun barely rises, is night and comes from the north (ibid. 34).

The names of months in the part of the year when Sakha are busy with subsistence are specific to those activities and the existing environmental conditions. *Kulun Tutar* (March) means "holding the foal" and is the time to keep newborn colts from their mothers in order to reserve mare's milk to make *kymys* for human use. *Muus Ustar* (April) literally, "taking off the ice," signifies the time to remove the ice windows from the winter home before they melt. *Yam Yia* (May) is "spawning month," named for the time that lake fish lay their eggs. *Bes Yia* (June), "pine month," means it is safe to harvest pine pulp for food without harming the trees. July is *Ot Yia* "hay month," and marks the beginning of the hay harvesting season with *Atyrjakh Yia* (August), or "pitchfork month," the time of stacking hay. September is appropriately called *Balaghan Yia* to mark the move from the *saiylyk* (summer home) to the *kystyk* (winter home). *Altynn'y* means both "hunting month" from the paired word, *bult-alt*, and also "sixth month," based on the Sakha word for six, *alta*. The rest of the months, November through February, are numerical: *Setinn'i, Akhsynn'y, Tokhsunn'u, Olunn'u* (seventh, eighth, ninth, and tenth, respectively) and times of low activity in their environment for Sakha (ibid).

Word variants within the vernacular language reflect how a culture shapes the symbolic forms to reflect local and regional differences. Sakha's summer activities, although relatively universal, also vary from one place to another. A 1965 expedition in Suntaar documented how inhabitants called *Yam Yia* (May): *balyk yar yia* (fish spawning month) and *tirge yia* (snare month), the latter to designate the time to hunt hares. *Bes Yia* (June) also had variants: *byrdakh yia* (mosquito month) and *bes sular yia* (month to halter the pine, referring to harvesting pine sap). *Atyrjakh Yia* (August) was also known as *kydama yia* (longest pitchfork month), *kydama suuiar yia* (longest pitchfork washing month), *ot mas khagdaryiyar yia* (month that trees and plants yellow), *ardakhtaakh yia* (rainy month), and *tongoruulaakh yia* (month with frosts) (IHRISNA 1965: 1).

The Sakha words for "cold" is from the Tungus language, one of several terms Sakha adopted for conditions and phenomena they did not know in the south. They developed variants of the term to be more specific to environmental conditions and to communicate important information. It is important to know the variants for the word for cold (*tymnyy*) to be prepared for the right conditions: *bytarghan tymnyy* (crackling cold), *jybardaakh tymnyy* (frosted cold), *aan küden tymnyy* (strong foggy cold), and *ulakhan kyraadistaakh tymnyy* (very big temperature cold) (ibid. 2). The same is true for variants of the extremes of summer heat (*kuiaas*): *ümürük kuiaas* (narrow heat), *öngürük kuiaas* (intolerable heat), *buhar kuiaas* (boiling heat), *buhuruk kuiaas* (half-cooked heat) *syralghannaakh kuiaas* (scorching, unbearable heat) (ibid. 3). Land names are also diverse: *sir khotu baha* (the land's northern end), *ürekh baha* (river's headland), *ürekh tördö* (river origin land), *uhun sinn'iges sir kuturuga* (long thin land tail), *sir khotu kuturuga* (land's northern tail), and *baranar baha* (the used-up end) (ibid. 36).

Toponyms also have Tungus influence. It has long been known that the names of the two villages where I conduct most of my research, Elgeeii and Kutana, are Tungus, as is their regional center, Suntaar, itself named after a mighty Tungus *oiuun* (see map 2).

Other toponyms of Tungus origin are only recently being discovered. In the settlement Togusskovo of the Viliuisk region, researchers recently substantiated that the village's toponyms are clearly divided into Sakha and Evenk (Tungus) names. They were able to do so by correcting the existing

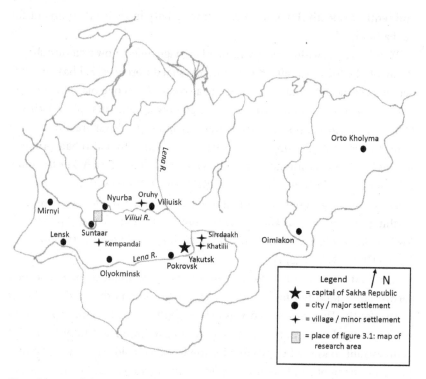

Map 2 Map of the Sakha Republic showing locations mentioned in the text. Map by author.

Russian toponyms of the GIS database with the historical names used by local inhabitants. This not only produced rich information for each place-name location but also showed how Evenk toponyms dominated one half of the settlement and Sakha the other (Filippova and Bagdariin 2018).

Sakha's Forecasting and Prediction Practices

Toward the end of 2010 summer research, Martha said she had recently heard several reports from a *bilge* (Sakha weather predictor, from *bil* 'to know') on the radio. He was providing an explanation about why there was so much water on the land. I was eager to know more. I contacted him and arranged a meeting.

There is the *kuturuksut* [*oiuun*'s helper] who follows and learns all the *oiuun* does for 6 or 7 years. Then the *oiuun* gives a sort of exam to the *kuturuksut* and, with that, knows what they will be and tells them . . . I was told that I am a *bilge* . . . I can tell if the month will be dry or wet. I know how to read everything in nature, the sun, the moon, the trees . . . that is what I read . . . I watch and learn and study it and tell . . . I know it. I have been watching this for 30 years . . . I know where the sun comes up and goes down and the moon cycles . . . and I study four stars that also tell me . . . I don't write it down . . . none of it . . . I have it all in my head. (Vasili Yegorovich Vasiliyev, interview in Kundeii village, August 12, 2010)

He proceeded to draw a schema of the *aar baghaakh* (central structure in the *yhyakh* festival) and to explain how it acted as a compass for Sakha life and the changing weather patterns.

These vernacular ways to predict weather are another rich insight to a culture's knowledge system (Orlove et al. 2000). For Sakha, *bilge* can foretell the weather by reading the sky (day and night) and gauging the cyclical nature of the ecosystem based on a form of shamanistic power (Gogolev 2015a: 27). *Bilge* also know the wet and dry cycles of the permafrost system, both the longer forty-year cycles and the shorter wet and dry periods. This knowledge is crucial in an unusually dry permafrost ecosystem in which plants depend on water transferred up from thawing permafrost (Mikhaleva-Saia et al. 2013: 122).

For as soon as the crops are in, they spike and ripen in six weeks, for the sun in these latitudes in the summer sets for a short time or does not set at all and the soil receives warmth day and night. At the same time, the most amazing thing is that it doesn't rain here at this time, and the land, which, I must say, is thick and black here, thaws no deeper than a quarter or a half a quarter of an arshin.[14] In that way the roots receive moisture from below, and on the top the plants use the strong warmth and so they grow very quickly. (Vittenburg 1927: 17)

Bilge is another example of how Sakha continue to use their historical belief to work within the limitations of their permafrost environment. Of course, every person professing to have the gift of *bilge* may not actually be *bilge.* Since 1991 I have met Sakha individuals who possess a power beyond the ordinary who I can safely say possess one of the *oiuun* powers. I have also met charlatans, those who do not. One of my collaborators reported to me in July 2020 that a local *bilge* had predicted a period of dry heat and advised people who had cut their hay to let it cure a few more days. The next day it started to rain and continued for the rest of the week. The *bilge* sheepishly explained that they had consulted the Internet to make their forecast.

Another way to predict weather and environmental conditions is the use of Sakha proverbs. There are many to predict the cycles of wet and dry. "When it will be a *kuraan jyl* (dry year), the field mice go in their burrows," or "A spring without lightning means a dry summer" (Sosin 2010: 52). To predict a water time, "When a water year is coming, the bittern roars 7–8 times," or "If the birch has a lot of sap in spring, a rainy summer is coming." "When mosquitoes are many" foretells an *öng jyl* (bountiful year) (ibid. 54). Common knowledge of the wet season versus dry season determines the timing of the first and last snowfalls, with it snowing earlier in the fall and lasting later in the spring during the wet years and the opposite in dry years (Mikhaleva-Saia et al. 2013: 120). These time-tested ways were essential to survival for herders in the conditions of permafrost, and some use them to this day despite the modern reliance on instrumental data (Gogolev 2015a: 33).

Innovations Based in Ecosystem Constraints or Possibilities

Permafrost, in many ways like water, is a central element of life in the north and has both life-giving and life-detracting qualities. Knowing permafrost is critical to discern its beneficial and its deleterious properties. "Get up, get up!" my host Natalia beckoned when she saw me sitting in the circle with others, as the *choroon* of *kymys* was passed around. I suddenly wondered if I had sat in the wrong place or with a different group than I should have. It was my first *yhyakh* and my first time in Sakha. I assumed that since I was invited to join them, it was in line with custom. I looked around to see if anyone in the circle could give me a clue of what I was to do. By that time, Natalia had made it across the field to me. As she gently laid a decorated square of heavy felt by me, she made eye contact with elders in the circle who nodded in approval. She explained in a soft voice, "I guess no one told you yet . . . but women especially should not sit on the ground without protection. The cold will go right up through you." I had in fact noticed that there was a contrast between the coolness on the ground and the summer heat. I also saw that everyone else had a felt square. I got up, placed the felt square down, and sat just in time to receive the *choroon*.

Sakha use many innovations to take advantage of permafrost's life-giving qualities. A *buluus* is a frozen cellar made by digging down to the permafrost layer and excavating a large horizontal cavity. Typically, the storage area of a *buluus* is one to three meters below the land surface, with an angled stairway that leads down to the storage cavity and an above-ground structure that is well insulated to avoid any warm air coming through or into the passageway (Yoshikawa 2017). Once I learned about *buluus* early on in my research, I finally understood what all the tiny huts were by the older houses. They were not huts at all but rather the upper entry to a below-ground *buluus*. In the late 1990s, most cow-keeping households had a *buluus* that they used to store perishable foods (meat, milk, etc.) and ice (for drinking water) in the temperate months. By 2018–19, most households had abandoned using their *buluus*. "We have a *buluus* . . . we put our meat there . . . it is deep— but we have to watch it . . . in some places it holds the freeze and in others it doesn't . . . we know that the permafrost is thawing . . . we can see it in the *buluus*! It melts now . . . it is not like before" (Vasili Mikhailovich Lvov, interview, July 4, 2018).

I did find a few households still using a *buluus* in more recent fieldwork. When Mariya (Marusa) Pavlovna Afanaseyeva in Kutana told me that they still depended on their *buluus*, I immediately asked if I could see it. In part I was curious about what made it different from all the rest that were unusable owing to thawing permafrost. I also was visiting Marusa on a scorching hot day and thought it would give me some relief. Marusa looked surprised at my request, but she also knew from our decades-long relationship that I was prone to be curious about aspects of Sakha life that to her were routine. She led me to their home's entry room and handed me one of the two winter coats on the rack, "Believe it or not, you will need this!" I carried it with me as we walked outside and to a wooden hut on the edge of the forest. We donned our coats, and Marusa opened the door to reveal another door a few feet behind it. The second door was much more substantial than the first, with heavy insulation that went beyond its edges. Marusa opened it, and a

Figure 9 Entryway into Marusa's contemporary *buluus*. Photo by author.

wave of frosty air escaped. Once that cleared, I saw a downward canal into an icy chamber.

When I mentioned that so many others had abandoned their *buluus* because of flooding, Marusa explained that their *buluus* was still usable because its permafrost is protected from the thaw. They had built it in a place with forest cover to shield the ground from the sun's rays and where the ground has a less ice-rich permafrost. She added that many households are not using their *buluus* because everyone now prefers the convenience of an electric freezer.

Oibon is another innovation Sakha use to work within their permafrost ecosystem. *Oibon* is a wide hole cut in lake or river ice where herds can drink. It is covered with hides and insulating materials that keep the opening ice-free from one day to the next. In both Elgeeii and Kutana, *oibons* are used by many households, and there is usually a person who tends it to keep it accessible in case of storms, and to keep the opening ice-free. In Tumul, the tiny hamlet where Edjay lives, there are no *oibon* tenders. I know intimately about *oibon* from my own experience. I was in Tumul for a week one winter to learn cow-keeping practices from Edjay. One day I asked Edjay if I could video her taking the cows out to the *oibon* for water. She agreed and off we went, slowly out the gate to the road and down the road to the trail that led to *Ebee* (literally "grandmother" but used as an endearing name for lakes, here for Kÿÿkei Lake). Once at the lakeshore, we followed the path out to the *oibon*. She easily hoisted off the cow-skin covers, and the cows circled around and began taking long steady draws of water. Edjay kept busy using a short shovel to clear ice from the edges of the *oibon* that had formed in the several hours since she was there earlier. I was filming the cows drinking and Edjay was working when I took a sweep around behind myself to capture the lake and surrounds. Suddenly I heard "Aa-eee! . . ." I spun around to see that one of the cow's two back legs had gone into the *oibon*. Edjay was there immediately, grabbed the cow by its tail, and with one huge heave (and a lot of adrenalin) she jerked it back out. It's important to remember that Edjay stood four foot ten and maybe ninety pounds, if that. I had no time to even get over to help. I stood with my mouth agape. Our eyes met and she chuckled. I asked what happened. She said the cows are shy around new people and that one had gotten confused. It all happened so fast, and she extracted the cow with such dexterity that I suspected that it was not the first time.

Unless winter temperatures go below −40 degrees Celsius, contemporary cow-keeping households continue to water their herds at one of several village *oibons*, located on the lake in Kutana and on the Viliui River in Elgeeii. Today *oibon* are a simple construction, but in the past Sakha had more variations on the form, including *silaas oibon* (a warm *oibon*), and *oibon-khoton* (an *oibon* with barn), *oibon mojoghoto* (an *oibon* with a threshold for livestock to access water), and so on (IHRISNA 1972: 170).

Sakha also innovated ways to forage year-round to take advantage of the annual cycle from freeze to thaw. Depending on the time of year, they forage the small lake fish, *sobo* (*Carassius carassius*), using either *kuiuur* (a long wooden pole with a basket shape at one end), *ilim* (standing nets), or *mungkha* (a large sweep net). In January and February, in the depth of winter's cold, when *sobo* float in torpor (semi-sleep) just beneath the lake ice, Sakha cut a two-foot-wide hole in the lake ice and swirl a *kuiuur* to scoop up

Figure 10 Cows drinking at one of several *oibon* on the Viliui River in Elgeeii. Photo by author.

the fish. They use *ilim* when lakes are ice-free from June through September, harvesting from them daily. In early winter, once lake ice provides a firm foundation, they work in a large team to fish with a *mungkha*.

After hearing description after description of *mungkha*, I asked Montyor, an organizer of local *mungkha* in Elgeeii, if I could come along one day. He seemed reluctant but told me he would let me know when they were to set out. I thought maybe he was being polite in the moment and would not contact me after all. I knew that historically *mungkha* is an all-male activity. Women are prohibited from participating in the *mungkha* because they are considered unclean and bearers of bad luck. Perhaps he was uncomfortable because of my gender and worried about how the rest of the team would feel if he allowed me to come and potentially jinx their prospects. But in a few days, he did call and announced when he would come pick me up.

We arrived at Ulgutta (map 1), and the *mungkha* team was already in position, one man every ten feet or so, encircling the lake's ice. Each stood and chipped a hole at their place. They would use their hole to help move the net across the lake, from one end of the lake to the other, under the ice. At each end of the lake were two gaping holes. At one, several men worked to carefully lay out the net. Once the team around the lake signaled that they were ready, several men lowered the net into the hole, extending the ropes that kept its mouth open to either side. One by one the team took the ropes under water via the ice holes until it had reached the other side. As the attendants at the far end began to gather the net to pull it out of the lake, the previously silent crew started to hum with comments to each other about how many fish there might be. Anticipation was high. I started to feel really self-conscious . . . what if there were no fish because of me? The team drew up the net. It moved with flopping fish, and I felt relieved to see there was a catch. In the same moment a low groan emanated throughout the team. I noticed a few men glance my way and shake their heads. Next thing I knew, Montyor had quickly made his way to me over the ice, waving his hands as he approached, "No, not the best catch but we got some, and we are all happy that you are here to see how we *mungkha*." Despite his effort to quell the disappointment, after a few days I learned via village gossip that many did blame my presence on their slight catch. Soon after that experience I heard of other women who have participated in *mungkha* and the catch was far beyond expectations. That made me wonder about the historical practice of not allowing women to the *mungkha*. I decided right then to think that my observation of *mungkha* was well worth a bit of short-lived humiliation!

Sakha's Food System

Recipe books for Sakha's historical meat, milk, and forage foods inevitably open with words such as these, "The cold, which once isolated Yakutia from the central Russian culture, cultivated a specific lifestyle for the inhabitants of this extreme outback. This also applies to their food culture" (Fedorova 1991: 3). The "cold resource" not only provides everything in terms of transportation, access to subsistence resources, and the living resources themselves but also influences the cultural practices surrounding the storage and preparation of food (Suleymanov 2018). One Sakha food that succinctly illustrates the use of the cold resource is *tar*.

Tar is one of several soured milk concoctions also made by many Mongolic and Turkic tribes, as documented in linguistic and archaeological data (S. I. Nikolaev 2009a: 135). What is unique about Sakha *tar* is their innovative method of using soured milk to preserve other nutritious food stuffs in temperate months to be used later in a frozen state (Mikhaleva-Saia et al. 2013: 146). The process involves mixing the souring/fermenting milk with leftover milk products, plant products (wheat and porridge tailings), and animal parts (bones of water fowl, fish, and other hunting catch) for use in winter when food supplies are low (Savvin 2005: 99). The brew is kept in a large barrel-size container, with products added beginning in late summer and through the fall. The mass gradually freezes and is then cut into slabs to be used as needed for *khaahy* (porridge) and other dishes in the winter.

A 1913 study provided a highly technical explanation of the process:

> In summer, excess *suorat* is collected in a wooden barrel in a cool *ampaar* [shed] to continue to sour into November. On the top grows a smooth mold, below it a layer of serum and further down a protein precipitate. A form is made with snow to drain off the mold and serum and leave the protein precipitate in the shape of a tub, each weighing 5–8 *pood*.[15] That form of food from soured milk is called *tar*. It is eaten in the winter mixed with fresh cream or its sourness neutralized by cooking with barley and sweet roots of swamp grasses. In terms of the latter, most common is licorice. (All Russian Hygienic Exhibition 1913: 14–15)

Contemporary Sakha explain it differently. I heard many descriptions over the course of the fifty-five elder oral history interviews in my 1999 research. Elders talked about *tar* as being key to their survival and health. The depictions that stay with me most from elders' testimonies are, "*Tar* is great! We ate it all winter and never got sick!" and "*Tar* was how we were able to survive. It took the bounty of food we had in the harvest time and kept it for us to eat in the winter when food was scarce." I wanted to try *tar* just like I wanted to try *mungkha*. But no one makes it anymore. The making and use of *tar* diminished greatly in the Soviet period with the move away from a total reliance on home food production and the later importing of a

Figure 11 *Tar* in its final frozen slab state. Notice the man standing by the building to give perspective. Photograph by I. V. Popova, in Savvin 2005: 99.

variety of foodstuffs to village stores. Finding a Sakha who makes *tar* today is extremely rare, if not impossible.

Another Sakha food, *agharaan*, also relies on soured cultured milk and frozen temperatures, but it is solely used to preserve fish (S. I. Nikolaev 2009a: 126). Surplus fish from the summer's daily catch are mixed with sour milk reserves in a large birch container that is stored in a *buluus*. The flesh and bones break down over the course of the summer to produce a highly nutritious winter food (ibid. 127). It can also be made without the soured milk, instead using a base of bitter berries, either red currants or unripened black currants, whose acid preserves the fish (S. I. Nikolaev 1961: 43).

Sakha's Permafrost Knowledge from Explorer and Colonizer Accounts

The historical records of "visitors" to the Sakha's area in the early colonization period give some information about Sakha's permafrost knowledge. Many of them mention Sakha's adaptation to their extreme environment in the context of the challenge that the new dry and extremely cold climate posed to Sakha pastoralism (Savvin 2005: 203). Some descriptions reflect a certain stereotype, for example: "On the 9th of December," said Wrangel, "in the −33C we spent the night in the open, wide pastures, with nothing to protect us from the northern wind, around a fire set below the clear night sky. Here I was able to see how Sakha are hearty to the extent they can endure cold and discomfort" (Gartvig 1866: 191–92).

Wrangel had the wrong impression of Sakha at the time. Certainly, Sakha had developed a level of acclimation to the environment, but it is doubtful that they "endured the cold and discomfort' of −33C." More than likely, Wrangel assumed that Sakha were less than human, a colonial attitude that many white explorers maintained at the time. Others' records reflect more insightful observation, focused on how Sakha innovated to make a living in their new environment. Jochelson proposed that the extreme dry climate had forced Sakha to diversify beyond horse and cattle pastoralism and to engage in the other subsistence activities of hunting and fishing (1895: 8–9). Shimanskii noted this also: "Now, under the effects of their new conditions, they have a new economic relationship . . . before it was all herding and now includes fishing and hunting . . . and also they must make fields to grow wheat for bread" (1886: 311). Jochelson went on to observe that Sakha kept more cows than horses, in contrast to their southern counterparts, and purported this as their adaptation to the swampy conditions of the thaw in summer months (1895: 8–9). Others understood Sakha's increase in cows relative to horses as a response to their more settled life in the north which demanded more bulls to work the land (Nedokuchaev 1927: 494).

Some visitors assumed that Sakha did not use wheat prior to Russian invasion, based on the fact that Sakha did not have bread that resembled a familiar form. However, Sakha's Kurykan ancestors were known as *sukha-hyttar* (people of the plow), who grew wheat in their southern homeland (Ermolaev 1991: 6). Contemporary Sakha food historians document at least a dozen ways Sakha used wheat and other grains in precolonial times, in the form of *khaahy* and several different kinds of unleavened flat breads (Alekseeva 2007: 65–66). Additionally, linguistic evidence traces Sakha's word for wheat, *burduk*, to Turkic origins, and archaeological remains include instruments associated with wheat, including a grinding stone (ibid. 15, 11). More than likely, Sakha grew less wheat in the north than their southern Turkic ancestors owing to the permafrost conditions of the soil and the shorter growing period. Instead they utilized the wild grains that grew on the *alaas* landscapes and plowed minimally to avoid damage to the permafrost system. Their intricate vocabulary associated with the different stages of permafrost change detailed earlier reflects a deep understanding of how disturbance altered the landscape.

Scientific Permafrost Knowledge

Scientific knowledge of permafrost had its beginnings around the time of Russian colonization across Siberia. This was a time of colonial infiltration and resource grabbing by Imperial Russian forces. A comparison of two Sakha area maps, one from the seventeenth century and the other from the eighteenth, provides clues to how quickly the area was assessed and "known" (maps 3*a* and *b*).

Cossacks made the first recorded observation of permafrost in Russia in 1601 on the Taz River, just east of the Ural Mountains (Baer 2000: 13). There they observed how the soil was frozen at a certain depth. They continued to make this same observation across Siberia as they pursued land claims and *yasak* (fur tribute in the form of *kiis* [sable] pelts) for Imperial Russia (ibid. 13). Over a century later, Johann Georg Gmelin consistently recorded frozen soil from the Ural Mountains to Yakutsk while participating in the Bering Second Kamchatka Expedition (1733–43). These observations compelled him to change his depiction of Siberia in the *Flora Sibirica* from a land of unending natural wealth to a land of frost and cold (Gmelin 1747). Gmelin conducted botanical research and collected specimens during the expedition, and he also engaged local Sakha to explain how they used their frozen resource. In one excerpt he depicts a *buluus*: "There were berries covering the land. Sakha use them all year round by storing them in a cellar below the soil and in which they do not spoil even though the cellar is only a little over 2 meters deep" (Baer 2000: 107). On the same expedition Gmelin observed a century-old well in Yakutsk that the Cossack Yakov Svetogorov was hired to dig in 1685 to supply water for the Russian stronghold. Svetogorov had worked for four days, reaching a depth of 28 meters without breaking through the solidly frozen ground to water (Gmelin 1751). Between 1828 and 1837, Fedor Shergin also attempted to dig a well for a supply of good water, reaching a depth of 116.4 meters. He failed to reach water but

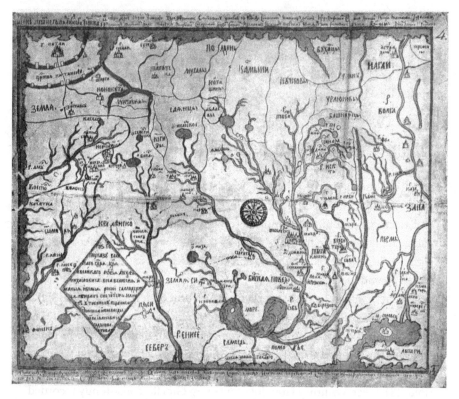

Map 3a "The first Russian map. North at the bottom, South at the top." Drawing of Siberia by Peter Godunov, 1667 (from L. Bagrov). Source: Vittenburg 2013.

the feat brought him recognition by the Russian Academy of Sciences and by academics worldwide interested in understanding the frozen soils (Baer 2000). Soon thereafter, the St. Petersburg Academy assigned naturalist Karl Ernest von Baer[16] to prepare the background information on frozen soils for an expedition intended to

> communicate the temperature data of the frozen layer, penetrating the Yakutsk shaft [that Shergin dug] and also in different places documenting the melting, strength and frozenness of the soil ice in Siberia; measure the temperatures to which the sun and atmospheric moisture warm the summer soil of the soil above the ice at different depths and in different places; determine the kinds of plants that are able in that context; determine the relationship of the sources to the soil ice; to the extent able, increase the number

Map 3b "Part of the Ice sea with the mouth of the Lena river and the Northern part of Yakutsk County." Map 6 from *Russian Atlas*, 1745. Source: Vittenburg 2013.

of observations of soil temperature in which the frozen condition of the water only presents part of the effect; and finally, train fit people to produce observations in those places where the expedition cannot go. (Ibid. 25–26)

The leader of the expedition was A. F. Middendorf, an expert in ethnology and natural history. They made temperature observations in *Shakhta Shergina* (Shergin's Mine), at the full depth of 116 meters and calculated the thickness of the permafrost in the Yakutsk area (ibid. 26). Baer used the expedition data to write the first theoretical survey of Siberian permafrost

(Tammiksaar 2002). Later studies on lake development (Zubrilov 1891) and on the native vegetation and soils (Abolin 1929) further enriched scientific knowledge of the frozen soil.

The most substantive advance of scientific permafrost knowledge was in the wake of Soviet period mining and construction activities. Mikhail I. Sumgin founded the new scientific discipline, "frozen soil science," or the "systematic and comprehensive study of permafrost soils." He published *Permafrost Soils of the USSR* (1927) and cofounded the Obruchev Permafrost Institute and the Yakutsk permafrost station directed by P. I. Melnikov (Alexander Nikolayevich Fyodorov, interview, December 10, 2018). Research areas included hydrogeology (Melnikov and Efimov 1953), the formation of the ice complex, _yedoma_ (Shumskii 1952), the origin of *alaas* (Solovyev 1959), and the physical and the mechanical properties of permafrost (Votiakov 1961). Sumgin's work to increase scientific knowledge of permafrost and to delineate "the region of permafrost" was not just research for research's sake but was also a highly political effort. His work contributed to many Stalinist five-year plans to advance the USSR as a major industrial power by demarcating the exact geographical area that needed to be transformed and by developing the scientific tools to do so (Chu 2015: 398).

There were observations made of frozen soils outside of Russia. For example, Sir Martin Frobisher made observations in 1577 on Baffin Island during his second voyage to find the Northwest Passage. While digging for gold ore, he noted how the ground stayed frozen to depths of "four or five fathoms, even in summer" (Ray 1973). But Russia and the USSR were always historically the center of permafrost science. In the twentieth century the United States Geological Survey (USGS) and the Army Corp of Engineers knew that. When they began the planning for a Permafrost Division in the US Arctic, they recruited Inna Poire, a Russian permafrost scientist. At that time, all the permafrost expertise was in the USSR, and most permafrost documents were in the Russian language (Chu 2020: 4–6).

The Complexities of Permafrost

Since Sumgin's era, permafrost has been defined as "soils that are frozen for at least two continuous years." Those frozen soils come in a myriad of compositions, depending on specific geological, hydrological, and climatic

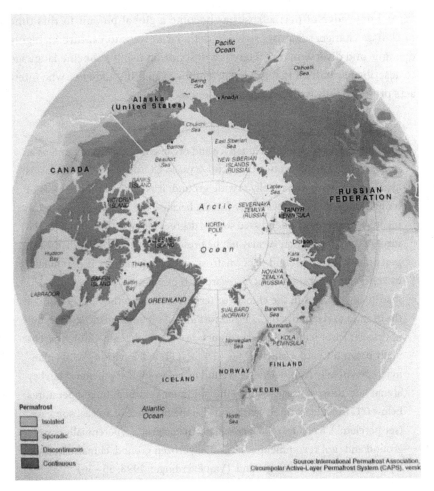

Map 4 Permafrost map. Varying shades on a continuum from dark to light indicate whether the permafrost is continuous, discontinuous, sporadic, or isolated. Source: IPA (International Permafrost Association).

conditions. Furthermore, permafrost can be continuous, discontinuous, sporadic, and isolated, as illustrated in map 4, showing permafrost's distribution on the planet according to those four parameters. Each of those are further delineated into permafrost types according to altitude, thickness or lack thereof of overburden cover, and ground ice content. It sounds counterintuitive, but it is a fact that not all permafrost has ice in it. In fact, most does not but instead is made up of frozen rock, sand, and other elements.

As knowledge of permafrost has become a global pursuit in this time of climate change, scientists strive to define it in ways to capture its highly dynamic and diverse nature. Here is a description using a specific language to describe permafrost in its global extent for a scientific audience who interacts professionally with permafrost science.

390. permafrost

Ground (soil or rock and included ice and organic material) that remains at or below 0°C for at least two consecutive years. COMMENT: Permafrost is synonymous with perennially cryotic ground: it is defined on the basis of temperature. It is not necessarily frozen, because the freezing point of the included water may be depressed several degrees below 0°C; moisture in the form of water or ice may or may not be present. In other words, whereas all perennially frozen ground is permafrost, not all permafrost is perennially frozen. Permafrost should not be regarded as permanent, because natural or man-made changes in the climate or terrain may cause the temperature of the ground to rise above 0°C. Permafrost includes perennial ground ice, but not glacier ice or icings, or bodies of surface water with temperatures perennially below 0°C; it does include 56—DEFINITIONS Revision—2005 man-made perennially frozen ground around or below chilled pipelines, hockey arenas, etc. Russian usage requires the continuous existence of temperatures below 0°C for at least three years, and also the presence of at least some ice. (see pereletok). SYNONYMS: perennially frozen ground, perennially cryotic ground and (not recommended) biennially frozen ground, climafrost, cryic layer, permanently frozen ground. (Van Everdingen 1998: 55–56)

A definition for laypeople that communicates permafrost's essential qualities is perennial frozen ground with an *active layer* (freezes and thaws annually), a *transient layer* (a typically ice-rich layer between the active layer and the upper permafrost), an *intermediate layer* (between the transient and the permafrost layers), and a *permafrost layer* (freezing and thawing at century to millennial scales) (French and Shur 2010: 191).

Overall, the scientific knowledge of permafrost evolved based on the historical, political, economic, and cultural context(s) in which it took place. "The shifting meanings of frozen earth in the scientific imagination" (Chu 2020: 9) are critical in order to grasp how this knowledge exists today. Early colonial permafrost knowledge developed in the process of either invasions, or extraction, be it the Cossacks' observations while establishing a fort for Imperial Russia in the 1600s or Frobisher's 1577 observation while digging for gold ore. Knowledge progressed along with further colonial development, from the digging of wells in Yakutsk to twentieth-century industrial efforts to extract resources from below the ground. However, long before scientific permafrost knowledge came to be, humans had expert Indigenous knowledge and local knowledge systems in place via a long history of adaptation to their permafrost environment. For Sakha, that expert knowledge is best exemplified in their ongoing relationship with *alaas*.

Alaas

Sakha's Home on Permafrost

Foundational to Sakha's knowledge system of *alaas* is their historical belief system and its entanglement of the living and nonliving. An understanding of their historical belief system is critical to fully perceive what Sakha do from day to day. Knowledge is socially produced and, in that process, works to imbue what is being known with particular cultural values and associations. Cultures that assign sentience to all animate and inanimate beings also practice social relations with those beings and thereby extend their "social world" to them (Cruikshank 2005). I came to this realization early on in my research.

Sergei pointed to the swirls of frost on our living room windows when I came down for morning tea: "The frost on the windows is different today . . . it is moving in concentric swirls across the panes. You probably need an extra layer now." I nodded in recognition and took my place at the table just as a wave of frosty steam spread across the kitchen floor from the entry door. The daughter from the kin household next door, where the cows were kept for both families, had entered to deliver morning tea milk. I knew from the cow-keeping households I was working with regularly that the arrival of new frost patterns and frozen waves of steam signaled that the time of slaughter had arrived, the time when temperatures stay below freezing day and night to enable storing meat in unheated outbuildings. At the time, I was documenting household food production activities via surveys, interviews, and participant observation. I was also using visual documentation in my research, which meant documenting Sakha's cow and horse slaughter. During tea, the phone rang. It was Ailita from one of my survey households telling me to come over if I wanted to document the slaughter. I jumped up and started to get ready. I had learned the art of protecting myself from the *albyn tymnyy* (deceptive cold) during my first winter in the early 1990s when it frostbit my cheeks without me knowing it.

The process of dressing for the outside takes time, starting with long underwear topped by leggings and a turtleneck shirt topped by a wool sweater and cashmere wrap on the back body, all covered by a heavy insulated calf-length coat. This along with *unty* (reindeer boots), insulated gloves, a fur hat, and a scarf to cover nose and mouth was how I "suited up" to venture out for various research activities. Once out on the street, I hustled to get over to Ailita's. As I walked, I saw a huge cloud of steam rise up from behind a solid wooden fence surrounding the household's yard across the street. I instantly knew that the steam was from opening the initial slit down the belly of a cow in the process of slaughter. I realized that other households had decided to slaughter that morning also.

Upon arriving at Ailita's, I was greeted by her husband and two other male kin in the yard preparing the ground and gathering tools. "Where is Ailita?" They motioned to the *khoton* (barn). I was confused at first. All the milk cows were in the pen with their udder covers on (used to protect them when it got colder). The *khoton* door was slightly ajar. As I approached, I could hear Ailita speaking in a low voice. I stood outside and waited so as not to interrupt. I wondered who was in there with her. She soon emerged from the *khoton*, acknowledged me with a nod and smile, then opened the back gate and led the rest of the herd out. After she was out of sight with the herd, one of the men came to lead the cow out of the *khoton* to the side yard. I wondered what had gone on in the *khoton* and where Ailita was taking the herd.

I stayed to document the slaughter, which begins with hitting the cow's forehead with the back of an ax. This knocks them out, which lets their heart continue beating so that the blood can be captured for *khaan* (blood sausage). Ailita returned twenty minutes later and got to work pouring the blood into the large intestine casing. I held open the mouth of the casing as she poured the blood in. She used twine to tie it up in foot-long sections. This was stored in the out building. She then picked up the pot with the liver and signaled me to follow her inside. We shed our outermost layer, and she began to fry up the liver. "May I ask what you were doing with the cow in the *khoton*?" Not looking up from cooking, she smiled and nodded, explaining, "I was preparing her for slaughter. I was explaining that it was nothing to be afraid of. This was her destiny . . . that *Ieiiekhsit* [deity protector of humans, horses, and cows] would take her on to the next place and that she should know that and be calm. I took the rest of the herd to another place so they would be protected from seeing or hearing it." I knew of this practice but this was the first time I had witnessed it. I was both taken aback to realize that she had done this and also comforted that the belief continued. I knew that the Soviet government repressed all outward expressions of Sakha belief. But this and other similar expressions of belief in daily life helped me to understand that Sakha's historical belief not only survived that period but also continues to provide a grounding for many to this day.

Sakha's historical understanding of an all-inclusive sentient world informs how permafrost and *alaas* knowledge "came to be" and continues within their cultural understanding. Sakha's historical belief system is animistic and aligns with other ancient understandings of humans' relationship within the natural world (Maak 1994: 280–97; Seroshevskii 1993: 593–655; Jochelson 1933: 103–6; Gogolev 1994).[1] It posits Sakha as guests on a planet inhabited by sentient beings, both living and nonliving. Sakha's belief facilitates survival in their extreme climate through the enactment of annual rituals and daily practices. These practices placate the earth and sky spirits, who, in turn, provide for them. It divides the world into three realms: the *khallaan* (upper world), *orto doidu* (middle), and *allaraa doidu* (lower) worlds. The *aiyy* (gods) live in the *khallaan* and are organized in a nine-tiered pantheon. Inhabiting the highest tier is *Ürüng Aiyy Toion*, the creator of all the universe. The deities below are various manifestations of that essential power. The most highly regarded are *Jühügüi*, deity protector of horses who sends horses to the middle world (Pekarski 1959: 854); *Ieiiekhsit*, the deity protector of humans, horses, and cows; and *Aan Alakhchyn*, spirit mother of nature (Gogolev 1994).

Human and nonhuman animals, plants, and *ichchi* (spirit keepers) inhabit *orto doidu*. *Ichchi*, inhabiting mountains, clouds, insects, trees, water, rocks, and the like, are able to think, be joyful, be offended, dream, and help someone (S. I. Nikolaev 1995: 98). Many aspects of the non- and metaphysical world are also *ichchileekh* (spirit-filled). Perhaps most importantly, words are *ichchileekh*, a phenomenon that explains the power of the words, from mundane usage to the texts of the *ohuokhai* dance:

...the power attributed to *ohuokhai* is not only in the aerobic release, but also in the power of the language that, according to Sakha belief, has its own *ichchi* (spirit), referred to as *tyl ichchite* (spirits of words): "Spoken words turn into a prophetic bird that flies according to the meaning of the words uttered and retells the original words" (Kulakovski 1979: 45). The act of speaking words gives them the power to fulfill their meaning. (Crate 2006b: 168)

Sakha invoke the spirit of words in their appeals to the fire, forest, earth, and the other *ichchi* when appeasing them. The spirit of the words interacts with the spirit being addressed. For example, water is *ichchileekh*, and "with the right words of respect, river water is said to braid itself in delight" (Kulakovski 1979: 189). Water is the conduit to the spirit world. Sakha place a cup of water by the deathbed to let the soul jump into the *ölüü uuta* (water for dying) (Gogolev 1994: 4).

Uot ichchite, the fire spirit, is a gray-haired elder man who requires regular feeding of the household's best food and drink to protect the hearth and home. *Jaajai Baraan Khotun* (commonly known as *Aan Alakhchyn* but also known by other names, this one specific to Viliui Sakha [see Ergis 1974: 117]), the keeper of all earth, oversees foraging, haying, and activities at the summer home. *Jaajai Baraan Khotun* is an old woman, an image carried over "from the times when women held a central role in society" (ibid.). The spirits of plants, in the form of tiny children, assist her by cleaning and dusting the leaves and grasses. *Baianai*, the spirit keeper of the taiga, forest, and all wild animals, is a jolly red-or black-haired elder wearing a coat of reindeer skin.

Allaraa doidu (the lower world) is an impassable swamp, inhabited by steel plants and *abaahy*, who are in constant pursuit of middle-world inhabitants. *Ichchi* and *aiyy* protect Sakha from *abaahy*. In more challenging circumstances, Sakha summon an *oiuun*, a person born with the powers or trained to have the powers to mediate the spirit world. The *ürüng oiuun* (white shaman), first documented in the eighteenth century (ILLA: 1), are holy priests whose main role is delivering the *algys* (sung prayer) to elicit plentiful conditions for summer harvests from the sky world deities during the *yhyakh* (Romanova 1987: 15). The *khara oiuun* (black shamans) travels across all three worlds to combat illness and the bad fate of humans. Once they discern the *abaahy* causing the bad fortune, they travel to fight it with spoken and sung incantations on their "spirit horse," which canters with the beat of the *düngür* (shaman drum) (N. A. Alekseev 1975: 162). In pre-Soviet times the *khara oiuun* conducted an annual blood sacrifice of horse or cattle to the *abaahy* (Troshanski 1902: 130). An *udaghan* is a female *khara oiuun*.

For the birth of people, cows, and horses, there are specific rituals with appropriate *ichchi* and *aiyy*. *Aiyyhyt* (goddess of birth for humans, horses, and cows) is a female deity carried over from the Sakha's matrilineal clan structure of the Paleolithic period (Okladnikov 1970: 35–37). For humans, she arrives seven days before the onset of labor and stays for three days after the birth to ease the process. The mother and her female kin perform a special ceremony in her honor before she departs. They smear their faces with warm fat and laugh hysterically. The stronger they laugh, the more pleased *Aiyyhyt* will be and the greater the promise of lifelong happiness for the new born (Kulakovski 1979).

Sakha's historical belief infiltrates their practices of living "by the *alaas*." The family carries out the ritual *salama yiaahyna* (hanging of the *salama*) during their semiannual move in late May or early June from the *kystyk* to the *saiylyk*. *Salama* is a twisted rope made from black and white horsehair from which pieces of colored fabric, animal figures made from birch bark, duck beaks, and fish bones are hung. *Salama* is a gift to the sky deities and an invitation for them to visit the middle world and be present during various rituals. For the *salama yiaahyna*, family members first light a fire by their dwelling and feed their best foods to *uot ichchite* while one member sings *algys*,

> You, sacred fire, elder, gift giver,
> Protector of our place and our elder
> Who gives us strength and spirit
> And pardons, we will always bow before you
> Let joyful be, let joyful be.
>
> (N. Ignataev, interview, May 10, 1992)

Participants then move to the lake adjacent to the *saiylyk* and hang the *salama* as a gift to the lake *ichchi*. The *ichchi* are "fed" to the intoning of an *algys*,

> You, gift giver of the lake
> Who gives us food, and life and pleasure,
> And existence and being,
> And pardons, we will always bow before you
> Let joyful be, let joyful be. (Ibid.)

Salama yiaahyna marks the beginning of seasonal work: the tending of herds; the hunting of duck, hare, and other wild game; the gathering of herbs, plants, pine sapwood, and berries; and the storing of foods for winter, such as using excess milk products to make *tar*, gathering and storing berries and plants, and salting, drying, fermenting, and freezing fish. This is also the time to remove birch bark, once the trees' sap flows in late spring, to make a variety of containers and utensils. July marks the beginning of the cutting, gathering, and stacking of hay for winter fodder. A ritual also marks this event, a ceremony in honor of the earth spirits and sky deities.

> The rich time of summer has come
> All the heat of the sun has brought the strong green grass
> Give us the best grass
> So that in the winter our herds aren't hungry
> And so there will be more herds
> Help us to make the most grass
> We are joyful and we give you, through the fire,
> The sweets and fat meat and the richest cows' milk
> And the strongest *kymys* to you
> We praise you with that. (Ibid.)

The family returns to the *balaghan* in early September, a move also marked by ritual ceremony.

Adapting Southern Pastoralism to the North

> In looking at the settlement pattern of the first herders from the south, they settled advantageously on the sunny side of the *alaas* terrace in groups of 2 to 8 households. (Gogolev 2015b: 64)

Alaas landscapes were the primary areas where Sakha's Turkic ancestors settled to continue their horse- and cattle-breeding subsistence. In the process, they developed a highly refined Indigenous knowledge of *alaas*. They adapted the more mobile nomadism of their southern origins, moving between pastures in an annual round, to a seminomadic lifestyle, moving between a summer and a winter home. They lived in forested areas in the

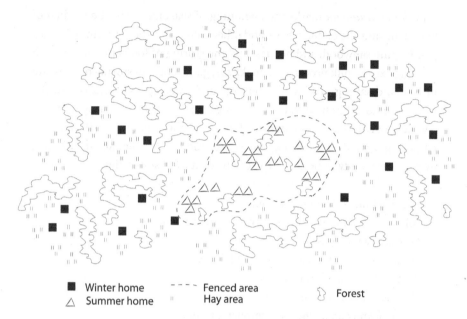

	Winter home	- - - - Fenced area		Forest
△	Summer home	⁞ Hay area		

Figure 12 Sakha settlement pattern showing summer and winter habitation. Drawn by author.

winter, where they had some protection from the elements, and then moved to the open *alaas* areas for the summer (figure 12).

Their social structure was highly stratified, characteristic of other pastoralist societies (Ruttan et al. 1999: 636). Wealthy Sakha *toions* (elite clan heads) with large herds exercised the right to use land, to keep others off that land, and to pass that land on to their kin. They depended on the poorer class for labor. Scholars claim that this was an indentured agreement wherein *toions* acted as provider-protectors, supplying food for the needy members of the population in exchange for labor (Pakhomov 1999). *Toions* also reaped "rents" from the middle class, smaller herd owners who used parcels of the *toions'* lands in return for a percentage of hay or animal produce. A predominant *saiylyk* social structure for these smaller herd owners was *kyttygas* (communal work) and *jukaakh* (living together, boarders) to accommodate the intensity of the work over the short summer period (Mikhaleva-Saia et al. 2013: 147). Smaller herd owners depended on a mixed subsistence mirroring the Indigenous Tungus strategies of hunting, fishing, and foraging. The poorest households, who could not afford cattle and had no *toion* to work for, relied solely on fish. This was so common that the word *balyksyt* (fisher) was used synonymously for "poor person" (Tokarev and Gurvich 1964: 250). On the Viliui River, Sakha who relied mostly on fish were referred to as *symahyt* (Ksenofontov 1992: 14), a name based on the word *syma* which refers to the preservation of small fish by layering them with larch boughs (Sleptsov 1972: 358).

Structures of Winter and Summer

Sakha's winter and summer dwellings contrasted sharply, a reflection of the extreme climatic differences between those two times of year. The main dwelling at the *saiylyk* was an *uraha*, a light, airy birch bark tent with a tall ceiling to allow for maximum air circulation. In winter Sakha lived in a *balaghan*, a heavily sealed wooden structure connected to their cow barn to maximize heat. Its location was critical: "Sakha located their winter home in a low spot that was most protected from the cold northern and western winds" (Gogolev 2015b: 72). In cross-section, the *balaghan* was trapezoidal in shape with vertical timbers placed at slight angles against a pole frame. Each autumn, household members sealed the structure with a mixture of fresh cow manure and clay, applied in three layers, each to a specific thickness, to produce an insulative, impermeable layer. From the time the first snow fell, they would pile snow up around the *balaghan* for greater insulation. The *balaghan* was divided lengthwise in two, with the main house for people to the south and, to the north, the barn area for herds. Its small area, an east-facing entry door that allowed the morning sun to warm the house, and the attached cow barn on its north side all maximized warmth (see figure 13).

The *balaghan* living space was arranged according to a hierarchy of age and gender. The light-filled south side was the place for men, considered the most respected household members, whereas the dark north side was the females' place (Danilova 2011: 46). Beds for household members ran along the walls of the main room, in order of the hierarchy within the household group. *Balaghan* floors were earthen, except for richer Sakha, whose *balaghan* had wood floors.

Sakha covered the *balaghan* windows in the fall and spring with woven horsehair to keep out insects, and in winter with either thick ice, cow stomach, or afterbirth, stretched tightly over a frame, to let in light (Kulakovski 1979: 88). They cut and installed ice windows about twenty centimeters thick

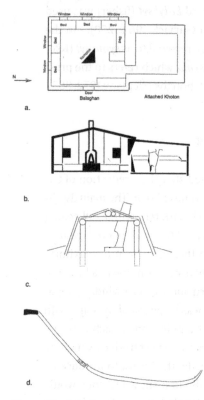

a.

b.

c.

d.

Figure 13 *Balaghan* structure and Sakha scythe: (*a*) top view showing layout, (*b*) long side view showing attached barn, (*c*) short side view showing *kömülüök*, (*d*) Sakha scythe, which was used by circling overhead and down to ground. Drawn by author.

and replaced them three or four times each winter, when they had thinned to several centimeters.

In addition to its southern orientation and heat from the herds, the *balaghan's* other source of heat came from a *kömülüök*,[2] an open-faced stove venting through the roof that stood in the center of the *balaghan*. Its chimney was made from larch limbs that were sealed over with a mixture of clay and dung on its outer surface and pure clay on the inside. Firewood was placed vertically in the pit to burn. With no flue, the *kömülüök* burned constantly to heat the *balaghan* and to purify the air that was often thick from the herds. Contemporary elders recall how it was their job in youth to gather wood from the forest floor for the *kömülüök*. In the depth of winter cold, the *kömülüök* was known to burn an entire sledge of wood per day.[3] The *kömülüök* also served as the sole source of light during the long dark winters.

Balaghan and their elements have a myriad of symbolic and spiritual meanings (cf., e.g., Danilova 2011; Romanova 1997; N. A. Alekseev 1975). For example, the *kömülüök* was considered the home's center around which life cycled. It was innately feminine, with its positioning in the structure's center, its function as the main heat source, and its role as the keeper of the home (Danilova 2011: 61). "Women received their productive energy from the *kömülüök*; the state of the *kömülüök* reflected the status and the conditions of the household; from the *kömülüök* began the path to the outside world" (ibid. 62). Its state also reflected a household's abundance or need. Those seeking a wife would often measure a bride's worth by the robustness of her family's *kömülüök*, kept by her mother and symbolic of how well the daughter would maintain the home fires elsewhere (Seroshevskii 1993: 342).

The yard around the *balaghan* had several *ampaar* to store tools, equipment, and food reserves, a *buluus* for perishables, and *dal* (corral) for herds. There was at least one, if not several, *serge* (horse-hitching posts) to secure riding horses. *Serge* were used as a ritual conduit between the three worlds, connecting the middle to the upper and, less often, the lower to the upper. The *toion serge* ("king *serge*" for the most important *serge*) was situated beside the house entrance and was reserved for the head male. As an example of the *serge* that served strictly ritual purposes, the *kiiiit serge* (bride's post) was erected the first day a groom visited his bride's home to symbolize a new patrilineal branch of the household (Danilova 2013: 189).

Sakha moved to their *saiylyk* after the spring floods subsided and the sun's warming rays had brought new grass. They situated their *saiylyk* on the *alaas* and adjacent to forage areas for berries, plants, and fish, and along their pastures so herds could graze between milking and food-processing activities. The *saiylyk* had to be far enough from the *balaghan* to preserve pasture for winter horse grazing.[4] The *uraha* beds were also aligned along the walls in order of the household hierarchy. In the center was an open fire pit made in a clay-lined wooden box. Smoke escaped through the peak of the *uraha*. On the floor to the right of the entry door, Sakha kept the tools for the women's work of milking and containing milk. To the left, they stored the tools for men's work of haying and pasture making, including all sizes of pitchforks, rakes, scythes, and shovels.

Typically the *balaghan* and *uraha* both had several pieces of simple furniture: short stools, chairs, and a table. Clothing and belongings were kept in boxes. Every household had a meat-chopping block. The arrangement of having one *uraha* and one *balaghan* was common, but there were also variations based on socioeconomic status. It was not unusual for wealthy households to have several dwellings in each place, and for the poor, without herds, to live year-round in a *balaghan*.

Foods from the *Alaas*

Sakha's main sources of food and materials were the meat, milk, and other parts (organs, skins, bones, horns, tendons, etc.) of their domestic horse and cattle herds. Wild plants and animals of the *alaas* supplemented Sakha's meat and milk diet.

Plants of the Alaas. Alaas pastures were rich in plant species including wild oats (*Bromus inermis* & *B. ciliatus*), barley (*Hordeum prateuse* & *H. jubatum*), rye (*Elymus dasystachys* & *E. excelsus*), couch grass (*Triticum repens*), oats (*Festuca elatior*), wormwood (*artemisia sr. r.*), various ranunculus (*Ranunculus achillea, R. millefolium, R. borealis, R. repens*), and over eighteen species of legumes (Seroshevskii 1993: 63–64). This plant diversity supplemented both fodder for herds and the food and medicine for humans. Sakha used the vegetative parts of sorrel (*Rumex acetosa*), wild angelica (*Angelica sylvestris*), silverweed (*Patentilla anserina*), horseradish (*Armoracia sisymbriodes Cayand*), rhubarb (*Rheum compactum*), broadleaf plantain (*Plantago major*), fireweed (*Epilobium angustifolium*), mugwort (*Artemisia vulgaris*), Siberian lily (*lilium dahuricum*), and various kinds of wild onions and garlic (*Allium sp.*) (Yonova 1961: 27). They used the roots and bulbs of flowering rush (*Butemos umbellatus*), bulrush (*Typha latifolia*), great burnet (*Sanguisorba officinalis*), and the aforementioned horseradish, lilies, onions, and garlic (ibid. 28). Although Sakha did grind wild grains into flour for unleavened breads, the flour they were more inclined to use was the inner white pulp of pine trees (*Pinus sibirica*),[5] which, when mixed with *tar*, water, and plant material, made a kind of *khaahy* (Savvin 2005: 192–94; Middendorf 1868: 789). During *Bes Yia* (Pine month or June), when the trees' sap was flowing, they harvested pine sap to add to drinks (Savvin 2005: 194).

Plants were also the main source of medicine. The post-Soviet period has seen a flourishing of knowledge pertaining to Sakha's medicinal plant use, which is often integrated with knowledge of shamanic practice. The healing qualities of the plants are attributed to the plants' sentience and different spirit presences.[6] One author documents over seventy-five medicinal uses of plants, all based on the teachings of the late contemporary healer/shaman V. A. Kondakov (Yakovleva 2009).

Fishing and Hunting "by the Alaas." Lakes of the *alaas* provided families with *sobo* year-round, in summer's temperate months using *ilim*, and when ice was on the lakes, by *mungkha* or *kuiuur*. Men hunted hare, duck, geese, and wood birds during *saiylyk* time and bigger game (moose, reindeer, bear, etc.) in early winter when at the *kystyk*. Sakha adopted much of their hunting and fishing techniques from local Tungus. However, archaeological findings of Kurykan cave paintings showing the hunting of moose, deer, and other game animals, and other remains attest to the use of pursuit, tracking, luring, and corralling, and also trapping by stationary (pits) and portable (traps and snares) means (Zikov 2013: 151). All hunting practices were preceded by offerings to *Baianai*.

Making *Alaas* Land

When I contemplate the historical uses of land and also think about the tumultuous changes in land use of the last century, from pre-Soviet to Soviet to post-Soviet, my mind goes back to one day in particular. It was early June 1993. We were having morning tea when we saw the village land expert enter our yard by the front gate. Normally the family would have waited for the visitor to enter to offer them tea. But Sergei sensed an urgency to the visit and so instantly stood up and went outside to greet him. Several minutes later he returned to announce that he had been asked to organize the divvying up of hay plots at Kÿöl Elgeeii. He said I could go along if it interested me. We packed up and rode the motorcycle out to the site, a long, relatively narrow tract nestled within a birch and larch forest. Inhabitants, mostly men, were already there, pacing about and deciding what parcel they wanted. We spent the morning divvying the area into plots, starting from one end of the field and gradually working across, as household heads staked their claims for a hay lot in the new system of household food production.[7]

While I watched and assisted as I could that morning, I also reflected on the history of that land place. Just a short two years before, Kÿöl Elgeeii was one of the Elgeeii state farm's many hay areas. Land management in the state farm period was based completely on mechanization, using tractors to cultivate and harvest. Forty-five years before that, it was a hay area of the Molotov *kolkhoz* (collective farm, itself an abbreviation of *kollektivnoe khoziaistvo*; *kholbohuktaakh khahaaiystyba*), which used mechanization in its later years but, for most of its forty-year tenure, was managed using draft animals and the time-tested techniques of pre-Soviet Sakha. In the early twentieth century, Kÿöl Elgeeii was inhabited by clusters of households living "by the *alaas*" (map 6*a*). The latter had been there for centuries and had survived thanks to Sakha's centuries-old knowledge of managing the land. Indeed, Sakha developed an intimate knowledge of their permafrost ecosystem, and specifically of *alaas*, through trial and error. Academics explain that the only way that a southern steppe culture could make it in the extremes of northeastern Siberia was via the "counteraction of the northern condition with innovations and the role of active human labor in the transformation of nature" (S. I. Nikolaev 2009b: 4).

In the Viliui regions there were three types of pasture lands: pasture located near a lake or in the place where a lake had dried up; floodplain, or pasture located along a river or stream; and swamp, or pasture located at the middle or upper reaches of a river around small lakes riddled with hillocks and tussocks (Mikhaleva-Saia et al. 2013: 164). Sakha managed these lands to maximize their production and make them more extensive using different techniques of "pasture making" or _lugovodstvo_ by either clearing a forest with fire, done to "clear the oceans of taiga," or by draining an existing lake (S. I. Nikolaev 2009b: 5–7).[8]

Burning had the benefit of producing highly fertile soils for the first years immediately afterward. Sakha used one of three methods to clear with fire, depending on the forest's conditions. For a relatively young stand, they scorched and cleared the trees, then uprooted and burned the stumps. For a mature forest, they first harvested larger trees for lumber and firewood and left the smaller trees to dry. They then burned and cleared the area. In the final method, they cut down all the trees, uprooted the stumps and roots, and left it all to dry. Once dry, they crushed up the turf and roots with a heavy hoe and burned it all. The latter was the most labor intensive but rendered the most fertile fields (Mikhaleva-Saia et al. 2013: 169). Fire was also important for managing the fields in early spring and late fall. Sakha used controlled fire on the hayfields to clear the fields of encroaching shrubs and forest saplings and to inoculate the soil with nutrient-rich ash. In the fall they used it to clear remaining plant matter to provide a clear area for the next spring's hay growth.

Sakha's second main method of _lugovodstvo_, draining an existing lake to increase pasture and hay area, was a much more complex and dangerous process. It involved expert knowledge of the land adjacent to the lake to execute the canal work to properly drain the water body. It also required the heavy work of canal digging. But first and foremost, it required spiritual intervention. The draining of an _alaas_ lake involved appeasing the spirit of the lake with the proper words, sacrificial foodstuffs, rituals, blessings, and dreamings (Mészáros 2012; Takakura 2015). All of this required the assistance of an _oiuun_, _udaghan_, or other individual versed in the _algys_ for this act (S. I. Nikolaev 1970; Sheludiakova 1961: 21). This appeasement was necessary to subdue the lake spirit, who was potentially angered by its predicament and might otherwise drown or harm those involved in the draining process (S. I. Nikolaev 1970). Once the proper rituals were performed, the work involved the digging of canals from the existing lake to adjacent waterways in order to drain the area.

The most challenging part of maintaining hay lands and pastures for Sakha was water management. Early Soviet-period scientists describe the unique conditions of the dry climate and permafrost that made maintaining a proper water balance in fields so difficult:

> ... the extreme and original climatic and hydrologic regime of this land creates here completely original conditions for the activities of flowing water ... [including] an extremely insignificant amount of precipitation, a very quick start of spring and rapid melting of snow, a colossal heightening of then emptying out of water in rivers, an insignificant amount of water in rivers in summer, and the presence of permafrost, which only thaws to an insignificant depth, despite the very high temperatures of summer. (Grigor'ev 1927: 47)

They also explained the way that the permafrost ecosystem "functioned" in this low water environment as a reliable source of water from under the ground:

> As the upper horizons of the soil dry up, the water collected below ascends by means of capillary action, and forms a reliable source of moisture for the normal development of vegetation. When this supply is consumed, it is replaced by the last stores of water, which had been frozen up in the preceding autumn in the deeper horizons of the soil, and which become available as the ice gradually thaws. Thus, the permanent frozen earth-layer presents a most beneficial apparatus for the conservation and very economical consumption of water. Without such an apparatus the whole extent of the Lena-Viliui plain with its 200 mm annual precipitation and its 19 degree (C) mean July temperature would be converted into an arid desert, incapable of cultivation and entirely destitute of forest. (Abolin 1929: 338)

However, in extreme droughts, the below-ground water source from permafrost did not suffice. In those times, Sakha used one of several methods. The most widespread practice was *nüölsüter* (managing water), irrigating fields with timber-enforced earthen *khoruu* (canals). The practice was brought to the north by Sakha's Kurykan ancestors (Ksenofontov 1992; Gogolev 1993; Okladnikov, 1955, 1970). Similar *nüölsüter* methods are found in the Altai mountains, where they use rocks and stones for canals instead of wood and earth (Sheludiakova 1961: 22). *Nüölsüter* involves the damming of fields to hold sufficient water in times of drought or the opening of the dam for excess water to run off in a system of canals when water is in abundance (Ermolaev 1991: 126). *Nüölsüter* was an exact process and required a careful understanding of the land and the local water system to be successful (Sheludiakova 1961: 21). In addition to *nüölsüter*, they used hay areas with supplemental water, located either adjacent to a forest or on top of a recently dried lake called *uolba* (S. I. Nikolaev 2009b: 11). Another method to deal with extreme drought was to create a dam in an adjacent stream and redirect its water via a canal to the fields. Sakha used this same technique to redirect the surface streams of the massive spring snow melt to their fields (ibid.). A final method, and last resort to deal with extreme drought, was to relocate home and herds to headwaters where there would still be water and productive pasture (ibid. 12).

Nüölsüter is also the main practice that Sakha used to adapt to their ecosystem's natural fluctuations of wet and dry cycles, by releasing excess water from their fields in wet years and holding what water there was in dry years. A "wetter than usual" period is referred to as an *öng jyl*, which can only be beneficial if people know how to manage the excess moisture (*nüölsüter*). If it was too wet to cut hay in the haying season, and canals were nonexistent or insufficient to release the water, inhabitants would do *muus oto* (ice haying), that is, waiting to cut until the standing water froze in early autumn.

Sakha's knowledge of the wet year/dry year cycle was how many inhabitants explained the excess water early on in our 2008 to 2012 climate project. In 2008, I starkly remember my sense of alarm when looking out the airplane window en route to the regional center Suntaar for summer research. The areas along the way were familiar to me after traveling over them for the previous eighteen years. In the three years since my last visit, there appeared to have been an inundation of water on the pastures and fields below. It was also clear once we landed and traveled across more familiar landscapes to find former fields turned into lakes. In our focus groups and interviews that summer, participants attributed the increased water on the land to four causes, with the most popular being "nature itself," explained as the wet and dry cycles of their ecosystem. Inhabitants' testimonies verified other Indigenous experts' documentation that on the Viliui, the wet and dry cycles occur in three-, seven-, twelve-, and forty-, and one-hundred-year cycles (Sirdik 2006; Kondratev 2007). The dry period from 1924 to 1961 transitioned to a wet period from 1965 to 2001 (Kondratev 2007: 55). These cycles also corroborate with meteorological data to show a dry period from 1984 to 1996 followed by a wet period from 1997 to 2009 (Crate and Fedorov[9] 2013a: 23). The years 1951–63 and 1973–83 were years of increased precipitation (ibid.). Although local inhabitants explained the excess moisture in 2008 focus groups as the wet cycle/dry cycle effect, scientific extrapolation at the time showed that 24–34 percent of the water on the surface was from the thawing permafrost below (A. N. Fedorov et al. 2014).

A third approach to pasture making that was not as widely practiced as the burning of forests and the draining of lakes was the creation of a new lake by activating the thawing properties of the permafrost. This approach is described in an academic account:

> Having found in the lowland taiga places of shallow occurrence of under-ground ice, the Yakuts, according to the versions of their legends, intention-ally let the forest fall. Moreover, they allowed fire to extend beyond the res-inous canopy to the pillars and stumps, which, when burning, in turn began to thaw underground ice, forming deep dips, [that] filled with water from the ice being drained. To further encourage the formation of a grassland, they then drained the basin. (S. I. Nikolaev 2009b: 7)

During my dissertation research (1999–2000), I heard several references to this approach in the context of elders' history at their birth *alaas*, adjacent to the Kÿÿkei Lake,

> Kÿÿkei, one of the greatest hunters in his time, challenged another fierce hunter to see who could shoot from the farthest distance. Both stood on the Batamai mountain and each shot an arrow at ducks in the fields below. Kÿÿkei, who was sure he had shot and killed a duck at a greater distance than his opponent, was unable to find his arrow and forfeited his victory. In his anger, he returned to the top of the mountain and shot a burning arrow into the fields below. This started a fire, which burned for three years to form the great Kÿÿkei Lake. (Yegor Mikhailovich Nikolayev, Elgeeii village, April 14, 2000)

About one-third of the village elders I interviewed at the time had grown up around the Kÿÿkei Lake, the largest lake in the Viliui regions. They spoke of how, when they were children, the lake and the surrounding abundant pasture and hay fields supported many *agha uuha* clusters of homesteads living "by the *alaas*," keeping cattle and horses, growing wheat and potatoes, and foraging for wild berries, plants, game, fowl, and fish. This final method of pasture making by creating new lakes was not practiced widely, but it was nonetheless important, considering how Kÿÿkei Lake and its surrounds have been sources of inhabitants' water, fish, waterfowl, hay, and pasture lands for centuries.

The Scientific Knowledge of *Alaas*

In the early 1900s, when the scientific community's knowledge of *alaas* began, scientists defined *alaas* as "any opening in the taiga forest regardless of its origin" (Desiatkin 2008: 18). As this understanding of *alaas* matured, the definition became one of debate.

> Although a number of authors dealt with the question of the genesis of drainless basins [*alaas*] the origin of the lakes on them is weakly understood. Some attribute them to the underground karst origins, some to the fluctuations of melting permafrost, another said the lake erosion is a dominant and sustained force of these lands, another says it is the work of the eroding quality of the water that flowed post-Pliocene that gradually transformed the river channel and isolated the chain of lakes in the periods between ice ages. (Grigor'ev 1927: 46)

The scientific understanding was swiftly refined when Soviet-era development projects were proposed on *alaas* landscapes. Two scientists conducted the research for an initial project, the construction of a Soviet-period European-style health spa by Lake Abagha, in the central regions. Their research showed that *alaas* existed on a foundation of "underground ice" and required a protective layer to maintain that ice (Efimov and Grave 1940: 70). Accordingly, they recommended that, prior to construction and land clearing for agricultural activities, directors engage a six-step process to determine ice extent in *alaas* areas. They urged that such projects only be planned and completed on ice-free landscapes (ibid. 77–78).

Another critical development in refining the concept of *alaas* was M. M. Yermolayev's 1932 introduction of the concept of "thermokarst,"[10] the degradation of permafrost toward thawing (enlargement of the active layer) due to the combination of high ice content and low relief (Czudek and Demek 1970: 103). Thermokarst develops from the natural effects of forest fires, where excessive moisture triggers an erosion process. Humans can also bring about the process of thermokarst by removing the permafrost's protective layer when clearing forests, plowing grass slopes, and damaging vegetation with vehicle and construction activity (ibid. 104).

The next significant development of the scientific understanding of *alaas* occurred with the increased industrialization and infrastructure activities of the postwar period, and the need to define and map *alaas*. "The nature of the northern part of the Lena-Amga middle river is related to a large population with a unique and strong relationship to agriculture in the Sakha Republic (YSSR). There we find wide areas of thick underground ice and connected to that, innumerable thermokarst *alaas*. Over the course of one generation appears a subsiding lake which subsequently dries up, at the bottom of which forms a hill" (Solovyev 1959: 3). This delineation of *alaas* areas was a work in progress, with the initial map designating the *alaas* areas extending across the central and Viliui regions (ibid. 4). More than likely, this wider distribution of *alaas* came about because all of the scientists determining *alaas* range were themselves Sakha and had the Sakha understanding of *alaas* etched deeply in their consciousness.

Not long after, *alaas* were newly defined as drained thaw lake basins (thermokarst depressions) with large areas of subsided ground surface resulting from the thawing of ice-rich permafrost (Solovyev 1973). With this in mind, scientists discerned that areas on the Viliui, although within the same ice complex as the central regions, did not have these technically defined *alaas*. The *alaas* zone was limited to the central regions, with the highest concentration between the Aldan and the Amga rivers (Desiatkin 2008: 24).

At this time scientists also delineated the *alaas* cycle. *Alaas* are a landscape feature unique to northeastern Siberia that form from the combination of the thermokarst process and its abundant moisture in the context of the extreme dry climate of the Sakha area (Troeva et al. 2010: 13). They cycle, approximately every 150 to 180 years, from a maximum rise of lake water, to its minimal, then to lake area desiccation, and finally to the complete disappearance of water from the *alaas* basin (Bosikov et al. 2012: 56). The

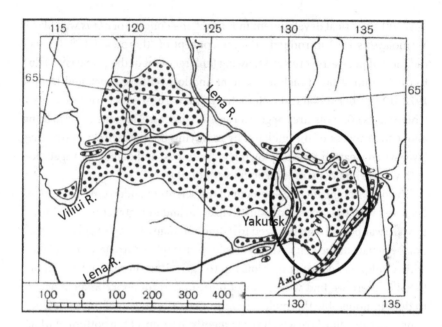

Figure 14 Distribution of *alaas* in Central Yakutia (Sakha Republic), with earlier scientific understandings in dotted areas and later confined to the area within the circle. Source: Solovyev 1959 (circle added by author).

area is then a base for vegetation and the gradual decline of the land surface as the thermokarst process begins anew and a new lake forms (Troeva et al. 2010: 13).

The Cultural Meaning of *Alaas*

Since learning the exact scientific definition of *alaas*, I have grappled with exactly how to talk about them. In Sakha's Indigenous knowledge frame, *alaas* have always extended throughout the Viliui regions. Viliui Sakha inhabitants describe them in the poetic and spiritual accounts of their birth *alaas*. The scientific understanding of *alaas*, on the other hand, categorizes them as an exact physical phenomenon. These juxtapositions are about how people know, how they build knowledge and to what ends. The scientific investigation was driven by Soviet-period economics, to understand the exact properties of *alaas* to enable industrialization and infrastructure development. The longer history of Sakha Indigenous knowledge of *alaas* similarly came about for economic reasons, those of a southern pastoralist culture's need be successful in their new environment. However, the two knowledge systems are qualitatively divergent. For Soviet-period development purposes, scientific *alaas* knowledge served the singular focus of economic development. For Sakha, knowledge of *alaas* involved not just a physical adaptive response but also a continual spiritual recognition. "Knowing" *alaas* meant acknowledging them as living, sentient beings, with all the qualities of emotion, will, and agency of humans. It is this inherent sentient quality of *alaas* that has maintained *alaas* to this day as a prominent cultural symbol of identity for Sakha: "*Alaas* are close to a Sakha person . . . we hold them close . . . before we lived spread out 'by the *alaas*' and in any case there is still something there . . . there is a good sense about the *alaas* for us . . . birthland—the *alaas* idea is in our minds and consciousness" (Valerian Yegorovich Afanaseyev, interview, June 13, 2018).

The thought of *alaas* elicits different responses based on the respondent's generation. Contemporary elders' eyes glaze over as they return to childhood memories of their birth *alaas*. Those born in the mid-Soviet period will well up with tears, reflecting on their ancestral birth *alaas* and the annual pilgrimages their elders taught them to make. Youth will think of their *saiylyk*, where they may have spent summers since early childhood, helping with the haying, foraging for berries, and learning to love the many Sakha *ürüng as* (literally "white foods," referring to all Sakha's dairy products). Some of this difference in intergenerational response can be explained by how each generation has lived and related to their *alaas*. I was able to map the generational change in settlement patterns in the process of eliciting oral histories of fifty-five elders in 1999–2000 research. Each elder recounted their early childhoods on *alaas*[11] and their gradual moves to the *kolkhoz* and then to the compact village where they had lived to that day (Crate 2006a: 166–87). I then located them all on a combined map of Elgeeii and Kutana to show how, during the Soviet period, all went from living "by the *alaas*" to resettlement in compact villages (map 5).

Although today Sakha do not physically "live by the *alaas*," their relationship to *alaas* is apparent in historical narrative, academic understandings, and contemporary ethnographic encounters.

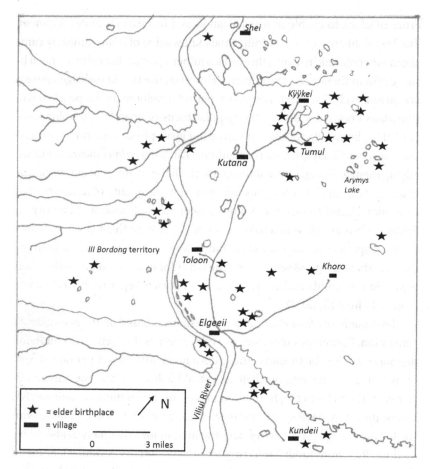

Map 5 Map showing former elder homesteads of elders now residing in either Elgeeii or Kutana. Drawn by author.

Sakha's Early Understanding of Alaas

The earliest written account of *alaas* is credited to E. K. Pekarski in his Sakha language dictionary. Born in 1858 in the Minsk province, Pekarski was exiled at age twenty-three to Siberia, to the Boturuskom *uluus* (modern Tatta) of Sakha for fifteen years of hard labor. He immediately began learning Sakha, because, as he put it, "I wanted to interact with the surrounding community" (M. E. Nikolaev 2009: 9). In the process of mastering the Sakha language he also became literate in Sakha's spiritual culture. He used his in-depth understanding of Sakha's Indigenous knowledge to create the first Sakha language dictionary, published in 1907 (N. M. Alekseev 1959: 3–5).

In addition to giving a general definition of *alaas*, "a meadow or spacious field, surrounded by woods, a piedmont valley, a long, clear glade among the forest, a field or meadow, surrounded by forest" (1958: 67), Pekarski includes other revealing details, for example, information about a parallel word in Altai or Kazak, *alan*, that clarifies *alaas*'s Turkic root, in addition to various *alaas* toponyms: *uulaakh alaas* (water-filled or flooded *alaas*), *kuranaakh alaas* (dry *alaas*), *büte alaas* (remote *alaas*), *amydai alaas* (namesake *alaas*), *üchügei alaas* (good *alaas*), *ynakh alaas* (cow *alaas*), *kyys alaas* (girl *alaas*), *udaghan alaas* (female shaman *alaas*), *jakhtar alaas* (woman *alaas*), and so on, and also a riddle: *angara kharanga alaas, angara sirdik alaas bar ühü* (they say there is darkness on one half of the *alaas*, and light on the other). For Sakha, any confined space, be it an *alaas* or a dwelling, is divided into two parts: southern (illuminated by the sun and light) and northern (in the shadow and dark) (D'iachkovskii and Popova 2014: 61). This relates also to the *balaghan*, where the dark side was female and the light side male.

Alaas in Sakha Consciousness

Alaas permeate Sakha's historical narratives, perhaps best exemplified in Sakha's epic poem, *Olonkho*:

> On the glorious primordial mother earth,
> in the very middle of it,
> with outskirts of a dark forest,
> the great alaas is located.
>
> (Emel'ianov and Illarionov 1996)

Aal Luuk Mas (the tree of life) connects the upper, middle, and lower worlds, growing up through the *alaas*; it symbolizes the cosmological axis of the universe (Danilova 2011: 14) and is associated with the goddess, spirit mother of the earth, *Aan Alakhchyn khotun* (figure 15).

Other Sakha narratives are similarly rich with depictions of living "by the *alaas*." Among them, the best known is *Bies Ynakhtaakh Beiberikeen Emeekhsin* (Old Woman Beiberikeen with Five Cows),

Figure 15 *Aal Luuk Mas* (Tree of Life) shown with the goddess, spirit mother of the earth, *Aan Alakhchyn khotun*. From the Sakha heroic epos *Olonkho* series. Artist: Timofei Stepanov, 1982.

One day Old Woman Beiberikeen with Five Cows went out on the *alaas* to milk her cows. In the field she saw a beautiful sardana lily and picked it and took it back to her house. She returned to milk and, in a few minutes, heard the sound of bells tingling and scissors cutting coming from her *uraha*. She hurried in and saw the lily in the same place she left it. She returned to milk and in another few minutes heard the same sound but this time when she returned, she found a beautiful girl awaiting her with coal-black hair and eyes. Old Woman Beiberikeen was overjoyed to have a companion! About this same time a young hunter, Khaarjit Bergen, the son of Khaikhamsik Khara Khan, came by hunting squirrels. One of his arrows fell near Old Woman Beiberikeen's uraha and when he went to get it, he saw the beautiful girl inside and ran back to exclaim to his parents that he would marry her. As all turns out, they married and lived with Old Woman Beiberikeen to keep her company, help with chores and raise a family, through all of her days. (Avvakumov 1973)

Sakha's cultural identification with *alaas* is strong in rural areas. But urban Sakha also identify with their ancestral *alaas*, some making an annual pilgrimage to their *saiylyk*, spending the summer months in the rural area where they were born. Although a majority of urban Sakha do not physically visit their ancestral *alaas*, they identify with the many images and descriptions of *alaas*, its physical and cultural meaning, that pervade Sakha culture. Songs are especially replete with *alaas* elements, from "Agham Alaaha" (My Father's *Alaas*), to "Min Doidum" (My Birthland) to "Törööbüt Alaaskyn En Taptaa" (Love Your Birth *Alaas*), to "Saiylyk" (Summer Place). Herein the subtleties of the Sakha language are important, to the extent that many expressive forms refer to *törööbüt doidu* (birthland), which in Sakha is synonymous with *törööbüt alaas* (birth *alaas*) (Danilova 2011: 15).

Academic Understandings of *Alaas*

The image and symbol of *alaas* are an important topic of contemporary academic discourse among both older and younger academics, a fact that further verifies *alaas*'s unique cultural meaning for Sakha. One example, written largely by older academics, is the 2015 publication *Alaas: The Sakha People's Cradle*, which integrates the cultural meaning of *alaas* with its scientific description in both the Sakha and Russian languages. The contrast of the Sakha and Russian translations of the front matter testifies to the powerful cultural meaning that *alaas* have for Sakha and the lack thereof for ethnic Russians:

> [from Sakha text] Every culture has a unique landscape that is revered as the one associated with their ancestral beginnings. For Sakha, without question, their original cradle is the *alaas*. *Alaas*—a land form made by the upper gods especially for Sakha to live and thrive. Our *alaas*, no matter the time of year, never lose their beauty as they are the true creative glory of our middle world. In them the Sakha person keeps their herds, makes their living, hunts and fishes, raises their children and the next generation, in this unique nature base with the green fields, the different plants and trees, the carpet of flowers, the animals of the dark forest, the birds of the field and lakes. . . . For the Sakha person it is their source of all life, their cradle of beginning, their original *ebe* [grandmother] . . .

> [from Russian text] . . . a truly nature-created ecosystem, that strikes human kind with its unrepeatable natural beauty, rich animal populations and diverse botanical wealth. It is an independent natural system with a pictur-

esque blue lake, bordered by moist meadows and stately eastern Siberian
taiga, which surrounds it with the bright green cover and plays the central
ecological role in the life of the northern person. (Savvinov and Makarov
2015: 4 and 5)

Another academic example is a linguistic comparison of Russian and
Sakha words that express the concepts of "homeland" and "birthplace." All
such concepts have parallel associations across a range of terminology in
both languages, except for the term *alaas* (Savitskaia 2017: 210) (see figure 16). The author uses this comparison to argue how Sakha's understanding
of *alaas* is unique and that it "played an important role in the formation and
strengthening of the Yakut [Sakha] ethnic group, the formation of its mentality and worldviews" (ibid. 213).

A first-generation post-Soviet Sakha social scientist further refines the
central place of *alaas* in Sakha worldview and culture. The writer frames
their understanding of *alaas* and its relationship to Sakha as a "cultural landscape," with ties to a settled subsistence:

In a traditional worldview, housing is a space in space, and its main function
is to protect human life in the natural world and to preserve family and
cultural values. The concentric development of the world is primarily due
to the sedentary lifestyle. An ethnological study of spatial representations in
various cultural texts showed that the process of mastering space in a certain
sequence repeats the order of creation of the world. . . . *Alaas*, as the native
land, acts as a component of life and social space. As a study of the structure
of living space in the Sakha tradition, the natural landscape determined not
only the economical-social activities of an ethnicity, but all of that ethnicity's
essence. For example, Sakha, the "marginal people" constituted the lower
level of the social hierarchy and were distinguished by their slow-paced and
non-social nature. *Tya kihite* (forest Sakha) . . . hunters of the middle social
status who commanded a vast space. Pastoralists, *alaas jono* (people of the
alaas) represented the upper level of social structure and had a broad and
social nature; they were called "people from the center." (Danilova 2011: 104)

This framing posits the importance of both space and orientation that allow
alaas to exist in both the physical and the cosmological worlds. Today, when
Sakha inhabit rural and urban settlements physically distant from *alaas*, these

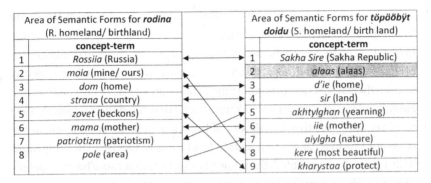

Area of Semantic Forms for *rodina* (R. homeland/ birthland)			Area of Semantic Forms for *töpööbÿt doidu* (S. homeland/ birth land)	
	concept-term			concept-term
1	*Rossiia* (Russia)		1	*Sakha Sire* (Sakha Republic)
2	*moia* (mine/ ours)		2	*alaas* (alaas)
3	*dom* (home)		3	*d'ie* (home)
4	*strana* (country)		4	*sir* (land)
5	*zovet* (beckons)		5	*akhtylghan* (yearning)
6	*mama* (mother)		6	*iie* (mother)
7	*patriotizm* (patriotism)		7	*aiylgha* (nature)
8	*pole* (area)		8	*kere* (most beautiful)
			9	*kharystaa* (protect)

Figure 16 The relationships of semantic fields showing no comparable concept of *alaas* in Russian. Source: Author's translation and interpretation of Savitskaia 2017: 210.

representations reify *alaas* in contemporary Sakha culture: *alaas* as Sakha's cradle, *alaas* as a center, *alaas* as the center of social, economic, and spiritual interactions and meaning. They provide Sakha with a sustained source of cultural identification in the midst of historical relocations and urbanization.

Other Sakha academics continue this analysis, citing how Omoghoi and Ellei, in Sakha's origin narrative, chose the wide-open area of the *alaas* for the first *yhyakh* because the *alaas* was "the center of the universe with its geo-architectural structures: the tree of life, *Aal Luuk Mas* and the horse-hitching post, *serge*" (Romanova 2015: 94). *Alaas* for Sakha are their spiritual core, key symbol, and "a cultural landscape perceived and observed through the prism of signs and symbols, coupled with a rational and emotional experience of space" (ibid). These ideas are also carried over into the next generations. Contemporary Sakha children feature the *alaas* as a central component of their world and the place of their home, charting the relationship as "*alaas*—home—microcosm" (Romanova and Ignatieva 2012: 66). *Alaas* are understood as a sacred landscape for Sakha that has important cultural meaning as a place where "local spirits and shamanic forces protect a [Sakha] person" (Prokop'eva 2015: 140). One contemporary Sakha linguist breaks down the word into *aal* (sacred) and *as* (food) to reflect its numinous meaning and its early conception as a provider of everything needed from both the physical and spiritual realms (Prokopii Mitrofanovich Yegorov, personal communication, June 12, 2018).

In an article analyzing the word's origin, meaning, and use, two Sakha linguists define *alaas* as both the landscape form that pre-Soviet Sakha depended on and as a symbol of cultural identity, synonymous with "birthland" and "birthplace" (D'iachkovski and Popova 2014: 58). They use the example of how, when traveling, Sakha often bring the spirit of their birth *alaas* with them by taking a handful of soil from their birth *alaas*, to smell, to speak to, to calm themselves, and to comfort their soul (ibid. 61). They also interviewed Sakha students at a university in Yakutsk who described their understanding of *alaas* using positive descriptors of homeland and security. Some of the students, however, described *alaas* in less favorable terms, associating *alaas* with a place that is haunted, the home of evil spirits that cause harm to people (ibid. 63). These negative impressions may be the result of the short stories of mystery and darkness popular with youth that are regularly featured in some Sakha-language newspapers, for example, the section "Nomokh" (Legend) in the newspaper *Kyym*. They may also be because the spirit of their birth *alaas* is offended by their lack of engagement.

Field Encounters with the Sacred *Alaas*

During my field research in 2018 and 2019, inhabitants articulated intimate descriptions of the multidimensional meaning of *alaas* as birthland, spirit protector, a micro-world unto itself where all needs were supplied, as a main ancestral link, and as a source of strength and power in the world. Several called themselves *alasny patrioti* (*alaas* patriots),

> We are *alasny patrioti*—we live on *alaas* . . . you can understand it from the basic scientific way or from the deep philosophical way . . . I am a child of the *alaas* . . . for a Sakha person, *alaas* means their birthland . . . every person here was born in an *alaas* and they think of it until they die . . . like the salmon that goes far from its birthplace and then eventually returns . . . it pulls them—and people, when they die, they want to be laid to rest at their birth *alaas* and if they die far away and cannot come back, soil is brought to their grave from their birth *alaas*. (Svetlana Gavrilovna Martinova, interview June 13, 2018)

> . . . *alaas* has a physical meaning and also an abstract meaning-birthplace and birthland . . . and when you say you are from *Suntaar* or Churapchi . . . they say the *alasny patrioti* live on. (Rozaliya Semyonovna Nikolayeva, interview, June 12, 2018)

In addition to such firsthand testimonies, another gauge of *alaas*'s central role in Sakha's cultural identity can be found in the legacies of two historical figures, one of Elgeeii and one of Kutana. The late Elgeeii resident and prolific writer Ivan Gerasimovich Ivanov (pen name Ivan Nolar) was a celebrated Soviet-period Sakha writer who published both short stories and novels featuring Sakha characters who worked and lived "by the *alaas*." The publication *Sakha and Alaas* records the presentations at a 2004 conference celebrating the late Ivan Nolar's seventy-fifth birthday and his lifework (Gerasimova 2008). The following quotations exemplify the participants' sentiments for the late author and for Sakha's sacred association with *alaas*:

Sakha people will never break from their identification with the *alaas*. (Ibid. 7)

The words "Sakha" and *alaas* are from one source of our bloodline. (Ibid. 20)

The meaning of *alaas* for Sakha is deep and wide. It is not just some symbol but rather a deeper philosophy of what it means to be Sakha. It is Sakha's essential identity, character, and source of origin with a mysterious primordial power for all who call themselves Sakha. (Ibid. 67)

Alaas, for the Sakha person, is their original homeplace. Our ancestors made us this original bounty in nature and from it we began as a people. It is our original cradle where we each began and come from. (Ibid. 68)

In nearby Kutana, the late Nikolai Innokentiyevich Ivanov, nicknamed *Kuola Uchuutal* (Teacher Kolya), left a legacy of teaching and promoting cultural identification with and ancestral linkages to *alaas* within his community. He was a renowned geography teacher who practiced "experiential learning" by taking students on field trips to study their ancestral *alaas* in both physical and historical aspects. Over his many-decade career he compiled multiple notebooks containing detailed maps and information about the historical occupants for one hundred *alaas* in the greater Kutana area. In 2015 his daughter transcribed his notes and published it in the book *Suntaar Kutana 100 Alaas*. The preface begins with Nikolai Innokentiyevich's words,

Every person has a birthplace. We, who are now older,[12] think often of our birth *alaas* and are happy only when we can see it. When we think of it, we

remember our childhood, all the people around us, these memories come
to us clearly. . . . I separated from my *alaas* a long time ago . . . and I think
and say to you that you are but my one and only, that which raised me, I will
never forget you and every year I visit you. (Pavlova 2015: 7)

Sakha's Turkic ancestors lived "by the *alaas*" upon arriving from the south
(Takakura 2010), and the narrative of living "by the *alaas*" remains, to this
day, just as central to Sakha identity, woven through historical and contemporary expressive forms. It is that narrative that feeds Sakha's spiritual sustenance, like acquiring the needed physical sustenance to survive. Although
most contemporary Sakha live physically far from *alaas* and the living "by
the *alaas*" livelihood, they nonetheless experience the cradle of the *alaas* as
their central cultural identifier.

Alaas and Change

A Tale of Two Villages

My first and second trips to the Sakha Republic, for three weeks in the summer of 1991 and for eight months from January to August 1992, were during the critical time of the breakup of the Soviet Union. At the local level, this was a period of intense transition as the administrators of the Elgeeii state farm decided to disband the state farm operation and divvy up the resources among inhabitants. But at the time of my first trips, I was not cognizant of these changes. My singular focus was on researching the *yhyakh* for my master's thesis. Although I now regret having missed the chance to document in real time how the breakup went, I have been able to weave the different strands of my fieldwork into a rich understanding of that time of transition. Sometimes I deliberately sought out those strands, and other times they came to me largely unexpectedly.

> I was walking with Tamara to the other side of Elgeeii to her mother's house for an oral history interview. The route took us through some back neighborhoods and then to a large open area, dotted with stumps of old construction on a landscape that dipped and dove. Tamara stopped when she realized the relevance, "This is called *Jogolookh*. Mom was a milker here during the state farm." I looked around at the vast open bare space. She must have noticed my confusion. "This used to be the biggest group of *khotons* on the Elgeeii state farm. In its day, this area was covered by a half dozen long *khotons*

housing hundreds of animals in the winter." I couldn't imagine how that could be . . . how a place so empty and quiet was once a bustling area filled with people and cows. We continued on, winding along the footpath through the remains of the former state farm activity. With her mother's and multiple others' accounts of state farm work at *Jogolookh* I gradually developed an understanding of that area that I had previously regarded as empty and quiet. Every other time since then, when I crossed *Jogolookh*, the area came to life with the sounds of cows, milk pails and bustle and with the images of workers going here and there around the long *khotons*, with cows moving through. (Journal entry, summer 1999)

These unexpected insights, in combination with my more detailed elicitations from local inhabitants alive during the early Soviet period, provide an image of the past in my two main research villages, Elgeeii and Kutana (see map 1): "My folks lived on their own . . . they lived well, they had twenty milkers . . . cows and horses . . . they had their *kystyk* and they had their *saiylyk* on their *alaas*, which is still there but other people hay there now. Before, we Sakha did everything by hand . . . then when the collective formed, my folks moved to near the *alaas* where I hay now" (Arian Andreyevich Kondratyev, interview July 3, 2018). Respondents like Arian (b. 1936) were relocated one or more times over the period of *kolkhoz* consolidation (see map 5) before moving to a concentrated village settlement of the state farm, in his case to Elgeeii.

Beyond inhabitants' testimonies and local specialists, I also used archival and secondary source documentation to understand the larger policy context of the period that affected life on the ground. These geopolitical transformations were not just physical, in terms of settlement patterns and food production practices. These consolidations forced Sakha to abandon their intimate knowledge of and centuries-old adaptation of living "by the *alaas*." The political changes also infiltrated Sakha's *alaas* culture, sometimes subtly and other times not, as reflected here in Mikhail Nikolayevich Timofeev-Tereshkin's 1952 poem, "Saasky Tüün" (Spring Night; from Mikhaleva-Saia et al. 2013: 413):

The *alaas*, surrounded by fields
The stallion neighs from afar
From the eastern woods the cuckoo calls

And the bittern sounds from the lake

. . .

The great Party's strength
And the warmth of the fiery sun
People's lives become abundant
We make the joyful life

To fully fathom how those changes came into and transformed the lives of Elgeeii and Kutana inhabitants, I provide an overview of the broader national policies at the time.

The Soviet Experiment in Brief

The Soviet period brought monumental change to Sakha's and other non-Russian peoples' lives and livelihoods. Lenin's policy of *korenizatsiia* (nativization) was aimed to support native languages and formally institutionalize ethnicity within the state apparatus (Suny 1993: 102). The *Narkomnat* (People's Commissariat of Nationalities), later known as the Committee of the North, negotiated *korenizatsiia* policy to ensure an independent cultural life for native non-Russians (Grant 1995: 71–85). However, the organization's members were divided on how to achieve a "backward" people's passage to socialism through an active proletariat. One group advocated a system of reservations, while the other encouraged assimilation. With Lenin's death in 1924, Stalin replaced his native village leadership protocol with administrative measures to perpetuate the great Russian culture, transforming the mandate of the Committee of the North from reifying native ways to efforts of "cultural construction" (Suny 1993: 108). Native language and culture were now branded inferior unless they could propagandize socialism. Historical belief systems, their attending practices, and other cultural particularities were to be extinguished. Stalin waged a "war against the past," reframed collectivization as a "revolution from above," and promoted the "socialization of the countryside" by integrating agriculture into the system of central planning (Pitassio and Zaslavsky 1985: 9). Peoples practicing native economies, including herding, hunting, fishing, and foraging, were forced to relinquish their resources and integrate into cooperative units with specialized "brigades" devoted to one type of economic pursuit (Slezkine 1994: 204).

Stalin introduced "dekulakization," the forced liquidation of wealthy land and resource holders, in the early 1930s. In response, many slaughtered their herds across the USSR, and in some cases, chaos ensued. Kazakh livestock holders slaughtered 80 percent of their herds, and millions more died from violence and starvation (Suny 1993: 107; Conquest 1986: 189–98).

World War II and the fight against fascism took attention away from Stalin's purges. All USSR inhabitants, including Siberian natives, participated. Men went to defend the war front and women, children, and elders stayed to work in their place. The economy boomed postwar, and native inhabitants' living standards began to rival Russians'. In the late 1950s collectives were consolidated into agro-industrial state farm operations with workers receiving paychecks instead of a portion of the collective production and having access to a variety of consumer goods.

Sakha's Transition from Living "by the *Alaas*" to Living on the State Farm

Sakha's transition to collective organization was predicated upon the government's careful analysis of their existing conditions. From 1925 through 1927, the USSR Academy of Sciences carried out 5,516 worker days in ethnographic, medical, economic, forestry, hunting, fishing, agriculture, geomorphology, hydrology, and meteorological expeditions across the present-day Sakha Republic to determine how to best maximize total production (Vittenburg 2013: xviii). The inspectors documented Sakha's pasturing and fodder system:

> . . . pastures are divided by the inhabitants into two groups: the first comprises lands of the type just described [*saiylyk*] usually adjoining the summer dwelling of the Yakut [Sakha]. Here graze in perfect freedom, cattle and herds [*tabun*] of horses. The pastures of the second group, *kharyakh* [protected area], are set apart for the animals used in farm work, and these pastures or really paddocks, being generally of smaller size, and providing better feed, are fenced in. (Poriadin 1930: 375)

Some of the inspectors in these early efforts noted Sakha expressions of their historical belief system: "Sakha live in yurts and before they make their

place, they ask the sky for blessings so they can be happy there . . . so they
and their animals will be free of all diseases" (All Russian Hygienic Exhibition
1913: 1). The also detailed Sakha's *alaas* management:

> They organize their nomadism in their family group having a specific area
> of land, and usually move 2 or 3 times a year . . . all near a water source that,
> in winter, does not completely freeze to have drinking water. In summer
> they move to their summer camp which is surrounded by pasture and has a
> water source and often has many brambles and so is not fit for haying. They
> cut hay and stack it near their winter home so they don't have to haul it with
> horses. They burn the old hay on the hayfields in the spring, which improves
> the hay growth and results in a gradual widening of the hay area due to the
> brambles and the incoming trees being burned. . . . Agriculture in this region
> only appeared with the arrival of Russians. Neither Sakha nor Tungus knew
> agriculture and even to this day both groups stay committed to their former
> activities. (Abolin 1929: 71–72)

The Academy of Sciences specialists concluded that Sakha's lifestyle
needed to be drastically changed in order to maximize production. Sakha
were considered backward and "still fairly primitive," to the extent that they
"stayed committed to their former activities" (Nikitin 1930: 361). They initiated the change with an issue that explorers had made note of decades before:
"Sakha lived with their *kömülüök* and their *khoton* in one place and all the
dirt and smell thereof, which bled into their clothing and, because they never
washed, stayed all the time" (Jochelson 1895: 16). The early twentieth-century
expeditions echoed this observation and criticized it in the name of hygiene:
"Their animals are with them inside their 'yurt' . . . they coat the 'yurt' with
fresh animal excrement in the fall to seal it. . . . They can smell [the stench of]
their yurt, but for the warmth and economical aspect of heating, they cannot
yet move away from it" (All Russian Hygienic Exhibition 1913: 2).

The solution was *Yraas Olokh* (literally, "Clean Life"), moving Sakha from
the *balaghans* they shared with their animals into Russian log homes separate
from the barns and heated by Russian stoves (Mikhaleva-Saia et al. 2013:
142). This change resulted in better health for families that were too poor to
manage the house and barn combination without spreading disease, but most
others were able to maintain the arrangement without health issues.[1] In truth,
the government's change had much loftier goals than hygiene. "Many are

fighting for the separation of barn from home . . . and of course it will result in cultural development and an increase in literacy" (All Russian Hygienic Exhibition 1913: 3).

This effort was one of many initiatives aimed to sovietize Sakha during their "Century of Perestroikas" (Grant 1995). Grant argues that _perestroika_ (restructuring) was not a one-time event of the late 1980s but rather a long and subversive process that extended over the seventy years of Soviet rule. The non-Russian ethnicities across the former USSR were to be indoctrinated into a culture of one Soviet people. He builds his Century of Perestroikas argument on his ethnography of Nivkh, an Indigenous people of northern Sakhalin, during the Soviet period and the effects of the major institution of cultural construction: state-mandated culture houses. Craig Campbell embellishes Grant's argument, detailing how these restructuring efforts involved a superficial retaining of outwardly expressed cultural differences while, at the same time, disciplining a people's foundational belief system and cultural identity to fit within the Soviet protocol (Campbell 2014: 2). I extend Campbell's argument further by arguing that, to the extent that cultural identity is in part based in a people's essential human-environment relationship, the forced consolidation into _kolkhoz_ and eventually state farms was part and parcel of these Soviet government disciplinary efforts to reconstruct culture. For Sakha, this involved the removal of inhabitants from their historical living "by the _alaas_" livelihood into larger and larger consolidated living and production centers.

The Soviet and Post-Soviet Periods in Close-Up for Elgeeii and Kutana

Until the late 1920s, Sakha of Elgeeii and Kutana lived "by the _alaas._" Contemporary Elgeeii and Kutana inhabitants recall those pre-_kolkhoz_ times when they understood, respected, and followed both the practical and the spiritual precepts of their lives.

> Back before the _kolkhoz_, people chose where they lived. Here there were many lakes and fields but of them they had three main choices . . . Kutana, Aranghastaakh or Diring Kunde . . . and they chose Kutana—they didn't like the other two places as much because each had only half the pasture—

and also they used a divining practice to decide. The head of the community threw the *tyrekh* [spoon of fate] three times, and if it landed with it's mouth upward, then that was good land and if it fell with it down, bad. Then they said *tusku, tusku, tusku!*, calling it *tuskulaakh* [blessed] land! (Svetlana Gavrilovna Martinova, interview, June 13, 2018)

The first collective farms were organized in 1929 in Elgeeii: Bastaky Sardanga (First Ray) and in Kutana: Bassabyyk (a Sakha-ization of the word "Bolshevik"). The mostly poorer households, those who stood to benefit the most from this government initiative to "level all wealth," eagerly joined first. They also worked to bring others in.

All upper, lower and middle class! The Bordong I [contemporary Elgeeii][2] *nehiliek*[3] [name for patrilineal clan area that now refers to a settlement] of Suntaar *uluus* invites you to join in the agricultural collective in order to work in common and provide for our households. By joining the work collective, you will be fighting the forces of the *kulaak* [wealthy class], who are the exploiters and the enemy of the people. (CSA: 6)

Households who joined the *kolkhoz* were allowed to keep a maximum of five milk cows for their own use, and the remainder they had to give to the *kolkhoz*. At first, Stalin used indirect protocols to force productive resources into the *kolkhoz* system, in this case exacting a high tax on household herds that put many into bankruptcy. Soon his efforts became more extreme, with the use of terror tactics to erase remaining *kulaak*. Local narratives describe how wealthy herders fled:

The Samsonov family lived in Kÿÿkei. They were very wealthy with many herds. My *khos khos ehe* [great-great-grandfather] took the Samsonov family's goods in three to four wagons to sell in Olyokminsk, where it was more developed with Russians and stores and all . . . he sold the meat and butter and bought tea and wheat. The Samsonovs lived well in Kÿÿkei. You could tell because of the characteristics of their *balaghan*—it had a *kömülüök* with two mouths and stood in the middle to send heat out in two directions . . . this means they had a huge wide house . . . they lived very well and then BANG! the October Revolution came . . . if you had thirty-plus animals . . . you were a *kulaak* . . . if you had sixty animals . . . you were a big *kulaak* . . . if you had a hundred animals, you were a very big *kulaak*. The Samsonovs ran immediately to Prokovsk on the edge of Yakutsk . . . where they all became scientists and teachers—it was good for their education—then after ten to twenty years later they came back . . . and the Kÿÿkei school there, to this day, has the Samsonov name. (Vladimir Nikolayevich Semyonov, interview, May 30, 2019)

Other local testimony tells of wealthy herders who were imprisoned:

Our *ehe* [grandfather] had many cows and horses and joined the *kolkhoz* but then he decided it was not the right idea and he left the *kolkhoz* and he took back his animals. Soon after the government started to tax private animals. Then one day, when going to water, all *ehe*'s horses fell into the lake . . . the ice was new and they went on it and all fell in and died . . . but the government still demanded tax even though they were dead! *Ehe* had no way to pay and so he went to Olyokminsk with his older son and in 1941 the *povestka* [summons] came to him to go to the war. But he couldn't leave the boy there alone in Olyokminsk and so they both came to Kharialaakh [settlement adjacent to contemporary Elgeeii] on foot to bring the boy back. He intended to then go to war. But they accused him of being a deserter and a *kulaak*, arrested him and sent him to prison in Olyokminsk. (Margarita Ilyinichna Zabolotskaya, interview, May 29, 2019)

Other testimony tells how some *kulaaks* were blatantly shot. "Our people were many in number and were cut down in Soviet times," remembers Nikolai Nikolayevich Martinov. "Take my five brothers who were shot. For what? Because they didn't want to go to work for the collective farm. They wanted to live independently as before and live the good life they had built for themselves. They were shot here on the river bank near where a small prison stood. Then they [the Soviet regime] separated the clans and tribal lines so we didn't know each other. I don't know where my people are" (interview, July 11, 1992).

Although Stalin's local purges went undocumented, the preliminary census for 1937 shows a precipitous drop in population (Arkadi Iakovlev, specialist consultation, September 20, 1999). Stalin's purges forced inhabitants into collective production. The *kolkhoz* grew a variety of crops including barley, rye, oats, wheat, potatoes, cabbage, and carrots. Members were paid once a year, on New Year's Eve, according to their year-long accumulation of *kuluhun kune* (literally "sweat days," days of work), a measure of work hours based on a *nuorma* (quota) of standardized tasks. Pay was in farm "profits," that is, what remained of the butter, meat, and wheat at the end of the year after the farm had paid its government taxes. Viliui region *kolkhoz* sometimes went years without making a substantial profit. Household survival depended partly on home food production, keeping the allowed quota of herds and foddering them by haying the marginal lands that were left after *kolkhoz* haying was completed.

As *kolkhoz* amalgamated into larger and larger operations, work grew increasingly specialized into brigades that engaged only a small sector of village populations, for example, to do all the fishing and hunting. This meant that Viliui Sakha no longer actively used their mixed subsistence herding, hunting, fishing, and foraging knowledge. In an effort to step up milk production, the Department of Agriculture introduced eight Simmental bull inseminators, a high-producing European breed, in the early 1930s to cross with the local breed. This move systematically assimilated the hardy aboriginal Sakha cattle. By 1960 the Sakha-Simmental mix was considered one of the highest quality and quantity milk and meat producers across the USSR (S. I. Nikolaev 1970).

World War II brought many setbacks to the Elgeeii and Kutana *kolkhoz*. Adult males left the farms for the front, leaving only women, children, and elders to run the nascent collectives (SRA, Annual Bookkeepers' Records). The year 1942, remembered locally as *achchyk jyl* (starvation year), was a year of devastating drought and consequent hunger. The nearby salt-rich Kempandai settlement (map 1), which had operated for over a century as a penal colony, stepped up its production of salt to preserve food for the war front. *Kolkhoz* workers who were sent there to work remember, "At Kempandai we worked cutting wood and mining salt. It was great because in 1942, starvation was everywhere but they fed us three times a day" (Elgeeii elder, 1999). By 1944 many Viliui area *kolkhoz* were growing tobacco and raising a variety of animals previously unknown to the subarctic climate, including pigs, chickens, geese, sheep, and goats.

After the war, the government introduced new mechanization methods of farming to step up production. In Elgeeii and Kutana, the first tractors arrived in the late 1940s. Superphosphates and other chemical fertilizers replaced the historical practice of burning fields and applying animal manures as

Figure 17 Monument to the first tractor that arrived in Elgeeii in the late 1940s, still standing today. Notice the Soviet propaganda on the far building, "СЛАВА (Т) РУДУ!" *SLAVA TRUDU* (GLORY TO LABOR). Photo by author.

fertilizers. *Kolkhoz* were further consolidated in the early 1950s. The number of Suntaar regional *kolkhoz* went from one hundred to twenty-five by 1952 (SRA, "Material of the January 1st Report").

The postwar period was also the time to step up industrial production, part of the government's effort to "catch up with the West." In the Viliui regions this was evident in the discovery and subsequent extraction of diamonds. The mineralogist Larisa Popogayeva discovered the first kimberlite "pipe" in 1954. This initiated the search for other diamond deposits nearby. This newly discovered diamond "field" was demarcated and deemed an industrial region. Botuobuya, home of the first diamond mine, became the Mirnyi (meaning "peaceful" in Russian) village and later the Mirnyi city proper in 1959 (Arkadi Iakovlev, specialist consultation, September 20, 1999).

The government disregarded the multiple environmental issues that resulted from the mining and processing of kimberlite to extract diamonds. The Viliui River was polluted with thallium, a heavy metal used in the final process of cleaning the diamonds from the kimberlite. The river also turned red from a significant input of phenols from the anaerobic breakdown of thousands of hectares of forests that were submerged to create the reservoir for hydroelectric power generation. Two of the eleven underground nuclear explosions, done for "peaceful purposes," resulted in above-ground fallout that had plutonium levels higher than Hiroshima. The environmental and human health repercussions of these activities severely affected Sakha along the Viliui River for decades, a fact that many at the time suspected but was only verified in the *glasnost* (openness) period of the late 1980s (Tichotsky 2014; Crate 2002).

Nikita Khrushchev directed the final consolidation of *kolkhoz* into agro-industrial state farms during his brief leadership from 1957 to 1961. The over one thousand *kolkhoz* in the Sakha Republic were consolidated into seventy state farms by the late 1950s. Three of them were massive in size in order to produce an excess for workers in industrial production. These farms were in the Lensk, the Nyurba, and the Suntaar regions (SRA, "Orders and Instructions"). These massive state farms were given abundant resources: unlimited fuel supplies, dozens of tractors and other farm machinery, and an entire corp of specialists including agronomists, veterinarians, economists, animal breeders, inseminators, medical doctors, and farm directors imported from western Russia and Ukraine.

The massive consolidation in the Suntaar *uluus* was the Elgeeii state farm, whose main objective was to "feed the diamond colonies" (Tichotsky 2014; Crate 2006a). To these ends, the government put in place a state farm director who could clearly align with this goal: "Before I came to work here as the director, I worked on the geological expeditions searching for diamonds. After we found the diamond wealth, we then had a new path to travel to lead us to our future wealth and prosperity. It is part of this great responsibility for the local Indigenous inhabitants to produce meat, butter, and cream to feed the working settlements. This is the Elgeeii State Farm's foremost objective" (Semen Zhuravlyev, quoted in SRA, "Material about Production Activities").

The Elgeeii state farm encompassed 150,000 hectares equaling 670 square miles, or an area approximately half the size of Rhode Island. With the influx of foreign specialists and the relocation of populations from the adjacent *kolkhoz*, the Elgeeii village population increased several-fold. Vestiges of the resettlement remain to this day: "My parents were in the Varishilov *kolkhoz*. In fact, this street we live on now in Elgeeii is named Varishilov because many who worked for that *kolkhoz* in III Bordong moved here to live on this street. They stopped everything in III Bordong except for watching steers.

All else was moved to Elgeeii" (Zoya Alekseyevna Novogitzina, interview, July 3, 2018).

In the state farm period, village inhabitants had access to a diversity of consumer products for the first time in their lives. Elders today recollect their relief from the constant work of making everything themselves.

> There were five *kolkhoz* around here before . . . Bassabyyk, Kommunar, Mai, Kyhyl Kekke, Stalyn . . . we were in Bassabyyk and I was working in the *kolkhoz* from age sixteen. Then those five *kolkhoz* joined into one and then that one joined with three or four others. Then there was one huge *kolkhoz*. Soon after, in 1957 that *kolkhoz* joined to the Elgeeii state farm . . . and from that time, *sühüökhpüttüger turbupput* [literally "we stood up with our own knees without falling"] . . . flour came to us already ground . . . we no longer had to grind it by hand with the *suoruna* [mill using grinding stones], and we had pay to buy bread from the store . . . from 1957 we were no longer poor . . . we had clothes and lots of varieties of food . . . we had it all—we got salaries and could go to the store and buy all we needed. (Mariya Leekenovna Ivanova, interview, June 13, 2019)

When the USSR ended in 1991, three generations had adapted to living in centralized villages with electricity, schools, hospitals, and all their needs close at hand. State farm managers were given a choice to continue their operation based on their own economic plans and resources or to disband. The Elgeeii state farm managers chose the latter and proceeded to divide farm resources, including animals, machinery, equipment, and hay land among the inhabitants. Overnight, the people of Elgeeii and Kutana lost their steady employment and secure food supply.

The early 1990s were a period of economic dislocation at the village level which had different manifestations from household to household. Some went from full employment at the state farm to participating in a *baahynai khahaaiystyba*, a form of collective meat and milk production aimed to supply local needs in the wake of state farm dissolution. Most households lost their employment and had no other option than to depend on their household's elder pensions and child subsidies. Even if a household had monetary resources, village stores were devoid of essential food stuffs, empty except for vodka, cigarettes, candy, vinegar, salt, and matches. A majority of households in Elgeeii and Kutana adapted by developing a "cows-and-kin" food production system. They used their share of state farm resources, including animals, equipment, and a hay land allotment, to produce food on an interhousehold level, exchanging products and labor with other households, most commonly through kinship associations (Crate 2006a). Cows-and-kin took many forms, but most typically involved one elder household keeping the cow herd and performing the daily cow-care duties and the other kin households, predominantly younger with day work, performing the intense harvesting of the hay to overwinter the herd in exchange for meat and milk products.

Now, several decades after the state farm dissolution, residents of Elgeeii and Kutana live a relatively more stable existence. Both have fully stocked stores and a handful of households who keep larger herds to supply the village demand for local meat and milk, largely thanks to local and regional entrepreneurial efforts. Households are modernizing, replacing wood heat with electric and installing large water reservoirs to have "running" water. There is high speed Internet and cell service. Youth are getting higher educations to become specialists.

But with this modernity also come questions about the future of these village settlements. Youth out-migration is ongoing, since many are unable or uninterested in returning from the city to work in their home village. The resources to continue breeding cattle and horses are increasingly difficult to access. Not only is hay difficult to harvest annually owing to the new erratic regime of climate change, but also because it is prohibitively expensive to bring hay from the distant hay areas. Hay land was also affected by the government's effort to drain hay fields during the wet period from 2005 to 2016. There is also a problem of resource access. In Elgeeii, the village hay land has always been inadequate for the population (approx. 2,500) and especially so with the above-cited changes. The majority of Elgeeii hay land is located across the Viliui River in III Bordong (map 1), which further complicates the process of cutting hay and hauling it back to the village. Kutana (population approx. 1,000) enjoys relatively better access to hay land, with a smaller population and a location among *alaas* ecosystems.

Today Elgeeii and Kutana inhabitants do not live "by the *alaas*" by being physically located on an *alaas* ecosystem during *saiylyk* and moving to a *balaghan* for the winter months. But contemporary inhabitants of Elgeeii and Kutana nonetheless perpetuate a relationship with their birth *alaas*, making annual and semiannual pilgrimages to "feed the ancestors," using birth *alaas* lands for hay and forage resources, and maintaining a continuing cultural identification with *alaas* in their daily lives.

The Tale of Two Villages

Elgeeii and Kutana are very different settlements based on their positions in the physical landscape, their specific histories, and their kin makeup. The latter came to my attention when comparing their cow-and-kin proclivities.

> The most sustainable[4] models of the cows-and-kin system are in the smaller settlements where there is not only sufficient land available to support a herd that supplies household needs but also *more intact kin networks* that are essential in providing labor. According to 2000 research results, 20 percent more Kutana households keep cows than in Elgeeii, averaging one more cow per household. This difference is in part due to the fact that Kutana house-holds have hay lands that are closer to the settlement and more abundant. Additionally, *Kutana kin groups are more locally clustered than in Elgeeii and so there is more interdependence among them*, which is essential to pooling hay land and other subsistence resources. (Crate 2006a: 165; emphasis added)

In addition to settlement size in relation to hay access, this difference is also based on both the stability and the composition of each population over time. Compared to Kutana, Elgeeii had a relatively sparse population in pre-Soviet times, which, in the process of gradual consolidations of the *kolkhoz*, increased several-fold with the final centralization of the massive Elgeeii state farm (ibid. 171). Kutana always had and continues to have a solidly kin-based settlement with little fluctuation of population numbers.

Another factor that differentiates these communities today is the pre-Soviet historical trajectories of each. In both places, horse- and cattle-breeding Sakha settled from as early as the eleventh and as late as the seventeenth century, either migrating from the south or from Sakha settlements in the central regions near present-day Yakutsk (Afanas'ev 2016: 16). What happened between then and the Soviet period in part shapes them in contemporary times.

"*Elgeeii*" is a Tungus word meaning "a long thin lake that lies along a river."[5] These lakes are an abundant feature, with forty-four in the III Bordong area alone. Early Sakha called Elgeeii "Tuoidaakh Alaas" (literally, "clayey *alaas*"), because of the high-clay content of its soils. The greater Bordong area was a grouping of five *nehiliek*. Contemporary Elgeeii is located within one, the I Bordong *nehiliek*. Of the five, it was III Bordong that flourished in pre-Soviet times. Both archival records and local testimonies credit this to the land management strategies of the seventeenth-century *agha uuha* leader Chokhoroon. He practiced *nüölsüter*, clearing the land and creating an intricate irrigation system.

Russians settled in I Bordong in 1761, but their tenure was short-lived. After two years of trying unsuccessfully to grow wheat, they relocated to the slightly warmer climes of Olyokminsk (southern Sakha Republic). In 1875, I Bordong was made home of the first of eight Orthodox churches in the Suntaar region. Both of these early colonial events took place in I Bordong because of its location on the only existing transportation link at that time, the Viliui River. Later that century, the government completed a road from Yakutsk, the imperial center, to the Viliui regions, that ran through Elgeeii to Suntaar proper. There are random patches of the horizontal wood-post road-bed across the river from the village to this day. I Bordong served as Suntaar's regional center from 1822 until 1898 when fire destroyed the administrative building. The regional center was then relocated to Kutana.

"*Kutana*" is also a Tungus word, roughly translated as "bright flowing water with a muddy shore" (Afanas'ev 2016: 15). The archaeological record shows that hunting, fishing, and reindeer herding Tungus migrated to Kutana from the Yenisei River of central Siberia at least 2000 years BP (ibid. 16). In 1714, five or six horse- and cattle-breeding Sakha households lived on the shores of the Kutana Lake (ibid. 15). Seven years later, Russian administrators formally established the greater Kutana area as "Khangalas," after the dominant *nehiliek* there (Yakovlev 2006: 48). To give some idea of Sakha's pre-Soviet living standards, in 1796 Khangalas inhabitants overall had 94 stallions, 300 geldings, 1,906 mares, 215 bulls, 2,174 cows, and 1,611 smaller cattle (Afanas'ev 2016: 49). When recollecting their ancestral histories, contemporary Kutana inhabitants repeatedly refer to several outlying *alaas* areas including Oghuruottaakh, the Kuukei Lake area, and Aryylaakh (map 1), the latter being where Chokhoroon also used *nüölsüter* to create productive hay lands.

In the Soviet period, Elgeeii and Kutana went through different processes of collectivization and later state farm establishment. Elgeeii was made a state farm center in 1957, largely owing to its riverside location which offered easy access to shipping. The adjacent *kolkhoz* populations were relocated to the Elgeeii state farm center, first by invitation and later by closing schools, medical stations, and other facilities to force the population to move. Elgeeii's population in the state farm period was made up of relocated *kolkhoz* workers and Russian and Ukrainian specialists imported from the western Soviet Union to act as farm administrators and technicians. In sharp contrast, Kutana had a several-centuries-long pre-Soviet history as a vibrant settlement. In the state farm period, it was designated as a state farm branch, with no substantial influx of adjacent *kolkhoz* workers or non-Sakha technicians.

The breakup of the Elgeeii state farm in the early 1990s accentuated the differences between the two settlements. One contrast between the two was in employment levels. Kutana was the base of the state farm's road-working division which, after 1991, became a licensed legal company called Aian Suol (literally "travelling road"). In the post-Soviet period, Aian Suol has been the economic backbone of Kutana, employing almost half of the village. In contrast, there were no such employment opportunities in Elgeeii. Most inhabitants struggled more to make ends meet than their Kutana neighbors in the immediate post-Soviet period. A second contrast between the two villages is in kin structure. Today, the Kutana community retains an extensive kin base. One Kutana resident, Anatoli Petrovich Fyodorov, claims an ancestral lineage with 50 percent of the village community. The Elgeeii administration has made efforts in the post-Soviet period to nurture community cohesiveness. One effort is by establishing *tüölbe* (literally "small round pasture" but used today to refer to small groups within a community who socialize and do activities together), which have made some difference but have also proven short-lived in comparison with the continuity of blood kin.

The contemporary testimonies of two historical settlements, III Bordong of Elgeeii and Tumul of Kutana, add additional insights about the similarities and differences between the two populations. They also depict how Elgeeii and Kutana inhabitants lived "by the *alaas*," how they moved from living "by the *alaas*," and how they maintain some form of relationship to *alaas* today.

III Bordong and Tumul: Two Villages, Change, and *Alaas*

My approach to understanding the past through local testimonies is to elicit oral histories from individuals who are of a certain age, a certain experience, or both.[6] Oral history accounts document an individual's personal recollections of their life in the context of change over time. What the individual chooses to remember and why are as important as the series of events they relay. Oral history accounts can make sense of how individuals situate themselves in the present: ". . . social memory and social space conjoin to produce much of the context for modern identities—and the often-rigorous contestation of those identities" (Hoelscher and Alderman 2004: 348). Public memories of specific events and individuals also diverge because they are shaped by the hierarchies of power, gender, and social position of those who are doing the remembering (Buyandelger 2013: 135). An example of how contemporary identities can both converge and diverge via oral history is the different ways that Chokhoroon, the clan head who initiated *nüölsüter* in III Bordong, is thought of today. To some, he is known to have transformed the conditions for everyone's good. Others recollect how badly he treated people and animals and also how he abused his power and took more resources for himself. The process is not to decipher who is telling about the "real" Chokhoroon and who is not. It is an exercise in understanding how all of these testimonies can exist at the same time. Most recollections describing Chokhoroon as a saint who saved III Bordong inhabitants come from contemporary individuals who are of his lineage. They were told these narratives by their kin. Negative descriptions come from those outside of Chokhoroon's bloodline. The important takeaway here is that oral history recollections are couched in multiple interacting temporal and cultural layers. They tell as much about a series of events as they do about the individuals recalling them.

Another consideration in interpreting oral history accounts in post-Soviet spaces is how recollections and memories passed down to contemporary inhabitants of the pre-Soviet past are often inconsistent and muddled owing to state-enacted "forced forgetting." "Not only does forced forgetting erase parts of the past and prevent their transmission to newer generations; it also creates anxiety about repressing the past, which weakens individuals' confidence in their own memories" (Buyandelger 2013: 67). Evidence of forced forgetting runs throughout my fieldwork and most prominently in how the generation of the early Soviet period were denigrated and even arrested for continuing to teach their ancestral legacy.

Inhabitants' testimonies of two Soviet-period relocations, of the *kolkhoz* populations from III Bordong to the Elgeeii state farm center and of households from Kutana and other outlying areas to the hamlet of Tumul, add finer details and a human presence to the general historical timeline of state farm consolidation. They also give insights into "the inextricable link between memory and place" (Hoelscher and Alderman 2004: 348). To "be" in those places via social memory calls up a different history than is found in archives and historical texts. This different history is adorned with cultural values, individual and community identities, and social mores. Amid the apparent chaos of multiple relocations and forced forgetting, oral history can trace the thread of a people's essential human-environment relationships by "looking away from what so often counts as history [that] embeds people in the chain of energy conversions foundational to all life" (Demuth 2019: 9), and a looking toward individual and collective memory as a guide to what is persistent through time. Inhabitants' perpetuation of a cultural identification with *alaas*, both physically and spiritually, amid the last century of <u>*perestroikas*</u> is testimony to how individuals adapted their relationship to *alaas* and how *alaas* represent a vibrant cultural symbol for Viliui Sakha of Elgeeii and Kutana.

III BORDONG

Many contemporary Elgeeii elders recalled[7] growing up in III Bordong and later relocating to Elgeeii proper in the state farm period. During my 1999–2000 fieldwork, and to a lesser degree today as elders pass away, there is a strong collective nostalgia for III Bordong, with its many *alaas*, plentiful hay land and pastures, firewood, berries, and hunting and fishing resources. It was home to two *kolkhoz* in the collective period which later consolidated and then relocated to join the state farm. After that, III Bordong was used for cattle raising and as state farm hay and pasture land. Following the early 1990s breakup of the Elgeeii state farm, the III Bordong land area was designated Dabaan *baahynai khahaaiystyba*, a cooperative formation that could access significantly greater hay, pasture, and resources than households could in order to produce a high level of meat and milk for the local community. Soon thereafter, Dabaan *baahynai khahaaiystyba* began a Sakha aboriginal cattle breeding program, one of three such operations in the Sakha Republic.

Long before the Soviet period, III Bordong was known as a highly productive area that supported a relatively dense population. Most attribute this success to Chokhoroon's original work establishing a *nüölsüter* irrigation system. An edited volume produced in 2017 by members of Chokhoroon's ancestral lineage includes an account of his success.

> The prince Bekeen Kniaz' lived near III Bordong. It was an *ugut jyl* [big water time] and the seasons were late. The sun did not show all summer and it remained cold and raining. The only hay that grew went under water. So, they cut it and put it on high wood racks to dry but it rotted. Water came in the houses and fire stoves were ruined and could not make fires. Bekeen Kniaz' took everyone in to live with him as *jukaakh*. They made a huge barn and *uraha*, with fires in the center. A bull pulled a sleigh with wood for the fire in one side and left empty out the other so they could have fires day and night. Their main foods were milk, *kymys*, fresh fish, pine sapwood and *syma* (fermented fish). They harvested willows by the river to feed the herds. The next year the weather turned for the better and they celebrated. Bekeen Kniaz' made his son, Chokhoroon, the next *kniaz'* (prince) who would now manage everything. Chokhoroon told his father that their land was too small to ever make them rich. He then burned and cleared huge areas and, on one side of the settlement, dug down to the permafrost so it would thaw to make a dam. This brought the stream water into their land in dry times. III Bordong was watered well and some of the water created a huge lake, named Emis Kÿöl [Fat Lake]. Takabyl was a big *alaas* where another large lake formed. Chokhoroon also dug canals to drain the lakes and fields in water times. (Ivanov 2017)

Elgeeii resident Arian Andreyevich Kondratyev, also a Chokhoroon descendant on his mother's side, was born in 1936 in his father's land place Sirsar near present-day Toloon (map 1). His life history includes details of Chokhoroon's life after III Bordong:

> My great-great-grandfather Chokhoroon lived in Takabyl, a land place in III Bordong. They say Chokhoroon was of Tygyn Darkhand's[8] bloodline and his ancestors came to III Bordong from Yakutsk. After two of Chokhoroon's sons died in Takabyl, he decided it was a bad place with dark spirits. So, he went to Viluchaan, also on the Viliui River but on the other side of Suntaar. There he also made the land like in III Bordong. There is a land name "Chokhoroon *khoruu*" [Chokhoroon's canal] in Viluchaan. (Interview, May 28, 2019)

Arian also recounted his memories of the time of state farm consolidation when the III Bordong community was relocated:

> There were lots of people in III Bordong from way back. In the early Soviet time, there were two *kolkhoz* there . . . Varishilov and Stalin. Most of the people who lived there were of Chokhoroon's lineage. Then, when the *sovkhoz* [state farm] formed, they called for households to move to the center. At first few households wanted to move. Then, in 1964, they closed the school. Mother's kin moved from III Bordong to Kyöl Elgeeii [map 6a]. (Ibid.)

Elgeeii elders, born in and around III Bordong, are few today. Marfa Koninovna Ivanova, also a Chokhoroon descendant, was born in III Bordong in 1929. She recollects the process of consolidation: "We had a school, stores, and *Sel-Soviet* [village administration]. Then the two *kolkhoz* became one *kolkhoz*, Varishilov. Then, after they formed the *sovkhoz*, everyone had to move to Elgeeii. Some built a new house and some brought their house with them" (interview, May 31, 2019). Marfa also recounted memories of her early life, an upbringing that was typical for most Viliui Sakha at the time.

> I was born at the land place Ingett Atagha [map 1]. We lived in a *saakh jiete* [literally "manure house," another word for the *balaghan*, since it is sealed with manure]. They say my mother was so very strong that she went to shovel manure three days after I was born! I was sickly and grew very thin . . . all my ribs showed . . . how did I survive? . . . my *ehe* was a healer and he took *kunaakh* [the black fungus from the birch], carved it into a tent shape, put it on my skin and burnt the tip. It healed by slowly drawing out bad blood. I was revived. Mother taught me work from age five. I learned to rake hay at nine, to cut hay at twelve and I cut until I was seventy! Father made a good scythe that fit me and that I kept very sharp. I used it all my life. We used a hand knife, a curved blade with a handle, to cut wheat. We cut and tied it into *tuutek* [standing bundles] a 10 by 15-meter area a day. We grew wheat in our yard. Back then we did it all ourselves. (Ibid.)

Her memories also add personal detail to the major historical changes of the war years and the further challenges: "Father went to the army in 1942 . . . 'I will leave tomorrow,' he said . . . 'and you will not have any money to pay the war tax so they will take our cows.' We had five cows. After father went to war, the government took four for the war tax since we had no money . . . where did our four cows go?" (ibid).

Another III Bordong descendant's story provided an answer to Marfa's query. Agrafina Vasiliyevna Nazarova has been a preschool teacher for twenty-five years in Elgeeii. The following description of her mother's life during World War II tells what happened to cows that were taken as tax from households and the injustice served her for doing the right thing,

> My adopted mom, Liana Timofeevna Siderova, was just a sixteen-year-old girl during the war. The *kolkhoz* representative had to go to the war and so they made her the *kolkhoz* representative. I guess because they knew she could read, write, and do math. In the war years it was forbidden to eat the *kolkhoz* cows, even if people were starving. Cows were to be sent to feed the front. Although it was a crime, she could not bear to see starvation and so allowed the III Bordong people to eat the cows. Officers came around from the region and Republic and arrested her for that—charged her with the crime and sent her to hard labor in Kempandai to cut the trees and make the road. Soon thereafter a twenty-year-old man, Timofee Grigor-ievch Nazarov, was newly appointed as the *kolkhoz* representative in nearby Kundeii [map 1]. He studied the official papers of her arrest. He understood that the girl had done nothing wrong. And so, he went to Kempandai to defend her and succeeded in getting her out. They both returned to III Bordong and worked together. In 1946 they got married. My stepmom was a very fierce woman . . . at III Bordong there is a statue of her . . . she was only a child! It was only when they made the statue to her honor, after the fall of the USSR, that we knew of her work feeding the starving . . . no one talked or told about it before then . . . she probably was left feeling very bad about it . . . she was only sixteen and had done the right thing. (Interview, May 30, 2019)

I told Agrafina that I distinctly remembered seeing the statue when I visited III Bordong to see the Sakha aboriginal cattle in 1993. As we traveled by motorboat down the Viliui River, I noticed on the left riverbank a huge white statue of a woman with an uplifted arm. I asked my guide what it was there for, and he remarked simply, "It is the heroine of III Bordong."

After years of separation from her birth mother and her and her siblings' upbringing in separate adopted homes, Agrafina finally came to know her III

Figure 18 Monument to "the heroine of III Bordong," honoring Liana Timofeevna Siderova. Source: Mironoff and Afanaseev 2017. Photo by author.

Bordong heritage in the post-Soviet period. That she didn't know the story of her kin line until recently is an example of forced forgetting.

Other people knew who my birth mother was, but back then no one talked about it. In those times people just never said anything . . . maybe a very old woman would talk but that was it. As young people and children, we were not supposed to ask and were not to listen to what grown-ups were talking about. And so, I and my siblings knew nothing . . . we didn't hear what they talked about but went out to play . . . we didn't ask where it all was . . . we didn't want to know then . . . now I want to know but can't find out . . . they didn't write memories or make a kin lineage. (Agrafina Vasiliyevna Nazarova, interview, May 30, 2019)

In the last decade Agrafina and her siblings have done the work to understand their mother's story and to piece back that part of their heritage. "We found out that our father was around but mother was sick with a bad liver . . . and so they gave me and my siblings to mother's younger sister to raise. Mother got better, but when she tried to take us back, our stepmother was stern and said she was still not well enough to watch us. She [my stepmother] raised us to adulthood" (ibid.).

Other life histories contribute to a greater understanding of the III Bordong relocation, articulating disdain for the move and regret for the loss of the resources and nature there. Afanasee Ivanovich Trofimov, although not born in III Bordong, spent all of his working life there as a *sylgyhyt* (herder tending horses). He is outspoken about the *sovkhoz* relocation and the opportunities missed with the relocation to Elgeeii.

Our ancestors . . . they lived slowly by the *alaas* . . . they had a *kystyk* and a *saiylyk* . . . then the *sovkhoz* gathered everyone in a big group to farm in one place. I think it was a mistake . . . they brought everyone from III Bordong into the Elgeeii center . . . and left all the outlying areas empty. I think today we need to follow the ancestors' old ways. We need to go back to those far areas. We can use solar energy and get all we need by ourselves. But there is no money for this. Our old traditions are very, very wise. They make sense . . . back then it all worked in balance with nature. (Interview, July 3, 2018)

Also based on his experience at III Bordong, he is opinionated about the government's haphazard and often unsuccessful efforts to relieve the water-logged fields in many parts of the Sakha Republic for the last decade.

The canals should have a gated dam to open and close. In the last years, they only dug canals and all the water went right away. Now we have drought and the water all went. Our ancestors dug canals with dams that they closed after the spring high waters went to retain the water. Now there is all this science and they still can't do it right. In 1973 specialists came to III Bordong and studied Chokhoroon's system. They designed a dam project with a canal that had a gate like Chokhoroon made. That is why the hay grows in III Bordong and people get all the hay they need there to this day. (Ibid)

Another Chokhoroon descendant with a deep knowledge of III Bordong is Vasili Mikhailovich Lvov. He was appointed director of the original *baahynai khahaaiystyba* called Dabaan and its later iteration, Tubei *baahynai khahaaiystyba,* and he continues to direct III Bordong's current operation, the Elgeeii *baahynai khahaaiystyba.* Both Vasili and the then newly appointed 1991 head of Elgeeii village are Chokhoroon descendants, which made Vasili the obvious candidate to direct the Dabaan *baahynai khahaaiystyba* when the *sovkhoz* disbanded. He makes his birth connection to III Bordong clear: "I hay there every year because if I don't, the ancestral spirits will get angry at me. Why didn't our boy come and cut hay?" (Vasili Mikhailovich Lvov, interview, July 4, 2018). Born in 1956, not long before the relocation of III Bordong to Elgeeii proper, he nevertheless recalls the process,

My parents worked on the Varishilov *kolkhoz* in III Bordong. My dad was first the *kolkhoz* representative and then the veterinarian. Mom counted the *kuluhun kune* and did the accounting for all the *kolkhoz* business. We had everything we needed there; hay, pasture, forage, hunting, fishing, water, a school and club. In 1964 they changed the school, so we all came to live in Elgeeii proper. (Ibid.)

The Lvov household gets their milk and meat products from III Bordong.

We stopped keeping personal cows because we get all we needed from III Bordong. We started the Dabaan *baahynai khahaaiystyba* for breeding horses then we brought Sakha aboriginal cows in an airplane from Ebem Taiga to start a breeding program here. This is a good place, since we are isolated from the village cows and can keep the breed pure. We started with six females and one bull and now have 108 head. (Ibid.)

Vasili also knows a lot about the III Bordong *nüölsüter* system from his almost thirty years of directing the *baahynai khahaaiystyba,*

We have a gated dam that opens and closes in III Bordong . . . we are the only ones in the entire Suntaar *uluus* with the gated dam for hay fields . . . Chokhoroon's gate is broken but still there in a farther place. It is very heavy and solid. I can't believe they dug it all with wooden shovels back then! From the dam, the *khoruu* circles around the entire settlement. Chokhoroon made an amazing system. The one we use now was made in the *sovkhoz* times. It copies his design. It has a gate and we open and close it . . . there is a mark and if the water goes above it, we open the dam. If the water is to the mark, we close it. We always have productive fields because of that gated dam. If we didn't have it, our land would be dry like everyone else's are during this dry period. (Ibid.)

His most powerful testimony about the advantage of having the dam was when he recounted how good the III Bordong hay growth had been in the last decade, a period of increasing drought that had caused hay yields to drop precipitously in most other places.

Our hay production has been great! We get 300 tons of hay which translates into 150 stacks. We make them the old way, in big stacks. Most people today make the hay into rolls. But our land is not flat and has lots of *dulgha* [hummocks]. In many places we still have to cut by hand with a scythe. We have two brigades. One cuts by hand with scythes and the other uses the "Isaakof" method. For the latter, a tractor cuts and two people stand on the tractor's trailer and stack the hay as it comes up. Most people now don't bother to cut the uneven areas by hand. They either use a weed whacker or just don't bother with it. No one today wants to do physical work. Only if you do it by hand can you get a lot of hay in the uneven areas. (Ibid.)

These narratives of III Bordong that Arian, Marfa, Agrafina, Afanasee, and Vasili shared are just some of Elgeeii inhabitants' many recollections. Three decades after the fall of the Soviet Union and six decades after Chokhoroon's descendants were relocated to Elgeeii proper, there remains a deep connection to the III Bordong land area for both its abundant resources and the ongoing cultural importance of living "by the *alaas*."

Whereas III Bordong was largely abandoned in the state farm period, the small hamlet of Tumul outside of Kutana grew into a highly productive farm that continued production through the end of the state farm. In the post-Soviet period, Tumul served as a bastion for cow-and-kin activities, a place where many people from the adjacent, hay-poor areas of Elgeeii and Suntaar came to help their kin hay and, in the process, to realize their own hay needs.

TUMUL

When I am in Tumul, I feel like I have gone back in time. Houses look pretty much like they have for decades, and people practice a slow-paced life in the cradle of the Tumul area *alaas*. My first visit there was in the summer of 1993, and afterward I spent many summer and winter days there. I stayed mainly with Edjay Olga and Lena, helping out as I could with their herd of sixteen cows and learning about contemporary cow keeping. There are several memorable households in Tumul. The first to come to mind is the home of Iruna and Dunya. I met the two sisters in the early 1990s when I first visited Tumul and Lena took me around to meet the dozen or so Tumul households. I formally worked with them a decade later when I collaborated with Lena on a project called *Kyrjagastaan Subetin Il* (Take Wisdom from the Elders). Lena explained that they continued to do everything "the old-timey way." I was so struck with the experience of visiting them to learn about all their activities, I wrote a journal entry about it:

We entered their yard down a steep bank and through a gate. To the right was their main house and to the left an old *balaghan*. Lena explained that the old *balaghan* was where we would always find them in the summer. We entered and they joked saying, "Welcome to our *saiylyk!*" They both sat at a long table to one side, Iruna making a *chabychakh* [wide, shallow birch bark bucket], sewing it together with white and black horsehair, and Dunya fashioning a larger mat of horse hair into a round sit-upon. We sat and chatted about their lives and how Tumul had changed. They explained that they had learned to make all these utilitarian items of birch bark, horsehair, wood and plants from their grandparents, who used them daily. Now they taught others. Lots of Sakha are interested in knowing the old ways now. After a while, Dunya asked if I wanted to see their "museum." I followed her out to a large shed, and she showed me all kinds of old equipment. There was a *suoruna*, what looked like a huge mortar and pestle made up of a *keli* [wooden base carved out a tree] and a *sokhokh* [a heavy wooden ram to crush grains in the *keli*], a *saar yaghas* [large birch bucket for horses' milk], a *siri ihit* [a large leather container used for *kymys* at the *yhyakh*], a butter churner, and an iron pot with a lid, which she promptly opened to show a bunch of razor-thin wood peelings. She put her hand in and lifted up a handful and let it lightly fall. "This is *tuos* [birch bark]." "Really? What do you use it for?" She pointed to her mouth and made a chewing motion, "*zavatchka* [chewing gum] . . . you just add a tiny bit of crème fraiche to it." She went on to explain that most of the old tools were in pretty bad shape but the kids said not to throw them away because they wanted to make a museum. (Journal entry, summer 2004)

Marusa was another memorable resident whom I worked with regularly in Tumul. Marusa hunted and hayed and "did everything like a man." Her life, like Edjay's, Dunya's and Iruna's, revolved around Tumul and the Kÿÿkei Lake.

Whenever I come from far away, I go and feed *Ebee* [endearing form of *Ebe*, here referring to the lake] and when I leave, I also do so . . . I was taught that practice. But it was when I was very sick that I truly learned it. I had a very high temperature . . . and I went to *Ebee* and said many good words, like "You are very powerful and you know all and please help me not to be so sick" . . . and then I went to the hospital in Suntaar. When I got there, my analysis was fine . . . they said to me, "You were pretending to be sick, eh?" But in Tumul I had a 36-degree temperature . . . didn't eat and laid about all the time . . . and I made a big request to the lake spirit and after that I knew that *Ebee* is very strong and powerful. (Mariya Gavrilovna Zakharova, interview, July 6, 2009)

There is something truly magical, spiritual, and energetic about Tumul, a certain dynamic of the place that sets it apart from other places. The process of recounting my time there—of working with Edjay Olga, and Lena, of visiting Iruna and Dunya's craft workshop in the *balaghan* and their "museum," of sitting with Marusa and learning of her latest hunting adventures—call forth in me a visceral sense of place. It is not just the glorious setting of an immense lake surrounded by green pastures, fields, and forests. There is a definite energy in Tumul that is unquestionably founded in its long history of Sakha settlement and living "by the *alaas.*"

In sharp contrast to the emptying out of III Bordong to consolidate workers and herds in the Elgeeii state farm center, in the state farm branch of Kutana there was a deliberate effort to bring workers and herds out to productive areas. Of them, Tumul is best known because of the unrivaled production of its director, "Hero Dmitri": "At that time [1961], Tumul had 3 or 4 elderly households and nothing more . . . then, the first year after deciding to start the cattle operation, they built an apartment building, a club, a *medpunkt* [medical station], a store, a bakery. Soon 150 people lived there and we were raising over 1,000 cattle" (Andreev 1995).

Like III Bordong, the greater Tumul area is rich in origin narratives about the pre-Soviet Sakha *agha uuha* who lived there "by the *alaas.*" Tumul sits eight kilometers from Oghuruottaakh[9] (map 1), a centuries-old Sakha settlement area rich in hayfields, lakes, and abundant subsistence resources. With the 1957 consolidation of the state farm, many households relocated from Oghuruottaakh to Tumul. Mariya Pavlovna's ancestors were among them:

My parents had come from Oghuruottaakh to Tumul in the 1960s to work for Hero Dmitri. There were lots of people in Tumul then and also a club, a store, a bakery. It was wonderful . . . in spring it was all bright green with cuckoos cooing and lots of butterflies . . . everywhere . . . lots of birds . . . I lived there until I moved into Kutana for school. I still went every summer to Tumul to hay. (Mariya Pavlovna Afanaseyeva, interview, June 6, 2019)

Hero Dmitri's son, Osip Dmitriyevich Andreyev, lives in Tumul today and is one of Tumul's two year-round households, along with Iruna's. His father figures large in his memories:

Back then, there were so many people in Tumul. All worked well together. I was ten and I worked hard . . . in those times, all the children worked . . . haying and helping with the animals . . . dad was born in 1912 and worked all his life for the Soviet farms. He was first a *kolkhoz* representative and then a brigadier. He did not go to the war because his work here was too important. Then in the 1960s they enlisted him to head up the cattle production in Tumul. He received the highest honor for his heroic work. (Osip Dmitriyevich Andreyev, interview, May 21, 2019)

When asked about his decision to live in Tumul and not in Kutana, where he and his household could access needed goods more easily, he dismissed the idea. He explained that his choice was based on a deeper understanding of place attachment, on how Tumul was his sacred *alaas* and that by living there he was respecting his people's ancestral practices:

When I was young, I didn't do the Sakha practices . . . it has only been since I have gotten older that I do them . . . when I was young I didn't believe in those things . . . partly it's because we were raised in the Soviet time . . . no belief, no devils, no religion, nothing of that at all . . . it was a different ideology. Then when I got older, the practices my mother showed me and my father told me came back to me. I understood their importance and I practice them in my life. (Ibid.)

One of Hero Dmitri's workers, Mariya Leekenovna Ivanova, recollected many details that add to an understanding of the richness and pulse of life in Tumul:

We married in Kÿÿkei and moved to Tumul when Hero Dmitri formed his brigade in 1962 . . . I worked in the bakery and husband Semyon worked for the Hero as a brigadier. Back then it was so great! There was a hospital, a club, a bakery, a store . . . lots of people . . . and over 1,000 head of cattle. And the nature was so full with lots of foraging for *jeijen* [wild strawberry], *oton* [lingonberry], *moonn'oghon* [black currant], and *khaptaghas* [red currant] . . . it

was the best place. In '70 we moved to Kutana for the kids to attend school
but we still spent every summer in Tumul. As soon as school finished, we
moved back to Tumul. Now there are only two families . . . Iruna and Osip.
It is too bad. (Mariya Leekenovna Ivanova, interview, June 13, 2019)

Marusa's recollections also suggest a certain sacred element of life in Tumul
that she did not find in Kutana:

In the spring in Tumul there was so much excitement in nature. I always
hung the *salama* before the cows birthed. I rolled the horsehair on my leg to
make the rope, then tied colored rags and birch bark figures to it and hung
it. My *salama* are still hanging in the Tumul *khoton* to this day! We hung
salama when we lived in Tumul, but not when we lived in Kutana. Somehow,
it's not the same in Kutana. (Ibid.)

A decade after the state farm disbanded, Marusa's husband, Semyon,
explained how there were plans for further development in Tumul. He talked
about a late Soviet plan that never came to pass:

I worked as a brigadeer for Hero Dmitri and we had 1,200 head of cattle
there at one time. I really would like to see a cooperative in Tumul. The hero
worker, Dmitri Gavrilovich Andreyev, proposed one in 1990 called *Buluu
Programmata* [Viliui Program]. They had plans to build an airport, a hospital, a school, and everything the community needed. Then the *sovkhoz*
broke apart and so did that plan. (Semyon Petrovich Yegorov, interview,
July 7, 2000)

Instead, the post-Soviet period in Tumul has been a time of gradual depop-
ulation, as elders who had lived there most of their lives have passed away,
and inhabitants chose to move closer to their needed amenities in Kutana.
There have been other changes also. Osip's lifelong experience there gives
him a unique perspective on how Tumul has changed with the post-Soviet
population decline and also other changes as they have developed in more
recent years:

There are lots of changes . . . I grew up here when there was no *tekhnika*
[machinery of all kinds] to ruin everything. It was relatively untouched here . . .

now with all the *tekhnika* the land is ruined . . . and now, with the permafrost thawing, more holes are appearing in the ground. I see these changes in the land . . . previously very flat lands are now wavy and full of holes . . . as the permafrost thaws, it forms *ungkachukka* [here meaning "cavities"] where the land then falls in. Then the *tekhnika* goes over those lands and breaks the land more. The other issue is the last decade of deforestation. I have lived here for sixty-four years . . . I see how they have cut so many trees and spoil the nature here. In the Sakha Republic . . . the trees do not grow fast . . . they are slow to grow. Before when people had no *tekhnika*, they didn't ruin nature. (Osip Dmitriyevich Andreyev, interview, June 26, 2018)

Although Mariya Leekenovna Ivanova no longer lives in Tumul, she goes there when she can to pay her respect to her ancestors. Her testimony adds to Osip's, speaking to the contrast between how things were then and how they are today:

Before I was working all the time, the cows, the kids, the house, the work . . . I had no time to think about things. Now I sit and think a lot. When I go in the forests and on the land of Tumul, I remember what it was like before, and I can see that so much has changed. In some places, all the trees are cut down. The places where I have gone all my life, I now see where the once flat land now goes up and down and, in some places, new small lakes have appeared. I see these changes when I go to Tumul and Kÿÿkei alike. There is a new lake in Tumul and when I walk around it, I can see how the land has fallen down. It was completely flat before and now it is all holes that fill with water . . . I think it will all fall . . . this land. (Mariya Leekenovna Ivanova, interview, June 13, 2019)

In addition to more *tekhnika*, better access to Tumul is another reason for the increasing use of its resources. People commonly remark about how it used to take five or six hours to get to Tumul from Kutana owing to the poor Soviet-period road conditions. In the late 1990s, Aian Suol did extensive work to construct a properly drained and paved road system between the regional centers of Nyurba and Suntaar. Once main roads were done, they began the project of improving the roads out into resource-rich areas like Tumul. Today it only takes twenty minutes to get to Tumul from Kutana.

Map 6a One of four maps that greet visitors in the entry room of the Tuoidaakh Alaas Museum. Each map shows the historical settlements of Sakha living "by the *alaas*." This one shows the homesteads in and around Kÿöl Elgeeii. Map title reads: "Kÿöl Elgeeii: Until 1930 families lived dispersed." In the lower right area is the present location of the Elgeeii village. Source: Tuoidaakh Alaas Museum, Elgeeii. Photo by author.

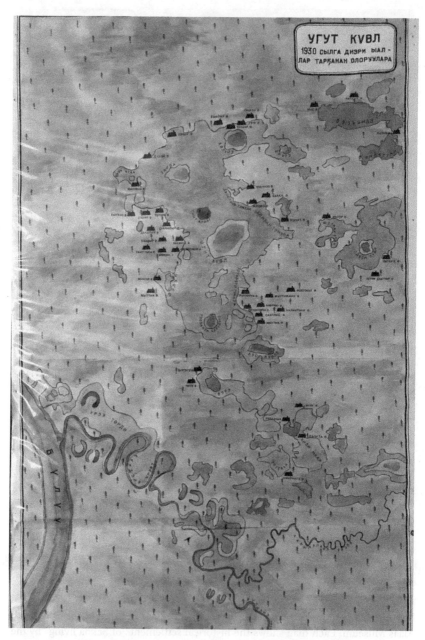

Map 6b Another one of the maps that greet visitors in the entry room to the museum. This one shows the homesteads in and around Ugut Kӱöl. Map title reads: "Ugut Kӱöl: Until 1930 families lived dispersed." Source: Tuoidaakh Alaas Museum, Elgeeii. Photo by author.

III BORDONG, TUMUL, AND *ALAAS*

These two villages have very different histories of change over the span of time from the pre-Soviet period of living "by the *alaas*" to their contemporary settlements. In both places, inhabitants continue to have a strong cultural identification with the *alaas* in their outlying areas. Descendants of Chokhoroon continue to identify with the myriad of *alaas* in the III Bordong area and reify their memories of place there. The *agha uuha* descendants of Oghuruottaakh and the greater Kÿÿkei Lake area perpetuate the living "by the *alaas*" heritage of Tumul, either by living there and enacting ancestral practices or by making regular pilgrimages to feed their ancestral spirits. In addition to the work of Ivan Nolar in Elgeeii and Nikolai Innokentiyev-ich Ivanov of Kutana to teach and write about Sakha and *alaas*, Elgeeii is also home to a museum dedicated to village history called Tuoidaakh Alaas. Upon entering the museum, the visitor sees six maps of the outlying *alaas* areas displayed on one wall of the entry room. Each map identifies the *alaas* area toponyms, including the various *ötökh* of pre-Soviet inhabitants. These are the ancestors of Elgeeii's contemporary residents (maps 6*a* and *b*). The rest of the museum documents these *agha uuha*, their beginnings and the generations up to contemporary times.

Inhabitants express their identification with their *alaas* in other ways besides recalling their ancestral lineages, writing about the Sakha *alaas* relationship, or substantiating local *alaas* history in a museum. Arian Andreevich Kondratev explained to me that he grew up in a musical household and was playing *bayan* (a button accordion) and writing songs from a very early age. When I asked what his first song was, he smiled broadly and said, "Törööbüt Alaahym" (My Birth *Alaas*) and sprang up to retrieve his bayan and play it for me.

I think of my birth *alaas*
The soft wind in the birch grove
My small Sakha *balaghan*
And the flowers in layers all over the yard.

I think of the birch shade
And making the small hay tent

Burning a strong *tüpte* fire
Relaxing in the peaceful playing

I think of the *tühüulge* [social gathering of *yhyakh*] in the evening
Ehiekei [sound of *ohuokhai* singing] with so many beautiful words
My *alaas* has ten different colors in it
With the beautiful flowers growing

I am homesick for the joy and cheer
My dear mother's beautiful-sounding *khomus* [Jew's harp]
I think of the relaxing swimming
In my little lake with "*khomus*" [type of reed]

I think of my birth *alaas* Sirsar
The first tractor coming
He brought it driving
My brother who did not return from the war.
> (Kondratyev Arian Andreyevich, interview, May 28, 2019)

The contrast of time and place was stark. The moment before he sang his song for me, I was in his home in 2019, a time when living "by the *alaas*" had long been a vestige of the past. By way of his song and his intricate sensory depictions, I traveled to his *alaas*: I could hear the *khomus* music and *ohuokhai* song, I could see the birch grove and soft grasses, I could smell the *tüpte*, and I shared the grief of his brother's death. More than words, song is a sonic medium that connects humans with their sentient world (Brabec de Mori and Seeger 2013). For Sakha, who consider all parts of the animate and inanimate world sentient, song also proves a powerful medium to maintain the essential relationship with one's birth *alaas*. Arian's song left a strong impression on me of just how resilient *alaas* are for Sakha cultural identity.

Chapter 4

Community-Level Understandings

From Climate Change to the Complexity
of Change and Back

I had my first epiphany about the deeper implications of climate change for Viliui Sakha in the summer of 2005 as I listened to elders explain how *Jyl Oghuha* (the Bull of Winter) no longer arrived.

> *Jyl Oghuha* is a legendary Sakha creature whose presence explains the turning from the frigid winter to the warming spring. The legend tells of how *Jyl Oghuha*, who keeps the cold in winter, loses his first horn at the end of January as the cold begins to let go to warmth; his second horn melts off several weeks later, and finally, in another few weeks, he loses his head, as spring is sure to have arrived. It seems that now, with the warming, *Jyl Oghuha* no longer is . . . (Sakha elder [b. 1935], 2005)

I knew the historical narrative of *Jyl Oghuha*, which Sakha had used for centuries to explain the frigid, dry, windless three-month period of winter. In 2005, the situation had been turned around. Since then, inhabitants retell this story, not to explain how the seasons go in their permafrost ecosystem, but rather to contrast with how the seasons have changed. *Jyl Oghuha* has become a prophecy of climate change. In winter 2018 I saw an abundance of *Jyl Oghuha* in a range of contexts, from refrigerator magnets to a substantial statue complete with multiple details of the *Jyl Oghuha* narrative in the capital city Yakutsk.

Figure 19a *Jyl Oghuha* statue erected ca. 2015 in front of the Kulakovski Theater in Yakutsk, complete with the bull's legend. Photo by author.

Figure 19b A 2018 refrigerator magnet featuring *Jyl Oghuha*. Photo by author.

When I first recorded the elder testimonies of *Jyl Oghuha* in 2005, there was ample scientific information about the physical effects of climate change (cf. ACIA 2004; IPCC 2001). But these elders were not framing the change they witnessed using scientific knowledge; rather, they were using their Indigenous knowledge to explain how the change worked to alter a long-standing cultural narrative of seasonal change (Crate 2008). After hearing elders' testimonies in the summer of 2005, I had the following questions: Will *Jyl Oghuha* no longer explain how the seasonal cycle works but rather represent some antecedent to the present? What happens to cultural narratives that underpin a people's way of understanding the world when disruptions caused by climate change work to undermine those narratives? I saw the need to "reaggregate" Viliui Sakha's natural, social, and cultural worlds (Cruikshank 2005: 4) to understand the reciprocal relations between those worlds and how *Jyl Oghuha* fit within them. My questions that summer led to two formal research projects, one investigating inhabitants' overall perceptions of change (Crate 2013, 2011b), and the other their understandings of changing seasonality (Crate 2012).

After four years focusing deeply on those projects, one day I "looked up" to notice that there were no cows on the Elgeeii streets—at least not in the numbers that supported the findings of my dissertation research and the cows-and-kin adaptation (Crate 2006a). I immediately assumed that the presence of fewer cows was because of the local effects of climate change, specifically the flooding of hayfields and pastures that disrupted haying. Soon after, when I realized that even the stoic and steadfast cow herders, with whom I had worked since 1992, were also "freeing themselves from the *khoton*," I decided to investigate what was going on. I added several questions about cow keeping to the climate change interview questions that summer. What I found was that, yes, climate change was a factor, but there were two other main drivers: youth out-migration and fully stocked stores. In both Soviet and post-Soviet times, village youth had routinely gone to the capital city Yakutsk for a higher education, but the majority had also routinely returned home once they completed their education. In the last decade, a majority stayed in the city. With their youth gone, cow-keeping households lose an important part of their summer labor force for hay cutting and also have less demand for cow products. The second driver, fully stocked village stores, decreased the demand for home food production, which for many was the only way to feed their household in the early '90s period of food scarcity. In short, climate change was one along with two other main drivers of change precipitating the decrease in cow numbers. I expanded my research gaze to include these other drivers, referring to this threefold assemblage as the "complexity of change" (Crate 2014). When I realized that the complexity of change concept could be a useful analytical tool in contemporary global change research, I saw how others were also engaging a similar approach.

Because anthropology and specifically ethnography require the researcher "to follow, observe, and explain what people actually do in their daily lives" (Puri 2015: 268), it opens the way to deeper understandings of how individuals and communities make decisions in the face of change. Many anthropologists are analyzing the diverse drivers of change affecting the daily lives of communities to understand the dynamics of climate change, for example, interfacing energy extraction activities that lead to environmental justice issues (Maldonado 2018) or the change brought about by disasters not directly associated with climate change (Oliver-Smith and Hoffman 2019). Anthropologists defining change at a local level show how multiple drivers of change interact with and affect ritual practices (Shaffer 2017) and also how eliciting community input about drivers can link to future scenario-building exercises in collaboration with affected communities (Tschakert et al. 2014).

In many cases anthropologists are collaborating with other disciplines to investigate multiple drivers (Jorgenson et al. 2019). Such studies focus on eliciting an affected population's understanding of relevant drivers to show how climate change is often considered less of a priority issue for affected peoples, for example, how issues of mining, logging and infrastructure development are at the forefront of people's concerns (Boissière et al. 2013). One approach to prioritizing an affected community's perceptions explores how inhabitants' vernacular knowledge systematically interlinks changes through codifying, valuing, and prioritizing the biophysical, cultural, and socioeconomic drivers within their living system (Yletyinen et al. 2020; Reyes-Garcia et al. under review). The process of defining community understandings of change based on their tacit knowledge of that change clarifies how affected populations identify drivers not recognized in the environmental change literature, bringing to light the drivers that research has overlooked (ibid.). Anthropological interdisciplinary research shows one way that this oversight can be ameliorated is via culturally sensitive boundary work and knowledge exchange that engage practitioners' and outside experts' epistemological orientations (Dannevig et al. 2020).

My process of talking to local inhabitants about the important drivers of change in their lives made clear that although climate change is certainly a threat challenging their long-term survival, it is often not their first or even their second concern. Identifying and engaging what local communities are prioritizing not only expands but makes more relevant an investigation that can begin as a myopic focus on climate change to become an investigation of the many drivers of change that a community recognizes and that affect their lives. Scientific knowledge and inquiry can tend to prioritize climate change to the detriment of understanding the multiple drivers affecting communities, some of which are having more of an immediate impact. Climate change is an existential threat, but one that cannot be addressed without understanding its many implications within the context of the set of drivers that affected communities recognize and often prioritize (Hoang et al. 2019; Barnes et al. 2013).

The Complexity of Change in Community Perspective

After understanding how the complexity of change worked in my two research villages, I was curious to know whether regional data reflected similar trends. In my decades working in the Suntaar *uluus*, those who played a role in the local and regional Soviet apparatus have always held me suspect. For some, it has taken almost thirty years to understand what I do. The bookkeeper from the Elgeeii state farm openly told me in a 2018 interview that she only recently realized that I wasn't a spy. I had the same sense from the Suntaar regional statistician, that is, until I went to speak with him in late summer 2012. After I explained the trend of youth out-migration that I had documented in Elgeeii and Kutana, it seemed his previous sense of suspicion fell away, as if he realized that I had finally gotten what was going on and perhaps was doing good work in the villages. He proceeded to expound on how youth out-migration in the last years was unprecedented. He next explained how the trend was the result of post-Soviet politics, with young people pressured not to return to the village once they'd gone away for a higher education. He said that in many cases it was their parents encouraging them to stay away to find a "good" job in their profession. He then searched his computer to bring up the demographic tree he had created based on the last decade of out-migrations and the trend lines into the future, should things stay the same. By his estimate, the villages in the Suntaar *uluus* would cease to exist in twenty years (Crate 2014: 57). I followed up with the Suntaar regional statistician in 2018 and learned that he maintained his stance. He used visual graphs to show the continued decline in numbers of youth in the villages.

After my 2012 meeting with the statistician, I met with specialists in the Department of Agricultural Statistics to see if the trend in dwindling cow numbers in my research villages was corroborated by findings in other regional villages. They verified the same drop in cow numbers that I documented in Elgeeii and Kutana and added, "Cow care is too much work now . . . the current cow-keeping work force is elderly and the next generation is not interested. In the Soviet period we had a ready-made work force . . . 700 kids would finish school and work for two years on the farms and later 50 percent of them would go into farming" (ibid. 56–57).

Village youth are also cognizant of these trends. A Kutana tenth grader conducted a study in 2014 to understand his peers' aspirations for their future (S. Fedorov 2014). He developed a set of questions to discern whether they planned to keep cows like their parents and ancestors had. One hundred of the 104 students interviewed said no, giving three main reasons: they were lazy; they planned to live in the city; and they would choose a different profession. The four in favor said they would take up cattle breeding because they wanted to make a profit. The student researcher didn't probe further to understand the exact ideas that the four had about making a profit. However, based on my own observations of village trends, it could be that they were aware of the dozen or so households in both Kutana and Elgeeii who were not only continuing to keep their cows but also expanding their herd in response to a nascent local market. Most local inhabitants prefer the taste and quality of local meat over the meat imported from Central Asia and Australia available in the village stores. Some of these entrepreneurial households also sell *ürüng as* to their neighbors, which satisfies many elders who long for it now that fewer and fewer of their households are holding cows. This nascent entrepreneurial trend shows how there is a specialization of cow keeping among a percentage of village populations. This suggests that the cows-and-kin adaptation served as a bridge for households to feed themselves in a time of food scarcity to a time when stores were full, and this specialization evolved.

Settlements smaller than Elgeeii (pop. 2,400 in 2018) and Kutana (pop. 1,100 in 2018) are addressing the cow-keeping issue differently. Inhabitants of Kundeii (pop. 750) and Kÿÿkei (pop. 325) are keeping cows cooperatively, in one common *khoton*. In these arrangements, cow-owning households pay workers a nominal fee to tend their cows in the nonpasture months (approx. September through late May). Then, from June to early September, these cow owners manage their herd, milking in the morning before the cows head to pasture, and again at night when they return home. In Kundeii the present-day cooperative is a continuation of a group that worked together during the Soviet period *sovkhoz* and continued to work together after the 1991 breakup. Both the long-term relationships of the cooperative and the way they nurture their youth, the next generation of cow keepers, to stay involved appear to be the keys to their success. "They [Kundeii] are a great community . . . they understand each other and trust each other . . . they help each other . . . from long ago the elders have gotten the youth to work with them. They say because of some very wise person who planned the school work . . . the kids are very smart and are very active in the community!" (Agrafina Vasiliyevna Nazarova, interview, May 30, 2019).

Engaging youth early, as in the Kundeii case, can help to perpetuate cooperative efforts at the village level and bolster the next generation's relationship with both the physical and cultural meaning of their *alaas*. A similar cooperative system of cow keeping has failed in both Elgeeii and Kutana. Inhabitants explain that their villages are too big to maintain the trust and interdependence of a village-level cooperative. Size is a factor, but there are also issues specific to each village that impede such efforts. In a 2017 publication, my co-authors and I contemplated this question and argued that the future of *alaas* depend on engaging Sakha youth: "In rural communities in the Viliui Regions and Central Sakha there needs to be investigation examining the decisions of members of different generations whether to leave or stay (along with the economic and legal aspects that stand behind these). Who will work in the *alaas* in the future?" (Crate et al. 2017: 101).

A young Sakha woman contacted me, adamant that youth were by no means abandoning the *alaas* or cow care, citing how she and many of her acquaintances go to their birth *alaas* to help in the summers. What she failed to understand is that summer help is not a substitute for the year-round arduous work of horse and cattle breeding, the practice of which is dropping precipitously in a majority of villages.

The Complexity of Change in Close-Up

In the remainder of this chapter I show how the complexity of change is understood by Elgeeii and Kutana inhabitants through content analysis of

2018 household interviews. I designed the interview questions to capture an overall picture of change: historical, cultural, intergenerational, economic, environmental, and climatic (see appendix: 2018 Household Interview Instrument). The questions were also tailored to gauge inhabitants' essential *alaas* relationship, on both a physical and a cultural level. The majority of interviews were with the longitudinal households I had worked with for over twenty years. I also interviewed several households in each village who had a particular specialty or expertise of high relevance to the study. In all, I conducted twenty-six interviews in Elgeeii and twenty-two in Kutana.

Community-Level Perceptions and Responses to Change

I first asked participants to discuss overall change in their own lifetimes, and their perception of changes in their parents' and their grandparents' times. In their own lives, changes mostly revolved around births and deaths in their immediate and extended families and their personal experience of getting older. Looking back, many fell into a certain nostalgia when they contrasted the present with their memories of childhood, which is considered the best time of life in Sakha culture, a time of resilient health and strength. Interviewees' childhood experience was of a time spent outdoors, making up games, learning sports, and being in nature. Many interviewees juxtaposed their youth experience with today's youth who spend their days inside on computers. Elder interviewees recollected a past that was disciplined by the Soviet-period rule of law, a time when all had work, and productivity was high. Middle-aged participants praised the more open system of today: "Now there is progress . . . in the Soviet period it was work, work, work . . . now you also work but it is for yourself. A person can make their own life now and you can work as much as you want and only you reap the benefits" (Spartak Ivanovich Spiridonov, interview, June 26, 2018).

When exploring perceptions of their parents' lives, most conversations focused on the struggles during World War II, how men went to the front and women, children, and elders were left to do the farmwork. Several detailed the local reality of the *achchyk jyl*: "During the war time, our mother worked on the farm . . . haying . . . she and all the other women worked in place of the men who went to the war . . . the women worked from when the sun rose until it set . . . and there was drought in the early years and it was horrific with no food and many, many people starving" (Rozaliya Semyonovna Nikolayeva, interview, June 12, 2018).

The main way that people survived was by increasing their existing resourcefulness, finding ways to harvest from nature and using alternative foodstuffs. "We listened when they talked about how back then there was nothing . . . they had to find it all and make it all themselves . . . bring it in from nature . . . they made their own clothes and food . . . they had no stores . . . they had to have herds and to hunt . . . only then could they survive" (Oksana Petrovna Sofronova, interview, June 12, 2018).

Interviewees perceived their grandparents' lives in less detail. Some had never known their grandparents, either because they were already deceased when they were young or because their parents had been orphans. Others had a solid knowledge of a close relationship with their grandparents and depicted specific moments in time.

My grandmother was born in 1891 and she had ten siblings. Back then it was common to share children[1] and so her parents put her in a *tuos yaghas* [medium-sized birch bucket] and took her to Kÿÿkei to give her to another family. She lived with them by an *alaas* and, for some reason, she learned the Latin alphabet. What I remember most was that she used to read English to us! We would say proudly, "Our Grandmother can read English" . . . she talked a lot about how the war time was an incredibly difficult time . . . how they worked like men—she died at 103. (Ira Prokopiyevna Fyodorova, interview, June 25, 2018)

Some talked about how their grandparents had relayed a sense of doing well in the context of their historical time. "She told me how they lived on their own . . . not like now when we all live in one place—they lived by the *alaas* with a small group of households. My grandparents only moved to Kutana in the 1950s. When my grandmother talked about life before, it made me cringe. But she told me they lived well . . . at that time they didn't think life was hard. They worked and strived and for them that was living well" (Oksana Petrovna Sofronova, interview, June 12, 2018).

Following these questions about intergenerational change, I asked about cows: if they kept them, their care, important Sakha cow-care practices, and the issue of how to best keep cows today in the villages. Twenty-nine percent of households across both villages had cows in 2018, a significant decrease from the 80 percent who kept cows in 1999–2000. Those who had stopped cow keeping did so either because of difficulty getting enough hay, absent youth, or stores being fully stocked. Some of these households explained that they got rid of their cows but continued to keep horses because they don't require the daily work that cows do. Others don't have cows but get their meat and milk from their kin who do. Others simply eat less or no meat.

All of the interviewees knew the main Sakha cow-care practices. They explained the importance of making *uohakh alaaji* (small round pancakes made from the colostrum or first milk) after a calf is born and sharing them with others to ensure the health of the calf; the necessity of burning *seppereek* (ledum or labrador tea) in the *khoton* to clear out the bad spirits before the cows come in from summer pasture to begin overwintering in the fall; the importance of hanging *salama* for *Aiyyhyt*, the deity of birth, when a cow is ready to calf, so she can enter and protect the newborn calf and mother. Interviewees explained that the main way they learned these practices was by growing up in a cow-keeping household:

> When I was little, I helped in the *khoton* . . . *that is where all the wisdom came into me* . . . I helped all the time with the family cows . . . that was when I knew about hard work and I learned that if you treat the cow in the best way, that they will do the same back to you . . . I never had problems with the cows . . . they always treated me very well, as I treated them. When I was working with the cows, I felt there were spirits helping me and my cows. The cows understood me and they never came late. Also, when a cow gives birth for the first time in their life, you need to run the *ytyk* [utensil to whip cream and yogurt made of a cow horn] down their spine so there will always be plenty of milk. (Oksana Petrovna Sofronova, interview, June 12, 2018)

With fewer and fewer households keeping cows and today's youth not taking up cow keeping, it is unclear whether this knowledge will be transferred. Certainly, anyone can learn the Sakha Indigenous knowledge of cow care from a book, but learning *in situ*, where "all the wisdom comes," results in a qualitatively different kind of knowing.

The final cow question, of how to keep cows in villages today, was a particularly contested one. Most said they desired a cooperative arrangement like in Kundeii but have not been able to achieve it. Participants want to hold cows in common because then elders could access *ürüng as* without having to do the daily cow-care work. A cooperative would also free others to do their day jobs. Keeping cows in a village cooperative was also efficient, since caring for three cows or for ten took essentially the same amount of time.

What they didn't agree on was why it wouldn't work for their village. There were different issues in the two villages. Elgeeii interviewees argued that cows had no future there, since the village hay land was not sufficient for everyone and was continuing to shrink because of the excess water of the wet year floods, the paucity of water from the present drought, and the government's haphazard canal digging. Also, most of the hay land that was usable was across the river in III Bordong, presenting a transportation problem. Another issue was the sprawling size of Elgeeii and the concern that cows would never learn to go to the other side of the settlement to a common *khoton* when all their lives they have returned to their household's *khoton*. Others detailed reasons that came down to issues of trust ("I don't want a stranger watching my cows because they don't care about me and therefore won't take good care of my cows"); concerns about "freeloading," when some work very hard and others do not; and differences in resource inputs ("My haystack is bigger than yours, so I am contributing more hay"). There was an overall sense from Elgeeii respondents that their village population couldn't come together to work as one. Kutana interviewees' main reason that a cooperative wouldn't work there was much more straightforward: with a high percentage of village households employed by Aian Suol, people no longer had the incentive to keep cows. They could make a good salary and purchase all their needs.

In this same conversation, a few interviewees shared their ideas about possible alternative ways to keep cows in the villages. One was particularly innovative:

> What if we organized a place for them to live in the south, considering that they don't do well here in the winter and it is so much work to keep them here in winter. We could take them to a warmer place where they would produce more and could live better. A place where they could be in pasture on their own all winter like they do here in summer. My son said to me, "Mom, there is a railroad . . . why not, like the migrating birds, take the cows to the warm places in winter on the train and then bring them back here to summer?" (Margarita Ilyinichna Zabolotskaya, interview, July 2, 2018)

Cow-care issues segued into questions about access to and changes in hay land. Many talked about how hay lands had shrunk because of the extremely wet period followed by drought conditions. These conversations were dominated by complaints about the canal digging that the government initiated toward the end of the wet period to drain the flooded hay lands. It was done haphazardly to achieve a quick fix, without consulting the locals who knew the land and the proper *nüölsüter* methods.

> The canals they made now are no use! No one should make a canal like that . . . they did it with no thinking at all . . . and so they ruined the land . . . they could have followed the old ways of doing it . . . now they just do it quickly and aggressively to make their money and run . . . but they ruin the land. Before Sakha made *khoruu* based on how they knew the land and how the water moved. They did it by hand and with a shovel. They let the water go its natural way and knew to hold some of the water. The recent canal makers released too much water and now it has gone completely . . . they could have followed what the elders used to do . . . the elders know how to dig the *khoruu*. They know how the water flows and they thought about it. . . . Now it is all about money and doing it fast!!! (Nikolai Makarovich Semyonov, interview, July 3, 2018)

Several argued that the haphazard approach to canal digging further exacerbated the current dry cycle. I reflected on how elders in 2010 and 2011 warned that if the fields' waters were drained completely, there would be no water at all when the dry cycle came. By 2018 the elders' prognoses had become a reality. Further complaints were about how the canal makers had no understanding of how the land and water system worked, so they simply drew a straight line from the flooded field to the nearest water outlet (stream or river). This resulted in extremely deep canals, some over ten meters by the time the canal reached its outlet. Several grazing livestock had fallen to their death in the deep canals (figure 20).

I next asked interviewees about their perceptions of changes in weather and seasonal patterns. Most confirmed that the nine main changes of our 2008–11 climate project had continued: warm winters, water on the land, a lot of rain, cold summers, more floods, seasons arriving late, more snow, temperatures changing suddenly, and fewer birds and animals (cf. Crate 2013: 117). They explained that the issues of water on the land had persisted even though there had been a drought in recent years. The fields stayed water-

Figure 20 One of the many canals made in 2012–13 to drain flooded hay fields, with some so deep that livestock who accidentally fell into them drowned. Photo by author.

logged because they didn't have any relief that would allow drainage. Interviewees also added new observations in addition to the ones in our previous study. They cited constant wind, greater intensity of hot and cold in summer, more dried lands, more fires, and more dead plants and trees. Of these, the constant wind concerned them the most.

> The weather has completely changed from before . . . the winter is warm, and
> the spring is very windy and cold—very cold . . . snow falls all winter and is
> also very, very windy . . . I don't remember there being this wind . . . back then
> the winter was normal . . . the temperatures held at −60 degrees Celsius for
> several months and it was calm and windless. Now it almost doesn't go below
> −45 degrees Celsius and there is wind all the time! I also don't remember
> wind in the summer . . . before there was no wind when we hayed, but now,
> the *buguls* blow over constantly . . . so you have to work fast to get it stacked
> before it all blows away . . . we used to make the *buguls* and they stood for
> two to three days . . . now they do not stay! In the last few years there is a lot
> of wind . . . before it came every once in a while . . . but now it is constant.
> (Paulina Ivanovna Zahkarova, interview, June 26, 2018)

Others added that the constant wind also made their early winter work of clearing snow difficult, especially now that it tends to snow all winter. Formerly, snow fell from late September to early December, and snow management involved a daily routine of clearing paths from the house to the street, from the house to the *khoton*, from the house to the outhouse, from the house to the wood pile, and from the house to the ice pile.[2] From December, *Jyl Oghuha* ushered in the cold, dry, snowless season, which held until early to mid-March, after which snow fell and signaled spring's arrival. For over a decade the former pattern has changed. It now snows later in the year and continues to snow throughout the winter months. This means that householders work daily to clear snow and pathways and, considering the constant wind, that daily work takes longer and is more challenging.

The wind not only interferes with the precipitation patterns of winter but also in the temperate months:

> It is very different . . . for example, the rainfall and the wind . . . before we had very good rainfall . . . now when it rains it is heavy and huge winds blow—this spring we had so much wind . . . the weather has really changed. Now the rain falls in huge amounts and very fast and very, very strongly . . . before we had nice warm gentle rain that fell for several days . . . now when the rain falls it is cold and it falls in buckets, very fast. (Vasili Mikhailovich Lvov, interview, July 4, 2018)

Several interviewees described how the intensity of both hot and cold in summer had changed. "When the sun shines, it is very, very hot. But then, when a cloud comes and covers it, it turns very, very cold . . . I don't remember it being like that before. And also, now the sun is burning your skin. It never did that before. Yes, summers were hot before but the heat back then did not burn like it does now. Now when it is above 30 degrees [Celsius], it burns you" (Nadyezhda Ivanovna Zakharova, interview, July 2, 2018).

On this topic, half of all respondents made some reference to how cold the summer nights are compared to before. "Another new change is that now the summer nights are very cold. Summer nights used to be warm. We played outside in the evenings and no one wore sweaters like we do now. It used to be so hot some nights that you could not sleep in the house! Now we sleep inside with blankets. They say the cold summer nights are why the hay and our gardens do not grow like they used to" (ibid.).

These new patterns and changes in the specific climatological parameters to which Sakha have adapted their subsistence practices (cattle and horse breeding, gardening, hunting, fishing, and gathering) render those practices either more labor intensive or prohibitive. This then leads to changes in Sakha's land practices, which affect the ecosystem. With fewer and fewer people haying in outlying areas and not managing the lands as before, surrounding forests encroach into the fields, reducing the amount of hay land.

Other changes also affect Sakha's land management practices. After the recent increase in forest fires across the republic, the Sakha government banned Sakha's practice of controlled burning, a technique Sakha used annually to clear the fields of dry grasses and invading trees and shrubs and to let them soak up nutrients. This makes matters worse.

> In the last years we have had lots of fires . . . the land is burning! Part of it is because no one hays anymore in the farther lands and so a lot of dry hay accumulates there, which acts as fuel for the fires. Before we were allowed to practice controlled burning. We would burn the area so we could hunt well and so that later there would be good hay for our herds. Now when it is dry in the summer, a fire starts and it has all the fuel it needs and nothing or no one can stop it. But the government has prohibited controlled burning . . . it is a mistake. Sakha lived on the land here for a long time and did well—if they don't let us do what we know works in our environment, there will be trash in the fields and there will be bad pastures and there will be fires . . . and the animals will be few. (Viktor Yegorovich Vasiliyev, interview, June 13, 2018)

Some interviewees linked factors of change together by associating weather, climate, and seasonal change with management, demographics, and economic change. For example, one explanation of why youth were not taking up Sakha practices on the land linked the trend with young people's lack of experiences in nature. "I remember being a boy in summer—it was great back then . . . we boys did not come out of the forest! We hunted chipmunks with slingshots[3] then we made a fire and put them on sticks and ate them. We also fished. Kids these days don't do that . . . they just want to go to the city but for now stay inside on the computer and TV . . . and they don't go in the forest or even outside" (Alexander Nikolayevich Semyonov, interview, June 12, 2018).

Interviewees' observations of changes in their local landscape and in the contour of the land differed between the two villages. In Kutana, interviewees consistently moved one hand in a wavy horizontal line while they described how the land surface had changed from flat to being bumpy like a roller coaster. These once-flat lands were on the outlying *alaas*, on the *ötökh*.

> The land has changed . . . there were these very flat areas near the *alaas* that we knew from our childhoods that now are with dips and rises . . . which I guess means it is thawing underground. This is happening most of all in the outlying *alaas* lands. We used to cut hay with a tractor on one of our hay tracts and now a tractor cannot even go there at all . . . the once very flat places are now wavy. (Valerian Yegorovich Afanaseyev, interview, June 13, 2018)

> The land is thawing and it falls . . . the once higher places have suddenly fallen . . . I see a lot of lands like that—some sink a meter deep . . . and a lot near the Kÿÿkei lake . . . I would go there to the sawmill in the 90s when I was doing building and it was on a flat piece of land . . . now that area is completely up and down and falling . . . it has only been in the last few years that the land has fallen like this. (Anatoli Petrovich Fyodorov, interview, June 25, 2018)

In Elgeeii, only a few professional herders, those who frequented the distant fields where the old *ötökh* were, voiced similar sentiments. Most Elgeeii interviewees responded by talking about others' failure to make the land: "At Ulgutta, where the strawberry picking is . . . the trees are coming in . . . people no longer make the land and so the forest is taking it back . . . making land takes hard work and people today are not going to do it" (Arkadi Nikolayevich Semyonov, interview, July 14, 2018).

Others responded with a more all-inclusive explanation that detailed the long-term effects of industrialization.

> Now that people are not working the land, the forests are encroaching into the hay fields. There is also the massive cutting of the forests that the government is doing . . . and the industrial growth is more and more . . . the government keeps digging holes in the earth [mining diamonds and exploring for oil and gas] . . . because of that, I think the permafrost is thawing . . . and if the permafrost thaws, there will be a cataclysm . . . not just for us here . . . also in the city with the very tall buildings with many floors . . . it is because

the government is making the holes for the mining and drilling for the oil and gas . . . there will be problems . . . a poet came through and wrote that the diamonds are like tears . . . to the extent that the land is ruined. (Margarita Ilyinichna Zabolotskaya, interview, July 2, 2018)

This discussion of land change led into questions about permafrost knowledge. In both villages, interviewees had very basic knowledge: they knew permafrost was there, under the ground. Several said they heard on the news and on social media that it was thawing: "Whatsapp shows that the northern areas are thawing . . . it tells about all the areas of the Sakha Republic and the permafrost . . . they showed a picture of how it was thawing and falling down" (Oksana Petrovna Sofronova, interview, June 12, 2018).

The geography teacher and the biology teacher in Kutana were the most knowledgeable of all the interviewees. The geography teacher said,

Permafrost has a huge role in our lives . . . it is like the sphinx in Egypt . . . like the pyramids there, it is our foundation and it supports everything . . . all of our nature, the growing of plants, the animals . . . it affects it all . . . our larch trees have horizontal roots to adapt to the permafrost. A person needs to protect themselves from the cold below the ground . . . and also needs to keep it cold, for example, give the greenhouse legs to be above it . . . it is cold and so the plants and trees grow slowly . . . it has a direct connection to our lives. (Svetlana Gavrilovna Martinova, interview, June 13, 2018)

The Kutana biology teacher framed her response within her pedagogical approach with students: "I know a lot about it and I teach the students . . . and I tell them that with climate change, the water is increasing on the land, the *alaas* are changing and the underground ice is thawing" (Nadyezhda Yegorovna Savvinova, interview, June 12, 2018).

This discussion segued into questions about interviewees' knowledge of *alaas*. All respondents but one explained *alaas* in the context of their life experience of *alaas*. The outlier used language to express the more recent scientific understanding:

Alaas is a big field that dips . . . Sakha in the central areas have a lot of *alaas* . . . we Sakha who live on this side of the Lena . . . we talk about *sihii* [field] and *ötökh* . . . the land that dips is an *alaas* . . . my brother's land

"*Ungkur*" is a dipped land . . . that may be an *alaas* . . . here we talk about *sihii* and *khonuu* [field] . . . not *alaas*. (Alexander Nikolayevich Semyonov, interview, June 12, 2018)

The majority described *alaas*'s cultural meaning for Sakha as a self-contained world where there is access to and control over all needed resources:

It is a hay land . . . the main meaning . . . a wide field . . . to the extent it has good conditions, then the hay will grow . . . if the *alaas* is good, there will be abundance and there will be cows and food and riches and all will be well . . . It has a huge meaning to Sakha—"Törööbüt Alaaskyn En Taptaa" [Love Your Birth *Alaas*] is a song . . . we are *alaas* children . . . which means that we clothe ourselves and eat from the *alaas* . . . to the extent that the *alaas* has hay, there can be cows and horses and that means food. (Nadyezhda Ivanovna Zakharova, interview, July 2, 2018)

Some include philosophical depictions:

Sakha depended on *alaas* for their physical and spiritual sustenance. Sakha are children of the *alaas* . . . every Sakha has an *alaas* in their spirit—and we carry that *alaas* with us all our lives . . . the *alaas* is connected to our roots . . . our beginnings . . . the birthplace . . . the homeland . . . why is that? Because Sakha lived by the *alaas* long ago . . . they had *alaas* . . . they protected it and lived from it. (Margarita Ilyinichna Zabolotskaya, interview, July 2, 2018)

Discussions of *alaas* segued to participants' knowledge of their ancestral lands. In Elgeeii, all respondents except one knew where their ancestral lands were, but most said they were too far away to visit regularly. In contrast, all Kutana interviewees knew their ancestral lands and visited them at least annually when they hayed or berried. Many Kutana respondents considered their ancestral lands to be their sacred *alaas*.

The next questions were about interviewees' knowledge of Sakha historical lifeways and culture. Most said they knew and practiced Sakha rituals, including feeding the land to appease *sir ichchite* (the spirit of the land), feeding the *khoton* to please *Aiyyhyt*, and feeding the home hearth to please *uot ichchite*. Several respondents detailed aspects of character that reflected "being Sakha," specifically relating to the Sakha understanding that words are *ichchileekh*.

> I practice what the Sakha do . . . you don't talk about yourself . . . I am great or I am bad . . . it is all middle . . . you do your best . . . even when something goes well you don't talk about it. Also, if you have a bad disease you don't talk about it . . . because the disease will hear it and get worse . . . Sakha have that understanding. You also don't talk about your child as being this or that . . . you are careful and don't talk about it. If you can do a lot, you do a lot but don't talk about it. Also, you don't count . . . for example . . . I have this many this and this many that. You don't count your grands or great-grands . . . because people will be jealous and you will make people feel badly. Most everyone does that! If you go somewhere far . . . you don't talk about it . . . when you get back, you talk about it . . . it is the Sakha character . . . Sakha are *naghyl* [calm and not emotional on the outside]. You may wonder why is that? We follow the sun. The sun here is that way . . . it takes a long time to rise and a long time to set. In other countries, the sun rises quickly and shines right away and also gets dark very quickly and so people need to go quickly so they can get everything done . . . and so their lives are organized that way. (Svetlana Gavrilovna Martinova, interview, June 13, 2018)

Svetlana's association of Sakha's character aligning with the deliberate and steady pulse of their ecosystem has important parallels with the claims of other northern peoples. "He who hurries in the taiga hurries to his death" is one of Nenet's ways to express how they live in a similarly paced rhythm with that of their environment (Golovnev and Osherenko, 1999: 40). Survival in the north depends on going slowly and observing in order to ensure your movements and actions are measured to prevent injury or death. For Sakha, this deliberate approach includes an awareness to what words you speak, and even whether you should choose to speak at all.

Another gauge of interviewees' knowledge of Sakha lifeways and culture came in their responses to the next questions, which were about Sakha's summer festival, *yhyakh*, and Sakha's circle dance, *ohuokhai*. *Yhyakh* occurs around the summer solstice, the time of year just before the hay cutting begins, when Sakha must appease the sky deities for all the right conditions to have a bountiful harvest. The *yhyakh* went through many changes in Soviet times, then reemerged in the post-Soviet period as a central symbol of ethnic revival and historical belief (Crate 1994, 2006b, 2019). My interviewees' responses gave a sense of the extent to which households retained an active, public practice of being Sakha.

A majority attend because *yhyakh* is the single most important time of year for them to gather in large numbers, to socialize, and to celebrate getting through the long winter with their community. A few described their commitment to attending the *yhyakh* by drawing attention to the festival's spiritual aspects.

> It is our request to the higher spirits . . . it is the new time of the year . . . all is new . . . all the new greens and the hay is growing that we need to feed the animals . . . and so the tradition is to request from the higher spirits . . . all the good conditions and help of the spirits and for our thoughts to be clean . . . we all gather and are together as one . . . it happens once a year . . . it is our new year. (Ludmilla Nikolayevna Pavlova, interview, July 3, 2018)

When asked about how the festival had changed over time, respondents framed their responses with their childhood memories. Middle-aged respondents in both Kutana and Elgeeii remembered the *yhyakh* of their childhood as a large gathering at Ugut Kÿöl for the state farm *yhyakh*.

> In the *sovkhoz* times *yhyakh* happened in Ugut Kÿöl. I went with my parents on a motorcycle and we stayed overnight . . . I remember so many tents, all arranged in kin groups . . . the horses that were to race stood in their stalls, and we kids all went to look at them. There was a lot of *khorchop* [food stalls] and the *ohuokhai* never stopped . . . we children would go into the center of the dance and look at the people dancing and then weave our way back out. Sometimes there were even two circles . . . one person would sing and two circles . . . in the evening, there was the horse racing. It was a huge holiday . . . lasted two days. (Svetlana Gavrilovna Martinova, interview, June 13, 2018)

Some compared past to present to show how the festival had changed.

> No one stays all night anymore . . . before it was so good and the horses raced . . . in the last years the horse race area has been either underwater or dried and ruined . . . before, the horses ran and there were so many flowers and butterflies and so much *ohuokhai* . . . as kids we would run in and out of

the dance circle and no one told us to stop or that we interfered . . . we went in and out of the circles—and in the evening when our parents told us to go to sleep, we got in our tents and as we were going to sleep, the sound of the *ohuokhai* came to us through the air . . . it was so wonderful—that is the memory that has stayed with me the most . . . Ugut Kÿöl . . . lots of people, lots of *khorchop* . . . the *yhyakh* and how the *ohuokhai* was so great back then. (Mariya Leekenovna Ivanova, interview, June 26, 2018)

Questions about *yhyakh* led to discussing *ohuokhai*, Sakha's circle dance fueled by improvisatory singing that originated as the collective response to the white shaman's appeal to the sky deities. Much of the power of the *ohuokhai* is attributed to the spirit of words. Interviewees said that *ohuokhai* was where they could enter the circle and feel as one and equal with others. Some talked about the energy they got from dancing and singing the *ohuokhai*. Many commented about how both the *yhyakh* and the *ohuokhai* had changed over time, contrasting today's festival and dance with the past.

It is our ancient practice . . . before, when our ancestors lived by the *alaas*, *yhyakh* was the one time a year that people saw others outside their kin-clan group . . . back then they lived far from each other . . . so it had a huge role . . . one time to gather . . . and the *ohuokhai* was also that way . . . people danced and got to know each other . . . that was even how people met and married! (Valerian Yegorovich Afanaseyev, interview, June 13, 2018)

Some described the forced changes to the dance and the improvisatory singing during the Soviet period.

It is our Sakha practice . . . in the last decades our language has weakened . . . back then, the *ohuokhai* was where we practiced our language, singing about nature and *alaas* . . . then in Soviet times, we had to sing about the Soviet party . . . about how Soviet laws are good and communism is good and socialism is good. Before we sang about the nature and our *agha uuha*. (Anatoli Petrovich Fyodorov, interview, June 25, 2018)

Others explained the artistic mastery and the spiritual connection needed to be an *ohuokhaijit* (singer of the *ohuokhai*) and lead the circle in improvisatory song.

Ohuokhai is our central tradition . . . and it is all based on creative imagination . . . nothing is written on paper . . . right away the master improvisator
sings directly from their mind . . . they must be so masterful, some can sing
about one phenomenon for hours . . . writers write drafts and then second
drafts but this is the direct communication with the spirits and improvisa-
tion from that. (Afanasee Ivanovich Trofimov, interview, July 3, 2018)

The closing question of the interview elicited opinions about the future of
the villages, beginning with ideas about village development. This was another
question that elicited divergent responses between the two villages. In Kutana,
many respondents continued to talk about how their village needed to create
a cooperative to hold all their private cows in one place.

Every year it is more and more expensive . . . before all was cheap. . . . for example water is now 200 *solkuobai* [rubles] a barrel and before it was a few *kopeiki*
[kopecks] . . . and people can't afford to hay now . . . it is so expensive to do it all
on your own. If we hayed in a common practice, working together and sharing
tekhnika, it would work. It is very difficult if you don't have the equipment for
haying, for example. You have to ask people to help, to use their tractor to cut
the hay for you. But if we had a centralized system to do that it would be good
for all. (Svetlana Gavrilovna Martinova, interview, June 13, 2018)

Other Kutana interviewees made a similar argument but tied it to the need
for government support and the issue of youth leaving the village.

We need to get support from the government to develop the agriculture
here . . . nothing else is needed . . . and then the youth will want to stay and
be involved in the village and our agriculture will develop . . . cows and
gardens . . . for that we need to have funding—nature here makes farming
difficult . . . if you are growing potatoes and they don't do well, you will go
bankrupt because the government gives you no support. If they support you
and you have a stable salary . . . you will be able to live. There has been no
progress in agriculture . . . no production like before . . . everyone lives as
they can . . . households can only make a small amount of money by selling
their milk . . . but they have no chance to do any better than that. They only
have enough money to keep their houses running and their families fed . . .
that is it. (Osip Dmitriyevich Andreyev, interview, June 26, 2018)

Some talked about attracting young families from outside Kutana who had farming expertise so there would be development. Overall, most Kutana respondents wanted the pooling of resources and labor in order to resolve the problem of how unfeasible cow keeping and other agricultural pursuits had become for individual households. At first this unanimous desire for a cooperative and further development of agriculture in Kutana seemed incongruous with interviewees' earlier sentiments about why a cooperative would not work in Kutana. The difference is that the former is their desire and the latter is their perception of why it has not worked so far, specifically because their village has relatively robust employment that works to disincentivize cow keeping.

The Elgeeii responses to the question of village development were emotion-laden, with people blaming other inhabitants for the village's lack of development. Some put the blame on individual actors: "People here just need to work . . . there is a lot of work to do in Elgeeii but no one here wants to work . . . people in Elgeeii run away from work. People could be busy with keeping cows . . . but they run from hard work and so few people now have cows" (Nikolai Makarovich Semyonov, interview, July 3, 2018). Others described the failure in terms of the Elgeeii community's inability to work as a team: "We just need to come together and to understand each other and to work together and to be good to each other . . . we are trying to do this with the *tüölbe*—there are seven in all. But nevertheless, we just don't seem to be able to break our factions" (Nadyezhda Ivanovna Zakharova, interview, July 2, 2018).

Several pinpointed the issue of youth retention as the reason that there was no development in the village:

> Work places for our youth are the most important right now. Our children are all going to the city because they can't get work here. For example, my daughter wants to come and work here. She has training as a pharmacist and she went for her practicum at Sakha Pharmacy in the city and they kept her. She wanted very much to come here. (Agrafina Vasiliyevna Nazarova, interview, July 2, 2018)

One respondent blamed pensioners for double-dipping and exacerbating the youth unemployment issue: "I can only say that if the youth come to live here, it would be best . . . but there are many who are older and have a pension but also keep their salaried work . . . I think they need to stop working so that the young people can come and have the work" (Daria Ivanovna Grigoriyevna, interview, June 12, 2018).

Respondents in both villages considered youth out-migration in both a positive and a negative light. Some encouraged their own and others' youths to leave, saying that youth today have more opportunities than in the past and should take advantage of them by studying and developing a specialty. This group praised youth for how savvy they were, navigating the new world of information and technology. On the negative side, interviewees complained that today's youth just want to go to the city for the "easy life" because they don't know how to and don't want to do the hard work of village life. Opinions were also polarized in both villages about whether youth should stay or go. Most thought they should go if they could not find work in their specialty in their village. Others felt that the youth's birthland could benefit from their expertise if only there were jobs.

> If the conditions can be here, it is better here . . . the air is clean . . . but there needs to be work here for them . . . that is the main reason they do not stay . . . they want to work! They are resourceful and know how to do things and work well! There is no work here so they do not come. If they all leave, the village will fall apart . . . if they go, fewer and fewer newborns . . . all the people here are older who are holding horses and cows. (Mariya Leekenovna Ivanova, interview, June 26, 2018)

The final query asked respondents how life would be in the villages of the future if the trends of youth out-migration and lack of development continued. Although many said that these changes did not make them hopeful, most respondents were resolute that, considering all the rural areas have to offer, young people would find their way back to the villages.

Ten Years After "Gone the Bull of Winter"

In addition to interviews with longitudinal households, in 2018 I repeated the focus group inquiry of the initial 2008 climate project investigation. My justification was that although the other drivers of the complexity of change—youth out-migration and economic globalization—were, to some extent, unprecedented and threatened the stability of village community life, inhabitants still had a certain amount of agency to address them. The drivers of the local effects of climate change were largely outside their realm of local control. I wanted to gauge not only what different observations of change people were seeing ten years later but also *how* they were perceiving them. In 2008, most respondents had attributed the nine main changes to three drivers other than climate change: the presences of the Viliui GES (hydroelectric station reservoir), nature itself, and "too much *tekhnika*" (Crate 2011b). Only a few in each village mentioned climate change. Repeating the earlier inquiry would help me understand if they were attributing the changes any differently.

My first meeting with the head of Kutana village suggested that people were much more informed about the local effects of climate change. Once he learned that I was collaborating with a permafrost scientist, he described to me how many of their territory's formerly flat *ötökh* in the outlying *alaas* had become roller coasters from the permafrost's thawing due to global climate change. I had already gotten a sense in interviews conducted earlier that same summer when asking about seasonal changes and permafrost that inhabitants had gained a greater understanding of the effects of climate change since 2008. The focus groups brought those differences into greater relief.

2018 FINDINGS

Similar to what we did in 2008, we facilitated two focus groups in each village, one of men and one of women, with a combination of youth, the middle-aged, and elders. We also replicated the process of asking participants to first fill in a chart to record each of their observations of changes in nature, weather, and cycles, what they thought was causing each change, how each was affecting them and their household, and their thoughts on what it would be like in ten years if each change continued. The purpose of these written documents was twofold: they allowed us to elicit ideas from each participant and avoid issues of dominance by one or two persons, and they gave us a written record of each participant's initial thoughts, which we could use in our analysis and also follow up on later, if need be. Overall, the 2018 focus groups reported that they continued to observe the 2008 groups' nine main changes. Below I detail what new observations the 2018 participants reported in relation to those of 2008.

All 2018 focus group participants cited the presence of very strong and destructive winds that blew off roofs, knocked down trees, and downed electrical lines, causing power outages. Several described how, in the spring thaw period, the winds took all the moisture for spring growth. They referred to this evaporation process as the wind "making the moisture fly," taking precipitation not only from rain and spring meltwater but also from the very thick snow that they said would literally "disappear" before their eyes.

They also talked at length about how nights in summer were now very cold and how this had a huge impact on Sakha subsistence. In this discussion, elder participants commented how summer nights used to be *ip itii* (very hot). Some recalled the Sakha proverb, "*Üs kununen ot üünner*" (The hay grows in three days). They explained that daytime temperatures in the height of summer are sweltering and far too hot for hay to actively grow. During that time, the hay grows at night. It gets sunlight throughout the night and it is not as hot, so it can mature over a short period of days, perhaps even three.

Another big difference from 2008 was participants' knowledge of climate change. Ten years earlier, only a handful of village teachers and well-read elders attributed the changes they observed to global climate change. In contrast, most of the 2018 focus group participants attributed the changes they observed to climate change. They explained that the last ten years had seen a steady increase in public information about climate change and the thawing permafrost in newspaper articles and on TV and radio programs.

Two focus group participants seemed oblivious to the changes, remarking, when they were asked to share their opinion, that "everything [for them] is fine." At first, I was confused. I thought maybe they lived in isolation or spent little time outdoors. Then I interpreted this as their taking to heart the Sakha understanding that words are spirit-filled. The pure act of talking about a phenomenon assigns it power and agency. They were trying to avoid angering the spirit of words and making the effects of climate change worse.

Gone the Cradle of the *Alaas*?

Several participants in the focus groups and interviews commented that there were not as many stars in the winter sky as there were before. They said that this was because of the warming winters, so different from the clear, crisp, cold winters of before when there were many, many stars. This discussion triggered a memory of my first winter in Elgeeii in 1993, when I was so in awe at my first sight of the night sky. I was in the backyard of my host's home, a place where the surrounding forest made my window to the sky quite limited. To get a better view, I walked to the nearest open area and stared up. My mouth gaped open in awe (and nearly froze)! There were so many stars, they seemed to overwhelm the dark sky. On another night I walked with my host to the river to see even more stars and *Jükeebil* (the northern lights).

Although in many places in the world light pollution cancels out starlight, there has been no increase in night lighting in these regions. The focus group participants who commented that there were fewer stars went on to say that as the stars go, so go the *alaas*. This sounded so familiar to me at the time. Later I recalled how, early on, I learned a Sakha simile to express the vast number of *alaas*, "There are as many *alaas* on the land here as there are stars in the sky." Today I cannot help but wonder, given the rapid change of *alaas*, how such interactions of physical phenomena and the cultural meanings relate to *alaas* for contemporary Sakha?

Scientific knowledge shows that climate change is thawing the permafrost, and since *alaas* are founded upon permafrost, its thawing results in dramatic physical changes to *alaas*. In what ways do the physical transformations of *alaas* affect Sakha's continued identification with the cradle of the *alaas*? Based on my 2018–19 field materials, people do not need to physically live "by the *alaas*" in order to identify and perpetuate *alaas* as a cultural identifier. However, considering how other drivers of change are coming into Sakha's worlds, both rural and urban, will Sakha's main cultural identifier of the cradle of the *alaas* continue?

These contemplations on the cultural meaning of *alaas* and how the physical *alaas* are rapidly changing mirror my earlier contemplations of the cultural meaning of the *Jyl Oghuha* and how its function as an explanatory narrative had changed. In both cases, climate change not only affects Sakha's physical environment but also their cultural perceptions of their world. *Jyl Oghuha* was their explanatory story for seasonal change. The *alaas* is their cultural identification, their sense of place, and their way of knowing who they are. My argument in 2008 remains valid:

If we agree, as Keith Basso convincingly argues, that human existence is irrevocably situated in time and space, that social life is everywhere accomplished through an exchange of symbolic forms, and that wisdom "sits in places" (1996, 53), then we need to grapple with the extent to which global climate change is transforming these spaces, symbolic forms, and places. It follows that the result will be great loss of wisdom, of cosmologies and worldviews, and of the human-environment interactions that are a culture's core (Netting 1968, 1993; Steward 1955). As anthropologists, we need to look closely at the cultural implications of the changes that global climate change is bringing. (Crate 2008: 573)

Our understanding of the complexity of change drivers that are transforming the physical *alaas*, and how *alaas* nonetheless continue as a central Sakha cultural identifier, underscores *alaas*'s critical importance today.

Windows into the Complexity of Change

Individual Life Histories

Both Kutana and Elgeeii appear to be abandoned "sleepy towns" when you first arrive. The streets are empty except for a few people and several cows and dogs. You may wonder what inhabitants' lives are like and what keeps them in such a seemingly empty and forgotten place. If you are curious and take the time to know individuals, you will begin to appreciate how rich their lives are and the many changes they have negotiated over their lifetimes.

Hearing contemporary inhabitants' life histories can trigger a sense of time travel, across generations, through historical changes, and within the ways that a culture has and continues to adapt to their environment. It is through life histories that the intimate knowledge individuals have developed and refined, to not only survive but to thrive, can be known. Life histories show how the complexity of change comes into a people's time, place, and daily livelihoods. They also bring to light the role that culture plays and the forms it takes.

One individual's life history can also open the way to hearing similar experiences from others. Marusa not only invited me into the historical space of her life's memories and reflections, she also taught me about a pretechnological Sakha mode of adaptation by describing the sound of cold. Soon afterward I heard others describe the same phenomenon:

There is no more *tymnyy tyhyrgaar* [sound of cold] . . . it is the sound the air made when you walked—like shaking dry hay, *tys-tys* . . . also, when the air

broke open and made a sound. We don't hear it anymore. (Svetlana Gavrilovna Martinova, interview, June 13, 2018)

It has warmed greatly . . . my *ebe* and *ehe* talked about the cold making a
sound when you breathed . . . they said that, you knew it was –50–55 degrees
[Celsius] . . . your breathing made a sound like dry grasses blowing . . . later
I understood that it was really the sound of the steam falling and freezing
instantly . . . now there is no sound . . . in winter it only goes below –40 C for
three days. (Afanasee Ivanovich Trofimov, interview, July 3, 2018)

These finer details and adaptive modes that link to a culture's vernacular knowledge are one important contribution that life history investigation
bestows. But I would argue that the most relevant insights of life history
engagement are how they bring individuals to life, opening just one of many
separate chapters of the collective tome of the history of a place. Elgeeii and
Kutana inhabitants' life histories illustrate the extent to which individuals
have seen change over time, in weather and climate, foodways, animal care,
work organization, youth, politics, and history. These inquiries span the generations to include elders, whose longer histories detail how early Soviet and
pre-Soviet politics came into life at the local level. Their long experience
also brings a local gaze to individuals negotiating the fluctuations of climate
and other changes that affect local ecosystems and cultural mores. Younger
residents contribute important insights to how the complexity of change
interfaces contemporary life in the villages. Those with professions reliant
on the specific climatic particulars of their home place are robust sources of
their culture's historical knowledge of and adaptations to change. A focus on
younger professionals is where we begin.

Snow Is Horses' Home

I remember the first winter I spent in Elgeeii. It was 1993, and when we
drove to another village, I became fascinated by seeing groups of horses in
the wide fields, standing together in one place and rhythmically digging. I
was amazed at their ability to stay outside all year round, especially in the
frigid winter conditions. I knew Sakha bred horses for meat and learned that
the combination of extreme temperatures and this gentle digging exercise

produced a perfectly marbled meat. But it was not until I probed the issues of a changing climate with Valerian Yegorovich Afanaseyev that I appreciated how intimately connected horse breeding was to the specific conditions of Sakha's extreme ecosystem. Valerian had repeated the same mantra each time we met in the last decade of my climate research: *"Khaar sylgy jiete,"* or "Snow is horses' home." "They are to work and dig. They need 30 to 40 centimeters of snow so they don't freeze. If it is less than that, they can't work, and so they start going from place to place and they get thin. They are to stand and dig and eat. Those are the best conditions for the foal inside and the mare herself. In short, *"Khaar sylgy jiete"* (Valerian Yegorovich Afanaseyev, interview, May 21, 2019). By sharing his life history, Valerian made real to me the lived experience of Sakha horse breeding and its baseline reality: that horses cannot survive the winter and breeding them is problematic unless they have the specific seasonal and climatic conditions of the historical ecosystem, most importantly, the exact quantity and quality of snow.

I had known Valerian since 1992 when my master's research on the *yhyakh* led me to an interview with his sister-in-law Marusa, a well-known singer of the *ohuokhai*. I began formal work with him as a household in my Kutana

Figure 21 Valerian Yegorovich Afanaseyev with one of his two riding horses, May 21, 2019. Photo by author.

random sample for my 1999–2000 dissertation research. At that time Valerian and his wife kept five milk cows to, as they put it, "have food during the hard times." They got rid of their cows in 2005 because of the significant amount of time required for cow care, and expanded their horse herd to trade horse meat for cow products. Although they don't get all the *ürüng as* they would like, they don't have enough time for cows. Valerian manages the herds of Aian Suol, the Kutana-based road building organization, for his salaried work in addition to his personal herd of five mares and a stallion. He works with his brother, also a professional *sylgyhyt* with a personal herd of the the same size, to harvest the ten tons of supplemental hay they need annually.

Valerian explained that understanding Sakha horse breeding starts with knowing the annual cycle. In early summer, horses are out in their harems, made up of an *atyyr* (stallion) with four to six *bie* (mares) with their new *kulunchuk* (foal) born in late spring. Early summer is the time of mating. The harems continue to roam and pasture throughout the summer. The *sylgyhyt* begins harvesting and storing hay in July and August. Even though horses pasture year-round, in winter digging through the snow to the fodder beneath, the winter fodder does not last all season. There are critical times in winter when horses need supplemental hay. The horses continue to pasture into autumn and, as the first snows fall, begin to dig underneath for fodder. In November the *sylgyhyt* prepares for slaughtering by separating the *ubaha* (yearlings, the new foals from the spring) from their mothers and supplementing the *ubaha* food to fatten them. If the *sylgyhyt* wants to begin a new harem, they hold a male and several female *ubaha* aside. They slaughter once the temperatures are holding well below freezing both day and night. The *sylgyhyt* starts to provide supplemental hay, first in January to any remaining *ubaha*, in mid-February to pregnant mares, and by March to all the herd until the first green grass appears in the open pastures. When mares' udders fall down full of milk, it is a sign that they will foal in twenty days. Birthing begins in April and lasts through May. By then it is early summer once more. The one-year-old *ubaha* that were saved from slaughter are now ready to be mothers, and the cycle repeats.

I asked how he got into horse breeding, and Valerian said he has it in his blood. His father and grandfather were *sylgyhyt*. Although his father was retired when Valerian was old enough to work with him, his passion bloomed watching his father leave and return from work, hearing his stories about his daily *sylgyhyt* experiences. Valerian's first paid job was in 1985 as a *kochegar* (coal stoker). He quit after a year to follow his heart and work with horses. At the time, the best option was working as a *sylgyhyt* for the *sovkhoz*. When the state farm broke up, he continued to work as a *sylgyhyt* for the road-building department (later called Aian Suol).

Valerian talked at length about the changes he had seen as a *sylgyhyt* over those thirty-five years. He began with the change from breeding horses in the state farm system to breeding them now. On the state farm, horses were kept in distant pastures, far from the villages, as a way to control their wanderings and keep them away from grazing in the cattle pastures and hay fields. Today that system no longer exists, and resource access, except for hay lots, which are assigned, is a free-for-all. Horse and cattle breeders tend to keep their herds close to their village to monitor them. This overcrowds the pastures adjacent to settlements. Having horse herds close is also met with a certain amount of resentment by inhabitants who are fearful of the fiery-eyed stallions that roam the streets.

To Valerian, these changes are negligible in contrast to the bigger challenges of the changing climate. The fall season is now much longer than before, and with many freeze and thaw events as temperatures rise and fall, often on a daily basis. This temperature fluctuation creates an ice layer that prevents horses from accessing the fodder beneath the snow. The elongated fall season also prevents the horses' coats from thickening as they should, exposing them to the bitter winter temperatures later in the season. These hides are also of poor quality when harvested and often unusable. The spring season is late. Before, April 25 was the usual time that new green grass emerged and *sylgyhyt* stopped giving supplemental hay to their herds. Now, spring arrives on time but stays cold and grass does not grow, forcing *sylgyhyt* to continue supplemental feeding an average of two weeks longer. Harems often roam far from their home village and end up starving, since finding them to give them supplemental food is not possible. Because of this, more *sylgyhyt* are keeping their harems close to the village.

Valerian explained how hay and pasture quality and availability are affected by the changed climatic regime. From 2007 to 2017 there was excess water on the land, after which came a drought period, which is made worse by the recent climatic change of constant wind. These recent drought conditions are further exacerbated by the government's efforts to drain the water-logged fields. "The *khoruu* digging has dried up the streams and now willows grow in the stream beds. If the government had made the *khoruu* correctly with dams and such it would not be this way. They said they had no money for that, but now all is drying up" (Valerian Yegorovich Afanaseyev, interview, June 13, 2018).

For me, the most profound understanding of how exacting the conditions must be for successful horse breeding in this extreme ecosystem came from hearing Valerian's discussion of *kencheeri* (aftermath). After the hay cutting in July, the remaining hay grows another six inches before the first snows fall. This is called *kencheeri*. It stays green beneath the snow. *Kencheeri* is what horses dig for in the snow, what they get fat on, and what gets them through the winter. Before climate change, *kencheeri* could be found under the snow all winter, providing horses their main nutrition. *Kencheeri* now does not grow because of either too much or too little moisture, which are both also affected by the elongated fall. The *sylgyhyt* could supplement *kencheeri* with *boruu* (horsetail), growing on lake and river edges, but boruu is also now scarce. No *kencheeri* means horses need more supplemental feed for more of the year.

Kencheeri is also critical for generating the heat horses need to withstand the bitter cold of winter. As alluded to in Valerian's mantra, "Snow is horses' home," the horses depend on the movements of rhythmical digging and grazing for the *kencheeri* to keep them warm as they make their way across the fields. Without it, horses do not dig, and they freeze. The new pattern of constant wind freezes them further. This prompts them to find shelter in the adjacent forest. All these factors make them thin and sickly. Valerian yearns for the past conditions with ample conditions for *kencheeri* to grow well, the gradual temperature change as fall moved to the deep cold winter, a snowfall in the autumn of about thirty centimeters that stayed through the snowless winter, and the still or windless quality of the deep winter.

Hearing Valerian's powerful testimony to *kencheeri* sensitized me to hearing others talk about it. One *sylgyhyt* commented that even though their hay land was not affected by the government's *khoruu* digging, they still had issues with a lack of *kencheeri*. "I don't have land near a stream, and so the hay depends on water from the snow and rain. I am a horse keeper and in the last years there has been no *kencheeri*. It only grows if there are the exact conditions . . . with the floods and now this drought, there is no *kencheeri* and the horses do not fatten" (Spartak Ivanovich Spiridonov, interview, June 26, 2018). A second *sylgyhyt* put the onus not only on the present climate conditions but also on Sakha's contemporary settlement pattern, which prohibits them from adapting as their ancestors did.

> Our fall is longer and now it does not rain so the *kencheeri* does not grow and the horses starve. Sometimes it will grow, but then it dries up. The horses have gone into bad conditions every year for the last time, and we have to feed them all the time. Our ancestors never kept all their animals in one place, and they also fenced in the winter pastures. Also, when they had drought like this, they relocated their animals to the headwaters where they knew there would be water and pasture and *kencheeri*. Now moving that way is not possible. (Afanasee Ivanovich Trofimov, interview, July 3, 2018)

I left Valerian's home that day with an expanded understanding of his mantra "Snow is horses' home," and a deep appreciation for the important six inches of green hay that hides under the snow, *kencheeri*.

It Is the Wind, Not the Water

Sardana Mikhailovna Gerasimova, like Valerian, has developed an in-depth knowledge of change via her life experience. Sardana's household was part of my 1999–2000 household sample in Elgeeii. At that time, she was thirty years old and lived with her three boys, her mother, and her uncle. Her husband and father had passed a few years before. She was unemployed and depended on the monthly subsidy she received for losing her husband and on her mother's pension. Over time I grew to appreciate the depth and breadth of Sardana's local knowledge of change, much of which she learned from her older kin.

> When the Viliui River water came close to the top of the banks in 1998, the elders told about the flood of 1959. My mother and her friend talked about how they remember going in boats. Mom worked at the village administration and took a boat to the post office and the store. . . . So in '98 when the water was rising, they told us how to prepare—take the children and cows up hill . . . to take all your documents and be ready . . . I prepared . . . got the kids and their winter clothes uphill to the relatives . . . I did not sleep all

Figure 22 Sardana Mikhailovna Gerasimova, May 28, 2019. Photo by author.

night . . . the next day we were fine. (Sardana Mikhailovna Gerasimova, survey, June 4, 2009)

Sardana repeatedly shared the elders' wisdom. During one interview on the topic of climate change, she relayed a proverb and its meaning: "The permafrost will melt and the big water will come from there." She also has keen observation skills that led her to talk about the pattern of unusual and constant wind long before anyone else. Although it was not one of the main nine changes of our 2008 focus group results, Sardana was witnessing new wind patterns early on: "There is a lot of wind . . . no one talks about the wind . . . everyone is only worried about the water . . . but I notice that the wind is especially strong this year . . . I watch the wind going this way and that . . . it does a lot of harm" (ibid.).

She explained how she had been tracking the wind patterns in a diary for over a decade. Her data showed the change from relative calm to strong and constant winds over that period. Her "instruments" for gauging the wind changes were her observations of how the smoke moved out of the chimneys near her home and by how often birds were thrown off their course in flight.

As a forty-year-old who was tracking meteorological observations and citing elder wisdom, Sardana was an anomaly for me. Furthermore, she was the only one in her age group to use the Bull of Winter narrative when she explained how the winters had changed: "The *Jyl Oghuha* . . . brings the deep cold and then the horns fall and the cold is less . . . and I also watch if that happens but now it doesn't work . . . it doesn't get cold . . . it doesn't happen as it used to . . . the big cold does not come anymore" (ibid.).

Sardana was raised in an extended family-clan group who all were active in horse and cattle breeding and in hunting, fishing, and foraging. Her father received several cows as his share after the *sovkhoz* breakup, and he bred a herd of ten from that. Sardana's 1999 recounting of how her household

used their cow products both to feed themselves and to barter for products they did not raise, including eggs, pork, and horse meat, reflected how
many households survived in the immediate post-Soviet period. Her kin also
formed a *baahynai khahaaiystyba* immediately after the state farm breakup,
which allowed them access to a larger hay area and helped them coordinate
the exchange of work and tractor use. Sardana slaughtered the household
herd after her mother and her grandfather passed away in the late 2000s.

Sardana also knows a lot about change because she grew up in nature.
In the 2018 Elgeeii women's focus group, the first change she volunteered
was "fewer ducks," and she immediately recounted her recent duck hunting
numbers: 2015 (58), 2016 (58), 2017 (47), 2018 (38). Later I asked about her
duck hunting activity, and she replied:

My father was a duck hunter and caught many, many ducks when I was
little . . . I watched mother see him off and he stayed away many days after
which he came back with sooo many ducks! He would put two or three in a
net and send me off to give them to this and that neighbor . . . I took them all
around. My love for nature started with that experience. I go duck hunting
to this day—but there are no ducks anymore . . . they fly very thinly . . . they
come very early and so are already gone when the season opens . . . we don't
get any now. (Sardana Mikhailovna Gerasimova, interview, May 28, 2019)

Her early love for nature gives Sardana an increased sensitivity to more
subtle changes of late. She talked at length about the recent issues of *setienekh*
(last year's grasses or hay), a topic that I had only heard seasoned herders
discuss.

Now people don't hay all the areas every year and there is a lot of *setienekh* . . .
that is the dried up, leftover hay from the year before. It builds up year after
year and is a huge problem! Sakha, from long ago, practiced controlled burning to clean the fields of *setienekh* and prepare them for the new growth in
spring. But the government has made burning the fields against the law with
all the recent forest fires. (Ibid.)

I also credit Sardana's in-depth knowledge for her drive to understand her
place in the world. Recently she talked about tracing her genealogy. I asked
her where she was doing her archival research, knowing that many Sakha

were working in the local, regional, and republic archives to those ends. She responded, "I don't work in the archives! I'm doing it by talking to people!" She showed me several folders of documents she had already created based on local people's testimonies. As of 2019 she had reconstructed her lineage back to the fifth generation. When I asked her how her ancestors came to Elgeeii, she explained,

> My *ehe* Pyoter came with my *ebe* from Olyokminsk with my mom when mom was two years old. *Ebe* was born near here (Elgeeii). However, her family had many, many children and her mother and father were desperate for food to feed them. *Ebe* had just come into child-rearing age and so her parents traded her for one-and-one-half sacks of wheat. The traders took *ebe* to Olyokminsk and she grew up there. She met and married *ehe* there and then they came back here, to Elgeeii. (Ibid.)

Sardana was not able to learn her ancestry directly from her parents. They had passed away without telling her anything. In the Soviet period when she asked questions about her heritage, her relatives said, "Why do you want to know about the past and for what purpose?" Sardana's was one of many testimonies I had heard verifiying the local reality of the Stalinist era protocol of banishing the past and forced forgetting, including ancestral heredity. Like many other Sakha today, Sardana is working to piece her heredity together. She told about one excursion she took last year to Kÿÿkei to learn about her *ehe*, Zakharov Nayum Ivanovich, nicknamed Kak-ka Oghonn'or (literally "Kak-ka old man"). She asked the inhabitants of Kÿÿkei and nearby Kutana about him until she found an eighty-year-old man, Pyotor, who had known Kak-ka Oghonn'or. Pyotor took Sardana to find Kak-ka Oghonn'or's *ötökh*. After a long search through the overgrowth, Pyotor located the posts of the old *balaghan* where Kak-ka Oghonn'or had lived. He also told Sardana many stories about Kak-ka Oghonn'or's life.

Sardana is reconstructing her heritage for herself but also, more importantly, for her sons, who live and work in Yakutsk. Sardana's extensive knowledge of local nature gives her an understanding of the ecological issues of the Viliui regions. In her opinion, the continued contamination of the Viliui River and its effects on drinking water and other aspects of local life make Elgeeii an undesirable place for her sons to settle and have their families. Although she does not want her sons to come back to Elgeeii to live, she considers it critical that they know their heritage, their ancestral roots, and their early lineage living "by the *alaas.*"

Sardana's attention to the changes, in climate and in history of place, illustrates how Sakha are living with changes on many fronts and finding various ways to maintain their essential connection to homeland, heritage, and *alaas*. Being relatively young, Sardana is unique among those researching their lineages. A majority of those occupied with lineage work are older, and often already receiving their pensions. The best example I have met is Anatoli Petrovich Fyodorov.

A Lifetime of *Perestroikas*

Anatoli Petrovich Fyodorov is a building expert by training and, by passion, an expert in local history. He has written three books detailing his ancestral lineage based on his careful archival research (Fedorov 2012a, 2012b, 2009).

In addition to the forced forgetting of ancestral lineages, another Stalinist-era protocol was to break up kinship groups in an effort to create one Soviet people (Alexopoulos 2008). Anatoli Petrovich has worked to expand and fill out his family tree since the end of the Soviet period. His knowledge is impressive.

I know my lineage fifteen generations, all the way back to the time when my ancestors lived near Yakutsk in the area called Khangalas.[1] After Russians arrived around 1632 or so, our people could pay no more *yasak* because they already were giving what they could. So, the Khangalas Sakha fought a war with them. The Russians won, of course, because they had guns and we only had arrows. Some of our people went to the north, there are Khangalas there in Orto Khalyma. My

Figure 23 Anatoli Petrovich Fyodorov with his three books on local kinship lines, May 21, 2019. Photo by Kathryn Tuyaara Yegorov-Crate.

lineage's people came here to live on the Viliui . . . first to Shei then settling in Oghuruottaakh. (Anatoli Petrovich Fyodorov, interview, May 21, 2019)

Oghuruottaakh and the areas adjacent to it near lake Arymys (map 1) were abundant with hayfields and other resources. But the people didn't just happen upon it. They were led.

Oghuruottaakh . . . that was the first area my people came to live. They settled in a place there called Odun. It was named after the white shaman who lived there, the same one who led our people to Oghuruottaakh from Yakutsk. He was a *sirjit* [literally "land-knower," one kind of shamanistic knowing]. My ancestors had left Yakutsk in the late summer, and so it was already winter when they arrived in Oghuruottaakh. Therefore, they had had no cow manure to seal their houses as was the tradition for a *saakh jiete* and so they sealed their houses with snow . . . and called them *khaar jiete* [snow house] . . . and wintered that way. (Ibid.)

I met Anatoli Petrovich Fyodorov in 2005 when he was referred to me as the Kutana land specialist. He had worked as the head of all construction for the Kutana *sovkhoz* branch. From 1991 he worked for six years as Kutana's village head, after which he became Kutana's land specialist until going on his pension in 2009. He commented that there was no such specialty in the Soviet or pre-Soviet times because "there was never the issue of who got what land before that . . . our ancestors used the land as they needed, and in the Soviet period, all the land belonged to the government . . . after 1991, households had to have land so they could feed themselves" (ibid.). He was asked to be the land specialist because of his extensive knowledge of the greater area, both of his ancestral lands and of the Kutana village.

Kutana was once huge . . . from 1900 to 1920 Kutana was the center of the Suntaar *uluus* . . . there were many stores, lots of people, schools, it was a big success here . . . then in 1920 a Russian man named Bolaksin ran the Post Office where we had a telegram using Morse code. Bolaksin started complaining, saying he would not drink the lake water because it was rotting. So, he moved Kutana to the Aranghastaakh place [map 1]. But when they got there, they realized their mistake. The closest pastures were ten kilometers away, in Kÿÿkei and Tumul. So, after three years, they returned. However, by then the *uluus* center was moved to Shei. (Ibid.)

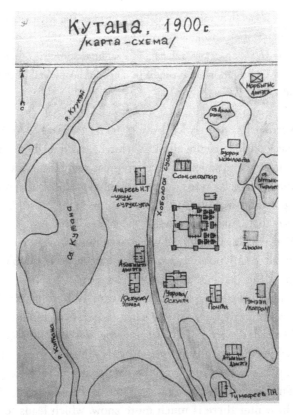

Map 7 Map of Kutana circa 1900. Drawn by P. N. Timofeev from A. P. Fedorov 2012b: 89. Photo by author.

Anatoli Petrovich spoke about the historical changes in the early Soviet period, the time of consolidation into larger and larger collective operations. A schema of early Kutana, in the 1900s, shows a settlement based on extended *agha uuha* groups living "by the *alaas*" (map 7).

One narrative from his life history includes details about consolidation during World War II.

In 1942, when all the men went to war, my mother became the head of the Khangalas and Aryylaakh *kolkhoz* areas. She was twenty years old! She served as head until 1947 and then married an Elgeeii doctor and moved to Elgeeii. Their first child died. Mother was offended that her doctor husband could let that happen, and so she divorced him. She was pregnant with me at the time. She returned to Oghuruottaakh, her home *alaas*, and soon I was born. When I was two, mother was made head of the Khangalas *kolkhoz*, which by then was a consolidation of the former Khangalas and Aryylaakh *kolkhoz*. The *kolkhoz* workers relocated to Kutana. Soon the other *kolkhoz*, Kÿÿkei and Mochuhun, were brought in, and she headed all of them until 1954. (Ibid.)

Anatoli Petrovich's ancestry work also benefits many others in Kutana and adjacent areas, considering the number of kin he has traced. "I cannot count them all! But if I do count them, then on my great-grandfather's side there are 360 individuals I am related to and, on mother's side, 500. This research has me counting, and it turns out that in Kutana I have the most kin of anyone. I can safely say that I am related to half the village" (ibid.).

Anatoli Petrovich has organized several reunions at Oghuruottaakh with extended kin attending not only from contemporary Kutana but also from other regions of the Sakha Republic and Yakutsk.

His knowledge of his kin and the landscape of Kutana and surrounds makes him particularly aware of the local impacts of climate change. He comprehensively described these changes in focus groups and interviews. He explained that during the most intense period of the water times, from 2007 to 2017, the excess water came from the combination of the wet-dry cycles and the recent changes in precipitation patterns due to climate change. He added that in winter there is much more snow, which leads to increased

Figure 24 Fyodorov extended family reunion at Oghuruottaakh in 1995, on the fiftieth anniversary of victory in World War II. From A. P. Fedorov 2012a. Photo by author.

spring meltwater. This excess water
and the water from the thawing of the
permafrost in the *alaas* made the wet
cycle that much more wet. During
the dry cycle ten years later, Anatoli
Petrovich was outspoken about the
further drought conditions caused by
the canal projects.

It was bad! First in 1997 when the wet
cycle started . . . from '97 to 2008 we
had the water years—all the *uluus* in
the Viliui, the central and some northern regions needed relief from the
water. The resources and money was
not enough . . . we pushed for them to
make the *khoruu* based on *nüölsüter*
as our ancestors made them . . . but
they just dug straight canals . . . hay
land appeared . . . they only planned
to drain . . . they had no idea to make a
dam and a way to control the water . . .
and now, in this dry cycle, all the water
has gone . . . and I say to all . . . let's make a dam and a way to control it but
no one wants to. (Ibid.)

Figure 25 Anatoli Petrovich at his ancestral *alaas*, Toloon. He is standing in a dip in the land resulting from the thaw of permafrost underneath to demonstrate its depth. 2018. Photo by author.

He could very well be the local expert to advise these needed *nüölsüter* activities, given his detailed knowledge of the surrounding lands.

He also understands the issue of changes to the land surfaces: "The once
flat *ötökh* are now dipping and diving" (interview, June 25, 2018). He used
the example of the once *dekhsi* (flat) land at the Toloon *ötökh*, the land place
that he has spent his summers haying from an early age, which is now riddled with waves. I asked Anatoli Petrovich if he would show me these lands,
remembering the Kutana head's offer to provide transportation to do so. The
next day I traveled with Anatoli Petrovich and one of his kin to the *ötökh* at
Toloon. There we traversed the rippled landscape while he described how
it used to be, going back to his early memories of where they camped and

set up a cook kitchen. Every once in a while, he would step down into the depressions to more effectively illustrate their depth (figure 25).

From there we traveled to Oghuruottaakh and the Arymys lake, the large *alaas* area where his ancestors came when they settled from Yakutsk. We then drove overland to see the old Kÿÿkei sawmill site, another place where the once-flat lands had rippled from permafrost thaw. It was a working sawmill up until a few years ago when the irregularities of the landscape made the sawmill work impossible.

In a later discussion he described in detail what he does to reify the relationship with his birth *alaas*, making the required regular pilgrimages there to feed the ancestral spirits. He then told me about his wife Valentina's pilgrimage to her birth *alaas*. I think this was because Valentina was with us that day during our discussion, and her presence brought it to Anatoli's mind. In the process, he explained an important Sakha ritual to make restitution with your ancestral spirits if you have neglected to visit them regularly: "Valentina had not been to her birthland for ten years and went last year. Before she did, she found a stone with a hole in it. The first thing she did upon arrival was look at her birthland through the hole, saying words to appease the spirits. If you have not been regularly, you need to go to the river and find a stone with a hole in it and do this" (Anatoli Petrovich Fyodorov, interview, May 21, 2019).

Anatoli Petrovich's life story is an example of how contemporary Sakha engage their past and their present simultaneously, of how they can move between the temporal and the spatial to perpetuate *alaas* as cultural identifier. In stark contrast, there are also individuals who have come to settle in the village from far away and have found their sacred *alaas* without the deep ancestral lineages like Anatoli's. They can also see change, in its many forms, based on having a stark before picture when they first arrived.

This Is My Home Now

I met Tatiyana Constantinovna Zhanova in early 2000. That day, I was completing a household survey with her husband, Valeri Kirilovich Aleksandrov, as part of my random sample of households in Kutana. About halfway through our work, Tatiyana came into the house from the outside cold and immediately began preparing tea.

Figure 26 Tatiyana Constantinovna Zhanova under her *cheremukha* (bird cherry) tree with garden beds in the background. She makes a compote of the cherries, but leaves some on the tree for the birds. 2018. Photo by her friend.

As she cut bread, opened pickles, and sliced meat, she supplemented Valeri's responses to my questions about household food production, recounting the kilos of tomatoes, cucumbers, squash, and potatoes that they had grown and put up that year. As she arranged everything on the table, she identified each item under her breath so as to not interfere with the survey responses. At the time, Valeri was in his third year as the head of the Kutana village. The couple had been keeping cows since the breakup in 1991, "in order to have food to eat." Valeri did the bulk of caring for the cows because Tatiyana had health issues at the time.

When I recently learned that Valeri had passed away in 2014, I asked Tatiyana if she planned to return home, to her birthland, Petrogorsk, near the Caucuses in western Russia. She immediately and enthusiastically responded

"No!" and commented that she had visited a few times and each time realized that her roots were now here.

> I am fine for the first week visiting home but then Kutana pulls me . . . and what is most interesting . . . Kutana is not my birthland. I say sometimes I will go back to the Caucuses . . . so beautiful and warm and with a health spa and all. But then I go there and Kutana pulls me back. Here I have my _dacha_ and house all in one, with no need for a car. I love it here and the air here is much cleaner. . . . This is my home. (Tatiyana Constantinovna Zhanova, interview, June 6, 2019)

Tatiyana came to Kutana from western Russia for work. Her path to Kutana was quite a winding one. She was given a choice of where in the USSR she wanted to practice after she finished her medical training as a nurse in 1970. She delayed a bit in deciding, so when she went to make her choice, there were only ten places left, all in the Yakutia ASSR (the Soviet name of the Sakha Republic). She was not deterred. "I knew it as a place of exotica—Siberia . . . the north . . . the snow . . . the tundra!" She and two other nurses arrived at the health ministry in Yakutsk to learn that their choices were limited to posts in the Suntaar region. Tatiyana, somewhat randomly, chose Kÿÿkei because it had a big lake and was adjacent to the Elgeeii state farm where she knew she could get vegetables. Her peers went to another settlement in Suntaar and both left after six months. She heard that they disliked the food, the climate, and the Sakha ways, the same aspects that Tatiyana found herself fascinated by. She was also assigned to work under a Russian head doctor, which meant she could communicate freely with her boss. Her next challenge was how she would communicate with patients, most of whom did not know Russian. She greeted a Sakha woman on the street in Kÿÿkei one day who responded to her in Russian. Tatiyana asked the woman if she would tutor her in the Sakha language, and the woman agreed. Tatiyana was pleased with how quickly she picked up Sakha, and one day it hit her why. She spoke Russian with her father and mother growing up, but they spoke a Turkic language, like Sakha, with her grandmother.

> I realized how well it served me then. I sat there, and my host explains to me where to go for a call . . . and she spoke in Russian and in Sakha . . . and I wondered why she spoke in a Turkic language and, for that matter, not very

well . . . turns out, in our language back home, that *su* is water whereas *uu* is water in Sakha . . . the same sound! Also, the word *suokh* means "no" in Sakha and is *uokh* in our language. For *kyys* [girl], we say *gyys*. Then I realized that I could already explain the things I needed to explain to my patients . . . I got the language so quickly! (Ibid.)

In December of 1970, Tatiyana went to Kutana to cover when the head nurse there fell sick. She never returned to Kÿÿkei. Shortly after arriving in Kutana, she was invited by a local man, Valeri, to go *mungkha* fishing. They fell in love. They courted for several months, and he helped her find her way around Kutana. Her memories of that courtship included details of how different conditions were at that time compared to now.

There were no roads, no good communication, and no medicine back then. It took six hours to drive to Elgeeii and six hours back. Today it takes twenty minutes each way! Back then we only had two or three cars in all of Kutana, and they were always being used for state farm business. My work was extremely demanding and included everything a doctor and a nurse does . . . even pulling teeth! I was a psychologist, a gynecologist, a pediatrician . . . and even much later, when I moved to work as a teacher at the preschool, people would ask me to come and birth their child or perform an operation . . . there was nothing I didn't have to do . . . it was very hard work. (Tatiyana Constantinovna Zhanova, interview, June 25, 2018)

Over the years, Tatiyana's yard has increasingly been dedicated to food production. Today it is end-to-end garden plots and raised beds. She boasts of how many kilos of this or that vegetable she harvests. She also forages for the full seasonal variety of wild berries and mushrooms. All this requires her mastery of how and when the seasons change, what the local practices of gardening and foraging are, and how she can improve upon them. It is this intimate local knowledge that enables her to know how the local climate and seasonal patterns are changing,

One big change is how the nights in summer are cold now . . . before, when June and July came, nights were warm and sometimes very hot . . . now they turn cold and that affects the plants . . . the vegetables and fruits are affected . . . they start to get the energy to grow through the day and then, just when they are about to grow, it gets cold . . . and so they grow poorly. Because of that, we harvest less . . . also now there are very few berries to forage. Before we picked so many berries! In the Soviet period, Valeri and I picked 500 kilos in ten days one summer. We sold them and used the money to buy a living room furniture set, a Ural motorcycle, a book shelf . . . that was in the 1980s. (Ibid.)

Tatiyana is another one of the few inhabitants, like Sardana Gerasimovna, who have been outspoken recently about the prevalence of strong wind. "Did we have these strong winds before? I have no recall of winds like these since I came here in the '70s . . . it is just in the last few years that we have these unbelievable winds—we never had before" (Tatiyana Constantinovna Zhanova, survey, June 3, 2009).

In addition to her extensive gardening and foraging, which give her insights into environmental change, Tatiyana's memories of when she came to Kutana in her twenties give her a solid "before" picture to contrast with now, decades later.

So much of what we need to do is connected to protecting the forests. If I compare with when I first came here forty years ago, the forests have been cut far too much. It takes at least thirty trees to build a house and without the forests there are no more birds or berries and the waters flood more. Also, recently many former residents of Kutana are coming here to cut and take the wood to Yakutsk because they want a _dacha_ [summer house] there. Then there is the huge quantity of wood that we burn to heat . . . I alone have four stoves. All of that together and there goes the forest and the birds and all! Every April 22 we go and get wood . . . think of how much I burn in my house . . . I have stoves in the garage, house, _bania_ [bathhouse], my _teplitza_ [greenhouse]—I am sad to think about the forests. (Tatiyana Constantinovna Zhanova, interview, June 25, 2018)

By 2019 most Kutana households were heating with electricity. Although this relieves pressure on the forests, some inhabitants are concerned about how dangerous it would be if the electricity failed in the deep cold.

Tatiyana knows Tumul and the surrounding lands very well, having spent much of her free time there with Valeri, who was born in Tumul. She sees the contrast when she goes to Tumul today:

We often went by motorcycle to Tumul—to gather berries or to just go for fun. For a few years we planted potatoes on a piece of land by the lake. We cut our hay there and we would help local people stack hay there in summer—for one day we raked it all and made the stacks . . . and there were so many wildflowers . . . gorgeous . . . so beautiful there!!! I go there today it is not like it was in the '70s. Back then there were no cars or tractors and there were so very many wild flowers. I know now that there were many medicinal flowers and they were mixed in the hay . . . when we fed our cows, we saw how they only needed a small amount . . . because the hay had more calories and nutrition . . . it made the cow's *süögei* taste like it had sugar in it . . . there was such a huge difference. Others in Kutana had big tall haystacks to winter their herds but ours was shorter . . . and full of flowers . . . we gave it to our chickens and no one else had eggs in the winter but we did because we fed them that hay. We never had sick cows . . . because they ate medicinal plants! There was *deviasil* [elecampane or *Inula helenium*] for cough . . . and krapiva [nettle or *Urtica dioica*] and this and that . . . they ate it all! Today there is no hay like back then. There has been so much disruption of the ecology and the use of the tractors and driving on the fields with the cars. So much is damaged now and has changed. (Interview, May 22, 2019)

There is a rootedness to Tatiyana's character that goes beyond all her activities and accomplishments to learn the language, to understand the local customs and mores, and to develop the skills and abilities to produce food. She has made herself integral to the Kutana community. It is best explained by her strong belief in fate and a sense of destiny that guided her on her path to Kutana.

My grandmother escorted me with all the others when I left for Yakutia. There were 35 people at the airport! They made a table and we ate and toasted to my new life. When she kissed me, she said, "You will not return from there." I thought to myself, what does she mean I will not return? I could only think of bad things. Then she said, "All that I taught you . . . how to deliver children and to work on teeth . . . you are going to do in a village there." Now I understand that she was preparing me so that when I got here, I would not be afraid . . . I would be ready. She told me that I would gain great experience and I would marry but that I would not return. I had two other experiences telling me this was destiny. During my practicum in a small settlement in the Petogorski krai . . . I met two _tsyganye_[2] and they said . . . "Come on, let us predict your future . . . let us predict." One of them took my hand and looked at my palm and said to me . . . "you will travel very, very far away and there you will live and you will have four sons." And, do you know what? That is how it went. Shortly after that, my friends and I made predictions of the future on the sixth of January, as is the Russian tradition. We all wrote men's names on pieces of paper. After 12 midnight we each picked a paper. I chose the name Valeri. I was not happy . . . my girlfriends picked really good names but I got this unfamiliar name . . . but I forgot about it until I arrived in Kutana and met Valeri. All those signs before coming here told me my fate. I had a husband named Valeri and four sons . . . and have been here for 50 years. (Ibid.)

Tatiyana's recognition of these clarion signs based on her ancestral belief opened her to Sakha belief. In 2019 she explained to me the series of events leading up to Valeri's passing. I knew he had been sick with diabetes for years but never fully understood his sudden death until she explained,

When you go to Tumul, Valeri's birth house used to be there on the right. He showed it to me when we married. I remember thinking then—how wonderful . . . so beautiful there! In 2014 Aian Suol came to him to ask if they could remove his Tumul house to widen and fortify the road. Valeri was too nice! He agreed and they took it down. Valeri died that same year. I know that, according to Sakha customs, if you take away an old structure, a house or _serge_ or otherwise, something bad will happen. There is something to that belief. When I was a nurse, our elder patients told us constantly that, according to Sakha ways, you should never remove an old structure. You must leave them to fall on their own. If you remove them, bad things will happen. (Interview, June 6, 2019)

This was not the first time I had encountered contemporary inhabitants very much engaging with their historical belief system and recognizing it in their daily lives. One might expect that all these past beliefs would be gone, considering the Soviet efforts to wipe them out. But today they are alive and well. But Tatiyana's testimonies were the first time I heard a non-Sakha expressing these understandings. Osip Dmitriyevich Andreyev's story provides an example of a Sakha who went back to his culture's historical beliefs later in life.

We Continue to Learn from the Elders

> It is important to look after cows and protect them . . . when they enter the *khoton* for the winter, you must feed the *khoton* spirits and ask them to take good care of the cows . . . we have that belief, it is the core of being Sakha . . . also when you go to the *saiylyk* you do another feeding of the spirits there with *alaaji*. I absolutely do it in the fall and in spring. We also burn *seppereek* in the *khoton* to extinguish the bad spirits so there will be no diseases for the cows. For horses we burn horsehair. Edjay Olga did it and I copy her . . . we continue to learn from the elders. (Osip Dmitriyevich Andreyev, interview, May 21, 2019)

Osip Dmitriyevich Andreyev and his family are one of two full-time households in contemporary Tumul. Osip is committed to living there and practicing the cow breeding and other household food production practices of his ancestors, all of which he learned from elders in Tumul. In turn, he hopes to teach young people so that his knowledge is passed on. I asked him if they hang *salama* in their *khoton*, and he explained they had one there from long ago.

> My mother wanted to hang it but my father was angry . . . he did not like it . . . he was a communist and against any belief and so hanging it was wrong. He stormed around saying how all the old ways were garbage and had no meaning. That was the politics at the time. But my mom hung it anyway, without making a big fuss and he did not bother with it or say anything . . . I think there was part of him that believed but he thought he needed to make noise about it to be true to the Soviets. Later he started practicing also, as belief came to him in his older years. (Osip Dmitriyevich Andreyev, interview, June 26, 2018)

He took me out to see the *salama* and explained its purpose, "It keeps away the bad spirits—tells the diseases not to come and protects the animals from them" (ibid).

Figure 27 Osip Dmitriyevich Andreyev in his household's *khoton*, standing by the *salama* his mother hung decades ago. 2018. Photo by author.

He made the point that he had not always followed these practices and detailed his path to them: "When I was younger, I didn't do them. It has only been since I have gotten older. We were raised in the Soviet time when there was not supposed to be any belief, or *abaahy*, or religion. . . . But as I get older, the stories my mother and father told me come back. They affect me and come into my life . . . our people's beliefs before. That is why I go now and learn from elders" (ibid.).

Osip emphasized that all the Sakha practices provide *kharyskhaal* (protection) throughout the day. "We go to *Ebee* [here referring to Kÿÿkei lake] and give *alaaji* and ask for all to be well . . . we feed the land and the spirits" (interview, May 21, 2019). Many Sakha, like Osip, who today are practicing their culture's original beliefs, have started to do so relatively recently. For others, however, like Margarita Ilyinichna Zabolotzkaya, it has been a life-long practice.

Through the Window

> I was born here in Elgeeii . . . I live with my mom and my brother, who is a professional herder so is not home a lot. My mother was born across the river in III Bordong, on the Tallalaakh [map 1] land place . . . she was the eighth child to be born to her parents. All the others before her had died. Because of that, they passed her through the window or performed *kureppit-ter* [to lead away, here "to escape the *abaahy*"][3] and took her to Kharialaakh near Kundeii to the Missika land place. My grandparents made a wooden doll and put that in the cradle in her place . . . to fool the *abaahy*. This is a Sakha custom to protect the child when there is a pattern of newborns dying after birth. (Margarita Ilyinichna Zabolotzkaya, interview, September 7, 1999)

Margarita Ilyinichna Zabolotzkaya's "through the window" story has stayed with me since that day when she and her mother sat in their living room completing a household survey. I had never heard of this practice before. I remember, while Margarita was telling the story, how I glanced up at one of the windows and then looked at Margarita's mother, who nodded and smiled when our eyes met.

I found out in later years that several other households I knew credited a family member's life to this practice. One said that his father survived because he was passed through the window when none of his mother's male newborns had survived. When the respondent's father was born, the parents did *kureppitter*, calling him "*Yt kyyha mooitoruk*" (dog's female puppy's neck scarf) so the *abaahy* wouldn't think he was human (Prokopii Mitrofonovich Yegorov, personal communication, June 12, 2019). Another inhabitant's recounting added a different nuance.

> A pregnant woman approached my *ebe* and explained to her that all the children she had birthed, had died. She asked if my *ebe* would pass her next one

through the window. She agreed and instructed her to make a new manure shovel, especially for the act. When the day came, the baby was born in the *balaghan* [the house and *khoton* were still attached then]. They wrapped the baby in rabbit skins, put it on the manure shovel and passed it through the window declaring, "This is manure!" They then put it on a sledge and took it far away, with someone following, sweeping the snow with a spruce bow to wipe away the sledge tracks and confuse the *abaahy*. (Izabella Nikolayevna Tretiyakova, interview, May 23, 2019)

Margarita said her personal story included another way that Sakha practiced to avoid the *abaahy*'s power over children: "My father and his birth brother were both named Aleksey. Sakha do this to confuse the *abaahy*, so they can't follow the trail. For my father and his brother, it worked! They both lived a very long time. You see how the traditions carry on" (Margarita Ilyinichna Zabolotzkaya, interview, May 29, 2019).

Margarita's contemporary life epitomizes the historical Sakha lifeways and belief. Most households today "modernize," getting the newest furniture, appliances, building materials, aluminum siding, indoor water tanks, and so on. But when you enter the gate to Margarita's household, to this day you have a sense of going back in time. I was struck by that sense when I entered on our interview day in 2019:

I arrived and the gate was open. Upon entering, I noticed that someone had scythed all the hay in the yard and stacked it into neat *buguls*, dispersed geometrically around the yard. I noticed how well kept the wooded exteriors of the house and all the outbuildings were. Several outbuildings had raised garden beds, approximately 2.5 feet deep and made from recycled wood, along them growing greens, beets, and carrots. Beyond was a small greenhouse of tomatoes and another of cucumbers. As I made my way to the door, I heard the brother's voice in

Figure 28 Margarita Ilyinichna Zabolotzkaya, at home. 2019. Photo by author.

the outer room. He was just leaving for work. Margarita welcomed me in to the house, which is exactly as it has been for the last twenty years that I have come there. She lay newspapers on the kitchen table to protect my papers from any dirt and we sat to do the interview. (Journal entry, 2019)

Margarita's life story reflects her deep respect for her ancestral history and her clear determination to live in awareness and pride of that history.

My *ehe* was a successful herder with lots of cows and horses. He joined the *kolkhoz* but it didn't work for him—they had tried to confiscate all his animals and so he left the *kolkhoz* with them. Then the government told him to pay tax on them but by then his animals had all drowned after falling through the ice when they went to the *oibon* to drink. The government still demanded tax, and so *ehe* went to Olyokminsk with his older son to make the money to pay the tax they demanded. It was 1941 and the beginning of the war. He got a war *povestka*. He decided he would go to war but did not want to leave his son alone in Olyokminsk. He was bringing his son back here, with his war paper in his pocket, when they arrested him for being a deserter and put him in the Olyokminsk prison. He soon escaped, hiding here and there. He finally made it back to his wife, my *ebe*. She hid him and gave him food . . . how could she not? The officials soon found them and sent them both to prison in Yakutsk. My *ebe* had to leave behind a newborn baby, and to this day, no one knows what became of her. When *ebe* was sent away, my mother was left an orphan at nine years old. She went from house to house to live but everyone labeled her a deserter's child and refused her. Some even took her by her collar and threw her out! She finally found one kin family who would keep her. Later the authorities in Yakutsk decided that *ebe* was not guilty of anything and freed her. She walked back here from Yakutsk . . . it took her half a year! She arrived in the fall. Her life was hard—she made their clothes from hare skins and somehow managed to find enough food not to starve. Later they sent *ehe* from the Yakutsk prison to Kempandai to do war mobilization labor. Conditions were very bad there and he died after the first year. (Margarita Ilyinichna Zabolotzkaya, interview, July 2, 2018)

Margarita's narratives also provide unique understandings of pre-Soviet life when Sakha lived "by the *alaas*" and often had to make a living by negotiating their skills and their limitations.

My *ebe* and *ehe* lived in the land place called Tallalaakh in III Bordong . . .
there were lots of families who lived there then. They lived by *alaas* and in
Tallalaakh there was a lake and fields nearby and many *ötökh*. *Ebe* would tell
us about a man named Taabara Suokh (literally "one without goods") who
made his living by taking other people's meat, butter, wheat, and goods to
Olyokminsk to sell. He got a percentage and that was how he worked. His wife
was blind and so they could not keep animals themselves. That was the only
work they could do back then to feed their kids. (Interview, May 29, 2018)

Margarita aspires to visit her ancestral *alaas*, but in the last years her
health doesn't allow it. She works in her yard and goes about the village daily.
A lot of the knowledge she has gained about how climate change is affecting
her village comes from her professional experience working as a nurse in the
Elgeeii health center since 1976.

Our winter is warm, not like when it stayed −50 or −60 C all the time in our
youth. There is too much wind all year. Before summer was very, very hot
and now it is cold. Ten years ago, the water was taking our land. Now it is all
dry due to both a dry cycle and how the government did so much damage
making the canals. The drought is why the plants are changing, the land is
changing, the animals and birds are changing . . . and this change is going
very fast. All my coworkers, they know these changes are happening and we
talk about them. I see, in my own work experience, how the disease patterns
are very different today also . . . the changes in weather and climate that
come so quickly is a strain on people's physical health . . . northern people
are not used to abrupt changes like we are having in the last years. Sudden
temperature changes are hard for people with high blood pressure and other
heart ailments. And I see how these problems are increasing. Also, ticks are
finding their way up from the south. We never saw them before and people
are now getting sick from them here in Elgeeii. (Ibid.)

Margarita associates the local impact of climate change with a myriad of
other changes, including changes in lifestyle, food, and the increased use of
transport and technology. In 2009 she explained how the thawing permafrost was contributing to the issue of water on the land and how this was due
to warming of the earth overall. Margarita's more global orientation is also
reflected in her philosophy of *alaas*.

Alaas is the Sakha's life. We are children of the *alaas* . . . every Sakha has an *alaas* in their spirit—and we carry that *alaas* with us all our lives . . . the *alaas* is connected to our roots . . . our beginnings . . . our birthplace . . . our homeland . . . why is that? Because Sakha lived by the *alaas* from long ago. Sakha have long had *alaas* and have protected them and lived from them. They are like one's own country. Why we could even think of the entire planet as a huge *alaas*! We are all born in that *alaas*! (Interview, July 2, 2018)

The ancestral roots of Elgeeii and Kutana inhabitants extend to adjacent and distant alaas and also far beyond the Sakha Republic. A different Elgeeii inhabitant's life history adds a different example of those more distant bloodlines.

The Ties that Bind

It was not until the summer of 2019, when I ran into Olympiyada (Lipa)[4] Nikanderovna Kirilina's nephew Volodya (Vladimir Nikolayevich Semyonov) on the street in Elgeeii, that I understood the winding trail of ancestral relations that he and Lipa shared.

My mother's *khos ehe* [great-grandfather], came here for prison from Belorussia . . . Kirillin Nikolai "*Beridatchit*" [literally "one who goes in front"]. It was long before Stalin's time, around 1880 when there was still a tsar in Russia. He came here for prison just like others we know well: Yaroslavski, Seroshevskii, Pekarski. . . . There were many prisons in Siberia back then. He stayed here after getting out and had a wife and boys . . . one son was my great-grandfather, Kirillin Semen Nikolaievich, nicknamed *Kutterer Oghonn'or*. He was wealthy with 150 animals, both horses and cows. He didn't watch them himself but employed others to. . . . They had plenty of meat and butter. But back then they had no stores like today . . . so what did they do? People had to take their goods to Olyokminsk to sell or trade for wheat and other goods to bring back . . . that was what my *khos khos ehe* [great-great-grandfather] did and why he was called *Beridatchit*, that name meant that he went in the front, leading all the merchants . . . he was the important person . . . if people had meat and butter but didn't want to go to

Olyokminsk, they gave it to him to trade. (Vladimir Nikolayevich Semyonov, personal communication, May 15, 2019)

Learning how Volodya was related to Lipa, I reflected back on her life history, which she had shared the year before. Her history of growing up as an orphan and becoming a regional _kino-mekhanik_ (a technician who shows movies) provides a glimpse of times gone by:

> I was born in 1931, in Kÿÿkei at _Kutterer Oghonn'or ötökhö_ [grandfather's homestead]. But soon we lived as orphans. Our father was repressed and went to prison in 1939 . . . he worked in the Soviet office and they found him there with bandits [those against the Soviet government]. So, the Soviets accused him of helping the bandits and they repressed him. They freed him in September '42, but mother had died that spring and we kids had all been sent to the Tobokhoy _detdom_ [orphanage]. Father soon found us and we lived together for a while. But then he was sent to the _trudovoi front_ [war front], where those who didn't go to the war worked for the army. After the

Figure 29 Volodya's heritage in photos. Far left: Kirillin Nikolai, _Beridatchit_, was Volodya's great-great-grandfather who came from Belorussia to Siberia for prison. Center top: Kirillin Semen Nikolaevich, _Kutterer Oghonn'or_, Volodya's great-grandfather, shown to left of Kirillin Nikandr, Lipa's father. Center bottom: Volodya's _ebe_, Volodya's mother Klavdiia, and, standing, Kolya (Nikolai), Volodya's mother's brother. Top right: _Ohuokhai_ scene, 1968, _Kihin ataary_ (Seeing off winter celebration), in front of old Elgeeii clubhouse; arrow points to Volodya. Bottom left: Volodya with his grandson Stepanov Yaroslav Savvich ("He spends summers here and I teach him Sakha"). Photos from Vladimir Nikolayevich Semyonov.

war he got us from the *detdom*, he remarried and we were a family again. (Olympiyada Nikanderovna Kirilina, interview, July 2, 2018)

Lipa only finished the first two grades of school at the *detdom*, so when the opportunity came for her to get training in a field where she could get a job, she took it without hesitation.

My stepmother introduced me to the director of the <u>*kino-mekhanik*</u> course who then trained me in the skill from 1951. I remember so well how I arrived for the training in Yakutsk in April by plane. All I had were *khaatyngka* [felt boots] that had holes in the bottoms. It was April and the time of the spring thaw, and so it was very wet all around. I really needed to wear rain boots but *khaatyngka* was all I had. The bookkeeper saw my *khaatyngka* and felt sorry for me. She gave me a <u>*talon*</u> [coupon] to buy skin boots. I wore them all summer. I studied hard . . . but it was extra hard for me because the whole course was in Russian and I only knew Sakha! I learned by doing, hands-on learning, and at the end of the course I was a <u>*kino-mekhanik*</u>! (Olympiyada Nikanderovna Kirilina, interview, May 28, 2019)

After the six-month training in Yakutsk, Lipa next fulfilled her practicum, working in Suntaar for a year and then in an adjacent village for another year. She was then assigned a ring route, traveling in a circle from one settlement to the next. Her memories bring to mind rich images.

They sent me to Khadanga to live. From there I crossed the river to Ilimneer and showed the *kino* in that village center and on its farm. I always went to the farms also to show the *kino*. After that, I continued to a farm on the way to Bordong then to show in Bordong and then in Tenkai. It was a ring trip. I got around with three horses . . . the *kino* motor was very heavy . . . that was carried by one of the horses and the other horse carried all

Figure 30 Olympiyada (Lipa) Nikanderovna Kirilina, in her home. 2019. Photo by author.

the films . . . they were also very heavy . . . and then the third horse carried all the other equipment . . . we used three horses. I say we because there was always a person traveling with me who took care of the horses. I mostly walked because the horses already had very heavy loads. In the summer, after the ice flow, we went by boat and over the land with the horses. We went all year round regardless of the weather! (Ibid.)

Lipa continued to show films in the ring route until 1957 when she married and started a family. She then settled first in Suntaar then in Elgeeii, where she worked as _kino-mekhanik_ for another thirty years until her retirement.

In 1999 she explained that she had never had cows because of her mobile lifestyle and the demands of her work. Then in 1996 she decided to keep them to have food to feed her children. She hired someone to care for them, since her severely arthritic knees made the work impossible for her. She slaughtered the herd once her children left home and Elgeeii stores were increasingly well stocked. Despite the ease of not having her own cows, she laments her lack of the Sakha _ürüng as_. She is not alone. Most interviewees have similarly longed for the Sakha _ürüng as_. The few households who continue keeping cows, enjoying the _ürüng as_ and local meat, have found ways to make a profit supplying their neighbors. Most of them say they also keep cows to have a safety net for when the next huge change, like the fall of the Soviet Union, comes. One person who is outspoken about this is Ksenya Prokopiyevna Semyonova. Ksenya's life history is a unique window into change over time and Sakha's living "by the _alaas_" in a contemporary context.

Living "by the _Alaas_"

I first appreciated how much of an entrepreneur Ksenya Prokopiyevna Semyonova was in the mid-1990s. I was facilitating a project at the Elgeeii Nature Museum, where she worked. Every day she would bring cow products with her to work—a jar of _süögei_ or _suorat_ to barter or sell, or a batch of fresh _uohakh alaaji_ to share, a practice believed to ensure the health of the newborn calf. I gained a fuller appreciation of her household's food production after she completed a household survey and kept an annual diary for me during my 1999–2000 research.[5]

Ksenya was born in Elgeeii and married an Elgeeii man, Arkadi Nikolayevich Semyonov. Between the two of them, they have near and distant kin
in Elgeeii that make up one-tenth of the village population. Above all, Ksenya
has a rootedness in place that is unique for someone in their fifties. I credit
it to the combination of her specific ancestry, her household's maintenance
of a cows-and-kin lifestyle, and her professional work, first at the nature
museum and now at the Zverov Museum of Sakha Culture.[6] Her specific
ancestry includes Nolar, the famous local writer who wrote extensively on
Sakha and *alaas*.

I presented Ksenya and her household, the Semyonovs, in my dissertation
as one of several examples of the cow-and-kin adaptation, specifically because
of the tightly nested interactions and reciprocities between hers, her mother's, and her in-laws' households to produce cow products and hay. Without fail, when I arrived at her house for an interview or diary check-in, she
would have the table laden with their home-produced foods, including a full
array of *ürüng as*. The combination fluctuated depending on the season but
could include *süögei*, *suorat*, *iejegei* (curds), *küörchekh* (sweetened whipped
cream), *khaiakh* (milk butter), *chokhon* (frozen *küörchekh*), and *bipak* (fermented cow's milk). She emphasized how
much their household relied on barter, be
it trading cow meat for horse, two sacks of
cabbage for a case of oil, or meat and cream
for having their wood hauled in.

One key aspect of her household's success is the interactions they have with their
kin, especially with Arkadi's parents. Arkadi recounted in a 2012 interview, "Elders
live well when they have their adult children helping and watching them . . . but
for me it is the opposite . . . they help me
before I help them!" Arkadi's parents are
another uniquely entrepreneurial household within Elgeeii. They grow and raise
most of their household food and sell their
goods locally. Arkadi's father even travels
to Suntaar to peddle their food products.
During an interview in the summer of 1999

Figure 31 Ksenya Prokopiyevna Semyonova, at Zverov Museum. 2019. Photo
by author.

he explained how he went directly to the Suntaar administration building and sold *sobo* from desk to desk. Arkadi's parents live in a house located on the street I take to go to the store. Each time I pass, his father is always outside working. I always stop to chat. He explains what work he is doing, for example, how he is putting ash on berry bushes as a source of fertilizer; removing crabgrass from their acre potato plot, a tedious job but one that results in a 200 percent better harvest; or finishing the work on a log home he built for their daughter to spend the summers in Elgeeii with their granddaughter.

Arkadi's parents also participated in keeping a daily home food production diary in 1999–2000. At the time, Arkadi's father practiced all the three forms of *sobo* fishing and also directed a local team to catch *sialihar* (burbot) in midwinter when they migrate up the Viliui River. Arkadi's mother foraged the full range of berries over the summer season, starting with *jeijen* in early July; then *khaptaghas* and *moonn'oghon*, *malina* (red raspberries), and *sugun* (blueberries) in late July through August; and *oton*, picked until the first snow falls.

Ksenya and Arkadi's entrepreneurial success is in part due to how their parents raised them. Ksenya also grew up in a cow-keeping household and learned household food production work from an early age. They have maintained a lifestyle that today is only carried on by a dwindling number of village households. Amid the quantum move away from cow keeping by the majority of Elgeeii residents, Ksenya explained why her household has kept on:

> It's simple . . . when you have your own herd, you have food and you don't need the store. And who knows when the store may not get supplies? As long as we can watch the animals, we will continue. We also do it to keep ourselves active. We will have more time when we retire, like Arkadi's folks. They have a lot of time, and if they had no animals, they would sit in their house all the time and not go outside! With animals you have to be active, to go out and feed them and lead them to pasture. We could supply Arkadi's parents with the products but they refuse. They want the activity and the income. (Ksenya Prokopiyevna Semyonova, interview, May 31, 2019)

Arkadi and Ksenya started keeping their own cows, chickens, and gardens in 1995 when they married and started their own household. Arkadi's parents gave them two starter cows. There have been many changes in Elgeeii since that time. For one, in 1995 their new house was in the woods and outside the bounds of the village, the last house on the way out of town. "From the first year we lived here, our house was so far from anything. In the evening I would come home from work in the dark and the house never seemed to arrive. It seemed I was going along this endless forest. I wondered for a long time, when will I get there? In winter it was like that in the morning going to work, and in the evening coming home also . . . it was so far then but now, with the many households beyond us, it seems close" (ibid.). This expansion is not because the Elgeeii population is growing but rather because more and more households have chosen to abandon the older houses in the center, many of which have not been maintained and also lack the modern aspects that can be built into new construction.

Ksenya and Arkadi depend on hay land that is not within the Elgeeii village hay area. The Elgeeii population is large in proportion to the village's hay area, much of which is across the Viliui River in III Bordong, requiring boat transportation. The village's hay area also continues to shrink from the water on the land, forest encroachment, and areas lost due to government canal digging. Many Elgeeii cow keepers work with their kin to use hay land in the smaller settlements, like Kÿÿkei and Khoro, where the ratio of hay land to households allows for larger lots. Ksenya and Arkadi hay on Arkadi's father's birth *alaas* in Khoro. They use a ten-hectare area on the ancestral *alaas* and recently built an *izbushka* (cabin) there where they spend several weeks in the summer to hay and to duck hunt in the spring and fall. They practice the Sakha allegiances: "When we first go in spring, we hang the *salama* . . . we make a small *yhyakh* there with our close kin . . . we berry there and hay all summer . . . I go there when I hunt . . . we have our *izbushka* there" (Arkadi Nikolayevich Semyonov, interview, July 14, 2018).

Both Arkadi and Ksenya have made decisions in their professional lives that reflect their values and commitments. Arkadi moved from an unfulfilling but secure salaried position in 2011 to start his own business. He began raising red worms to make starting soil and supply local stores and gardeners. Although he has to buy the worms, cow manure is a local resource that is in plentiful quantities.

I am an *Individualnaia Predprinimatel'* [IP, Individual Business], Semyonov IP. I make soil for growing by putting red worms in cow manure. The red worms make good products and they do not sleep. They work all winter and summer. I put the soil they make into packages and sell it to all of the Tatina stores in the Suntaar *uluus*. It is seasonal, only when people start their plants in late winter and early spring. I produce ten tons a year. The rest of the time I do tractor work for people, hauling hay, ice, you name it! (Ibid.)

In 2013, Ksenya changed her work from the nature museum to the Zverov Museum. She explained that she wanted more flexible hours. Later she explained how the new job resonated more closely with her passion,

> I could work from 10 a.m. and had flexibility to come and go. This worked better for me with four children. Also, I knew the director wanted to make a spiritual center and they needed workers there. I was drawn to the museum's focus, researching, teaching, and perpetuating the Sakha language and local folklore, and using the work of Zverov to do so. I wanted to gather the folklore of the Suntaar *uluus*: the *ohuokhai*, the *toiuk* and the *Olonkho* . . . When I first started, I took distance courses in museum pedagogy from the Russian Museum in St Petersburg. I earned a museum management certificate. (Ksenya Prokopiyevna Semyonova, interview, May 31, 2019)

She went on the explain that her passion for language and folklore is rooted in her lineage: she is descended from two well-known Sakha writers, Künde and Nolar.

> My uncle, my father's blood brother, was Ivan Nolar and their uncle was Künde[7] [Aleksey Andreyevich Ivanov (1898–1934)]. I never knew Künde but I did know Ivan Nolar. He lived with us when we were small children for many years when he worked here in Elgeeii. He was trained as a Sakha language teacher. He went on to work as head of the Shei school [map 1] and then worked in Kempandai. In the 1980s he came back here and lived for ten years in a house near ours with his family. He wrote all the time. I remember him telling us so many stories about our family and the past and who lived by which *alaas* in the areas adjacent to Elgeeii. He had health issues and so they moved to the city in the '90s and he passed away in 2006. (Ibid.)

Considering the depth of Nolar's thoughts and writings on Sakha and their relationship to *alaas*, it is not surprising that Ksenya gravitated toward work, both domestic and professional, in which she could perpetuate that ancestral passion.

Ksenya and Arkadi's physical and spiritual roots are firmly in Elgeeii, between their life rhythms with the seasons to produce most of their household's food, to their alignment with their ancestral ties—be it Arkadi's careful tending of his ancestral *alaas* in Khoro, or Ksenya's curation of a more philosophical ancestral lineage via her work at the Zverov Museum. They also have both been keen to speak to me about the myriad changes shaping their local world, be they driven by climate, sociocultural, or economic factors, or a combination thereof.

> For the last ten years, spring comes very early, by about twenty days, and then it freezes again. It never did that before. Before it gradually got warmer and went to summer. Now the snow melts very early and the winds take the water so that the snow water no longer soaks the ground. There are huge winds now that we never had before. Also, on May 9 we always went for *sahaan* [firewood] . . . we went by tractor and the snow was always up to our waists, so we tamped it down as we went. Now by May 1 there is no snow at all. It has been like that for ten years. Before, the river ice went between May 9 and 15. Now it goes between May 1 and the 9. That is a big change. (Arkadi Nikolayevich Semyonov, interview, July 14, 2018)

In 2018, Ksenya explained that the reason the permafrost is thawing is due to climate change and to the huge increase in clear-cutting in the last ten years. She knows through her social circles that many Elgeeii people who have relocated to Yakutsk come to take logs to build a _dacha_ outside the city. She also knows from village news that Aian Suol has been cutting forests nearby for the Russian government to sell to international companies for hard currency. In the midst of a rapidly changing landscape, Ksenya and Arkadi continue to practice a living "by the *alaas*" lifestyle, making all the *ürüng as* and producing a majority of their household food. They are perpetuating a lifestyle founded on their Sakha Indigenous knowledge in the context of village modernity. Their use and preference for Sakha *ürüng as* is also a draw for others, illustrated by the next life history.

I Would Still Be Eating *Tar* Today!

I met Mariya Leekenovna Ivanova (Marusa) and her husband, Semyon Petrovich Yegorov, in summer 1993 when I made my first trip to Tumul to help with my host family's hay-cutting efforts. Marusa and Semyon's home was the first house after we drove over the final cattle guard into Tumul.

Figure 32 Mariya (Marusa) Leekenovna Ivanova with her husband, Semyon Petrovich Yegorov, at home. 2019. Photo by author.

I remember clearly how their house was always bustling with their adult children, grandkids, nieces, and nephews who spent every summer with them in Tumul.

Marusa was born in 1932 on Küület *alaas*, an outlying area ten kilometers from Kÿÿkei (map 1). Shortly thereafter her family relocated to Kÿÿkei proper, to join in the first *kolkhoz*. Marusa knows her ancestry on her mother's side. Her father's parents died early, leaving their seven children orphaned. Each was adopted by a different family and given that family's name. She and her siblings have yet to trace their father's lineage.

Marusa clearly recalls how the *kolkhoz* functioned as a true collective, with workers paid in products, meat, and milk (mostly butter) at the year's end. Everything in domestic households and on the *kolkhoz* was done by hand—the making of clothing, food, and shelter. Nothing was wasted but rather used or put back into the life cycle. "Life was constant work, no different than it had been before the *kolkhoz* were organized. The main difference was that before you worked for yourself and close kin . . . now it was all for the *kolkhoz* and beyond, to the great Soviet cause" (Mariya Leekenovna Ivanova, interview, June 13, 2019).

Marusa shared a particularly thorough and ultimately poignant example
of the ethic that nothing was wasted and all went back into the cycle of life
with her account of *tar*.

> Mother's family had lots of animals before the *kolkhoz* and they lived by the
> *alaas*. We lived off the cows and, from my earliest memories, we had a *tar*
> *ampaar* [shed specifically for *tar*]. Inside was an *ungkachukka* [root cellar,
> cooled by permafrost] and we would pour the milk into there . . . there were
> no separators back then . . . we had a wide flat birch bark container which
> held five to eight kilos [800 grams = 1 liter] called a *chabychakh* . . . and after
> we milked, we poured the milk into there . . . and it stayed in the *chabychakh*
> in the *ungkachukka* for three days until the cream came up to the top. Then
> we would skim it off . . . we had three *chabychakh* and we poured the cream
> into a *yaghas* and with the *ytyk* we would whip it and make butter. We used
> the skim milk to make *suorat* or *iejegei* . . . it was still food . . . back then we
> never threw anything away. (Ibid.)

She explained that, starting in August, they poured any leftover *suorat* into
a large wooden barrel. Marusa's grandfather was a woodworker who made
barrels for *tar* for the family and for others in the community. Every family
had one. In late summer they also put fish bones in the barrel. As the fall
arrived and the temperatures fell, it was important to stir the barrel well
several times a day so it would not freeze. During the fall hunting season,
families would put the bones from their meals of hare and duck into the
tar. Those bones dissolved in a few days from the acidity and provided extra
protein. When the mass was frozen in winter, households cut off chunks
as needed and used the *tar* to make *khaahy* for the daytime meal and as
a drink with the evening meat meal. It lasted throughout the winter. By
May it was almost gone, with milking stopped in early spring as the cows
prepared to calve.

Marusa praised *tar*'s health-sustaining qualities. She could not recall many
instances of colds or other sickness, even though they went barefoot from
the spring melt until the first snowfall in autumn. She explained that this
was in part because they didn't have shoes like those available today—their
mothers and grandmothers made them *eterbes* (soft leather laced-up boots)
out of cow hides for the temperate months which, because of their fragility,
were used only for special occasions.

Discussing and explaining how to make *tar* made Marusa nostalgic for having cows and for having *tar*. She gave up the strenuous daily work of cow keeping when she turned seventy-five and passed the family cows to her daughter, who cares for them to this day and supplies her parents with products. However, *tar* is not in the daughter's resume. In fact, I have yet to meet anyone today who makes *tar*. That in and of itself reflects a change in how Sakha live today and how they lived in the not-so-distant past.

Another historical Sakha foodway that shows a similar trajectory of change is hunting. Although many Sakha continue to hunt to this day, a majority participate only in the spring and fall duck hunting. Fewer and fewer practice the seasonal round of hunting like Yegor Yegorovich Treti-yakov does.

They Call Me "Tungus"

I ask *Baianai* and I say an *algys* and then I feed *Baianai* before I go to hunt. If I do so, he provides. I am Sakha. I know my words are powerful, for good and for bad. I know people who spoke badly and in a short time after that, they died. I am very careful about what I say. (Yegor Yegorovich Tretiyakov, interview, June 18, 2004)

Although Sakha are predominantly a horse- and cattle-breeding people, they have always practiced a full cycle of foraging to supplement their household food stores. Their Turkic ancestors brought time-tested foraging practices to the north, and Sakha expanded them to supplement pastoralism, which was less productive than it was in the south. They also adapted foraging practices to the northern climate, to a large extent by learning the ways of the local Tungus, the Even and Evenk.

When I began research in Elgeeii and Kutana in 1992, many inhabitants practiced the full seasonal rounds of hunting beyond the spring and fall duck hunt. I worked with several in each village who went every year to the far taiga and stayed from October to December to hunt large mammals, including moose, bear, reindeer, and wood fowl—*bochuguras* (grouse) and *ular* (capercaillie). One elder hunter invited me to eat a cube of bear fat that he had preserved from the hunt years before, promising it would bring me good health and wealth.

Figure 33 Yegor Yegorovich Tretiyakov returning home from the hunt, 2019. Photo by author.

In 2019 I was unable to find any hunters in Elgeeii who practiced the distant hunting and only one in Kutana, Yegor Yegorovich Tretiyakov. I have informally tracked his hunting practices since 1992 when I interviewed his father-in-law about the *yhyakh* festival. After that interview Yegor and his family served me reindeer, moose, and duck, all from his catch. He proudly told me that, among the local hunters, his nickname is "Tungus," a title that reflects his mastery of hunting. He had to cut back on his seasonal hunting activities during his working years, when he could not be gone from October to December. During that time, he continued the twice annual duck hunt and the full year round of *sobo* fishing activities. Once he retired, he was often absent from the house, only seen leaving or returning from the hunt with his two horses packed for the trip. In 2019, I realized that he was one among very few left today who continue these seasonal hunting rounds.

Yegor came to Kutana in 1980 to work as an English teacher. Not long after, he married another teacher and they began raising a family. Yegor and his wife kept cows from the time of their marriage until 1995, when the work became too much. They decided to expand their horse herd to trade for cow products.

Yegor has always had a car, not such an anomaly today but definitely one in the 1990s. He used it to trade transportation for cow products and hay. Yegor's life story is reminiscent of Lipa and Volodya's, with their connections to the far west.

My mother's father came from Ukraine. His last name was Vashenko. I remember seeing him when I was in first and second grade. He had white, white hair and bright blue eyes. Vashenko Mikhaila, but they called him *Irigan Mikhaila* [literally "Skinny Michael"]. He came here as a political prisoner then married my grandmother and stayed. He lived here but his lineage was from Ukraine. (Yegor Yegorovich Tretiyakov, interview, May 22, 2019)

Yegor aspired to be a teacher, like both his parents, his mother of the Sakha language and his father of history. He learned his passion for hunting from his father's side:

In third or fourth grade we lived in Orto Khalyma [northern *uluus* in Sakha Republic], where my father was from. He took me in spring to hunt ducks in lakes close to the village. I carried the rucksack and the thermos and our snack. I was small. My father had two rifles, and one of them was not self-loading. It was my job to load it for him. I walked with the long stick that was used to load it . . . it was a long stick! We saw a huge goose and father shot it. I was small and the goose was huge and I held it over my shoulder and it almost touched the ground. (Ibid.)

The rest of his childhood and youth he spent in the Suntaar *uluus*, where his parents had various teaching assignments before they settled in Bordong village, south of the Suntaar regional center. All the while, he continued to hunt with his father. As a youth, he formed a hunting group made up of his peers, which he continued to do off and on throughout his university career and teaching practicum. After settling in Kutana in 1980, he established a more deliberate seasonal round.

When I first came here, I was teaching and so I only hunted on breaks. I got a horse and went for longer hunting trips with other hunters I met here. When I retired, I was free to go and hunt all the hunting seasons. Every September I get a license and hunt moose, going by horseback to the east side toward the

Botomoy stream, an area about seventy kilometers from here. In the winter we use a _baran_ [snowmobile] to set the traps and to check them regularly. I also hunt _taba_ [reindeer]. Starting in mid-October, I hunt _kiis_, _tiing_ [squirrel], and _solondo_ [in Russian, _kolonok_ or Siberian weasel]. I go with a group and we have many _izbushka_, so we go to one and hunt there a few days then go to the next and hunt there a few days and so on. In spring and fall I hunt ducks. I fish _sobo_ all year round. (Ibid.)

His familiarity with these areas farther from the village and his regular visits to them have sensitized him to the changes that are taking place. But Yegor's observation skills go back much further, to his earliest memories as a youth in Bordong and Viluchaan.

When I was a child, the Viliui River was crystal clear. Near Viluchaan there is the Nakhara land place, and when I was small, there was a fisherman named Nikolai Pavlov. His legs were paralyzed. We boys would carry him to the river and he would sit and fish and catch huge fish . . . and he would salt them. The river was crystal clear and full of fish back then. I remember skipping stones and seeing down a meter or two. But after the GES [_Gidroelectric-stanzia_ or hydroelectric station], it became thick and dark and you could see nothing in that water. (Ibid.)

Thanks to his early observations and his current hunting activities, Yegor is aware of this and other ecological issues of the Viliui regions, largely due to the unabated exploitation of diamonds in the Soviet period (Crate 2002) and afterward.

The Institute of Biology has asked hunters to send them animal parts for the last several years. I have sent parts of the moose I hunt to them for a few years now . . . I send the head, the liver, and the heart . . . and they analyze it for their ecological studies. These studies show the level to which the diamond and other environmental issues of the Viliui regions have affected the entire ecosystem and bioaccumulated in these larger mammals. (Yegor Yegorovich Tretiyakov, interview, May 22, 2019)

Yegor is also forthright about the local effects of global climate change. He testified about new species: "For example, I now see many new species of birds I never saw before, for example, *chibis* [lapwing, a crested plover], *küökh batakhtaakh köghön* [*kriakva* or mallard duck], and *poganka* [grebe]." He observes that the fur of certain animals no longer "ripens" sufficiently in the warming winter to be worth what they once were. The starkest changes he recounts are changes in the land in the context of the other drivers of change transforming the landscape.

> In some places the land is burned because we are having so many forest fires . . . in other places, where there were open fields thirty years ago, forests are now invading because people don't use the faraway places anymore. It is very expensive to bring hay from there . . . each hour costs a few thousand rubles. Those once familiar places are today unrecognizable. Additionally, in most places where there once were flat *ötökh* the land is now rolling . . . this is because the permafrost is thawing. (Ibid.)

Yegor's son, Vladik, also details how the land contour has changed from flat to rolling. After I heard both their testimonies, they took me to an area just behind the Tumul settlement. Vladik explained that he drives over the area several times a year to reach the farther areas to hunt ducks. In the last few years, he started noticing how it was more and more difficult to drive there, since the land was rising and falling where it had always been flat. Yegor identified several small trees growing in the dipped places. He estimated them to be ten years old and determied that the changes in the land surface had occurred over that period.

Another reason that Yegor and Vladik are more sensitized to the changes in the surrounding lands is because of the many years they lived with Iza's (Yegor's wife) father, Nikolai Innokentiyevich Ivanov. Iza's father's life work focused on documenting and tracing family genealogies and establishing which kin groups lived "by the *alaas*" in their ancestral homesteads, in areas adjacent to Kutana. There are approximately a hundred of these *alaas* homesteads in the greater Kutana area. Nikolai Innokentiyevich's work becomes that much more relevant in the context of the changing *alaas* of today, caused not only by thawing permafrost due to climate change but also by the abandonment of *alaas* as the inhabitants leave animal work and youth leave the villages. I learned much about Nikolai Innokentiyevich's work from his daughters, Iza and her sister Matryona.

Living with 100 *Alaas*

Izabella Nikolayevna Tretiyakova, Iza, is an extremely modest and soft-spoken person. She does not immediately come across as someone with a wealth of knowledge of change. It has only been over the course of three decades that I have come to know her keen understanding of change, in its many forms.

During the time of water on the land, she shared her awareness of the local effects of climate change and their impacts on her household's food production.

> Our garden grows late now, and it supplies all our winter food. Sakha have a saying, "One day in summer is worth a week of winter survival." But recently our garden sits under water. We used to have hay in the area but now a water grass grows because there is so much water. We used to get fifteen bags of potatoes but in the last few years only five at the most. (Izabella Nikolayevna Tretiyakova, survey, June 12, 2009)

Recently Iza shared her intimate knowledge of *alaas* via the legacy of her father, Nikolai Innokentiyevich Ivanov. I focus on Iza's father's work through both her recollections and his documentation to emphasize both how effective her father and his work were in the past and continue to be to this today.

Thanks to her father's vocation, Iza knows her ancestral lineage back ten generations. She has never moved from where she lives today. Iza and Yegor's present house is next to the house in which she was born and raised. Iza explained that her ancestral roots are in the *intelligentsia* [intellectuals] of the Soviet period. Being part of the *intelligentsia* did not in and of itself imperil individuals unless they chose to fight the Soviet system.

Figure 34 Izabella Nikolayevna Tretiyakova, at home. 2019. Photo by author.

My ancestors were studied people. In the Soviet time, with the 1930s repres-
sion, my kin went to Moldavia and other places to live, like Germany, America and France. My *ehe* on my mother's side taught in Kirgizia. He later came
back here to get his family and take them back to Kirgizia with him. But the
authorities caught him and accused him of being a Japanese spy. He was
shot, and his family came to Kutana to live. (Izabella Nikolayevna Tretiyakova, interview, May 23, 2019)

Iza's father, Nikolai Innokentiyevich, was born in 1915 near Kutana at
his family homestead on the Jonkuoduma *alaas*, toward Shei (map 1). He
finished school in Shei at age seventeen and moved to Kutana to teach. He
quickly earned the nickname *Kuola-Uchuutal* (Kolya Teacher) because he
was so young to be a teacher. When World War II began, he stayed home
from the front to care for his mother, a single mother who had suddenly lost
her sight at twenty-five. Iza clearly remembers her *ebe*:

Tatiyana was our most wonderful *ebe* . . . every night she told us such good
stories like *Bies Ynakhtaakh Beiberikeen Emeekhsin, Alam Oghus* [The splen-
did bull], and many she made up herself. She played the *khomus*. When she
made our *eterbes* . . . we would hold the skins for her while she sewed. She
also milked cows . . . dad would guide her with a rope to the *khoton* and she
milked. I guided her so she could go from house to house to have tea with
neighbors and know the village news. She also was called to do the rites at
funerals. She knew the *sier tuom* [Sakha sacred practices] . . . and I would
take her and we had to wear very fancy clothes and I would lead her in and
light a candle and feed the spirits with *alaaji* . . . I was not afraid . . . we did a
lot of funerals . . . at that time you would bring people to the sky world with
the Sakha *sier tuom*. (Ibid.)

As Nikolai Innokentiyevich's teaching career continued, his passion for
local history increased. That passion soon led him to start a museum, something he pursued outside of his already demanding teaching responsibilities.
He not only researched, documented, and displayed local and regional history in the museum, he also began a project to reestablish Kutana inhabitants' ancestral lineages. Although parents and grandparents at the time did
not tell their children anything about their ancestral lineage because of the

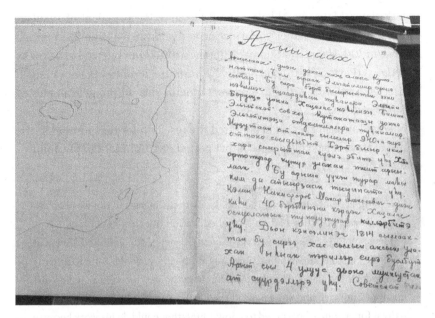

Figure 35 A sample of Nikolai Innokentiyevich Ivanov's notebooks, showing the clear penmanship that made it possible for his daughter to transcribe his work into a book. This page from *100 Alaas* shows the *alaas* Aryylaakh, on the road between Kutana and Elgeeii. The last sentences read: "People say that from 1814 there were huge *yhyakh* here with people gathering from four settlements for it. There were great horse races." Photo by author.

forced forgetting of the Soviet period, Nikolai Innokentiyevich was actively researching and documenting these lineages.

> He opened the museum in 1959 and he would stay there all the days when he was not teaching, sitting for long hours with the men and women of Kutana as they told him their ancestors. He wrote in many, many small notebooks, and luckily he had excellent penmanship. He made a special effort to get Marlboro cigarettes and Cuban cigars as *kehii* [gifts for host or participant] for the people who came to work with him. At the same time that he asked about their ancestral lineages, he also recorded the location and place-name of their ancestral *alaas*, charting it on a map in relation to Kutana and recording who lived there and when … eventually that information became the *100 Alaas* book. (Ibid.)

Iza's sister, Matryona Nikolayevna Pavlova, today a resident of Yakutsk, consolidated all their father's information and published two books, *Suntaar Kutanatin 100 Alaastara* (Suntaar Kuntana's 100 *Alaas*; referred to below as 100 *Alaas*) (Pavlova 2015) and *Suntaar Kutanatin Töröötere* (Pavlova 2012). The latter, *Suntaar's Kutana Ancestors*, documents all the genealogies of Kutana residents.

Nikolai Innokentiyevich had started the research for his museum in the 1940s. Matryona's recollections of that period give us insight to the political changes over time.

> Our people, before the Soviet period, knew their lineage all the way back to Tygyn Darkhand. They had no formal education but they could recite their lineages. Not everyone knew it. Just a few in each settlement and always at least one person. Case in point, there was a 100 plus-year-old woman from my husband Alosha's land of Orohu [settlement in the Verkhnyviliuisk region just north of Suntaar], and she knew all the Orohu people's lineages. She would write it for anyone who wanted to know. Our father could do his work because he started after Stalin's time. No one talked in the '30s–'40s because of Stalin's repression policies. That was the time when our greatest people, Oyunski, Ammosov, Kulakovski—smart brilliant Sakha *intelligentsia*, were accused of nationalism and went to prison to die. People saw that and were scared. Nevertheless, local people remembered their ancestral lineages and carried that knowledge with them. Dad started the museum in 1959, and by then it was safe to openly talk about this. There were sixty-to-seventy-year-old people in Kutana who remembered their lineages. The word got out that Dad was busy with this work. Local people trusted him. He was the Party secretary. They went to him and worked with him. We published the book of all the lineages in 2012. In Dad's time there were no books like this. But when there was an anniversary or a wedding, Dad would

Figure 36 Matryona Nikolayevna Pavlova at the National Library. Photo by Alexander Pavlov.

take a nice piece of paper and write out the couple's lineages as a wedding gift. People also came to him and ask and he wrote it out for them. (Matryona Nikolayevna Pavlova, interview, June 26, 2019)

When I asked Matryona where her father's fascination with tracing ancestral lineages came from, she explained,

Our mother was an orphan. In 1931, her father was labeled a Japanese spy and they shot him. Her mother then changed her name from Fillipova to Alekseyeva and ran away to Kirgizia and Belorussia. Our mother never knew many of her relatives. When Mom and Dad married, one or two of her kin came to the wedding and they talked about their kin. Dad started to trace her lineage based on what those people said. I think that is why he started writing other people's lineages. He was interested and saw that it needed to be done. After he researched and wrote up Mother's lineage, he then wrote his own and then started asking others and, in the end, it turned into writing the ancestral lineages for the whole village! (Ibid.)

If we consider the powerful way that political oppression worked to "uproot" people by discouraging and repressing their knowledge of their ancestral past, it is equally powerful to consider how Nikolai Innokentiyevich's work to reconstruct those lineages was able to reify those roots for many: "A woman named Fatina in Kutana was an orphan. Her parents died when she was very young. But it turned out her father had long before talked to our father and Dad had recorded all their lineage. When she found out, she was so happy! Before the book was published, she was like a floater in life with no sense of belonging and then she saw her lineage and suddenly had roots, suddenly had an identity" (ibid.).

Not only did his work bring new meaning to contemporary people's lives, as in Fatina's case, but it also provided insight to the rapid changes of the recent past, aspects of life in the last generation. For example, in the process of his interviews with local people and his own historical research, Nikolai Innokentiyevich documented information about Kutana's powerful *oiuun* (shamans), beginning in the thirteenth century up to the early Soviet period. One of them, Dmitri Afanaseyev, who went by the nickname *Khangkhachakh uola* (Pavlova 2012: 14), was the father of a man I met and interviewed when I first came to Kutana in 1992. *Khangkhachakh uola*'s son, Matvei Dmitriyevich

Afanaseyev, told me at length about his father's gift and how it was forbidden in Soviet times. The day after our interview he demonstrated how the *oiuun* does a <u>*kamlaniia*</u> (incantation) (figure 37). In the book, Nikolai Innokenti- yevich also speaks of how, up until 1918 when the Soviets opened a medical station in Kutana, residents relied on the *oiuun* for healing.

Nikolai Innokentiyevich had a very strong sense of connection to his birth *alaas* and to the healing power of *alaas* overall, expressed in a few lines of his poem "Alaaspar Sirittim" (When I Go to My *Alaas*),

> The fragrance of our *alaas* is everywhere
> Our hearts brighten
> The air there is cool and clean
> It strengthens our energy
>
>   (Pavlova 2015: 6)

Nikolai Innokentiyevich regularly took school groups on outings to study the *alaas*. In his writings, documented in *100 Alaas*, he states that the objectives of those outings were for students to learn the toponyms (place- names); who lived there in the recent past; the size of the fields and their expanse of hay; the fence lines; and how each *alaas* was used from the past to the present (Pavlova 2015: 9). But he was similarly intent on the students documenting ongoing changes: "The students didn't know the *alaas* names and he thought it was important for them to know them. Also, he saw the land changing, wondered why that was and thought the students should also know. So, he took them on outings to learn the *alaas* and to observe and know the changes, writing it all down. It is all in the *100 Alaas* book. Before our people lived on the *ötökh* by the *alaas*" (Matryona Nikolayevna Pavlova, interview, June 26, 2019).

Matryona Nikolayevna published her father's work in the *100 Alaas* book specifically to bring that important work to more people. Not only did her father record the birth *alaas* of those he wrote lineages with, he also mapped the *alaas* to locate who lived where.

I met and interviewed Nikolai Innokentiyevich in 1992 about his knowl- edge and understanding of the *yhyakh*. I knew nothing, at that time, about his work documented in *100 Alaas*. It was not until a 2008 focus group, that Kutana's geography teacher, Svetlana Gavrilovna Martinova, who had spo- ken knowledgeably about the effects of climate change on local ecosystems,

Figure 37 Matvei Dmitriyevich Afanaseyev, *Khangkhachakh uola*'s son, demonstrates for me how an *oiuun* heals. 1992. Photo by author.

Figure 38 Nikolai Innokentiyevich Ivanov leading one of his many school outings to teach students about their birth *alaas*. September 1, 1959. Photographer unknown. Photograph documented by author from Kutana school history display, 2019.

explained that she knew about this from taking students out to study the *alaas*. In an interview later that summer she said she was carrying on Nikolai Innokentiyevich's legacy. When I brought up the topic two years later, in 2010, she said she had stopped taking her students on such outings because the school administrators "decided this study had no future in it for the youth. They said youth need to focus on business and economics." In 2019 I suggested reviving these field trips to the *alaas*, especially with the once-flat *ötökh* on the *alaas* now rolling from the permafrost thaw. Svetlana explained that today they cannot take students on outings into adjacent areas for safety reasons. Bears have been coming close to the village in search of food, because of changes in their range and scarcity of food from the drought, both due to climate change. Today's young people also have no drive to explore the woods and fields around their villages as they did in the previous generations. They tend to stay inside on their phones and computers.

Tying It All Together

These windows into people's lives that life histories provide reveal individuals' vast knowledge of place and time and bring to light how change, in its many forms, comes into contemporary life. The life histories change what may appear as a "sleepy old town" into a place of vibrant life. They reflect knowledge of rootedness to place, as shown by Anatoli Petrovich's accounts of how his ancestors came to inhabit the area centuries ago, and by Tatiyana's strong sense of homeland despite her recent arrival from the other end of Russia. They document the in-depth knowledge people have of their environment, from Valerian the *sylgyhyt*, to Yegor the *bulchut* (hunter), to Sardana the fisher and nature lover. Some of the life histories convey how very different life is now and how much has changed, from Lipa traveling by a three-horse caravan to show films, to Marusa knowing cold by its sound, to Margarita's accounts of her grandfather's "deserter" status and her grandmother's six-month walk back to Elgeeii from Yakutsk. Ultimately the life histories show how, in many ways, Sakha continue to live "by the *alaas*" whether by practicing a household-level food production as Ksenya and her in-laws do, or by returning to the physical places of *alaas* as recounted by Osip, or by perpetuating knowledge of how inhabitants lived "by the *alaas*" through Matryona and Iza's efforts to keep alive the lifework of their father, Nikolai Innokentiyevich.

Sakha knowledge of *alaas* far predates the scientific understanding of *alaas*. In the vernacular understandings, Sakha continue to have a much broader understanding of *alaas* that encompasses most of the areas where Sakha's Turkic horse- and cattle-breeding ancestors settled to make their lives in the north.

I know that many people say that we don't have "real" *alaas* in the Viliui regions. They need to understand that we have a different understanding of *alaas* from the central regions . . . *alaas* is a not necessarily a big round place. Here we understand it as an area where people can live and where they have all they need to live . . . we call that *alaas* . . . others think of *alaas* as a huge area with specific contours . . . here we have big fields and such that we understand as *alaas*, many of which are smaller places, the *ötökh* and there is always a lake. (Izabella Nikolayevna Tretiyakova, interview, May 23, 2019)

In a contemporary context it is more important to focus on how individuals perceive *alaas* based on their tacit knowledge system. Most often there is an intergenerational difference. Oksana, the kin of Anatoli Petrovich who traveled with us to Oghuruottaakh, was living in Elgeeii when I first met her in 1992. In 2002 she moved back home to Kutana to care for her ailing mother and keep the family herd. Her and Anatoli Petrovich's understanding of their sacred *alaas* differ greatly. Whereas Anatoli Petrovich will immediately talk about Oghuruottaakh, Oksana waxes poetically about Kutana Lake, where her present house is located: "My sacred *alaas* is my contemporary yard. It is close to water, the lake. My parents came here from Oghuruottaakh in 1958 for the *sovkhoz*. I have lived here all my life except for six years in Elgeeii . . . I never noticed the lake until now that I am older. The lake is my teacher and a little world in and of itself . . . I have it all . . . my territory . . . my sacred *alaas*" (Oksana Petrovna Sofronova, interview, June 12, 2018).

Ksenya, of Oksana's generation, similarly understands her sacred *alaas* as her immediate home in Elgeeii: "Elgeeii is my birthland and my sacred *alaas*. Anywhere else I go, it is different . . . Elgeeii is wide with lots of fresh air and it sits on the river bank . . . it is good" (Ksenya Prokopiyevna Semyonova, interview, May 31, 2019). Younger inhabitants identify their birthplace, typically, within their village boundaries and its immediate environs as their sacred *alaas*, while those older describe their sacred *alaas* as the outlying areas of their contemporary village, most often also the place of their birth and youth.

These life histories also highlight inhabitants' knowledge of how climate change is affecting their lives and their ability to continue to live "by the *alaas*," from Iza's loss of household food production due to flooding; to the changes in duck hunting that Sardana observes; to Valerian's remorse over the changes in snow, the horse's home; to Osip and Tatiyana's laments of how logging and increased *tekhnika* are ravishing the local nature; to the several accounts of the change in the landscape due to thawing permafrost. Often these witnesses of environmental change are cognizant of the complexity of change, from Tatiana's explanation of the increased wind of late from both global climate patterns and the many trees cut for export, to Marusa's description of the interactions between climate change and deforestation that have led to permafrost thaw.

This intimate Indigenous knowledge is critical in the bigger picture of how longitudinal ethnographic findings matter. They provide the in-road to understanding how the complex global drivers of change are coming into and affecting not only the physical world of Viliui Sakha but also their cultural and spiritual worlds, their ability to continue, albeit in a more virtual form today, to live "by the *alaas*." Likewise, they also make clear the important role of engaging scientific knowledge of changing permafrost and *alaas* in concert with those local understandings. Ultimately, ushering in the necessary innovations and adaptations for the future is about the ability to engage all available knowledge systems.

Gone the *Alaas*

Knowing Permafrost and Alaas in the 21st Century

My depth of understanding about how climate change was affecting Sakha's lives reached a turning point when I met with Alexander Fyodorov in the summer of 2018. For the fourteen years of our collaboration, he had consistently greeted me with a warm, welcoming smile and handshake, after which we shared a few bits of personal and family news and then moved into our mutual work. This time he gave only a quick handshake and a nod then went right to his concerns about the pace of permafrost degradation. His distress was visceral. His mood was uncharacteristically solemn and his energy low. He showed me satellite images that illustrated the extent of thermokarst development, which visually appears as polygon formation in the *alaas* landscapes. My journal entry from that day describes it best:

> When I arrived to meet with Alexander today, he hurriedly showed me satellite and google earth shots of rapidly changing landscapes due to thawing permafrost. He next showed his work in Churapcha, documenting how land areas are sinking, and especially so in the Soviet-period agricultural fields. Next he showed me an overhead shot of a village runway that had completely turned to thermokarst, a 12-foot-wide strip of roundish humps with dips in between as the land sank and rose. He commented that planes cannot land in the settlement anymore. Next he showed me the "young families' neighborhood," and area in the same settlement that was established in 2013

for household plots, now riddled with same thawing thermokarst pattern. I asked why they would build it there under those conditions and he said, "they have no other land." Next, he showed shots from the Amma region, commenting, "All these areas are also falling. These areas used to be fields that produced a lot of food. Now it produces none . . . how can they live further? Entire fields are useless now from the combination of human activity and climate change." He then showed me forest areas devastated by the shelkopriad [the Siberian silk moth, *Dendrolimus superans sibiricus*], a pest that has been unleashed in the Siberian taiga due to warming temperatures. He explained that the defoliation from the silkworm negates the forest's ability to act as a protective cover for the permafrost. I wondered, where will it all end? (Journal entry, May 15, 2018)

He went on to explain that he and other researchers and policy people were pushing legislation to protect the permafrost. Their aim is to protect against the appropriation of land via two federal programs, the domestic program *Gektar* (Russian for "hectare" and referring to the Far Eastern Hectare [FEH] program which offers one hectare of land in the Russian Far East to Russian citizens), and the international program TOR (*Territoriia operezhaiushchevo razvitiia* or Territory of Advanced Development), aimed at attracting foreign investment by relaxing restrictions for resource exploitation. The results of the latter program were evident in the taiga forests east of Lake Baikal after Chinese interests were able to purchase and subsequently deforest thousands of hectares there. Multiple news stories, like "China's Voracious Appetite for Timber Stokes Fury in Russia and Beyond" (Meyers 2019), and the abundance of YouTube videos to educate people on the issue (e.g., "Siberia" 2018), document residents' inability to prevent the deforestation. Alexander stated that if such buy-ups of land and deforestation happened in the Sakha Republic, it would completely devastate the permafrost. My immersion in the array of new changes, including the acceleration of the thaw, the policy developments, and the implications of national resource grabs ushered in a new urgency to my own and our collective work.

I then asked Alexander how I could best prepare for my summer fieldwork, including the investigation of changes in the permafrost of Elgeeii and Kutana. I needed to understand what changes people would be seeing and talking about that I might be able to link to permafrost thaw. He explained that although the Suntaar *uluus* did not have the scientifically defined *alaas* found in the central regions, it nonetheless had a similar high-ice-content permafrost equally susceptible to warming. Therefore, I could expect to see changes in the plane of the land surface—holes where the ice had thawed and sunk down and rises where it had pushed up.

Toward the end of our meeting, I expressed my desire to see the scientifically defined *alaas* of the central regions, where Alexander had worked all of his professional career. I wanted not only to see the physical landscape but also to understand the communities' experiences and their perceptions of permafrost, *alaas*, and change. That August, on my way home from the field, we planned a December trip to the central regions, to Siirdaakh, where Alexander has conducted research since 1993, and to Khatilii, where he has worked since 2009.

Winter Journey

We left Yakutsk in a bitter cold −34 degrees Celsius fog on December 12, 2018, in a YAZ van (a Soviet-style jeep-van that is renowned for its ability on rural dirt roads). I sat in the front seat so I could be close to the only heat source. I still froze, with the wind piercing through cracks in windows and doors. Miraculously, for someone who is always cold, it didn't bother me. In fact, I was distracted by the clear views of the landscape and the changes in the central regions that the front seat afforded me. The changes were stark, with field after field riddled with humps and dips. I was not in the Viliui regions anymore! Two decades before I had been to the *yhyakh* in Tatta and Amma in the central regions. My encounters with these landscapes then contrasted greatly with what I saw now.

> Just back from the road trip with Alexander . . . I wanted to be sure to record
> how stunned I am by how much the landscapes there have changed. This
> is so different from what I remember when I was there in the late '90s and
> from the Viliui regions! Here we were driving down the road past field after
> field filled with humps and dips from the thermokarst polygons forming . . .
> Unbelievable . . . I posted some shots on Facebook and folks back home are
> also shocked. (Journal entry, December 14, 2018)

Shortly before arriving in Khatilii, our first village, we stopped at the boundary of the Churapcha region, taking a side road to a bank near the

Figure 39 View out the window as we drove to Khatilii. I was shocked at how the once flat fields were now transformed into a patchwork of thermokarst thaw. December 2018. Photo by author.

river. Alexander grabbed the bag of *alaaji* he had bought at the <u>*stolovaia*</u> (cafeteria) where we stopped for tea. We got out and walked to the bank, where Alexander lay *alaaji* in a circle to feed the *sir ichchite*. He said words asking for permission for us to be there and to do our work.

We arrived in Khatilii and were greeted at the school with a formal Sakha ritual of *alaaji* and *kymys*, and a performance of Sakha poetry and song by the students. The organizers led us to a large classroom, where we facilitated a "knowledge exchange" (for more on knowledge exchanges, see pp. 224–29). The next morning, we headed to Siirdaakh, located in the neighboring Ust Aldan *uluus*. There we also facilitated a knowledge exchange in the school auditorium. In both locations, we had audiences of thirty to forty residents, with the active engagement of community members, teachers, and students.

The knowledge exchanges began with audience members sharing their observations of change, describing landscape changes adjacent to their household and also in their ancestral *alaas* areas. Alexander then presented his research, explaining the overall changes to the Sakha Republic due to climate change, how permafrost was thawing to cause cataclysmic events in other areas of the Arctic, what these changes mean for the central regions, and the implications for inhabitants' settlements. Alexander then explained what people could do to help protect the permafrost. He recommended that people clear snow immediately after it fell in their yards to keep the permafrost exposed to the cold air and not insulated by snow. He used the aerial image of a household's yard which had been protected in this way as an example (figure 40). He said inhabitants could also counteract the thawing process by filling the holes resulting from thawing with available materials, including bark, manure, and soil. Seeing the extreme extent of landscape transformation so close to inhabitants' homes in Alexander's images, and how eagerly audience members took up these ideas to possibly postpone relocation, was a humbling experience for me. I was struck by how knowledgeable inhabitants were about the changes in the permafrost and their eagerness to do what they could to abate it.

Following Alexander's presentation, I spoke about my work with communities in the Viliui regions and the similar changes people there were

Figure 40 Aerial shot of dangerous thermokarst development in Sylan village, Churapchinskii *uluus*. Photo credit: A. N. Fedorov.

witnessing. I emphasized the critical place of individuals' and communities' knowledge, of the intimate and highly refined expertise that inhabitants had developed and used to negotiate life in this extreme climate. I further explained how important it was to engage that vernacular knowledge in consort with scientific knowledge, like what Alexander had shared, in order to have a more complete understanding of change and thereby be able to develop sounder plans for adaptation. We finished up with an open question-and-answer discussion.

After each of the two knowledge exchanges in the schools, we interviewed several inhabitants (two in Siirdaakh, three in Khatilii) to get a very preliminary understanding of how the complexity of change was affecting the local population. Questions included the status of cow keeping, perceptions of the three main drivers of the complexity of change (climate, youth out-migration, and economy), understandings of *alaas*, and opinions about youth's future.

All interviewees reported fewer and fewer cows in their village, and attributed the decline to two main causes: village youth not taking up cow care or leaving the village to pursue their future elsewhere; and the lack of incentive to keep cows, since prices for their products were too low. A few cited the increased difficulty of cow keeping due to permafrost thaw in the *alaas*. Those who still kept cows talked about how many of their neighbors were gradually transitioning to horses.

> Cows are fewer and fewer every year . . . we are trying to organize farming but this will only happen with the government's help. On Siirdaakh's west side, where I live, we used to have many, many cows . . . all the households there had cows . . . now only two or three households have them. We had two milkers but slaughtered one this year. But we have thirty horses. Others like us are changing their herds to horses. Horses are easier. (Yevdokiya Fyodorovna Olisova, interview, December 13, 2018)

The preference for horses over cows also came up when discussing youth. "Today's youth want to be free . . . if they keep any animals, they keep horses . . . horses are easier and don't need daily care . . . if you have cows you can't go anywhere" (Lidiya Nikolayevna Fillipova, interview, December 12, 2018). Several people tied their settlement's diminishing cow numbers to the bounty in the village stores, explaining that people now no longer had to produce most of their own food like they did right after the end of the Soviet Union.

Interviewees in both villages also testified about the changes in the landscape that they were observing and the implications for their food supply:
"We had lots of fields . . . we grew lots of grains here . . . our region was known
for the amount of grain that we grew . . . we grew the most per hectare than
any place in the Sakha Republic . . . now we don't grow because our fields are
useless . . . they are thawing and falling in . . . now all our food is brought to
us" (Valeri Ivanovich Danilov, interview, December 13, 2018).

I found myself feeling quite overwhelmed during these interviews. It is
one thing to learn about the changes in the land from the comfort of Alexander's office, viewing the satellite data. It is another experience entirely to talk
to people who have a deep connection to these landscapes, are living with
these changes and are trying their best to stay in their homeland. Inhabitants
have been learning from Alexander for several years now and trying the
techniques he shares to slow down the processes.

> At first our lands look good but then these holes appear . . . first they are
> small and then they grow larger and then the land falls down a meter or so.
> This is happening by my house. I fill the holes with trash and horse manure
> and tree bark so that they don't grow bigger. I never saw this before. It is
> from the warming that the land is thawing and falling in. (Lidiya Nikolayevna
> Fillipova, interview, December 12, 2018)

Several inhabitants' explanations reflected how they were combining their
intimate knowledge of place with what Alexander is teaching: "Where there
is a slant in the land, I know there is a set of polygons there and when water
gets in, then it all slides down the slope. I see it on the sides of the *alaas* . . . I
never saw this before!" (Nikita Nikolayevich Novgorodin, interview, December 12, 2018). Similarly, "The permafrost melts, the water comes up, the land
falls and makes a lake and then after that, it dries . . . it is a long process . . .
here we have many small, small *alaas*—we are in the middle of the three
rivers and are on a high place with many small *alaas*" (ibid.).

When I asked interviewees about the meaning of *alaas*, inhabitants of
Siirdaakh and Khatilii described both the physical and the cultural meanings.

> *Alaas* are where, long ago, the ice melted and the land fell to form lakes and
> hay fields . . . but lately with the fires and with the _shelkopriad_ that are eating
> the larches, the land falls faster and the water comes into the land from all

directions and fills the *alaas* with water. We also have lots of water from the very rainy summers now.... *Alaas* have a second meaning for all Sakha people. It means our ancestral birthplace. From long, long ago Sakha have been born and raised in the *alaas*. There they got hay and wood and were made into a person. All Sakha have *alaas* . . . and there is a summer *alaas* and a winter *alaas* . . . from long, long ago. Now we are in the village from the collective and state farm times. Nevertheless, I know my birth *alaas* and when I go there my spirit feels lighter, and I think about how my grandmother and grandfather lived there. There are small trails from one *alaas* to another and when I walk there, I think about how, as a child, my father probably ran along that path to the other *alaas*. (Lidiya Nikolayevna Fillipova, interview, December 12, 2018)

When the topic turned to the future for village youth, inhabitants shared a mixture of feelings. They both complained that youth were leaving and spoke with pride that their youth were making a life for themselves. "Many go to study and don't return . . . there is no work here. I have two children, and one works in Suntaar and one in the city. If they came to live here, there would be no work for them and so no progress for them either" (Yevdokiya Fyodorovna Olisova, interview, December 13, 2018).

Beyond these preliminary understandings of how inhabitants were perceiving the complexity of change in their lives and their understandings of *alaas*, another important moment for me was in the context of feedback on the knowledge-exchange process overall.

Thank you so much for coming . . . in the '70s there was a symposium here in Siirdaakh with foreigners—but we knew nothing about what happened . . . in the last few years people like you are coming to help us understand. For example, we now know so much from Alexander and you. We understand that we need to do a program here to plant trees and protect the permafrost . . . we need to do everything we can! (Ibid.)

The symposium in the 1970s that this respondent mentioned was part of the Second International Conference on Permafrost, held in Yakutsk in 1973. Siirdaakh was one of several fieldtrip sites after the main event. The trip to Siirdaakh was slated to show participants forest landscapes, sediments of the inter-*alaases* (yedoma)[1] with re-vein ice[2] and the organization of thermophysical studies of cryogenic processes at the monitoring station of the Permafrost Institute of the Siberian Branch of the USSR Academy of Sciences field station.[3] The conference organizers decided to bring participants to Siirdaakh because it was home to one of the most active lake/*alaas* systems. P. I. Melnikov, founder of the Institute of Permafrost in Yakutsk, promised the participants who chose to venture to Siirdaakh that they would see "the classic *alaas* landforms resembling the surface of the moon" (Melnikov 1978: 892). It is sobering to reflect today on Melnikov's closing words for the conference, held fifty years ago, considering how little of what he recommended has been done.

> Man's increasing encroachment upon the northern areas, the nature of which, strange as it may seem, is especially fragile and vulnerable, confronts us with the *urgent problem of developing, as quickly as possible, research connected with environmental protection and the efficient use of the natural resources of these areas.* Far too little attention is being devoted to problems pertaining to the relation of the cryosphere to the biosphere. *Economic activity in regions with exceedingly harsh natural conditions urgently calls for a fundamental solution to this problem as well.* (Ibid., emphasis added)

It is not for a lack of permafrost research activity that negligible actions have been taken thus far but rather because of a failure for those research findings to guide the Sakha Republic's economic activities.

We drove home after the last presentation, arriving in Yakutsk at midnight. In my follow-up with Alexander the next day, he explained more about local people's determination to stay: "They see the processes happening and they consider it their most important task to decide how they can continue to live there. No one wants to leave. They are in their homelands, by their birth *alaas*. We need to get the information to people about how they can protect the permafrost and continue to live in their homelands" (Alexander Nikolayevich Fyodorov, personal communication, December 14, 2018).

Alexander emphasized that educating people this way is critical not only so they can stay in their homelands but also so they can avoid the dangerous consequences as the permafrost thaw progressed. I immediately thought of one of the most striking images of Alexander's presentation, an aerial photo showing holes filled with water opening up right next to people's yards (figure 40). "These degraded areas are just going to get worse . . . take, for example, the house in this picture right next to an expanding hole of water . . . the ice underneath is continuing to thaw and the water will increase and take all the permafrost . . . to form a complete thermokarst area . . . a lake" (ibid.).

Alexander had used this same image to explain how residents could actively protect the permafrost under their yards by clearing snow as it fell. However, with the progression just outside their yards, it is questionable how long those kinds of prophylactic measures can work. Alexander underscored the importance of providing these affected communities with information they can readily access:

> This is my point: these are multiple academic journals about permafrost but very few are printed . . . for example, there are only 115 copies of the Russian scientific journal «Криосфера Земли» *Kriosfera Zemli* [Earth's cryosphere] across the entire planet. How can this information possibly get to people if only 115 copies are published? This low number of printings is true for most of the other academic journals on permafrost. But this is not the information inhabitants need—even if they could get these journals, they would not understand the information in them. (Ibid.)

I asked about the importance of projections and models to help local people understand future changes. Alexander does briefly mention trends and trajectories in his presentations, but he explained that it is important not to dwell too much on these. "Scientists are doing the public a huge wrong if they are not honest about the fact that we really do not know what will happen in the future. I focus on what we know from the science for today."

Equally important to providing affected communities with understandable information that they can use to continue to live and avoid danger is for scientific knowledge to be used in developing governmental protocols and future planning. In early 2019 the Sakha president introduced plans to develop the agricultural sector. This is a victory for Sakha who wish to continue rural cow keeping. However, the proposed development was in exactly the areas most sensitive to permafrost and *alaas* degradation, depicted by the dark areas of map 8.

When Alexander told me of this, I asked about trying to educate the government representatives so they would know how dangerous this is. He shook his head and commented that he has tried but to no avail: all his efforts

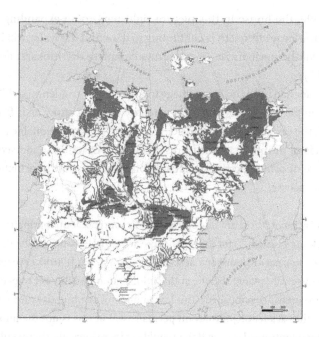

Map 8 Map showing ice-rich permafrost areas (darkened areas), the landscapes in Yakutia most vulnerable to climate warming and anthropogenic impacts. Map by A. N. Fedorov.

have landed on deaf ears. He recalled how the Yakutsk-based representatives of the Churapcha *uluus* were allocated funds to build an Institute of Physical Education and an adjoining Sports School in Churapcha's regional center. It was to be a complex unique across all of Russia. Alexander knew from the satellite data that the land where they intended to build the complex was completely riddled with thermokarst from thawing permafrost. He worked hard to educate the initiators of the project about the dangers, citing how quickly the thermokarst was progressing on the area of the intended complex (figure 41*a* and *b*). Despite his efforts, the project was completed and now awaits its problematic future.

The more I learned about the thaw and the urgency to educate people, from the local to the policy levels, the more permafrost took on a life of its own. It became a living being that humanity needed to appease and comfort to reverse its dangerous trajectory; a sleeping giant, under the ground, who had decided to turn over in very slow motion with few, if any, prospects of turning back. Anthropogenic climate change has set this process in motion,

Figure 41a Institute of Physical Education and adjoining Sports School in Churap-cha's regional center. Notice the ground already becoming uneven from thermokarst development (thawing permafrost). Photo credit: A. N. Fedorov.

Figure 41b Aerial view of the planned sports complex showing thermokarst development. Photo credit: A. N. Fedorov.

and it will be increasingly difficult to turn it around; if allowed to continue unabated, it will prove perilous.

Permafrost and *Alaas* Science in the Anthropocene

The scientific knowledge of permafrost made major advances with the onset of anthropogenic climate change. Attributing changes underground to a warming atmosphere is not straightforward. However, if considered on the global scale, and by integrating data of air, water and land changes, there is unrefuted evidence that climate change is the central driver of permafrost change (cf. IPCC 2019). Early on, scientists used landscape geography methods, developed in the 1980s, to understand the novel permafrost dynamics that appeared due to climate change and to gauge the extent of permafrost degradation. The approach entailed using spatial and temporal models to identify changes in permafrost development, its recovery after disturbance, and changing vegetation patterns (Alexander Nikolayevich Fyodorov, personal communication, December 14, 2018). Feldman and Shur introduced a new method of understanding permafrost dynamics by modeling heat transfer from the atmosphere to the lithosphere (Feldman et al. 1988; Shur 1988). This approach has proven crucial to today's urgent need to predict the development of thermokarst that signals global climate effects on underlying permafrost.

Today permafrost covers 22.79 million km^2 (approximately 14 million miles^2). Permafrost underlays one-fourth of the Northern Hemisphere and 17 percent of the planet's exposed land surface (Biskaborn et al. 2019). These permafrost areas are home to 35 million people, including three dense cities with over 100,000 residents (Chadburn et al. 2017: 342). Permafrost, in all its forms and manifestations, is highly sensitive to rising air temperatures and changing snow regimes, two ecosystem parameters that have been changing significantly in the last few decades owing to global climate change (ibid.; IPCC 2019). Considering how infrastructure in these permafrost areas is often highly, if not completely, dependent on the freezing and thawing qualities of permafrost, the implications of permafrost degradation for human settlements could be cataclysmic. However, aside from episodic sudden events, most of the changes in permafrost due to anthropogenic climate change are gradual and are significant only when seen over longer time periods. This fact initiated the global community's efforts to monitor permafrost change in the late 1990s.

Some posit that monitoring began in the city of Yakutsk in the F. Shergin mine (Chzhan et al. 2010). But it was only in the 1930s that the meteorological service of the USSR began widespread monitoring of permafrost, via the meteorological stations measuring soil temperatures to depths of 3.2 meters at specific sites. The Melnikov Permafrost Institute established the first monitoring station, the Igarka, in 1936, and, over the course of the next forty-five years, a total of thirteen stations were created, ending with the Chabyda in 1980. Scientific organizations within and outside Russia began regular monitoring of permafrost temperatures beginning in the 1980s, in Alaska (T. E. Osterkamp, V. E. Romanovsky), in Russia (A. V. Pavlov, N. G. Oberman, P. N. Skryabin, M. N. Zheleznyak, and others), and in Mongolia (N. Sharkhuu) (Alexander Nikolayevich Fyodorov, personal communication, February 4, 2019).

The international permafrost science community initiated global monitoring efforts when they understood the unprecedented warming of the permafrost, using the modeling paradigm of Budyko, the energy balance climate model (1970). In the late 1990s, international scientists began the Global Terrestrial Network of Permafrost (GTN-P) as the official global network for measurement of permafrost temperature and active layer thickness. The stated purpose of the GTN-P was "to establish an early warning system for the consequences of climate change in permafrost regions and to provide standardized thermal permafrost data to global models" (Biskaborn et al. 2015: 245). The GTN-P provided the first dynamic database that integrated two initiatives: CALM (Circumpolar Active Layer Monitoring) and TSP (Thermal State of Permafrost), all under the auspices of the International Permafrost Association (IPA).

GTN-P data showed that global permafrost temperatures had increased on the average from +/−0.29 to +/−0.12 degrees Celsius over the 2007−16 decade (Biskaborn et al. 2019). This may sound insignificant to a nonspecialist. However, much like the projections of a global temperature increase of 1.5 to 2 degrees Celsius sounds negligible to laypeople (IPCC 2018), to permafrost scientists this decadal change is extremely concerning and a clear sign of the greater ecological crises on the horizon. It signals a changing landscape and infrastructure for inhabitants of permafrost areas. It also means the release of substantial carbon and methane as the permafrost degrades, with methane a much more powerful greenhouse gas than carbon.

More recent modeling captures the dynamism of permafrost change, especially the trends of continuous permafrost areas degrading to discontinuous, patchy, and even vanishing. For example, the permafrost boundary in the Pechora lowlands of northwestern Russia shifted northward by thirty to forty kilometers and up to eighty kilometers on the foothills in the eastern part of the region over the last thirty-five years (Oberman and Liygin 2009). The same study shows how, in addition to a northward migration, what was continuous permafrost became discontinuous and in some places disappeared completely.

These finer tuned approaches to modeling add to the understanding of the urgency to respond. I ponder how much more impactful they could be for the public's understanding if they integrated the Indigenous knowledge and local knowledge of area inhabitants. This could add details about the specific ways local inhabitants have historically adapted to their permafrost environment, and how they are perceiving, understanding, and responding to both climate and the complexity of change today. Above all, by bringing affected populations' vernacular knowledge into these scientific models, policy makers could potentially be able to grasp that climate change is deeply human and that reversing it requires not only technological fixes but behavioral and cultural responses.

Scientific Knowledge of the Changing Permafrost in the Sakha Republic

Permafrost change in the Sakha Republic can be viewed in the context of the Russian Federation. Map 9 shows permafrost distribution across Russia over pre-Holocene and Holocene timescales. Permafrost had a very different distribution 10,000 years ago, relatively recently in a geological time frame.

Today permafrost is changing much more rapidly and over smaller time scales. Permafrost scientists have generated future projections based on contemporary monitoring data that show how the permafrost change we are seeing today may play out in the future. Maps 10*a*, *b*, and *c* show changes in mean annual ground temperatures at the bottom of the active layer from 1990 to 2100.

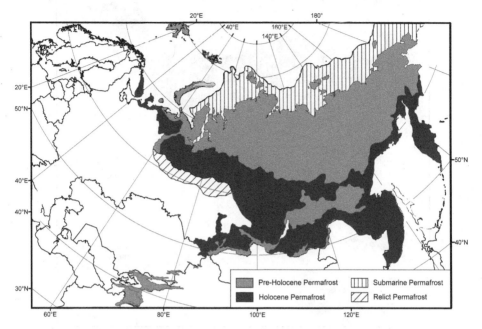

Map 9 Present-day distribution of permafrost of different ages in Russia (after Lisitsyna and Romanovskii 1998). Map by Vladimir Romanovsky.

The scientists' justification for using ground temperatures shows just how complex the processes of permafrost are.

> Due to this model's spatial resolution (0.5 × 0.5 latitude/longitude) it is practically impossible to reflect the discontinuous character of permafrost in the southern permafrost zones. That is why we choose the ground surface and soil properties for each cell that will produce the coldest possible mean annual ground temperatures within the cell. This choice means that all results produced by this model reflect permafrost temperatures only in the coldest landscape types within this area. It also means that if our results show thawing permafrost somewhere within the domain, we should interpret this to mean that permafrost is thawing in practically all locations within the area. It also means that in the stable permafrost area identified in Figure 8 [maps 10*a*, *b*, and *c* in this text], partial thawing of permafrost may occur at some specific locations. (Romanovsky et al. 2008: 1517)

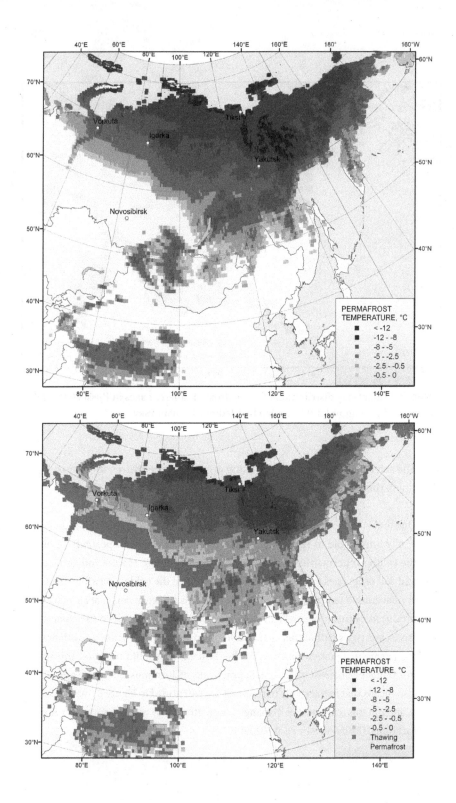

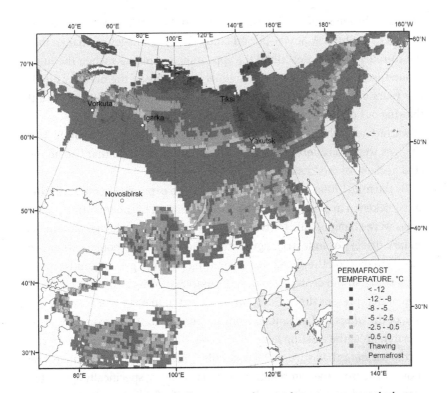

Map 10 Calculated distribution of mean annual ground temperatures at the bottom of the active layer in northern Eurasia averaged for three time intervals: a. 1990–2000 (top left facing page), b. 2040–50 (bottom left facing page), and c. 2090–2100 (above). The area with widespread permafrost thawing from the top down is shown in medium gray. Map by Vladimir Romanovsky.

The timescales in these maps are not long. For example, the middle map is twenty years out from the time of this writing. The third map is also in the near future and projects significant changes in a half-century time frame. Sobering, concerning, and giving rise to the question of how the people on the ground can adapt.

Scientific Understanding of the Changing *Alaas*

Alaas form in areas of high ice-content permafrost and cycle through a process of lake formation to dry land to lake formation every 150 to 180 years.

Scientists began noticing different changes outside these cycles in the early twentieth century. A Soviet-period study showing images of change in the micro-relief of fields described the appearance of hillocks when the underground ice began to thaw: "The gradual swamping of the fields ensu[ed] a few years after the clearing of the forest. Inhabitants attribute this to the thawing out of the frozen layers of the subsoil due to an increased accession of warmth after the removal of the timber stand" (Nikitin 1930: 360). These changes were considered part of the "natural" *alaas* cycle that had accelerated because of the loss of the protective layer.

By the mid-1900s, changes in *alaas* had both expanded in physical extent and quickened in pace. Sakha permafrost scientists began investigating how *alaas* were changing due to the combination of climate change and the secondary drivers of industrial agriculture and large-scale construction projects. One method they used was comparing past and present landscapes. A 2009 study, in the central region of Churapcha, compared a 1945 map to a map of that present time (Gorokhov et al. 2011). In sixty-five years, the lake area of the *alaas* had expanded from 1.3 percent to 9.4 percent of the total research area, the existing lakes were three times larger, and dry field areas within the *alaas* had shrunk 2.5 times (ibid. 12). These drastic changes were shown to be from the combination of human activity, specifically agricultural practices, and climate change. These site-specific findings were then extrapolated to similar landscape change identified by satellite imagery of *alaas* ecosystems to show that much of the Sahka Republic's arable land used for agriculture was turning into thermokarst.

Additionally, the presence or not of a protective layer, either an intact forest or an uncultivated natural *alaas* field, could be used as a proxy for permafrost thaw. The advent of 1950s industrial agriculture and large-scale construction projects removed much of the protective layer on *alaas* landscapes. Today the re-establishment and maintenance of a protective layer is considered a critical action to slow the thawing process (Konstantinov et al. 1996; Iijima and Fedorov 2019; Shepelev et al. 2016: 38–39). Scientists are able to compare the changes in permafrost temperatures of *alaas* areas that have protective layers intact with those that do not and can see that although the latter speeds up the thawing process, the permafrost temperatures have increased in both contexts. Maintaining the protective layer will not prevent thawing due to a warming planet, but it will significantly abate it.

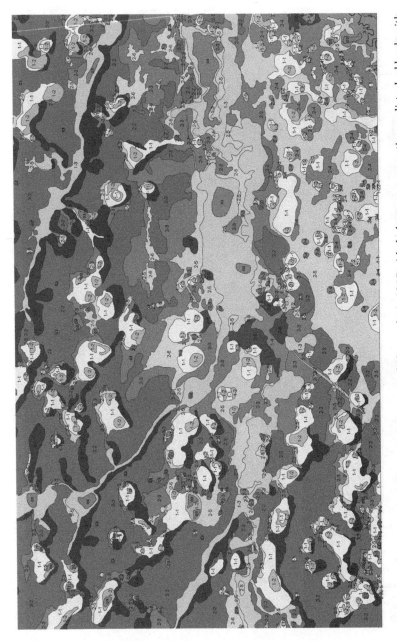

Map 11a Landscape map of the surrounding area of Churapcha in 1945 with dark areas representing undisturbed lands with little development and intact permafrost. From Gorokhov et al. 2011.

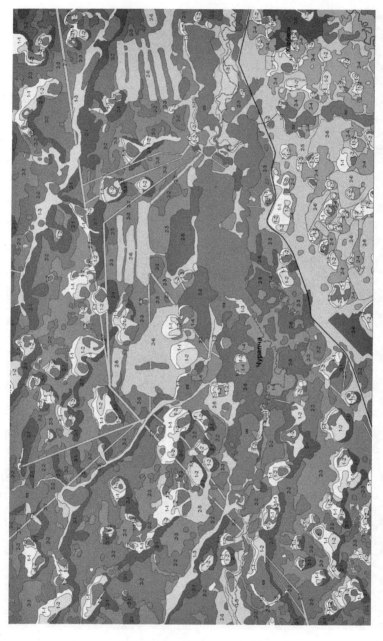

Map 11b Landscape map of the surrounding area of Churapcha in 2009 with dark areas of the 1945 map now disturbed with agricultural development and thermokarst development. From Gorokhov et al. 2011.

Another method to gauge *alaas* change due to permafrost thaw is to analyze the standing surface water on a given *alaas* site to determine the percentage that originates from below ground. Studies using this approach show that ground ice thaw water often made up one-third of the land surface water, be it in contributions to existing lakes or the formation of thermokarst and lake evolution (Fedorov et al. 2014).

Indigenous Knowledge and Local Knowledge of Permafrost and *Alaas* Change

Viliui Sakha inhabitants have a keen understanding of permafrost change. The first local testimony of land surface change that I heard was in 2010. A professional herder spoke of the changes he had seen over the course of the decades that he had traveled the land, caring for his and others' horse herds:

> I am a cowboy and hunter—the land has changed—where there never was a ravine there now is—all is caving in—where the flat hay lands were, the same is happening—the land's plane has changed—where there never was a hill, there now is—where there never was a hole, there now is—the erosion of our lands is happening very quickly—in just the last few years. (elder inhabitant, 2010)

His description, of the sudden formation of valleys and hills where once there were flatlands and of the raised areas that once were low, was an anomaly within local inhabitants' observations at that time. By 2018, it had become common knowledge. I was most surprised to hear a similar account from a thirty-year old resident, since my experience so far was that this kind of knowledge came from middle-aged and elder inhabitants.

> The land is changing . . . the pastures, the old homeplaces . . . the land relief is changing . . . they all used to be flat and now are up and down. We can no longer drive on them and it is getting worse and worse. It is happening very close, in Tumul and also in Kÿÿkei . . . the permafrost is thawing. I will show you. All those places we can take you there to see (Vladimir Yegorovich Tretiyakov focus group interview, June 7, 2018)

These testimonies from local inhabitants are a critical part of gaining a comprehensive understanding of the local to global effects of anthropogenic climate change. Indigenous knowledge and local knowledge contribute critical information which must be considered in concert with scientific data. They not only provide a down-scaling, a way of ground truthing the more generalized scientific knowledge of change but also translate change into the human context. Once this is understood, the big challenge is exactly *how* to do it. Based on my experience, it has to be done in a case-by-case context, engaging local communities and scientists to work together, to aspire to hear each other and use language that can be heard, to work across disciplines and differences or, as Donna Haraway succinctly says it, to "stay with the trouble" (2016). In the immediate case of Sakha and *alaas*, my and Alexander Fyodorov's experiments with knowledge exchanges serve as one example.

ONE APPROACH TO USING ALL AVAILABLE KNOWLEDGE SYSTEMS: KNOWLEDGE EXCHANGE

In 2010, Alexander Fyodorov and I embarked on an experiment, to design and facilitate "knowledge exchanges," community events designed both to elicit local inhabitants' observations of change and to share Alexander's research documenting the scientific knowledge of local change (Crate and Fedorov 2013b). The rationale was as follows: Our 2008 and 2009 field research showed that inhabitants were extremely knowledgeable about local change but that only a few attributed these changes to climate change. Furthermore, there was a paucity of information available to inhabitants about the local effects of climate change.

We conducted eight knowledge exchanges in the summer of 2010, four in Viliui regional centers and one in each of our four research villages. I was completely caught off guard when, after the fourth knowledge exchange, Alexander told me that this was the first time he had presented his research to affected communities and the first time he had ever spoken about his research in his native Sakha language. Until then he had only presented in the Russian language and at academic conferences. I realized then that our knowledge-exchange experiment had more benefits than I had expected.

After the eight events, we spent the next three years collaborating with the research communities to create a booklet, in the Sakha language, to emulate the knowledge-exchange process (Crate and Fedorov 2013a). We distributed

3,000 copies throughout the Viliui regions to the schools, libraries, local ecology offices, and administrations. We conducted two additional knowledge exchanges in the central regions of the Sakha Republic in December of 2018, described at the beginning of this chapter.

According to participants' feedback, these events were critical to their permafrost knowledge, facilitating their understandings of permafrost science in the Sakha Republic and specifically in the areas where they lived. Participants remarked that the events gave them an understanding of how a global process was having real effects in their lives, a message communicated by Alexander Fedorov's images that showed changing landscapes, structures, and forest stands that were familiar to them. The knowledge exchanges were also key moments for inhabitants to share their observations of change, and to understand that they had valued expertise that added important details and nuances to the scientific knowledge. It also provided a forum for community members to voice what they were seeing and for others to similarly recognize change and to build community awareness.

In the eight Viliui Sakha settlements in 2010 and in the central regions in the winter of 2018, we began each event by inviting local people to share their observations of change. In Elgeeii, in addition to the professional herder quoted above, a middle-aged woman spoke of local change based on her experience as a gardener.

> I am a gardener. For the last five years some brand new birds have come— *drozd* [thrush] and *grach* [rook] and they are moving in—from one village to the next, year by year. There have been two nests outside my house for a few years, and this year it seems that 100 came—they eat insects—but they also eat my tomatoes, choosing the very ripest—they suck the juice out—never before did the birds eat our vegetables! (elder, Khoro focus group, 2010)

It is challenging to successfully grow tomatoes in Siberia. As a keen observer of her garden, this woman was quick to notice the arrival of new bird species, especially ones that ruined her crop. Each knowledge exchange began with half a dozen or so similar local testimonies based on inhabitant's expert knowledge of place. Inhabitants' testimonies resonated with audience participants, who were often then moved to share their own observations.

With these local observations in mind, Alexander presented his locally oriented scientific knowledge of change. He began with an overview of the last fifty years of change in the Russian north, showing how average air temperatures were amplified in northern areas, including the Sakha Republic. According to data from the Yakutsk Meteorological Station, the average annual air temperature in the city of Yakutsk had risen three degrees Celsius since 1985, from −10.4 to −7.5. He explained how this change in air temperatures directly impacts permafrost temperatures. He showed images of several examples of permafrost degradation that have captured international attention, including the Batagaiski hollow in the Sakha Republic, the Yamal funnel in western Siberia, the numerous examples of coastal erosion involving entire masses of land in Alaska, and the failing of buildings' foundational structures. From there he discussed various efforts to model permafrost degradation in order to project and prepare for the effects of future changes on infrastructure. In 2002 scientists estimated that over 300 buildings in Yakutsk had already been damaged because of uneven subsidence of the permafrost (Anisimov and Belolutskaia 2002). One author caused panic in Yakutsk by projecting different models of when the pile foundations of the major buildings in northern cities will be in critical condition, with one estimation showing such degradation as early as 2020 (Shiklomanov et al. 2017).

Alexander next brought the topic of permafrost degradation into the local and regional context by focusing on the specific ecosystem that Sakha's horse- and cattle-breeding livelihood depends on, that of the *alaas*. In terms of permafrost, the *alaas* ecosystem is founded on a type of permafrost that has a very high ice content, making it even more susceptible to thawing than other permafrost types. He explained how land clearing for agricultural fields has stripped the protective layer and exposed permafrost to warming air. To illustrate, he showed images of the expansive fields cleared in the Soviet state farm period that are today areas of intense thermokarst development; in some cases with lakes forming where they had never been before. To complicate matters, in some *alaas* areas there have also been outbreaks of _shelkopriad_ that denude the larch trees of their needles, amplifying the effect of the loss of a protective layer. The last outbreak in 1999 was the largest ever recorded in the Sakha Republic (Vinokurov et al., 2001). The combination of the removal of the protective layers in the mid- to late twentieth century and the warming of the air temperatures due to climate change now has resulted in rapid thermokarst development in many areas, which threatens inhabitants' ability not only to practice horse and cattle breeding but to continue to inhabit their homelands. To drive this point home, Alexander shared a

Figure 42 Thermokarst destruction of arable land in the area of Syrdakh village, Ust-Aldan district of the Sakha Republic. Photo credit: A. N. Fedorov.

striking image of thermokarst development on a former state farm field in Siirdaakh, Ust Aldan (figure 42).

The next part of the knowledge-exchange process was educating people about what actions they can take, including clearing snow from their yards and filling growing holes with local materials. He also showed images of how they could build new or retrofit existing houses to keep the permafrost beneath them cold. For new construction, he showed a picture of a home built upon a meter of soil, with several pipes running parallel between the ground and soil. Not only did the meter of soil provide a buffer between the warmth of the house and the permafrost, but the pipes brought freezing air in during winter when they were open and prevented the penetration of warm air by being closed in summer. For existing structures, he showed an image of a pipe in the ground, angling toward a house's foundation into which the homeowner was to pour solvents to decrease the ground temperature.

Once Alexander explained the actions individuals can take, the knowledge exchanges went into lively question-and-answer sessions. The feedback we received from participants not only provided important information but also fostered community understanding at a deeper level. Inhabitants commented that they came away knowing a lot about their neighbors' thoughts and concerns about the changes that they too were seeing.

Bringing knowledge systems into community conversations this way also highlights the importance of interpreting and contextualizing what people say. Alexander and I decided to see if we could corroborate the nine main changes that inhabitants reported in the 2008 project with instrumental (scientific) data. The attempt to corroborate one change in particular helped us understand how knowledge systems are not just about data but also about how cultural predilections shape perceptions of change. In 2008, a majority of inhabitants observed that there was "too much rain." However, precipitation data for the previous twenty years did not support this. Instead of assuming that inhabitants were wrong because of the hegemony of instrumental data, we instead pondered the possibility that both inhabitants' observations and the instrumental data were "right." Based on my experience, I knew there were patterns of rain throughout the year that Sakha depended on to be successful in their environment. This was especially true for a successful summer harvest. I also knew that in the several summers leading up to the 2010 knowledge exchanges, the hay seasons had been unusually rainy. This helped us to see that it was the changes in the seasonal pattern of rain, and specifically the way that the changes interfered with Sakha's subsistence patterns, that prompted inhabitants to perceive "too much rain." What at first appeared as a contradiction across these two knowledge systems instead became a way to appreciate the two ways of knowing and the cultural embeddedness of Indigenous knowledge. Whereas scientific knowledge is based in a generalized and quantitative approach to knowing, Indigenous knowledge is only relevant within its *in situ* cultural context. To fully understand global change, it is critical to value and consider on-the-ground observations, elicited by respecting and understanding the knowledge system(s) relevant to an affected people, in parallel with scientific knowledge.

Another unseen outcome of the 2010 knowledge-exchange events was the possibility of engaging village youth in permafrost monitoring. Somewhere over the course of the eight knowledge exchanges, Alexander mentioned how he wanted to establish a permafrost monitoring site in the Suntaar region. A few months later, in September, he and his colleagues P. Ya. Konstantinov, Yoshihiro Iijima, and Hotaek Pak-San installed equipment at one site in Kutana to measure permafrost temperature at a depth of three meters. From that time on, students of the Kutana school took measurements of the soil temperature three times a month. Several Kutana teachers collaborated to develop a curriculum called "What the Permafrost Can Tell Us," designed for students to investigate how changes in permafrost temperature extrapolated to change in their ecosystem overall. The students wrote papers based on their findings and presented their work at regional school competitions.

The Moving Target of Permafrost Change

In late July 2019, I met with Alexander, this time on my way home from the field. Of the news we shared, several items immediately come to mind. First is his experience presenting at a June seminar in Churapcha called, "People on the Permafrost Landscape." Most memorable from his account was how the local people responded to his recommended plan to stay safe in the context of their rapidly changing permafrost. After giving a brief version of the most salient points about climate change, he then presented a slide that showed his proposal for how the community could begin to pursue a much safer alternative (see figure 43).

He explained that the light areas were the *alaas* landscapes and the dark areas Jurassic sandstone. Both had permafrost, but only the *alaas* landscapes had high-ice-content permafrost, the kind that is rapidly degrading and presenting problems. The permafrost beneath the Jurassic sandstone was ice-free and would not change significantly. He recommended that inhabitants move their agricultural activities to those blue areas, beginning with a trial in the closest lands, the light leg farthest north in the dark region on the map. He had calculated that they could use 5 percent of their budget to build five houses for five young families who could farm 1,000 hectares, making ten 100-hectare fields. As he told me the next part of this story, he head began to rhythmically move from side to side. The local Churapcha community responded to his proposal with fierce opposition, rejecting his idea of moving from their *alaas*. They told Alexander that they appreciated his plan and that it was good to know about in case they needed to relocate in some future time, but for now, they would continue to use the *alaas*. Alexander tried to reason with them, explaining how they would stay at a high cost. Their *alaas* were rapidly declining in productivity and becoming increasingly dangerous

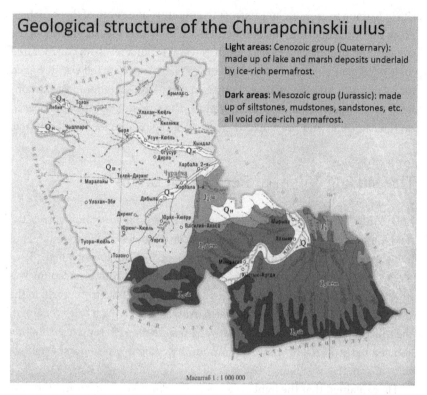

Figure 43 Geological structure of the Churapchinskii *ulus*. Light areas: Cenozoic group (Quaternary), made up of lake and marsh deposits underlaid by ice-rich permafrost. Dark areas: Mesozoic group (Jurassic), made up of siltstones, mudstones, sandstones, etc., all void of ice-rich permafrost. Photo credit: A. N. Fedorov.

for human and animal use. He reminded them of how, before their current permafrost crisis, they made all their own silage. In the last years, they have been importing silage from the Altai and the Amur at a great expense. Despite his appeals, they remained resolute, interested only in Alexander telling them how they could stabilize the *alaas* where they were.

Further into our discussion that July day he mentioned other ways that the Institute of Permafrost has been called on recently to share their expertise with local communities challenged by permafrost degradation, and more and more all the time. The head of Saniiakhtakh village, in the south of the Sakha Republic in the Olyokminsk region, requested advice from the institute concerning the recent formation of a seventeen-meter-deep, forty-meter-long ravine that threatened their cemetery. Thorough inspection by institute specialists' showed a thermo-erosive process, driven by both thawing of the permafrost and erosion from increased precipitation. Such ravines have appeared widely in the last decade in other areas of the Lena River (Pokrovsk, 2004–6; Sinsk, 2007; Tit-Ary, 2008; Olyokminsk, 2015). The team recommended reclamation immediately involving various steps to restore the frozen layer, using block stone and other materials. This type of reclamation work could only be completed effectively in the below-freezing times of winter. The work also included creating canals and other diversions for run-off from the site to address the surface-water erosion processes (Alexander Nikolayevich Fyodorov, personal communication, December 14, 2018).

Passing a Permafrost Law

Another update during our July meeting had to do with efforts to protect the permafrost on a larger scale. A few years earlier, Alexander and several other scientists and activists had created the Law on the Protection of Permafrost in the Republic of Sakha (Yakutia) in an effort to enact specific rules and guidelines for agriculture, development, construction, and so on, that would preserve the protective layer and delay the period of thermokarst development. The initial idea to create such a law came from a former Elgeeii resident, Eduard (Edik) Romanov, now living in Yakutsk. Edik proposed that they work on this law after attending Alexander's lectures and asking lots of questions. The stated overarching objective is "to establish the legal basis for regulating relations in the field of permafrost protection in order to preserve it" (Sakha Republic 2018). The eighteen articles of the law spell out in detail the principles, procedures, and processes for protecting permafrost: principles of public and state administration; the powers of executive bodies of state power and of local governments; the regulation of permafrost and the other environmental factors affecting it; the rights of citizens, legal entities, and public associations; requirements for economic and other activities affecting the state of permafrost; measures to protect the population in the event of a change in the state of permafrost, threatening the life and health of people; accounting for levels of impact and monitoring of permafrost; state supervision and public control; and responsibility for the violation of the law and compensation for damage caused to health, property of citizens, property of legal entities, and the environment by violation of the maximum permissible level of exposure to permafrost. The law was adopted on May 22, 2018.

Despite the law's adoption more than a year before our meeting, Alexander said that a committee established to implement the law had yet to bring all of its articles into full force. The first priority, as established by the committee, was to abide by the law's requirements for buildings and construction, considering the amount of new, ongoing construction and the dangers it posed to populations.[4] The other aspects of the law would take time to bring into action.

Beyond the importance of the law in slowing down thermokarst development, Alexander was also interested in its ability to decrease the impact of the Far Eastern Hectare (FEH) program on the Sakha Republic. The FEH program

> enables any Russian citizen who is also a resident in Russia to petition for and receive a hectare of land in the Far East Federal District, for the purpose of pursuing agricultural, small-business or other development. Groups of up to 10 individuals (including children, with their parents) can apply for contiguous plots. The applicant submits a proposal for what purpose the FEH will be used, and what land he or she desires, through a simple, web-based application process. If the proposal is accepted, the applicant receives the land parcel at no cost for five years. If the recipient of a FEH develops the land as per proposed within the five-year time frame, he or she can then apply to receive the land as property, or to lease it, for an additional 49 years. (Fondahl et al. 2019: 51)

At face value, the FEH program appears to be in the best interest of citizens. The law authorizing it, Russian Federal Law No 199-FZ, was signed into action by President Putin on May 1, 2016 (Russian Federation 2016).[5] However, the possible allocation of FEHs in the Sakha Republic ignited protests and turmoil. Many feared the encroachment onto Indigenous areas, and others feared land grabbing by outsiders (Fondahl et al. 2019). The Sakha government took action to try to minimize the effects of FEH, suggesting amendments and modifications to the draft federal law that would advantage residents. These included allowing residents earlier access to land, harnessing another set of laws to reduce the area available to foreigners, and

expanding the total area that residents could receive. Once it was apparent
the amendments would be adopted, it used the exclusions to ensure that 59
percent of the republic was not eligible for FEHs (ibid. 54). Alexander intends
for the Permafrost Law to further limit the extent of land that citizens or
other stakeholders can acquire within the Sakha Republic. The law states one
of its principles as "requirements for economic and other activities affecting the state of permafrost" that would mandate a thorough assessment of
thermokarst development and degradation due to the warming climate prior
to use of the lands and disallow activities that exacerbate those processes.

Social Scientists Investigating Permafrost and *Alaas* Change

Several Sakha social scientists have begun to document Indigenous knowledge and local knowledge of inhabitants' observations of climate and permafrost change. In the far northern areas of the Sakha Republic, flooding
is much more extreme and coastal erosion is a major issue, compared to in
the Viliui or the central regions. Research from 2011 to 2013 in two Sakha
villages, Betenkes in the Verkhoyansk *uluus* and Aby in the Aby *uluus*, documents how the combination of ice thaw and rock erosion along the Adycha
River is affecting the settlements. In Betenkes, "The village is gradually losing
its coastal lands. People are forced to move their houses and outbuildings
due to the constant breakage of the shore" (Ignatieva 2014: 88–89). Despite
these differences in latitude and ecosystem characteristics, many of the local
testimonies of change sound similar to Viliui Sakha's.

> Recently, the sun is very hot and in places our *buluus* have melted. I see
> many terrain changes. In some places, ravines have formed, in others, the
> earth has swelled into hills and ice has appeared, and in another a small lake
> completely disappeared. In the forest, there are now piles of felled trees, and
> the forest around is absolutely swampy. . . . Everything that I have seen with
> my own eyes testifies to the warming of the climate. (N. N. Chirikov, hunter
> from Betenkes, qtd. in ibid. 89)

Inhabitants also report observations of new species, which are moving
northward with the warming. Since 2010, inhabitants have sighted the river

otter, previously known only in southern Sakha, frequenting their northern waters. These northern Sakha communities also are similar to those in Viliui and central Sakha in their resolve to remain in their ancestral homelands and to adapt, no matter the changes. Additionally, their testimonies reflect a similar recognition that the world is sentient: "How is it possible to feel bitterness to the river, from which we drink even if, at the same time, it brings us the increasing threat of a flood?" (ibid. 95).

Sakha inhabitants in settlements of the Oymyakon, another northern area, are observing similar changes to Viliui and central region inhabitants but with an important caveat. The northern *alaas* are wetter than their counterparts to the south, and the increased water from climate change has rendered them in a constant super-saturated state (Solovyeva 2021). Hay is now impossible to cut in the temperate months. The communities have adapted by haying on ice, waiting to harvest hay once the water has frozen in the high meadows. They also need to supplement their hay with grain and nutrients because of the low yields.

A team of Sakha social scientists recently studied how rural populations were being affected by the landscape changes from permafrost thaw in the central regions (Svinoboev and Neustroeva 2017). They chose seven settlements located near areas of greatest change, in both climatic variability and permafrost landscapes, over the last decade. From those settlements, they selected survey households who had lived for at least ten years adjacent to the most extreme landscape change. Of these, 85 percent said their homes had subsided or settled due to permafrost change. One-third complained that their homes flooded in spring and autumn. Many reported changes in their yard, either seasonal thawing of the land, subsidence of rock, or soil unevenly distributed due to heaving, all processes that are inherently dangerous to the stability of land and home. A majority also noted similar changes in their village territory.

Social scientists from outside the Sakha Republic are also investigating the changing *alaas*, focusing on their geographical and spiritual importance. They cite inhabitants' testimonies of the possible dangers when a Sakha person fails to regularly visit and feed the spirit of their birth *alaas* or to treat their *alaas* spirit with reverence (Takakura 2015: 107–10; Takakura 2010: 64–66). Dangerous incidences can happen when a person suddenly returns to visit their ancestral *alaas* after a long period, or when a person is too noisy while visiting, or speaks their ancestral *alaas*'s name loudly and without respect, all of which offend the *alaas*'s *sir ichchite* and result in sudden sickness or other tragedy to the person (ibid.).

Another social science study highlights the unique interdependent relationship Sakha have with *alaas* as compared to other landscapes, with Sakha serving as both caretakers of and beneficiaries from *alaas*. Sakha's relationships with other land ecotypes where they hunt, fish, and gather are one-way and purely for procurement. Sakha's relationship with *alaas*, on the other hand, is characterized by one author as "direct economic control and mutual interdependence" (Mészáros 2012: 10). For example, inhabitants of the Tobuluk settlement of the central regions "consider the areas surrounding their village as controlled islands of *alaas* in a sea of uncontrolled forest" (ibid. 1). The author also emphasizes the power of the *alaas* in the Sakha mentality: "The *alaas* possess an immanent power that local people claim is hard to understand. This power can be personified as a beautiful girl or remain shapeless. This power must be respected, and therefore, it is strictly forbidden to shout, run, or curse when being on an *alaas*. If someone does not obey these rules, he or she may easily break a leg, or fall ill" (ibid. 18).

This same study further discusses how Sakha's perception of *alaas* has changed over time. The last century of relocations has seeded stark intergenerational differences in rural Sakha's understanding of their relationship to the land. Those born before the late 1950s state farm centralization tended to live part of their lives on *alaas* and, to this day, largely maintain Sakha's historical spiritual practices on the *alaas*. The most recent generation, those born in the post-Soviet period, may only go to their ancestral *alaas* to help with summer hay cutting, if that, and may follow their elders' *alaas* practices but tend not to initiate them themselves (ibid. 26). Although some of today's Tobuluk youth describe *alaas* as "hostile" and "untamed," Tobuluk inhabitants overall continue to perceive their homelands as a "small dwelt-in island [of *alaas*] within an alien environment [of forest]" (ibid. 30).

A final project on *alaas* and change engages both Sakha and non-Sakha natural and social scientists in an international interdisciplinary collaboration (Crate et al. 2017). This project's main objective is to integrate current natural and social science findings to illuminate how climate change is affecting an ecosystem historically manipulated by humans. In other words, how to develop an interdisciplinary understanding of global climate change in the context of an ecosystem that humans have manipulated for centuries. The project nests the history of Sakha *alaas* use within a background detailing the natural evolution of permafrost landscapes, and the specificities of the formation and cyclical processes of *alaas*. With this as a context, the study focuses on how global changes, most notably those due to anthropogenic climate change but also those due to rural-to-urban migration and economic globalization, are transforming *alaas* ecosystems and how that is in turn affecting Sakha land use.

How Language Loss Increases the Complexity of Change

In 2012, I noticed how youth out-migration and economic globalization were interacting with climate change in the complexity of change. Although my understanding of late has been focused on the issues of rapid permafrost and *alaas* change, I am noticing another source of rapid sociocultural change, which inhabitants first articulated in 2018 focus groups.

> I want to talk about the change in people, in people's characters . . . now it is very rare to find receptive and interactive people here, for example, on the village streets—they are hard to find. Before, people used to take the time to converse with each other. You would meet someone on the street and stop and talk and know the news from each other . . . now everyone walks along staring at their phone—no one needs anyone anymore . . . there is no interaction now . . . today people only interact over WhatsApp! (middle-aged man in Tolon, May 31, 2018)

My experience in the villages for the last few years compels me to associate this change with the sudden access to information and communication on devices in rural Sakha areas. This implicates sweeping changes if compared to how people learned the news a generation ago.

> Before, people would visit each other a lot and have tea. This is where people learned the latest news and connected with each other. It was how we lived. Now it is already not accepted. When someone enters a house, the inhabitants ask . . . "What did that person come in for?" and "What do they want?" Also, most households today don't even give tea . . . they just ask, "What did

you come here for?" and then, when that is decided, they shoo the person away . . . it is a huge change in our culture. Before when a person came in, they used to right away pour tea . . . I did this and saw my mother practice it also . . . she would go to see neighbors a lot. If she didn't go for a few days, she would get in a bad mood . . . she had to go and listen and chat. She always came back in a very good mood with all the news of the village! (Svetlana Gavrilovna Martinova, interview, June 13, 2018)

In addition, another of Sakha's historical modes of communication, the improvisatory singing during *ohuokhai*, also appears to no longer retain its important functions: "Before there was no communication like there is now—today all the cell phones, WhatsApp and Instagram—attention is elsewhere—before it was within the *ohuokhai* circle that so much was told about . . . before it was the only time we heard news and told it to each other—now it is not that way . . . and *ohuokhai* was where we heard news and learned the Sakha language" (elder, focus group, May 25, 2018).

Cultural change resulting from the widespread use of phones and social media is a global phenomenon. In rural Sakha settlements the sudden access to cell phones and high-speed Internet is threatening more than Sakha's social fabric. Our 2019 summer research suggests it may also be endangering Sakha language perpetuation, a finding that defied my long-held belief that because there were 450,000 Sakha people and that books are regularly published in the Sakha language, the Sakha language was somehow "safe." I thought that language loss was a phenomenon reserved for languages with few speakers. This is no longer the case. Today, the sudden access to high-speed Internet in the villages combined with parental disregard for the impact that that constant access has on their young children's lives may be threatening Sakha language perpetuation.

I gained a greater understanding of the impact of access to the Internet in the villages and its effect on young people's language acquisition in the summer of 2019. We developed a set of five questions about how the Sakha language was being perpetuated at the village level. Most interviewees remarked that their children and grandchildren knew Sakha, but their acquisition of the language had changed. Elders commented that their grandchildren were either not speaking Sakha very well, that they mixed Sakha and Russian, or in some cases that they only spoke Russian. An Elgeeii preschool teacher for twenty-five years was especially outspoken about this:

The kids in the kindergarten where I work speak more Russian than Sakha. They speak like they're in a cartoon. «_Oh, nyet_!» [Oh, no!] they say all the time. We talk to them in a group in Sakha, and they go off into their smaller groups and only speak Russian among themselves. They say, "We understand Russian better than Sakha, so we're going to speak Russian," and it's because of the phones. (Agrafina Vasiliyevna Nazarova, interview May 30, 2019)

The teacher went on to explain how she reads them stories in Sakha and they complain that the story is too long, and they don't understand, and to please give them a Russian interpretation of the story's main points. She also observed that her preschoolers aren't focused and can't sit still and concentrate like before. She related this change to the ubiquity of phones but also to the lack of parental control and overall parental disregard. Before parents always came into the preschool to settle their children and check in, both in the morning and when they collected them at night. Today's parents visit briefly, if at all. The parents also give their children phones as soon as they get home to occupy them while the parents stay busy on their own phones. Most online cartoons and other things of children's interest online are in the Russian language. As a result, children have started to enter the first grade speaking only Russian. This is in sharp contrast with just a few years before, when the rural Sakha areas were considered safe havens for the language as compared to the urban context (Ferguson 2015: 16).

Sakha language perpetuation is also affected by a lack of attention to it in the higher grades. High school students now have no incentive to learn Sakha because they are no longer tested for it. Most parents today consider Russian to be the language that their children need to get a good job. The high school Sakha

Figure 44 Electronic devices are increasingly present in the hands of very young children in both urban and rural settings. Elgeeii _yhyakh_ at Ugut Kÿöl, 2018. Photo by author.

language teacher in Elgeeii commented that the prerevolutionary insights of A. E. Kulakovski still apply today: "He said it himself in 'Shaman's Dream' . . . 'the small people [i.e., Sakha] living with big people [i.e., Russians] together, will be gone' . . . so the idea that Sakha could go is from long ago and I think it applies also today" (Ludmilla Nikolayevna Pavlova, interview, July 3, 2018). But perhaps this is the situation only in Elgeeii and Kutana. "What language will be emphasized is decided at the regional level, and Suntaar has chosen Russian over Sakha. That is why Suntaar is one of the most Russified regions. The regional powers that be thought their children needed Russian to be successful and so all went for it" (Ivan Shamayev, interview, June 25, 2019). This decision is surprising to me, considering that the Suntaar *uluus* prides itself as the nexus of Sakha folklore, the *yhyakh* and the *ohuokhai*, all of which are founded upon an intimate knowledge of the Sakha language.

I then realized that I had heard similar concerns during interviews in Siirdaakh and Khatilii in December 2018 when inhabitants talked about the younger generation's acquisition of the Sakha language.

> I am a teacher and I know that children, even as recently as ten years ago, thought very deeply. Now they are just thinking about one day and all is very fast . . . there is no depth . . . life has changed and moves very quickly . . . the cell phones are very problematic. Our language is dying . . . students have phones and watch TV and it is all in Russian and so when they get to school teachers all speak Sakha and they respond in Russian. They can't write in Sakha . . . I think in twenty years our language will disappear. (Yevdokiya Fyodorovna Olisova, interview, December 13, 2018)

Using Russian in the place of Sakha is much more than switching out for another language. It has implications for a person's ability to "be" Sakha. Half of all respondents to our 2019 language questions expressed this sentiment: "If it's a Sakha person, they definitely ought to be able to speak Sakha. Their thoughts and dreams should all be in Sakha. How they think and solve problems and what they decide . . . all in Sakha. Only then will they understand other Sakha people. They'll be in a Sakha mindset" (Osip Dmitriyevich Andreyev, interview, May 21, 2019). Some commented that a person's loss of the Sakha language also has implications for their ability to enact Sakha belief and a Sakha interdependence with the land: "Only if a Sakha person knows the language will they actually realize their life. If a person does not know the Sakha language, they cannot speak the words they need to and they will never get help from above. And they will have no connection with the land" (Izabella Nikolayevna Tretiyakova, interview, May 23, 2019).

This directly implicates a Sakha person's relationship with *alaas*: their ancestral beginning in the far north and that continued identification through to contemporary times. To the extent that *tyl ichchileekh*, or that words are spirit-filled, *alaas* cannot be perpetuated as Sakha's main cultural identifier without those words.

In part, the possible threat to the Sakha language can be linked to new federal language protocols. In the summer of 2018, residents of Yakutsk protested against a new law that would abolish mandatory Sakha language classes in schools (cf. Siberian Desk 2018), a response to Putin's 2017 statement that

> learning these languages is a constitutionally guaranteed right, [but] a voluntary right. Forcing a person to learn a language that is not native to them is just as unacceptable as reducing the standard and time of teaching Russian. I want to remind you, dear friends, that for us, the Russian language is the state language, the language of interethnic communication, and it cannot be replaced with anything as it is the natural spiritual framework of our entire multinational country. Everyone should know [Russian]. (Putin 2017)

Following his declaration, Russian officials visited Tatarstan and the Sakha Republic to tour the schools in the main cities and to discourage and decry the teaching of ethnic languages (Ivan Shamayev, interview, June 25, 2019). A Sakha language activist in Yakutsk connected this to Russia's larger effort to gradually strip away the republic status of the Sakha area.

> Russia is working so that this will no longer be the Sakha Republic but part of the Far East edge. They are doing it gradually. In 2005, YAGU [Yakutia State University] was changed to simply Northeastern University . . . they did this in preparation . . . they are trying to rebrand our republic . . . if we have the Republic status, we can have our state language . . . this is in our Republic's constitution . . . if we have no Republic, then it would be against the law to speak the Sakha language . . . they are also taking other actions, for example, they fired a teacher for talking to a student's *ebe* in Sakha . . . we hired her back but they fired her again! (ibid.)

The rapid loss of languages has worldwide attention (cf. Harrison 2010, 2008; Grenoble and Whaley 1998). There has been some success in bolstering threatened languages, engaging youth by using the Internet and social media (Lee 2016; Cru 2015; Cunliffe and ap Dyfrig 2013). But this may not be enough. UNESCO's "Interactive Atlas of World's Languages in Danger" gauges the degree of a language's endangerment based on intergenerational language transmission spoken in the home. Accordingly, a language is "safe" when it "is spoken by all generations; intergenerational transmission is uninterrupted"; and it is "critically endangered" when "the youngest speakers are grandparents and older, and they speak the language partially and infrequently" (Moseley 2009: 6). The Sakha language could be in the critically endangered category if the trend in Elgeeii and Kutana, and in other rural Sakha settlements, continues.

Language is one of a culture's many symbolic forms. It not only is a communicative tool but also an embodiment of cultural values and mores. A person realizes their life as part of a specific culture through their people's language. It follows that the perpetuation of language is directly linked to a people's cultural vitality. In the Arctic Social Indicators project (Larsen et al. 2010; Larsen et al. 2015), language retention was declared to be not only one of three important indicators of cultural vitality (Larsen et al. 2010: 105), but the one of the three that could serve as a stand-alone indicator (Larsen et al. 2015: 43). People stop using their language because of forced or chosen resettlement and necessary assimilation into a dominant population to survive. It also occurs when a population's numbers are low to begin with, and youth choose to learn the dominant language to succeed. In Elgeeii and Kutana it appears that language loss could occur by assimilation via electronic devices. Young people choose to interact on social media that is largely conducted in the dominant language of Russian.

Change is having profound effects on Sakha life and culture in Viliui Sakha and other Sakha rural settlements: not only the unprecedented change of permafrost and *alaas* due to the local effects of global climate change, but also the overall changes due to the past "century of perestroikas" and more recent post-Soviet drivers of globalization. Sakha's relationship to *alaas* has changed because of the gradual consolidation of Sakha's historical adaptation to the extreme north via living "by the *alaas*" into state farms and then the dissolution of those agro-industrial efforts into household-level and small-group collective food production activities. Sakha's relationship to *alaas* was further disrupted via Soviet-period industrialization efforts, which despoiled landscapes and removed the permafrost's protective layer, among other ecological changes. Post-Soviet socioeconomic changes transformed the rural Sakha living "by the *alaas*" adaptation of that time, as households stopped cow keeping in exchange for their new access to goods in village stores and because of their loss of youth labor. Recent changes in language perpetuation now threaten to further unravel Sakha's intimate relationship with *alaas* by taking away the spirit of words needed to maintain that relationship.

Alaas as Cultural Keystone of Sakha Identity and Resilience

> The attractiveness of the keystone concept is the focus on the entire assemblage and the recognition that one species can have a disproportionate effect on its many associates. It appeals to biologists because it synthesizes substantial natural historical information into relatively simple managerial protocols. For resource managers and conservationists, it may be successfully applied to issues ranging from ecosystem function to community restoration. (Paine 1995: 964)

Permafrost and *alaas* can both be considered as keystones for Sakha. Permafrost is an ecological keystone in its foundational role in the environment, both physically and climatologically. *Alaas* are Sakha's cultural keystone.

> "People of the Deer," "Town of the Wild Plums," "People of the Wild Rice" . . . all around the globe, humans identify themselves and each other by their cultural and economic affiliations with particular species of plants and animals. . . . These significant species play a unique role in shaping and characterizing the identity of the people who rely on them. . . . These are the species that become embedded in a people's cultural traditions and narratives, their ceremonies, dances, songs, and discourse. . . . [W]e . . . propose to identify them as "cultural keystone species," a metaphorical parallel with ecological keystone species. (Garibaldi and Turner 2004: 1)

Accordingly, Sakha are "People of the *Alaas*." This harkens back to the many rich descriptions of contemporary Sakha's relationship with *alaas*, be it to the specific birth *alaas* that a person makes an annual pilgrimage to or spends their *saiylyk* time in, pasturing their animals and haying, or to the cultural understanding of *alaas* so central to Sakha identity, which brings an immersion of memories and understandings, fragrances and panoramas when one of the many contemporary *alaas* songs play in an urban apartment.

Both the keystone's overall ecological status and its at-risk status suggest that its designation as a keystone might not be sustainable (ibid. 9). *Alaas* have both a threatened ecological status and a high at-risk one, limiting Sakha's continued physical use of them. Despite these physical limitations, the inherent value of assigning *alaas* cultural keystone status opens pathways to understanding the association between Sakha culture, their environment, and their Indigenous knowledge system (ibid. 9). As the cultural keystone concept evolved, a refined definition spoke to the inherent interdependencies of the physical and the cultural: "A cultural keystone is in no case directly equivalent to a biological species. Even if based around a single species, a cultural keystone is a complex, whose contribution to system structure also depends upon a range of other factors, including other biological species, artefacts, knowledge, and social practices. More importantly, it also depends upon a range of purely subjective factors: beliefs, ideas, norms and values concerning social identity and its enactment through culturally appropriate practices" (Platten and Henfrey 2009: 498).

The meaning of *alaas* for Sakha is integrative and includes the entire complex of physical, social, cultural, and cosmological attributes. The contribution of *alaas* to Sakha culture and identity depends upon more than the biological species of the *alaas* ecosystem. Especially today, in a time of rapid physical changes to the *alaas*, they represent assemblages of cultural meaning, historical legacy, and an entire annual cycle of ritual practices. *Alaas*, as Sakha's cultural identifier, require the Sakha language to enact those culturally appropriate practices and to beckon the sentient aspects of a person's relationship to *alaas*.

The cultural keystone concept further broadened its meaning to include a physical place of specific cultural meaning, a cultural keystone place (CKP) (Cuerrier et al. 2015), which is defined as "a given site or location with high cultural salience for one or more groups of people and which plays, or has played in the past, an exceptional role in a people's cultural identity, as reflected in their day to day living, food production and other resource-based activities, land and resource management, language, stories, history, and social and ceremonial practices" (ibid. 431).

Clearly, the CKP concept applies to Sakha and *alaas* but to what end? What agency does such a designation have in this era of rapid change, including not only climate change effects on *alaas* but also the drivers of the complexity of change, and more recently, language loss? We could argue that *alaas* provide Sakha cultural agency, "the development of an identity and agency specific to practices and activities situated in a historically contingent, socially enacted, culturally constructed 'world'" (Holland et al. 2001: 7).

Living by *alaas* is Sakha's central cultural identifier, from their beginnings in their northern lands, through the tumultuous changes of the Soviet period and, perhaps more so, the post-Soviet period, to the last thirty years of reclaiming and reviving their cultural identity. *Alaas* also provide Sakha with agency within their context of rapid environmental, sociocultural, and political change. "Culture becomes a vehicle for agency. . . . Agency runs interference, demands flexibility, tolerance and humor, all of which are inimical to coercive regimes" (Sommer 2006: 13–14). *Alaas* can also serve Sakha as a viable form of cultural resilience, "the ability to hold on to traditional [historical] beliefs and practices in the face of constant pressures to assimilate exerted by a dominant society" (Fortier 2009: 2), as Sakha, and other non-Russian peoples, confront increasing pressures from the Russian state.

Chapter 7

We All Live on Permafrost

Sakha's Predicament in the Greater World Context of "Knowing" Climate Change

International media first reported Sakha's predicament to the rest of the world in 2019 with the *New York Times* article "Russian Land of Permafrost and Mammoths Is Thawing." The author used simple prose to communicate to a broader public, articulating with clear descriptors and images what he saw so that readers could "see" the on-the-ground situation.

> The village road was once straight, with log houses and *khotons* lined up perfectly along its length. Now the muddy road is all potholes, winding among the new-formed hills, it has no resemblance to a road. Tossed around houses, sloping at different angles. "It's like after the war," says Makarov, whose new home stands on stilts embedded 16 meters deep, where there is still permafrost. "Soon there will be no flat land left in this village. I have only 30–40 years to live, I hope my house will last for this time." (MacFarquhar 2019)

Two months later, on October 3, the *Washington Post* published another article, "Radical Warming in Siberia Leaves Millions on Unstable Ground": "The permafrost that once sustained farming . . . and upon which villages and cities are built . . . is in the midst of a great thaw, blanketing the region with swamps, lakes and odd bubbles of earth that render the land virtually useless" (Trianovski and Mooney 2019).

I was interviewed by the *Washington Post* reporter who wrote the second piece. He was interested in my assessment of Viliui Sakha's situation, based on my long-term research there. After the initial interview at a café in Yakutsk, the reporter contacted me with follow-up questions to finalize the article. He explained that the social and natural scientists in Yakutsk said that few populations in the world were feeling the impact of climate change as intensely as the people of the Sakha Republic. I disagreed. There are many examples of human populations across the planet today challenged by unprecedented change, many who are being displaced and forced to migrate in response to the local effects of climate change. I cited some examples from my own scholarship, two edited volumes on anthropology and climate change (Crate and Nuttall 2009, 2016), and the recent IPCC Special Report on Ocean and Cryosphere in a Changing Climate (IPCC 2019), both of which used examples of communities in high-altitude, high-latitude, and near sea-level areas globally. He next asked my opinion of Yakutsk scientists' understanding that the local effects of climate change in the rural areas were the main reason why Sakha relocated to the city. I disagreed with that as well. Based on my experience, people relocated for a variety of reasons. Young people relocated first for a higher education and then, realizing they preferred the city life, either found a job in their field or in other work in order to stay. The elderly relocated because they wanted to have the comforts of central heat, running water, and good access to health care in their later years. Still others relocated because they had found work or because all their kin had moved to the city. But people moving specifically because of the local effects of climate change was not something I had witnessed in my own work.

These two 2019 newspaper stories, and other efforts to convey what is occurring in the Sakha Republic due to climate change, are critical to communicate the urgency of actions needed not only for Sakha's but for all of our future. But in order to be most effective, they must communicate those changes in their full depth and breadth. In both of my clarifications to the reporter, I had hoped to communicate the complexity of local to global change on the planet today and our mutual interdependency within that complexity. Instead of seeing one people's experience as worse than another's, it is more realistic to see each case as one part of the greater challenge of our mutual life on Earth. Instead of attributing climate change as the central driver of change on the planet, it is more accurate to include it in the multitude of other changes occurring simultaneously and often in interdependence. It is also critical to keep in mind the human tenacity to adapt when considering the narratives of people globally who are challenged by unprecedented change. Sakha continue to find ways to work with their challenges, "but people here are used to adapting. They survived the forced collectivization of the early Soviet Union. Gulag prisoners taught them to grow potatoes. After the Soviet Union collapsed and the state farms closed, they shifted to a greater reliance on hunting and fishing" (Trianovski and Mooney 2019). This is by no means to downplay the seriousness of climate change and the need to act in order to avoid its worst consequences, but rather to remember and reify humanity's inherent capacity to innovate and adapt. Humanity's tenacious adaptive capacity is mirrored in the Even's half-joke that if it continues to warm, they will change from herding reindeer to herding camels (Vitebsky 2006).

The Global Importance of Knowledge Systems and Narratives

"It is this dance of cross-pollination that can produce a new species of knowledge, a new way of being in the world. After all, there aren't two worlds, there is just this one good green earth" (Kimmerer 2013: 47). When Robin Wall Kimmerer wrote these words, she was contemplating the "energetic reciprocity" between the complementary colors of purple asters and goldenrod in order to emphasize the complementarity of Indigenous knowledge and scientific knowledge. Kimmerer argues that, similar to how complementary colors invoke each other, knowledge systems do the same, in a relationship she calls "lived reciprocity": "Its wisdom is that the beauty of one is illuminated by the radiance of the other. Science and art, matter and spirit, Indigenous knowledge and Western science . . . can they be goldenrod and asters for each other?" (ibid.).

How can Kimmerer's concept of lived reciprocity inform our discussion of Sakha's physical (permafrost) and cultural (*alaas*) keystones? Our biosphere is a single interactive system, evidenced by both past planetary climate change events (Blois et al. 2013; Trotter et al. 2015) and the plethora of global change knowledge to date (IPCC 2001, 2014, 2019). One part of the planet is not disconnected from any other part on the planet.

The ocean and cryosphere regulate the climate and weather on Earth, provide food and water, support economies, trade and transportation, shape cultures and influence our well-being. Many of the recent changes in Earth's ocean and cryosphere are the result of human activities and have consequences on everyone's life. Deep cuts in greenhouse gas emissions will reduce negative impacts on billions of people and help them adapt to changes in their environment. Improving education and combining scientific knowledge with Indigenous knowledge and local knowledge helps communities to further address the challenges ahead. (IPCC 2019: 92)

Testimonies such as these help to make the case that, metaphorically speaking, **we all live on permafrost.** This is both a physical and a cultural reality. Not only is the planet one interdependent biosphere, in which we all live on permafrost, it is also a dynamic and interacting ethnosphere, "the sum total of all the thoughts, dreams, ideals, myths, intuitions, and inspirations brought into being by the imagination since the dawn of consciousness . . . humanity's great legacy . . . all that we've achieved and the promise of all that we can achieve as the wildly curious and adaptive species we are" (Davis 2014: 1). Our human planet is a systematic patchwork of culturally diverse ways that humans have interacted with their environment and each other and innovated to adapt to change over time, both deep and recent. This idea is captured in the concept of biocultural diversity, "the diversity of life in all of its manifestations: biological, cultural, and linguistic, which are interrelated (and possibly coevolved) within a complex socio-ecological adaptive system" (Maffi 2007: 269). If culture is "a distinct ensemble of mutually interacting symbolic and material practices that a human group uses to survive and thrive in the world" (Powell 2016: 45), then the ethnosphere also represents humanity's cultural and innovative potential.

Because of our interdependence, living within our planetary biosphere and ethnosphere, our common future depends not only on "fixing" the physical issue of climate change but also on the multiple cultural issues, on a greater awareness of how the world's other peoples are affected by and responding to unprecedented change. Part of that awareness requires that we frame others' experiences in the context of their Indigenous knowledge or local knowledge. By engaging and reifying affected peoples' knowledge systems we are repatriating those ways of knowing within the world from which historically they were systematically disqualified and subjugated under the hegemony of "Western culture's domination of nature" (Scott 1996: 85). Retelling and "re-presenting" what people know in their specific frames of reference can then contribute to achieving the impactful *resonance* (Meyer 2015) needed to bring about the critical work of social change toward regenerative living systems. How can other cases where peoples find themselves increasingly disowned from their critical eco- and ethno-system foundations inform the Sakha case?

Mongolian Herders' Mobility on a Land That Is Moving

> We don't see summer anymore.... Our ancestors said that the day will come when we will wear our fur vests in the summer. (Household head, Eg-Uur confluence, summer 2014)

Since 2012 I have collaborated on a project in northern Mongolia investigating how climate change is affecting fish populations of Lake Hovsgol and several adjacent watersheds. Previously, members of the project team had all been natural scientists, concentrating on water temperatures, seasonal changes, and other liminal and riverine characteristics. One summer during their research they noticed several Mongolian herders who were fishing in the lake, extending a net across the lake's incoming tributaries to catch all incoming fish. No longer was their work only about temperature and other variables of the aquatic systems. It now included humans. They needed a social scientist to discern the part humans played in the declining fish populations.

Through a colleague already collaborating with the team, I was asked to join. I enthusiastically accepted. I had traveled to Mongolia before, first in 1990 when the country was still under socialist rule and later in 2011, two decades after the end of Soviet control. I was anxious to get back and also interested in how Mongolian herders' challenges compared to Viliui Sakha's. At the time I knew mostly about one major effect of climate change in Mongolia's grassland ecosystems, the increased frequency of *dzud* (Mongolian: an extreme winter), a time either of too much snow fall that prevents herds from accessing their fodder or of no snow that causes the bare ground to freeze, ostensibly killing the next year's spring pasture growth. In 2010, eight million animals died from catastrophic *dzud*, and herders who were just making ends meet at the time were forced to leave herding, with most relocating to urban areas for work (Rao et al. 2015).

I joined the team and participated in fieldwork during the summer of 2014. Several of us focused on gauging local perceptions and adaptations to change, in its many forms, while the others monitored fish populations. We worked in summer herding camps on two river confluences, the Eg-Uur and the Eg-Selenga. We conducted interviews with a dozen herding households at each location. Overall, we found that, like in Sakha, these herders were keenly aware of the changes taking place, based on their daily and cyclical interactions with their environment, and that they were actively adapting as best they could.

In addition to *dzud*, herders enumerated many other ongoing effects of climate change, including the intrusion of invasive plants into the pastures because of an early cold spring; a change in precipitation patterns, most notably from constant measured rainfall over several days to sudden downpour events that resulted in erosion and drought conditions; and a new summer temperature regime of frequent frosts and cool days in contrast to the hot days and warm nights of before. Climate change was not the only driver threatening the future of their herding culture. "The number of young herders is decreasing because herding is hard work and also because they are 'listening to another world' and no longer to their parents and elders" (household head, Eg-Selenge confluence, summer 2014). Mongolian youth are leaving herding for the urban areas and their community of peers.

The complexity of change for herders at the Eg-Selenga site was further complicated by issues of extraction and development. Mongolia has been pursuing construction of a hydro-dam at the Eg-Selenga confluence since the 1990s. The project has been off and on over the course of the last thrity years because of a wavering commitment from the Chinese government, the project's main funder. Once the proposed massive hydroelectric station is completed, it will flood the summer pasture of some 700 herding households along the Eg River. We included a question for interviewees at the Eg-Selenga site about the dam and its implications for their future. Many initially responded by echoing the government's propaganda line that the dam project was justified for their people to "progress." Further inquiry about their plans for summer camp once the dam was completed revealed an overall disdain for the project that would force many of them off the lands that their family had used for generations.

On my last day in the field, the director of the dam project made a visit to the area. I wanted to tell him what I had learned. In my naivety I assumed that since he himself was Mongolian, that perhaps my representation of the herders' concerns would somehow move him to reconsider the flooding. It was quite the opposite. When I explained that the herders talked about using the lands for generations and about having no idea where they would go once the flooding began, he quickly responded, "They can just move; they have been doing it for centuries." End of conversation. His words stayed with me. Those unfamiliar with contemporary Mongolia and the Mongolian herding lifestyle may think he is right. Indeed, mobility is a critical part of herders' success. To an outsider, there also may appear to be lot of extra space across Mongolia's vast steppe.

The on-the-ground reality is quite the opposite. Yes, herders are mobile but across a regular pasturing pattern, often one that they and their families have used for decades if not generations. The vast Mongolian steppe may be physically unfenced and unbounded, but it is nonetheless cordoned off, based upon the historical and continued use by extensive mobile pastoralist groups. Herders at the Eg-Selenga confluence are losing ground not only because of how their lands are "shrinking" from the various effects of climate change but also because of the distorted cultural constructs of modern mainstream land use in a neoliberal capitalist society. The world over, there is a multitude of ways that humans make a living from the earth and live in interaction with and maintain place attachment to their immediate ecosystem. There needs to be an alternative to the formal land ownership paradigm of modernity through finding ways to document and secure the place-based livelihoods of mobile peoples, be they Mongolian herders or Arctic reindeer pastoralists or African Maasai.

Another critical issue for Mongolian herders, not one that I learned about in the 2014 interviews with herders, is thawing permafrost. Sakha have it foremost in their minds because the thawing is bringing obvious changes to the many once-flat *ötökh* that local people know. In Mongolia the change is not visually apparent. It is nonetheless life threatening. In Mongolia permafrost is a main source of water that often saves vegetation in drought periods.

Mongolia is one of the most southern permafrost areas on earth, along with high-altitude China and the Tibetan plateau. In contrast to those areas, most permafrost in Mongolia is discontinuous or patchy. Furthermore, Mongolian permafrost is found in a pattern of north versus south slopes, with the forested north-facing slopes on permafrost and the south-facing slopes devoid of it. The forest cover acts as the protective layer that perpetuates the permafrost. The permafrost on these north slopes "waters" the forests, via the capillary action that draws water up from the permafrost during dry periods. In addition, the water from the northern slopes also waters the southern slopes, the exact locations of the pastures so important to Mongolian herding. In short, permafrost is critical to the water needs of the grasslands and pastures on which Mongolian herders depend. Given the country's arid climate, without the upward exchange of water from the permafrost below to the terrestrial plants on the surface, the present-day pasturelands of Mongolia would quickly turn to desert.

Continuous monitoring of permafrost in Mongolia shows its retreat and the resulting desiccation of pasturelands. Researchers use monitoring data from a transect of boreholes from the north to the south of Mongolia to project how, in the next hundred years, the conditions present now in the south (arid desert) will spread to the north (Ishikawa et al. 2018). In other words, in a century, Mongolia's permafrost will have completely thawed, leaving all of Mongolia an arid desert. Only one place in all of Mongolia will retain its permafrost, the Darkhad Lake, an area next to Lake Hovsgol (Etzelmüller et al. 2006). Despite these dire projections, the rich literature of both meteorological and socioeconomic data documenting how climate change is affecting Mongolia's ecosystems and herding lifestyle lacks the correlation between thawing permafrost, changing forage resources, and herding livelihoods (cf. Angerer et al. 2008; Rao et al. 2015; Danzhalova et al. 2012). Nevertheless, the data show that Mongolian herders are directly affected by thawing permafrost, having adapted their livelihoods to a permafrost ecosystem and, like Viliui Sakha to their north, can therefore be thought of as "ice dependent."

Ice Dependence in Sakha and Labrador/Nunatsiavut Canada

Another way that humans have adapted to permafrost ecosystems and de facto developed an "ice dependence" is by locating their settlements on coasts to use sea ice for harvesting and hunting. I fully grasped this understanding of ice dependence during a project from 2009 to 2012 comparing perceptions and understandings of changing seasonality in Viliui Sakha and

Nunatsiavut communities of Labrador Canada (Crate 2012). The project's two main Nunatsiavut settlements, Makkovik and Hopedale, are home to communities whose ancestors developed specific adaptations, using the perennial sea ice to hunt sea mammals and fish and using ice and snow for inland hunting, fishing, and land transport. Success requires an in-depth knowledge of snow and ice conditions. Contemporary inhabitants speak extensively about the ways they know to read the ice, referring to white ice, black ice, yellow ice, ice that forms before it snows versus ice that forms after it snows, to name a few. They claim that the most solid, dependable ice forms during the season's first snowfall, when the freezing temperatures harden the water to ice, and the falling snow thickens that ice substantially. They report that there is no longer any reliable ice in the early ice season, because of the elongated, warm fall period. As a result, many people no longer hunt as they used to. Similarly, the *shina* (Inuktitut: the ice edge where sea mammal hunting takes place) has changed. Before it was several kilometers out beyond the land's shore, and now it is only one kilometer at most. Furthermore, the quality of the ice needed to travel to the *shina* is no longer dependable. It is a patchwork of solid and thin areas, making travel restricted and even dangerous. Travel on this unpredictable ice is also more difficult than before with the advent of snowmobiles. In the old days, sled dogs knew the ice and acted as natural sensors of thin ice, stopping the sled before going farther.

Land ice and snow are also important to Nunatsiavut villages for hunting, trapping, getting wood, and traveling between settlements. A snow cover, solid enough to travel on, was historically in place by November at the latest. It now is only in place by the New Year at the earliest. In the winter of 2010–11 it did not form until early February, pushing the setting of traps back several months. With snow and ice increasingly less dependable and predictable, and in some cases absent, inhabitants who continue historically based subsistence practices do so with increased effort, danger, and cost. Inhabitants also reflected on the loss of their recreational uses of ice: "When we were teenagers, we all would go and play on the pancake ice . . . sometimes you fell in but there were people all around to help you out if you did [. . .] haven't seen a good gathering for that for ten years . . . some people go and try but it's different with the ice changing so much now" (elder, Hopedale, Nunatsiavut, 2010).

There were many similarities between the changes the Nunatsiavut residents were observing and the nine main changes found among the Vilui

Sakha. For example, changes in winter temperatures parallel observations that *Jyl Oghuha* was not arriving: "It's been a long time since we had that old-fashioned cold [. . .] we just don't see it anymore" (elder, Makkovik, Nunatsiavut, 2010).

There were differences also. Whereas Viliui Sakha talk about the huge increases of winter snow, Nunatsiavut inhabitants report the opposite: "Not so much snow . . . used to be so much snow that it covered the houses . . . I remember the men coming and digging out our chimney and then digging tunnels to our doors so we could get out [. . .] it doesn't snow like that anymore . . . that much snow was good because it insulated and kept houses warm and we burned less wood!" (elder, Makkovik, Nunatsiavut).

Another similarity to the Viliui Sakha case is how Nunatsiavut communities were grappling with other drivers of change beyond climate and changing seasonality. However critical to subsistence these ice and snow conditions are, for the time being they remain secondary to the more immediate threats to local communities, namely, increasing economic uncertainty and a disinterested or absent youth not taking up the local subsistence ways. Like in the Viliui Sakha communities, Makkovik and Hopedale are relatively dense settlements, for them the result of being established to provide labor for the cod fisheries, which crashed in the late twentieth century. This foundational economic activity no longer supports local economies, yet the settlements remain. Unemployment and dependence on subsidies and pensions are a large part of how people get by. This in turn has spurred the out-migration of youth, who leave for higher education and employment elsewhere. Fewer and fewer people in the communities are continuing the subsistence practices.

Ice Dependence in the Andes, Kiribati, and the Chesapeake Bay

These next examples continue the idea of communities as ice dependent, but this time engaging communities located in temperate world regions. From 2008 to 2015 I was involved in the documentary *The Anthropologist*. I agreed to take part, despite my mixed feelings about camera crews invading my field site and issues of human subjects' protection for my collaborators, because I understood the need to give climate change a human face. What anthropologists and others were witnessing in the world areas hardest hit by climate change needed to be brought to audiences where the signs of climate change were less apparent. The documentary team first shot footage during our 2010 knowledge exchanges and also in less formal interactions with Viliui Sakha inhabitants. The film directors then requested my thoughts on two other world contexts where climate change was having similarly challenging effects for local communities, but where I had never worked. We ended up engaging with communities in the high-altitude areas of the Peruvian Andes and in the near sea-level location of Kiribati, a South Pacific island nation. I also made the case for working with affected communities closer to home to communicate that climate change was not just affecting peoples in distant lands. This took us to the watermen of the Chesapeake Bay in Virginia.

To be successful in the Andes, local communities continue to refine the specific adaptations their ancestors have been developing over millennia (Orlove et al. 2002). One constant is the continued dependence on glacial water for agriculture, making ice dependence in that context fairly obvious. Farmers maintain *chakras* (Kichwa: small agricultural plots) between 7,000 and 14,000 feet in altitude with different crops growing in the different ecotones. This practice is referred to as "verticality" (Oliver-Smith 1999: 78) and it requires an intimate expertise of the conditions at each level. During the documentary shoot, farmers testified about how, as the warming of the atmosphere proceeds, crops that before only grew in the lower altitudes, like corn, are now growing at higher elevations. While walking in the higher elevations to meet and talk with farmers, we more than once saw the pre-Incan canals that local inhabitants have used for centuries to channel meltwater from the glaciers to water their *chakras*. Several interviewees shared their concern about the rapid shrinking of the glaciers and what it meant for their water supplies and crops. The glacial meltwater is critical not only to local inhabitants' agricultural success but also to their spiritual relationships, since the glaciers are central to their cosmology, like *Jyl Oghuha* is for Sakha (Paerregaard 2013; Bolin 2009).

Ice dependence in Kiribati and on the Chesapeake Bay are not as straightforward. In both places, inhabitants are challenged by unprecedented flooding, extreme weather events, and in the case of Kiribati, saltwater contamination of the freshwater lens[1] that provides drinking water.

Kiribati is an island nation state in the South Pacific made up of thirty-three island atolls. Over centuries, I-Kiribati (the term for a native of Kiribati) have developed an Indigenous knowledge system to be able to subsist on ocean products and tropical fruits and vegetables and to thrive as a culture. Today they are witnessing unprecedented sea-level rise. The Kiribati government has successfully brought their situation to the world's attention (Loughry and McAdam 2008). In 2003 the Kiribati Adaptation Program received funding from the World Bank and other international donors to mainstream adaptation into national development planning. The central challenge was sea-level rise that threatened inhabitants' continued residence on the island atoll. The World Bank advisers and the nation's president at the time emphasized "relocation with dignity" and secured a land area on Fiji to move the community. However, local inhabitants voiced their preference to find ways to remain in their homeland (Donner and Webber 2014). Studies then focused on discerning how best to bring about place-based adaptation measures by prioritizing how I-Kiribati were perceiving change. In other words, researchers were forefronting I-Kiribati's vernacular knowledge system to find long-lasting solutions: "Furthermore, it is important to examine the extent to which certain knowledge systems about climatic change and water management are privileged in adaptation planning programmes and the implications for anticipatory adaptation among local communities" (Kuruppa and Liverman 2011: 668). Most pressing were I-Kiribati perceptions of the threat that rising sea-levels were to their critical freshwater supplies (ibid.).

The Chesapeake Bay watermen also depend on and regularly put into practice a centuries-old local knowledge system to be successful in their environment. Unlike their I-Kiribati counterparts, their homeland is not made up of near sea-level island atolls and their drinking water is not threatened by saltwater intrusion. Chesapeake Bay watermen also have more alternatives in terms of making their living and access to products. Nevertheless, they clearly have a deep understanding of how their environment is changing. One waterman described the changes as he understood them: "I don't know if it is because of global warming but we used to pull 2,000 pounds of lobster out of the Chesapeake Bay. We don't see lobster here anymore" (qtd. in Kramer et al. 2015). The watermen's testimony is founded upon their lifelong inhabitance in one place and their in-depth local knowledge of that place. A pivotal topic of discussion was how winters were, past and present. When I asked about his recollections of winter in his youth, one waterman slipped into a memory and a smile expanded across his face. "Me and my buddies skated every day after school for three months in the winter. There are several ponds nearby that we used." I commented that the youth must love skating on those same ponds today. His smile turned to a pout and he proclaimed, "They don't skate . . . there hasn't been ice on the ponds for twenty years!" He said that not only have the winter conditions changed but also the youth themselves. He and the other watermen expressed dismay that their youth were not interested in learning the watermen's ways and instead were choosing other professions.

Inhabitants of near sea-level areas, like I-Kiribati and the Chesapeake watermen, are ice dependent the world over, to the extent that sea-level rise is, in part, a result of the thawing of the earth's cryosphere, and especially the ice masses on Greenland and Antarctica.

We All Live on Permafrost

If taken in the context of Earth as a holistic integrated system, the planet's cryosphere is not just the frozen parts of the earth, but the frozen parts of the earth that are intrinsically interdependent, sustained by and sustaining of the other parts of the planet. In other words, when the permafrost thaws, it affects all of the planet and, by default, all of us.

Humans have inhabited permafrost landscapes for a very long time, long before the scientific understanding of permafrost. They have done so suc-cessfully based on using their indirect knowledge of permafrost to develop innovations and adaptations to an ecosystem founded upon the permafrost layer. This is only part of the story of success. Critical to their success are the cultural innovations and adaptations, the innate and intimate interde-pendences with the ecosphere they inhabit, and the essential relationships maintained via both physical and spiritual reciprocities. For Sakha, living "by the *alaas*" was, and continues to be, their central cultural identifier. *Alaas* have been agentive through Sakha's significant historical, sociocultural, geo-political, and economic change. The resilience of *alaas* as cultural identifier is reflected in how *alaas*, through the myriad of historical, political, sociocul-tural, and climatological changes, continue to provide contemporary Sakha a cradle, a sense of return to something so very essential, and even primordial, to their existence.

Like in Sakha, the Mongolia case also called up images for me of perma-frost as a slumbering giant. This time, the beast came to mind because of another of its characteristics—its silent and secret below-ground work. In Mongolia, the issue of permafrost thaw has received little attention outside of a very specialized team of permafrost scientists. Both the academic social science research and the press coverage of Mongolia's climate change issues give no voice to the disappearing permafrost upon which all life depends.

When I mention permafrost in casual conversations about my research, most people respond with a comment about how the thawing is problematic because it releases methane. That the world's glaciers are rapidly thawing because of climate change has been and continues to be well-covered in the media (Glick 2004). The impact of rapidly thawing glaciers is also viscerally understood by most when they learn that the Andean and the Himalayan glacial masses combined supply drinking water for several billion people. This glacial water also plays a critical role in crop irrigation and energy generation. What we hear little about and only very recently (as in the 2019 *Washington Post* and the *New York Times* articles) is how another critical water source, which also occurs in the earth's cryosphere, is rapidly thawing—permafrost. Perhaps because we do not see it thawing and perhaps because it exists far below the earth's surface, permafrost has received little attention and has not found a place in global awareness. At the same time, permafrost science is highly matured and shows unequivocally that permafrost is thawing and that this thaw presents monumental challenges for ecosystems and the cultures who depend upon them. That means all of us and it underscores how *we all live on permafrost*. And we each have a sense of belonging, deep inside, like Sakha have shown us about their connection to *alaas,*

I find myself in the expansive city
Trying to get used to the shallow existence
But I don't sleep day or night
Constantly thinking of my birth *alaas.*

With this, my tale for you has come to a close. I explained earlier that I consciously chose to title this book "Once Upon the Permafrost," not to perpetuate a colonial legacy by using a trope of European fairy tales but to resonate with the archetypal past of those I consider this book's main audience, participants in Western consumer societies. Cultural narratives inform our lives, whether we are Viliui Sakha, I-Kiribati, or American, more powerfully and completely than scientific evidence. I also chose the title to frame my overall appeal of the book, specifically that because *we **all live on permafrost***, our best chance for a future on this planet is to do all we can to protect it. In short, "this is my story, I've told it, and in your hands, I leave it" (Warner 1995: xxv).

Afterword

I began this book project in December 2017, two years before Covid-19 became our harsh reality. I sent the first draft in to my editor on January 28, 2020, and left two days later for a fellowship at University of Melbourne, Australia. What I remember so distinctly about how I got word of the gravity of the virus was how the Australian Public TV News changed so dramatically. I got to Melbourne when the horrific bushfire tragedy was in its final stages. In fact, my host had advised me to bring N-95 masks because on some days in the city when the wind blows a certain way, it is recommended that you wear one. I never needed them, at least not for the bushfire smoke! For the first several weeks I enjoyed the news stories that took me all around the country, learning about the wildlife, gardening, various local issues for farmers and fishers and such. Then, around mid-February began the stories of the two cruise ships that were returning to Australia from China and the strange virus that prompted the government to quarantine the ships. In a few days, this was all that was on the news. I was interested but I stopped watching. When I was on campus, I began hearing about how the university's Chinese students were not going to be allowed back after the summer break (their summer is our winter in the Northern Hemisphere). At the end of February, I co-led a storying climate change workshop at the university and in between our discussion of how to best communicate about climate, were comments about the virus and how it was multiplying. I started reaching out to friends back home and tried not to panic. One of my projects was to work with local communities and facilitate discussion of climate and the place of narratives. After several weeks of working on a plan to do this, on the morning of March 14 I took the train out to the LaTrobe Valley to work with the communities in Sale and Morwell.

> **March 14** up early to take the train to Flinders station and then the train to Sale. Darren McCubbin met me at the station and showed me the dock where he said they dug a canal long ago so the gold could come through there. Then we had coffee in a wonderful cafe in the community building and met up with Jo, his 2nd cousin. She took me to see The Knob, a sacred aboriginal place a few miles out of town. It was so beautiful but I had a hard time "being there" because I was really distracted by the virus. Afterwards we went back into Sale to a venue called "Dave's Place" for the community discussion with a group of 20 very interested people. Darren then took me to Morwell for the second event. I asked if he would stop at the pharmacy so I could buy a thermometer. I got the last one! While I was in there, Jo texted him so he could tell me that the New Zealand government had just announced that they were implementing a 14-day quarantine for all who come into the country. I had been asking the universe to give me a sign about whether I should go and that was the final straw. No New Zealand. All I wanted now was to go home.

I cut my fellowship stay short by two weeks and forfeited my five-week trip on the South Island of New Zealand to come home on March 17. Two days later, I flew to Austin, Texas, where Tuyaara was in grad school to drive home with her.

The year 2020 has been a time of reckoning on many fronts. Not only are we in the grips of a global pandemic, we are also continuing to let climate change proceed unabated. Each alone is overwhelming. Taken together they present a very real existential crisis. Making matters worse, we in the United States have floundered in our federal response in both areas. Nevertheless, there are those who choose to take on the challenge of both Covid-19 and climate change by following the most up-to-date science. Of course, we can only do so much as individuals, communities, regions, and states. Now, two weeks after the November 3 election, there is a new hope for federal guidance and policy. Nevertheless, it is easy to feel discouraged.

Despite these odds, I have chosen to maintain a positive attitude about these two challenges we face. In fact, I believe that our experience thus far with Covid-19 has given us a clear idea of how we need to confront climate change and also that we really have what it takes. Our experience with Covid-19 on a global scale has shown us that when we change how we act in the world, it can have a direct effect on containing the virus or not. We have learned that governmental guidance, policy, and protocol are critical to contain the virus. Interestingly, a remarkable early response was seen by female leaders, for example, New Zealand's Jacinda Ardern, Taiwan's Tsai Ing-wen, Germany's Angela Merkel, Denmark's Mette Frederiksen, and Finland's Sanna Marin. We understand the fact that science is the key to tackling the pandemic. If we scan the news and look back at how we have acted, especially first responders, we gain a sense of our capacity to be empathetic and to care about each other. And the early quarantining response shows that we can act quickly. These are the very same elements we need to respond to the longer existential crisis of climate change. And here I want to give a shout-out to the younger generation. At the end of *The Anthropologist* I remark that I believe it is Tuyaara's generation who will have the gumption to turn climate change around. I am not implying that the rest of us old folks should just throw our hands up and let the kids take care of the mess we have contributed to. My intent was to recognize young people's energy, creativity, innovation, and drive. And we have seen it emerge in the last years, especially with Greta Thunberg and the Sunrise movement, among other youth initiatives. In the end, the words of the Fourteenth Dalai Lama ring the truest for me:

> To remain indifferent to the challenges we face is indefensible,
> If the goal is noble, whether or not it is realized within our lifetime, is
>   largely irrelevant,
> What we must do, therefore, is to strive and persevere and never give up.
>   —Dalai Lama XIV

A Note on Methods

The Longitudinal Chronology of
Research with Viliui Sakha

This book is a longitudinal ethnography, a study of change over time within a specific cultural context. I am a qualitative researcher. I use interviews, focus groups, oral history, and participant observation with some triangulation using quantitative methods (surveys, time allocation, document and archival analysis). In the summers of 2018 and 2019, I conducted field research in Elgeeii and Kutana with the specific objective of assembling the loose threads of my findings over the course of almost three decades of fieldwork with Viliui Sakha to provide the longitudinal gaze for this book. I worked with the same set of Elgeeii and Kutana households who were in my 1999–2000 random sample for my dissertation research. For the original sample, I used a random number table to select 30 percent of all households from each village's "Household Book," a log of all households, each with a consecutive number (Elgeeii, n = 210; Kutana, n = 70). I began to develop longitudinal household accounts immediately after the dissertation with the 2003–5 project, and all projects since by basing my interviews and surveys on the same random sample from 1999 in both Elgeeii and Kutana. It is this process that allows me to describe and provide the anthropological window into how Sakha are perceiving, understanding, and responding to the myriad of change in their lives over time. Although I integrate some of what I found in past research projects into my overall account in this book, the majority of the book is founded upon my 2018–19 research findings. For the 2018 and

2019 interviews I requested and received permission to use participants' full names. All quotes prior to that time, except where the full name is present, are anonymous, according to my research protocol in the field.

Seeing Change

In addition to the methods described above, I also use visual anthropology. I find that images have a unique power to communicate. For example, I captured the composition for the picture of the *buluus* with the modern Kutana school in the background (figure 6) as I was returning to my host's home after a day of interviews. It spoke to me of the rapidity of change ever present in my field site. I capture images and use them (observing all proper ethical procedures to do so) to tell the stories about change for Viliui Sakha. I have also engaged in several experimental ventures. One was in 2018 when I retraced the steps I took in 1999–2000 to the 210 households in Elgeeii to visually document how they had changed over time. Another was after I started the climate project in 2008; I took photos in specific places to track the change in water on the land over the next years (figures 45 and 46).

Figure 45 House near the Toloon lake, showing proximity to increasing water on the land in 2009. Photo by author.

Figure 46 House near the Toloon lake in 2010, showing how its proximity to the increasing water on the land has changed dramatically in one year. Photo by author.

I use photos in this book to take advantage of their power to communicate and to bolster my goal to bring readers closer to understanding Viliui Sakha and their contemporary predicament. Nonetheless, like other research methodologies, images are subjective artifacts that I have chosen to represent what I have seen. I can only hope that my representations, both textual and visual, communicate what I have come to know over the last three decades with Viliui Sakha.

2018 Household Interview Instrument

First, please tell me your birth year, birth place, how long you have lived in
   this house and what kin do you have here.

*Бастаан, баһаалыста, эт эрэ: төрөөбүт сылгын, төрөөбүт сиргин,
   манна төһө өр олоро5унуй уонна манна туох аймахтардаахыный.*

Did I work with you before? Focus groups, interview, survey?

Урукку сылларга эн миигин кытта үлэлэспитин дуо?

—If yes, when?

Ол хаһан этэй?

How has your life changed in the last 10 years?

Кэнники 10 сылларга эн оло5ун хайдах уларыда?

What was life like when you were growing up?

Эн эдэр эрдэххинэ Олох хайдах этэй?

What was life like when your parents were growing up?

Эн төрөппүттэрин эдэр эрдэхтэринэ Олох хайдах этэй?

What do you think life was like when your grandparents were growing up?

Эн эбэҥ-эһэҥ кэмнэригэр Олох хайдах этэй дии саныыгыный?

Do you have cows?

Эһиги ынахтааххыт дуо?

—If yes, how long have you had them?

Өскө, баар буолла5ына, хас сыл тутта5ыный?

—Tell me about your cow history—when did you start, why, who did you
   learn from?

*Кэпсээ хаһаанныттан ынах ииттэ5эний, то5о ииттэ5эний—уонна
кимтэн үөрэмиккиний?*

—If no, did you have them before?

Суох буолла5ына, Үрүт ынах ииттэр этинг дуо?

—If yes, when did you stop and why?

Сэп буолла5ына, хаһан уонна то5о эспиккиний?

—If no, why not?

Өскө, эн хаһан да ынах туппатаах буолла5ына, ол то5о?

—If no, where do you get your meat and milk?

Эт -уут хантан ылагыный?

Do you practice any special ways to care for them? Hang salama, or other?

Ынахха сыһыаннаах ханнык сахалыы үгэстэри тутуһа5ыный?

Do you work with your kin to keep them? Cow care, haying?

Кимниин ынах ииттэ5эний? Аймахтарыҥ көмөлөһөллөр дуо?

Where do you hay? How much land do you have?

Ханна оттуугунуй? Төһө оттуур сирдээххиний?

In the last 10 years, how has the hay grown there?

Кэнники 10 сылга, от хайдах үүммүтэй?

In your opinion, for your village what is the best way to keep cows?

*Эн санаа5ар, ынах сүөһүну иити эһиги нэһилиэккитигэр, ханнык
ньыма ордук буолуой?*

Do fewer people keep them now or more? Why?

Билигин эһиги нэһилиэккитигэр, хас ыал ынахтаа5ый?

Do you think your village will continue to have cows in the future?

*Эн санаа5ар, эһиги нэһилиэккитигэр, кэлэр кэмнэргэ ынах сүөһү
элбиэ дуу, а5ыйыа дуу?*

How have the last 5 years of canal digging affected the land?

*Кэнники биэс сылга, хоруу хаһыыта сиргэ-дойдуга туох содуллаах
дии саныыгыный?*

Has the releasing of the water been good for your hay land?

Ууну ыыппыттара эн отуур сиргэр туһалаах дуо?

Do you spend time in nature?

Айыл5а5а сылдьа5ын дуо?

If yes, doing what?

Еске сылдьар буоллаххына, соругун-сыалын-дьарыгын тугуй?

What changes have you noticed in nature?

Айыл5а5а туох уларыйыылары бэлиэтии көрө5үнүй?

How is it different from, say, when you were a child?

Эн оҕо сааскыттан билиҥҥи Айыл5а туох уратылаа5ый?

What changes have you noticed in the weather?

Халлааҥҥа туох уларыйыылары бэлиэтии көрө5үнүй?

How is it different from when you were a child?

Эн оҕо сааскыттан билинни Халлаан туох уратылаа5ый?

What changes have you noticed in the seasonal timing?

Саас, Сайын, Күһүн, Кыһын кэлиилэригэр туох уларыйыылары
    бэлиэтии көрө5үнүй?

How are they different from, say, when you were a child?

Билиҥҥи Дьыл кэлиитэ уруккуттаан туох уратылаа5ый?

Please explain how the season used to change and what the conditions
    were like.

Баһаалыста, кэпсээ эрэ, үрүт дьыл хайдах уонна хаһан кэлэр этэй?

Have you noticed any changes in the land?

Сир-дойду уларыйыытын бэлиэтии көрө5үн дуо?

What do you think is causing the changes in nature, weather, and land that
    we are discussing?

Бу уларыйыылар туохтан төрүөттээх дии саныгыный?

What are the effects of those changes?

Уларыйыылар туох содуллаахтарый?

How do you adapt to those changes?

Уларыйыыга эн хайдах сөп түбэһэн үөрэнниҥ?

What do you know about permafrost?

Ирбэт тоҥ туһунан тугу биле5иний?

What meaning does permafrost have in your life?

Эһиги олоххутугар ирбэт тоҥ туох суолталаа5ый?

What does the word "*alaas*" mean to you?

'Алаас' диэн тылынан тугу өдүүгүнүй?

Do you know where your ancestors' homeplace is?

Өбүгэлэрин өтөхтэрэ ханан баарын биле5ин дуо?

If yes, where?

Билэр буоллаххына ханна баарый?

Do you visit it?

Ол өтөххэ сылдьа5ын дуо?

From what time have you visited?

Хаһаанныттан?

What time of year do you go?

Ханнык кэмнэргэ?

Why do you go?

То5о?

Who taught you to go?

Кимтэн үөрэммиккиний?

If no, why don't you visit?

То5о сылдьабаккыный?

Do you know any *sier tuom*?

Ханнык сиэри-туому билэ5иний?

If no, why not?

То5о билбэккиний?

If yes, of what you know, what do you practice?

Итилэртэн, эн ханнык сиэрдэри-туомнары тутуha5ыный?

Do you think it is important to practice the *sier tuom*? Why?

Эн санаа5ар, сиэри-туому тутуhар наада дуо? То5о?

Do you go to *yhyakh*?

Эн ыhыахха сылдьааччыгын дуо?

If yes, what meaning does it have for you?

Ыhыах диэн туох суолталаа5ый?

If no, why not?

Ыhыахха то5о сылдьыбаккыный?

How is today's *yhyakh* different from that of your childhood?

Эн о5о сааскар ыhыах хайдах этэй, билинни ыhыах туох ураатылаа5ый?

Do you dance the *ohuokhai*?

Оhуокайга кыттааччыгын дуо?

What meaning does it have?

Оhуокай туох суолталаа5ый?

If you don't join the dance, why not?

То5о кыттыбаккыный?

What do you think is most important for village life to develop?

Тыа оло5о сайдыытыгар, эн санаа5ар, туох нааданый?

Do you think there has been progress since the state farm broke up?

Совхоз ыhыллыбытын кэннэ, тыа5а сайдыы баар дуо эбэтэр сайдыы суох дуу?

If yes, what do you see coming next?

Сайдыы барар буоллаҕына, кэллэр кэмнэргэ ессе туох сайдыылар
   буолуохтарай?

If no, how can there be progress? What is needed?

Сайдыы суох буоллаҕына, сайдыыны хайдах ситиэһиэххэ сөбуй?
   Онуоха туох нааданый?

How do you think young people's mindset is these days?

Эдэр ыччат билинни өйө-санаата хайдаҕый?

Do you think it is important to have young people stay in the villages or
   better they go to the regional centers and cities?

Эн санааҕар, эдэр ыччат тыаҕа олохсуйара ордук дуу эбэтэр
   куоракка ордук дуу?

Why?

ТоҔо?

If all the young people go to the city, what will village life be like, do you
   think?

Эдэр ыччат бары куоракка барар буоллаҕына, тыа олоҕо хайдах
   буолуо дии саныыгыный?

Is there anything you think I should know about that I haven't asked
   about?

Миэхэ ессе тугу эбии этэрдээххиний?

Thank you very much!

УЛАХАН МАХТАЛ!!!!!

Glossary

The glossary includes all foreign words in the text except lists of linguistic variances for terms. R. indicates a Russian word.

Aal Luuk Mas: the tree of life

Aan Alakhchyn or **Aan Alakhchyn khotun**: spirit mother of Earth

aar baghaakh: central structure of the *yhyakh* festival

abaahy: devil

"abaahy ÿngkÿÿleebit": "evil spirits danced"

achchyk jyl: starvation year 1942

agha uuha: patrilineal clan

Aian Suol: literally "traveling road," name of road building organization based in Kutana

aiyy: gods

Aiyyhyt: deity of birth for all, increases offspring; specific name for humans *Kihi Aiyyhyt*, for cows *Inakh Aiyyhyt*, and for horses *Sylgy Aiyyhyt*

Akhsynn'y: December

alaaji: small round pancake

alaas jono: people of the *alaas*

alasny patrioti: *alaas* patriots (R.)

albyn tymyy: deceptive cold

algys: sung prayer

allaraa doidu: lower world

Altynn'y: October

ampaar: shed

as: food

Atyrjakh Yia: August

atyyr: stallion

baahynai khahaaiystyba: a form of collective meat and milk production aimed to supply local needs in the wake of state farm dissolution. Literally "peasant farm," and the Sakha form of *krest'ianin khoziaistva*

Baianai: the spirit keeper of the taiga, forest, and all wild animals before the hunt

balaghan: typically the winter dwelling, a wooden structure with a rectangular footprint

Balaghan Yia: September

balyksyt: fisher

bania: bathhouse

baran: snowmobile

bayjaraakh: or *baidarakh*, formations that resemble earth mounds as thawing progresses

belimien: from *pel'meni*, dumplings

bereski: from *pirozhok*, pies

beridatchit: one who goes in front, a Sakhaization of Russian *peredatchik*

Bes Yia: June

bie: mare

bilge: Sakha weather predictor, from *bil* 'to know'

bipak: fermented cow's milk

bochuguras: grouse

boruu: horsetail

buguls: small hay piles

bulchut: hunter

bulgunn'akh: or *bulguniakh,* a domelike hill that is founded on an underground ice core

Buluu Programmata: Viliui Program

buluus: storage for food and ice in the underground permafrost

burduk: wheat

byllar: high-centered polygons (ice wedges)

chabychakh: wide shallow birch bark container used to separate cream

chakras: Kichwa: small agricultural plots

chibis: lapwing, a crested plover

chokhon: frozen *küörchekh*

Chokhoroon khoruu: Chokhoroon's canal

choroon: wooden chalice made from birch wood

dacha: summer house (R.)

dal: corral

dekhsi: flat

detdom: orphanage (R.)

dölühüön: native roses *Rosa acicularis; R. dahurica; R. jacutica,* used to refer to rose hips

drozd: thrush (R.)

dulgha: hummock

düngür: shaman's drum

dzud: Mongolian: an extreme winter

ebe: grandmother

Ebee: endearing form of *Ebe*

ehe: grandfather

Ehee: endearing form of *Ehe*

ehiekei: written form to express *ohuokhai* singing

emeekhsin: old woman

Emis Kÿöl: Fat Lake

eterbes: soft leather laced up boots

Gektar: literally "hectare" and referring in this text to the Far Eastern Hectare (FEH) program (R.)

glasnost: openness (R.)

grach: rook (R.)

ichchi: spirit keepers

ichchileekh: spirit-filled

ieie: thermokarst, the degradation of permafrost toward thawing

Ieiiekhsit: deity protector of humans, horses, and cows

iejegei: curds

ilim: standing net used for lake fishing

Individualnaia Predprinimatel: (IP) individual business person (R.)

intelligentsia: intellectuals (R.)

ip itii: very hot

irbet tong: literally "nonthawing frozenness," referring to permafrost

izbushka: cabin (R.)

Jaajai Baraan Khotun: spirit keeper of all earth

jeijen: wild strawberry

Jühügüi: deity protector of horses who sends them to the middle world

jukaakh: living together, boarders who usually work for their stay

Jükeebil: the northern lights

jüöje or **diuedia:** a thawing lake

Jyl Oghuha: the Bull of Winter

kamlaniia: shaman's incantation (R.)

kehii: gift for host or participant

keli: wooden base carved out a tree, used with a *sokhokh* as a hand mill, a huge mortar and pestle

kencheeri: aftermath, referring to hay growth after hay cutting

khaahy: porridge, gruel

khaan: literally "blood" but used here to refer to blood sausage

khaar jiete: snow house

khaatyngka: felt boots

khaiakh: milk butter

khallaan: upper world, home of Sakha's pantheon of sky deities

khaptaghas: red currant

khara oiuun: black shaman

kharyakh: protected area—from the root *kharys* 'to save or protect'

kharyskhaal: protection

khomus: Jew's harp

khomus: type of reed

khonuu: field

khorchop: food stalls

khoruu: canal

khos ehe: great-grandfather

khos khos ehe: great-great-grandfather

khoton: barn

kiihile: sorrel (*Rumex acetosa L.*)

kiiiit serge: bride's post

kiis: sable

kino-mekhanik: kino-mechanic, a technician who shows movies (R.)

kniaz': prince (R.)

kochegar: coal stoker (R.)

kolkhoz: collective farm, an abbreviation of *kollektivnoe khoziaistvo*; *khol-bohuktaakh khahaaiistiba*

kömülüök: an open-faced stove in the center of the *balaghan* that vented through the roof

kopeiki: kopecks

korenizatsiia: nativization, a policy of the early Soviet period (R.)

kuiuur: a long wooden pole with a basket shape at one end used for lake fishing

kulaak: early Soviet wealthy class, mostly herders with many head of cattle

kuluhun kune: literally "sweat days," used to calculate days of work

Kulun Tutar: March

kulunchuk: foal

kunach: black fungus from the birch

küökh batakhtaakh köghön: or *kriakva*, mallard duck

küörchekh: whipped cream with berries or sugar sweetener

kuraan jyl: dry year

kureppitter: "to lead away," used for newborns to mean "to escape the *abaahy*"

kuturuksut: one who follows, helps, and learns from an *oiuun*

kylyhakh: Sakha throat singing

kymys: fermented mare's milk

kystyk: winter house

kyttygas: communal work

Kyym: literally "truth," the name of a major Sakha newspaper

kyys: girl

leppueske: or *lepeshka*, a soda-leavened flat bread

lugovodstvo: pasture making (R.)

maa muut: Finno-Ugric: earth rat

malina: red raspberries

medpunkt: medical station (R.)

"Min yngyrabyn, min yngyrabyn!": I will invite, I will invite

mooitoruk: neck scarf

moonn'oghon: black currant

mungkha: lake fishing using a large sweep net

muus oto: ice haying

Muus Ustar: April

naghyl: calm, unemotional on the outside

Narkomnat: People's Commissariat of Nationalities (R.)

nehiliek: name for patrilineal clan area, now refers to a settlement

Nivkh: an Indigenous people of northern Sakhalin, Russia (R.)

nomokh: legend

nüölsüter: managing water

nuorma: quota

oghonn'or: old man

«Oh, nyet!»: Oh, no! (R.)

ohuokhai: Sakha's circle dance

ohuokhaijit: singer of the *ohuokhai*

oibon: hole in river or lake ice for animals to drink from

oiuun: shaman

Olonkho: Sakha's epic poem

Olunn'u: February

ölüü uuta: water for the dying

öng jyl: bountiful or fertile year

orto doidu: middle world

Ot Yia: July

ötökh: places of old homesteads

oton: lingonberry

perestroika: restructuring (R.)

poganka: grebe (R.)

povestka: summons (R.)

saakh jiete: literally "manure house," another word for the *balaghan* since it is sealed with manure

saar yaghas: a huge ceremonial birch bark container

sahaan: firewood

saiylyk: summer home

salama: braided horsehair rope adorned with birchbark figures and colored cloth strips as gifts for a deity

salama yiaahyna: the hanging of the *salama*

Sel-Soviet: village administration (R.)

seppereek: ledum or labrador tea

serge: horse-hitching post

setienekh: last year's grasses/hay

Setinn'i: November

shelkopriad: the Siberian silk moth (R.) (*Dendrolimus superans sibiricus*)

shina: Inuktitut: the ice edge where sea mammal hunting takes place

sialihar: burbot

sier tuom: Sakha sacred practices

sihii: field

sirjit: literally "land-knower," one of the kinds of shamanistic knowing

sir ichchite: the spirit of the land

siri ihit: a large leather container used for *kymys* at the *yhyakh*

sobo: a small lake fish in the carp family (*Carassius carassius*)

sokhokh: a heavy wooden ram to crush grains in the *keli*

solkuobai: rubles

solondo: or *kolonok*, Siberian weasel

sovkhoz: abbreviation of *sovetskoye khozyaistvo*, state farm

stolovaia: cafeteria (R.)

sugun: blueberry

sühüökhpüttüger turbupput: literally, "we stood up with our own knees without falling"

süögei: crème fraiche

suokh: no

suorat: yogurt

suoruna: mill using grinding stones

sylgyhyt: herder tending horses

syma: fermented fish

symahyt: Viliui Sakha who relied mostly on fish; refers to the preservation of small fish by layering them with larch boughs

Taabara Suokh: literally "one without goods"

taba: reindeer

tabuns: herds

talon: coupon (R.)

tar: frozen soured milk concoction

tar ampaar: shed where *tar* is kept

tekhnika: machinery of all kinds

teplitza: greenhouse (R.)

tiing: squirrel

toion serge: king *serge*, the most important *serge*

toion: elite clan head

toiuk: solo improvisatory song

Tokhsunn'u: January

TOR: *Territoriia Operezhaiushchevo Razvitiia*, territory of advanced development (R.)

törööbüt alaas: birth *alaas*

törööbüt doidu: birthland

tramvai: river boat (R.)

trudovoi front: war front (R.)

tühüulge: social gathering of *yhyakh*

Tuoidaakh Alaas: literally "clayey *alaas*," the historical name for Elgeeii and name of a contemporary Elgeeii museum

tüölbe: literally "small round pasture" but used today to refer to small groups within a community who socialize and do activities together

tuos: birch bark

tuos yaghas: medium-sized birch bucket

tüpte: dung burned to ward off insects and used for ceremonial purposes

tuskulaakh: blessed

tuutek: standing bundles of harvested grain

tya kihite: forest Sakha

tyl ichchite: spirits of words

tymnyy: cold

tymnyy tyhyrgaar: the sound of cold

tyrekh: spoon of fate

tyympy: a *jüöje*, thawing lake that is full of water

ubaha: yearlings, the new foals from the spring

üchügei: good

udaghan: female *khara oiuun*

ugut jyl: big water time

ular: capercaillie

uluus: region

ungkachukka: usually refers to a root cellar accessed from inside the house and cooled by permafrost but can also mean a cavity in the land

unty: reindeer boots

uohakh alaaji: small round pancakes made from the colostrum or first milk

uolba: hay area on top of a recently dried lake

Uot ichchite: fire spirit

uraha: summer dwelling, a birch bark tent with a round configuration of postholes

Ürüng Aiyy Toion: Great Lord Master

ürüng as: literally "white foods," referring to all Sakha dairy products

ürüng oiuun: white shaman

Üs kununen ot üünner: "the hay grows in three days"

uu: water

vechnaia merzlota: literally "eternal frost," referring to permafrost (R.)

yalga: "to a family," "to a neighbor"

Yam Yia: May

yasak: fur tribute demanded by Russia in the form of *kyys* (sable pelts) (R.)

yhyakh: Sakha's summer festival

Yraas Olokh: literally "clean life," referring to a policy of the early Soviet period

"Yt kyyha mooitoruk": "dog's female puppy's neck scarf"

ytyk: utensil made of a cow horn and used to whip cream and yogurt

Ytyk Khaia: sacred mountain

zavatchka: chewing gum from *R. zvatchka*

Notes

Introduction

1. In this context, this word is a formal noun, referring to Lena's aunt, Olga Naumova Trofimova, so I am transliterating it as a formal name using its phonetic spelling. The Sakha term for "older sister" is *ejiii* (transliterated according to the basic word system). Although historically the Sakha language has a specific name for each relative, these names are not used today, and *ejiii* is used to refer to all older females in one's kin group, excluding mother and grandmothers.
2. Means "small gathering of people."
3. A few of the most prominent examples are R. K. Maak and V. L. Seroshevskii. In *Viliuiskii Okrug*, Maak refers often to the areas that Viliui Sakha inhabit as including plains, meadows, glades, ridges, riverbanks, valleys, river valleys, lake sides, etc. (1994: 22–28, 43, 45, 52–53, 57, 77–78, 319–20, 322). Although he does not specifically use the term *alaas*, he describes the areas he sees according to Sakha's understanding of them: "Along the river valley . . . thanks to the beautiful meadows and pastures, a relatively well populated place" (78). "Often you will come to such a tract, in maybe 10–15 versts through the thick forest and arrive again to an open place, covered by a lake, shrubs, and hay fields. In that moment, the guide will ask what the place is called and receive the answer that it is all one tract, extending in all directions by 15 or so versts, preserving the character of meadows with lakes interspersed in a forest landscape" (319). Similarly, in *Iakuty*, V. L. Seroshevskii also refers to the landscape chosen for settlement by Sakha, (1993: 1–11, 16–18). Like Maak, he does not use the term *alaas* but describes the places that Sakha chose to settle as they describe their *alaas*: "In some places the river valley is the kind of series of lake basin extensions . . . there are a number of such basins" (16–17). "It is understandable that,

as cattle breeders, when coming to a new country, to take places with pastures, meadows and along the river or by lakes" (214).

4. Although the SROCC uses the acronyms "IK" and "LK" for Indigenous knowledge and local knowledge, respectively, and I had them here originally, my colleague Julie Cruikshank made an important critique about the use of those acronyms that changed my use of them: "When I was more actively working on similar issues in the North, I sometimes felt that even some scientists who grasped the *principles* of Indigenous or local knowledge were sometimes using the acronym in a way that made it appear more 'technical' (in a bureaucratic sense) and less complex than 'knowledge' as we understand it—whether categorized as 'Indigenous knowledge' or 'local knowledge' . . . especially when routinely referred to as 'TEK' or 'IK' in conversations or policy documents. It's a kind of 'flattening' that sometimes seems to occur and may actually undercut the more serious issues about how various professionals and agencies think about or evaluate local understandings" (personal communication October 18, 2020).

Chapter 1

1. I use the term "others" intentionally to underscore how we can also enter into the ethnographic moment by assuming a culture's understanding. For Sakha, the world is filled with sentient beings, and thus the larch is also a co-inhabitant with them in the permafrost ecosystem. Today many are pursuing this idea with multispecies ethnography (cf. Kirksey and Helmreich 2010).

2. I acknowledge that scientists may question that permafrost is the underlying constraint in the frame of scientific "cause and effect." However this calls into question exactly how we understand causation in a cross-cultural context? This is an ontological issue that, once raised, engages philosophical disputes that litter the history of anthropology and the comparative human social sciences more generally, without a whole lot of resolution. Taking it up here would spiral into all kinds of ontology of knowledge issues, requiring more time, space, and study than I have available in this document.

3. Recognize that there are at least two main ways to define the Arctic: (1) a strict 66-degree circle and (2) a nonlinear territory that is defined by ecosystem characteristics.

4. Keep in mind that there are many types of permafrost, and permafrost extent is either continuous, partial, or spotty.

5. The latter site's age is estimated at around 40,000 BP (Pavlov et al. 2001), but it is designated as a Neanderthal site and is highly debated (Slimak et al. 2011).

6. It was previously accepted that humans inhabited Diring Iuriakh, an area in the contemporary Sakha Republic, some 260,000 years BP (Kuzmin and Krivonogov 1999, 1994; Waters et al. 1997). However, once more sophisticated dating techniques were developed, specifically the standard TL method, such earlier declarations were determined to be unfounded.

7. Tatars, or Tartars, are members of any of the various tribes or hordes, mostly Turkic, inhabiting parts of Russia and of central and western Siberia, loosely, any Siberian Mongoloid.

8. The headwaters of the Lena are in the mountains to the west of Lake Baikal and the Lena River flows north from there to the Arctic Ocean. Therefore "downstream" took them to the north.

9. An earlier variant describes Omoghoi as a Tatar descended from Tatar Saat from the family Sakhi. These stories represent a legend cycle that bolsters theories about Sakha's southern origins (Ksenofontov 1992).

10. See the writings and records of Gmelin, Miller, Lindenay, Middendorf, Maak, Seroshevskii, Troshansko, Pekarski Stalenberg, Fisher, Jochelson.

11. See the writings and records of Ksenofontov, Kulakovski, Ergis, Gogolev, Alekseev, and Utkin.

12. Other academics are currently claiming that Sakha's Turkic ancestors arrived in the area much earlier (cf. Bravina 2017).

13. Thermokarst is the term used to describe the degradation of permafrost toward thawing.

14. An arshin is an old measure that is approximately 28 inches. Therefore, they are saying that the land only melts 3–7 inches.

15. One *pood* = 36.11 pounds.

16. At the time, he was well known for his 1840 flora and fauna studies of Novaya Zemlya and extensive studies on the Russian Arctic climate.

Chapter 2

1. It is worth noting that the understanding of this fundamental human belief system that presided for most of human history is being called up anew today in response to the dire need for humans to rekindle their essential human environment relationship—sometimes under the name of Panpsychism (Mathews 2019).

2. I use the term *kömülüök*, since I have heard Sakha use that term when referring to the old open-faced stoves that their ancestors used in the *balaghan*. I found this transliteration of *kömülüök* in Pekarski (1958: 1886), under the entry for *osokh* (which is written *ohokh*, because the "s" changes to "h"), which is what contemporary Sakha call their stoves. *Kömülüök* is also in Sleptsov's Sakha-Russian dictionary (1992: 178).

3. In contrast, the modern, flued, multichambered, masonry woodstoves, introduced by Russians and used by Sakha to this day, are very efficient, burning relatively little wood and giving off convective heat for hours after the fire is out.

4. Hay is not prepared for horses to the extent that it is for cows, since horses live outside year-round and continue to "graze" under the snow into late January.

5. A practice also known to some Native American groups, which I learned while visiting the native plant area of the North Carolina Botanical Garden.

6. Work with Western herbalists suggests that one way to reconnect ourselves to our essential place as beings *of nature* involves engaging in "modes of learning care across biological difference," while simultaneously reframing overwhelming changes that appear insurmountable down to a human size (Boke 2016).
7. For a fuller description, see Crate, "The Great Divide" (2003).
8. Today it is broadly accepted that Sakha created more hay land and had various techniques to do so. However, in today's contemporary context of climate change and its effect on *alaas*, some academics wonder whether Sakha were involved in *alaas* formation, but this is more in the context of discussing how *alaas* progress and how that progression appears to have quickened (Takakura 2015: 27). Additionally, in the past, some academics disagreed that Sakha made the land. For example, Mikhail Nikolaevich Timofeev-Tereshkin stated definitively, "Pasture-making in the Viliui regions does not exist. All pastures are natural and exist in full dependence of the natural forces" (Mikhaleva-Saia et al., 2013: 164). Perhaps it was Tereshkin's era that kept him from understanding how Sakha made pasture or the fact that he was an intellectual who did not participate in the herding life.
9. I am spelling Alexander's name in my discussions and quotes from our communications phonetically, as "Fyodorov," though it is spelled "Fedorov" for his publications.
10. The term "thermokarst" was introduced into English-language use in 1944 by S. W. Muller.
11. This was in 1999–2000 when there were many elders alive who spent their childhood at their birth *alaas*. Few are still alive today.
12. He is referring to his generation, who still lived "by the *alaas*" in the early twentieth century and so grew up by their birth *alaas*.

Chapter 3

1. House barns, which keep herds and herders under the same roof to maximize heat, were not unique to Sakha, and in many places they are considered advantageous (Noble 2007; Loudon 1839).
2. "Until 1934, what we know today as Elgeeii was called Bordong I. In 1934, the areas of Bordong I, Bordong III and Khoro were called Elgeeii" (Arkadii Yakovlev, specialist consultation, Suntaar, September 1999).
3. *Nehiliek* is originally a Sakha word that, when brought into Russian, was spelled as *nasleg*. The word originally refered to an *agha uuha* (patrilineal clan). Today it refers to any small administrative center in the Sakha Republic.
4. Here I am using the term to refer to the ability of households to produce enough to subsist.
5. Some contemporary linguists also claim it as a Sakha word. The Sakha words *Elge* and *eeii* are joined together to make the word, *Elge* + *eeii* = *Elgeeii*, and its core meaning is deep, wet, on a high bank of a river or stream, where there is an

open clear area of *alaas* and swamp (Prokopii Mitrofonovich Yegorov, personal communication, May 15, 2020).

6. Oral history and oral historians tend to have a particular interest in oral sources for what they reveal about history and memory. Life stories and life histories are methods used by oral historians and other researchers interested in narrative and narrative identity (Jackson and Russell 2009: 172).

7. I use the past tense because in 2020 there are few elders of this generation left — the recollections I refer to were ones I captured mostly in 1999–2000.

8. Tygyn Darkhand is considered a Sakha hero, a king of the contemporary Yakutsk area who united the various Sakha clans at that time. However, when Russians came in the 1630s, he was defeated and died in prison.

9. The name of the area literally means "with gardens" or "garden-filled."

Chapter 4

1. In Western cultures that have a strong focus on the nuclear family as family unit, the idea of giving away or informally adopting out your children may be interpreted as parental disregard and uncaring. However, in many agrarian and other subsistence-based cultures, "giving" children to kin who have few or none has long been shown in anthropological studies to be quite widespread and is a way to maximize production capacity and to share the burden of child rearing (cf. Silk 1980).

2. Ice is a source of drinking water for many inhabitants in the winter both historically and today. If properly stored, for example in a *buluus*, ice can last into early summer. Many Elgeeii inhabitants prefer to use ice considering the high contamination levels of the Viliui river, the settlement's main water source.

3. He explained also that, at the time, young boys were given a "plan" of the task, to hunt chipmunks because they were a pest on the farms, eating the grain in the fields and in storage. The boys brought the chipmunk furs to be compensated, and then the farm sold the furs.

Chapter 5

1. Not to be confused with the earlier name of Kutana, which is also Khangalas. Tygyn Darkhand was chief of the original Khangalas clan in the early 1600s near contemporary Yakutsk. As the groups spread out into different areas, the name Khangalas also spread throughout the Sakha regions.

2. A word used to refer to the many ethnicities ascribed under the umbrella category of Roma.

3. Before, when a newborn died after a few days from birth, it was believed that the *abaahy* ate them. So the mother would ask another family to care for their next baby. When the next baby was born, they placed the newborn in a manure shovel and passed it out the window while announcing that it was only manure.

They then took the baby to the other family to be cared for. It was called *kurep-pitter* (to lead away) or *kyottarar* (to let them escape). It was the way to deceive or trick the *abaahy*. The practice came from the belief that the *abaahy* would go to the north window of the *khoton* but would not eat manure. So if the family passed the baby out the window and sent it to another family, it would survive. Once the child was healthy, it would be returned to the birth parents (Prokopii Mitrofanovich Yegorov, personal communication, November 4, 2020).

4. She told me in a 2004 interview that her father gave her that name because it is the name of a Russian tree that lives for a very long time. Because she has lived a very long time, she now thinks there is something to it!

5. This refers to one of my dissertation methods. I contracted with eleven households to keep a daily diary for a year. The households represented the spectrum of how households were making it, ranging from those who were living only off subsidies to those who were almost completely self-sufficient. The households recorded income, expenses, household food production, recipes, outings, and the like.

6. Sergei Afanaseevich Zverov was the most renowned improvisatory singer of both *ohuokhai* and *toiuk*. He was born in the Suntaar *uluus* in 1900 and lived until 1973.

7. Künde was a renowned Sakha author. He is perhaps best known for his poem that begins, "Native, birth language is like cool cream, it comforts the soul . . ."

Chapter 6

1. "Yedoma is a type of Pleistocene-age permafrost (formed 1.8 million to 10,000 years before present) that contains a significant amount of organic material with an ice content of 50 to 90 percent by volume. Thawing yedoma is a significant source of atmospheric methane." https://nsidc.org/cryosphere/glossary/term/yedoma.

2. Yedoma deposits were formed in waterlogged conditions (wetlands). When these yedoma deposits freeze, they crack, and in springtime, meltwater fills these cracks. Over many years, these cracks increase and create systems of polygonal (re)-vein ice (Alexander Nikolayevich Fyodorov, email correspondence, October 10, 2019).

3. During the USSR, there was a year-round field station in Siirdaakh. Staff from the Institute of Permafrost in Yaktusk travelled to Siirdaakh and conducted continuous monitoring, replacing each other at the station (Alexander Nikolayevich Fyodorov, email correspondence, October 10, 2019).

4. There has been a significant increase in construction of both high-rise apartment buildings and commercial buildings in Yakutsk, especially in the past decade.

5. The law's full, formal name is given in the References. It is commonly called the Law on the Far East Hectare.

Chapter 7

1. Islands receive freshwater from rainwater, which can collect in surface lakes
    and ponds or, more commonly, in a lens underground that typically stays sepa-
    rate from the island's surrounding saltwater. With sea-level rise, these lenses are
    increasingly contaminated with saltwater.

References

Archival Sources

CSA (Central State Archive). "Announcements and Notes from I Bordong Land Committee, 1930." Fund 1179, Op. 1, delo 19.

ILLA (Institute of Language and Literature Archive). "Opisanie Yakutskogo Ysyakha Gemlinim" [Gmelin's Descriptions of Ysyakh]. Fund 4, Op. 1, delo 12.

IHRISNA (Institute for Humanities Research and Indigenous Studies of the North Archive). 1962. N. K. Antonov, "Main Landscape Words in the Sakha Language." Fond 5, Op. 12, Ex 1.

IHRISNA. 1965. "Material of the Expedition of V. D. Krivoshapkin, in Suntar about Language." Fond 5, Op. 12, Ex 76.

IHRISNA. 1972. "Scientific Report by Theme: Yakutski-Russiski Dictionary Agricultural Terms: Terms of Animal Keeping." Fond 5, Op. 12, Ex 136.

SRA (Suntaar Regional Archive). Annual Bookkeepers' Records, Molotov *kolkhoz*. Fund 43, Op. 1, delo 63.

SRA. "Material of the January 1st Report, Suntar Region, 1952." Fund 9, Op. 1, delo 42.

SRA. "Orders and Instructions Concerning Formation of State Farms." Fund 33, Op. 1, delo 1.

SRA. "Material about Production Activities of the Elgeeii State Farm, 1957." Fund 75, Op. 14, delo 67.

Published Sources

Abolin, R. I. 1929. *Geobotanicheskoye i pochvennoye opisaniye Leno-Vilyuiskoi ravniny* [Geobotanical and soil description Leno-Vilyui plains]. Leningrad: USSR Academy of Sciences.

Abram, N., J.-P. Gattuso, A. Prakash, L. Cheng, M. P. Chidichimo, S. Crate, H. Enom-
oto, M. Garschagen, N. Gruber, S. Harper, et al. 2019. "Framing and Context of
the Report." Chapter 1 in IPCC 2019.

ACIA (Arctic Climate Impact Assessment). 2004. *Impacts of a Warming Arctic—
Arctic Climate Impact Assessment*. Cambridge: Cambridge University Press.

Afanas'ev, M. M., ed. 2016. *Kutana Nehiliege* [The Kutana village]. Yakutsk: Bichik.

Agrawal, Arun. 1995. "Dismantling the Divide between Indigenous and Scientific
Knowledge." *Development and Change* 26 (3): 413–39.

Alekseev, N. A. 1975. *Traditsionnye religioznye verovaniia Yakutov v XI–nachale XX
veka* [The traditional religious belief of the Yakut in the 19th to the beginning of
the 20th century]. Novosibisrk: Nauka.

Alekseev, N. A., N. V. Emel'ianov, and V. T. Petrov, eds. 1995. *Predaniia, legendy i
mify Sakha* [Traditions, legends and myths of the Sakha]. Novosibirsk: Science
Publishers.

Alekseev, N. M. 1959. *Edvard Karlovich Pekarski: On the 100th Year from His Birthday*. Yakutsk: Yakutsk Republic Library Pushkin.

Alekseeva, G. G. 2007. *S. I. Nikolaev-Somoghotto: First Scientist-Ethnographer of
Sakha*. Yakutsk: YAGU Publishers.

Alexander, C., N. Bynum, E. Johnson, U. King, T. Mustonen, P. Neofotis, N. Oettlé,
C. Rosenzweig, C. Sakakibara, V. Shadrin, and M. Vicarelli. 2011. "Linking Indigenous and Scientific Knowledge of Climate Change." *BioScience* 61 (6): 477–84.

Alexopoulos, G. 2008. "Stalin and the Politics of Kinship: Practices of Collective Pun-
ishment, 1920s–1940s." *Comparative Studies in Society and History* 50 (1): 91–117.

All Russian Hygienic Exhibition. 1913. *Housing, Clothing and Food of the Yakut (Sakha)*.
Yakutsk: Yakutsk Oblast Publishers.

Andreev, G. 1995. "Tumul Uchaastaga" [The Tumul area]. *Suntaar Sonnunnar*,
December 10, 1995.

Angerer, J., G. Han, I. Fujisaki, and K. Havstad. 2008. "Climate Change and Ecosystems of Asia with Emphasis on Inner Mongolia and Mongolia." *Rangelands* 30
(3): 46–51.

Anisimov, O. A., and M. A. Belolutskaia. 2002. "Otsenka vliianiia izmenyeniia klimata i degradatsii vechnoi merzloty na infrastrukturu v severnykh regionakh
Rossii" [Assessment of the impact of climate change and permafrost degradation
on infrastructure in the northern regions of Russia]. *Meteorologiia i gidrologiia*
(6): 15–22.

Argunov, V. G., and K. A. Pestereva. 2018. "Osvoyeniye Yakutskoi Artkiki: Voprosy
drevnei migratsii i mobil'nosti tsirkumpoliarnogo mira" [Development of the Yakut
Arctic: Issues of ancient migration and mobility of the circumpolar world]. *Obsh-
estvo: Filosofiya, istoriiia, kultura* 3:30–34.

Avvakumov, P. D. 1973. *Bies ynakhtaakh Beiberikeen Emeekhsin* [Old Woman Bey-
berikeen with five cows]. Yakutsk: Yakutsk Book Publishers.

Baer, K. M. 2000. *Materialy k poznaniiu netaiushchego pochvennogo l'da v Sibiri*
[Materials on the knowledge of the non-melting of soil ice in Siberia]. Yakutsk:
Institute of Permafrost.

Barnes, J., M. Dove, M. Lahsen, A. Mathews, P. McElwee, R. McIntosh, F. Moore, J. O'Reilly, B. Orlove, R. Puri, and H. Weiss. 2013. "Contribution of Anthropology to the Study of Climate Change." *Nature Climate Change* 3 (6): 541–44.

Basso, K. H. 1996. *Wisdom Sits in Places: Landscape and Language Among the Western Apache.* Albuquerque: University of New Mexico Press.

Biskaborn, B. K., J. P. Lanckman, H. Lantuit, K. Elger, S. Dmitry, C. William, and R. Vladimir. 2015. "The New Database of the Global Terrestrial Network for Permafrost (GTN-P)." *Earth System Science Data* 7:245–59.

Biskaborn, B. K., S. L. Smith, J. Noetzli, H. Matthes, G. Vieira, D. A. Streletskiy, P. Schoeneich, V. E. Romanovsky, A. G. Lewkowicz, A. Abramov, and M. Allard. 2019. "Permafrost Is Warming at a Global Scale." *Nature Communications* 10 (1): 264.

Blois, J. L., P. L. Zarnetske, M. C. Fitzpatrick, and S. Finnegan. 2013. "Climate Change and the Past, Present, and Future of Biotic Interactions." *Science* 341 (6145): 499–504.

Boissière, M., B. Locatelli, D. Sheil, M. Padmanaba, and E. Sadjudin. 2013. "Local Perceptions of Climate Variability and Change in Tropical Forests of Papua, Indonesia." *Ecology and Society* 18 (4): 13.

Boke, Charis. 2016. "Care." Editors' Forum: Theorizing the Contemporary. *Fieldsights*, July 12. https://culanth.org/fieldsights/care.

Bolin, I. 2009. "The Glaciers of the Andes Are Melting: Indigenous and Anthropological Knowledge Merge in Restoring Water Resources." In *Anthropology and Climate Change: From Encounters to Actions*, ed. S. Crate and M. Nuttall, 228–39. Walnut Creek: Left Coast Press.

Bosikov, N. P., A. P. Isaev, E. Iva-Nova, V. I. Zakharova, L. V. Sivtseva, A. P. Ivanova, S. G. Semyonova, V. N. Ammosova, L. N. Poriadina, and V. G. Isakova. 2012. "Ritmy razvitiia alasnykh ekosistem v Tsentral'noi Iakutii" [Rhythms of development of forest ecosystems in Central Yakutia]. *Nayka I Obrazivaniie* 2:52–57.

Boyakova, S. I. 2001. *Osvoyenie Artiki i narody Severo-Vostoka Azii (XIX v.–1917)* [The development of the Arctic and the peoples of Northeast Asia (19th century–1917)]. Novosibirsk: Nauka.

Boyd, B. 2009. *On the Origin of Stories.* Cambridge, MA: Harvard University Press.

Brabec de Mori, B., and A. Seeger. 2013. "Introduction: Considering Music, Humans, and Non-Humans." *Ethnomusicology Forum* 22 (3): 269–86.

Bravina, R. I. 2017. "Novaia staraia gipoteza o proiskhozhdenii Yakutov (k 100-letiiu etnografa folk'lorista i kraeveda AA Savvina)." [New old hypothesis about the origin of the Yakuts (on the 100th anniversary of the ethnographer, folklorist and local historian A. A. Savvin)]. *Vestnik arkheologii, antropologii I etnografii* 2 (37): 94–105.

Bremer, S., A. Blanchard, N. Mamnun, M. Stiller-Reeve, M. M. Haque, and E. Tvinnereim. 2017. "Narrative as a Method for Eliciting Tacit Knowledge of Climate Variability in Bangladesh." *Weather, Climate, and Society* 9 (4): 669–86.

Briggs, J. 2005. "The Use of Indigenous Knowledge in Development: Problems and Challenges." *Progress in Development Studies* 5 (2): 99–114.

Brown, B. 2020. "The Research Journey." Accessed October 13, 2010. https://brene brown.com/the-research.

Budyko, M. I. 1970. Comments on "A Global Climatic Model Based on the Energy Balance of the Earth-Atmosphere System." *Journal of Applied Meteorology* 9 (2): 310.

Buyandelger, M. 2013. *Tragic Spirits: Shamanism, Memory, and Gender in Contemporary Mongolia*. Chicago: University of Chicago Press.

Campbell, C. 2014. *Agitating Images: Photography against History in Indigenous Siberia*. Minneapolis: University of Minnesota Press.

Cash, D. W., W. C. Clark, F. Alcock, N. M. Dickson, N. Eckley, D. H. Guston, J. Jäger, and R. B. Mitchell. 2003. "Knowledge Systems for Sustainable Development." *Proceedings of the National Academy of Sciences* 100 (14): 8086–91.

Castree, N., W. M. Adams, J. Barry, D. Brockington, B. Büscher, E. Corbera, D. Demeritt, R. Duffy, U. Felt, K. Neves, and P. Newell. 2014. "Changing the Intellectual Climate." *Nature Climate Change* 4 (9): 763.

Chadburn, S. E., E. J. Burke, P. M. Cox, P. Friedlingstein, G. Hugelius, and S. Westermann. 2017. "An Observation-Based Constraint on Permafrost Loss as a Function of Global Warming." *Nature Climate Change* 7 (5): 340.

Chu, P. Y. 2015. "Mapping Permafrost Country: Creating an Environmental Object in the Soviet Union, 1920s–1940s." *Environmental History* 20 (3): 396–421.

Chu, P. Y. 2021. *The Life of Permafrost: A History of Frozen Earth in Russian and Soviet Science*. Toronto: University of Toronto Press.

Chzhan R. V., L. G. Li, and M. M. Shats. 2010. "Shakhta Shergina: Novie vremena–novie podkhody" [The Shergin mine: New time–new ways]. *Science and Technology in Yakutyia* 2 (19): 74–78.

Conquest, Robert. 1986. *The Harvest of Sorrow: Soviet Collectivization and the Terror-Famine*. New York: Oxford University Press.

Crate, S. A. 1994. "Dance of Life, Circle of Life: *Ohuokhai* as the Sakhas' Emergent Ethnic Voice." Unpublished master's thesis, University of North Carolina, Chapel Hill.

Crate, S. A. 2002. "Co-option in Siberia: The Case of Diamonds and the Vilyuy Sakha." *Polar Geography* 26 (4): 289–307.

Crate, S. A. 2003. "The Great Divide: Contested Issues of Post-Soviet Viliui Sakha Land Use." *Europe-Asia Studies* 55 (6): 869–88.

Crate, S. A. 2006a. *Cows, Kin and Globalization: An Ethnography of Sustainability*. Walnut Creek: Alta Mira Press.

Crate, S. A. 2006b. "Ohuokhai: Sakhas' Unique Integration of Social Meaning and Movement." *Journal of American Folklore* 119 (472): 161–83.

Crate, S. A. 2008. "Gone the Bull of Winter? Grappling with the Cultural Implications of and Anthropology's Role(s) in Global Climate Change." *Current Anthropology* 49 (4): 569–95.

Crate, S. A. 2011a. "Climate and Culture: Anthropology in the Era of Contemporary Climate Change." *Annual Review of Anthropology* 40:175–94.

Crate, S. A. 2011b. "A Political Ecology of *Water in Mind*: Attributing Perceptions in the Era of Global Climate Change." *Weather, Climate and Society* 3:148–64.

Crate, S. A. 2012. "Climate Change and Ice Dependent Communities: Perspectives from Siberia and Labrador." *Polar Journal* 2 (1): 61–75.

Crate, S. A. 2013. "From Living Water to the 'Water of Death': Implicating Social Resilience in Northeastern Siberia." *Worldviews: Global Religions, Culture, and Ecology* 17 (2): 115–24.

Crate, S. A. 2014. "An Ethnography of Change in Northeastern Siberia: Whither an Interdisciplinary Role?" *Sibirica* 13 (1): 40–74.

Crate, S. A. 2019. "Ohuokhai: Transmitter of Biocultural Heritage for Sakha of Northeastern Siberia." *Journal of Ethnobiology* 39 (3): 409–24.

Crate, S. A., and A. Fedorov. 2013a. *Alamai Tyyn: Bülüü uluustarygar klimat ularyiyytyn tuhunan uonna baar kyhalghalar* [Alamai Tyyn: Climate change and other change in the Viliui regions]. Yakutsk: Bichik.

Crate, S. A., and A. Fedorov. 2013b. "A Methodological Model for Exchanging Local and Scientific Climate Change Knowledge in Northeastern Siberia." *Arctic* 66 (3): 338–50.

Crate, S. A., and M. Nuttall, eds. 2009. *Anthropology and Climate Change: From Encounters to Actions.* Walnut Creek: Left Coast Press.

Crate, S. A., and M. Nuttall, eds. 2016. *Anthropology and Climate Change: From Actions to Transformations.* New York: Routledge.

Crate, S. A., M. Ulrich, J. O. Habeck, A. R. Desyatkin, R. V. Desyatkin, A. N. Fedorov, T. Hiyama, Y. Iijima, S. Ksenofontov, C. Mészáros, and H. Takakura. 2017. "Permafrost Livelihoods: A Transdisciplinary Review and Analysis of Thermokarst-Based Systems of Indigenous Land Use." *Anthropocene* 18:89–104.

Cru, J. 2015. "Language Revitalization from the Ground Up: Promoting Yucatec Maya on Facebook." *Journal of Multilingual and Multicultural Development* 36 (3): 284–96.

Cruikshank, J. 1997. "Negotiating with Narrative: Establishing Cultural Identity at the Yukon International Storytelling Festival." *American Anthropologist* 99 (1): 56–69.

Cruikshank, J. 2005. *Do Glaciers Listen?: Local Knowledge, Colonial Encounters, and Social Imagination.* Vancouver: UBC Press.

Cuerrier, A., N. J. Turner, T. C. Gomes, A. Garibaldi, and A. Downing. 2015. "Cultural Keystone Places: Conservation and Restoration in Cultural Landscapes." *Journal of Ethnobiology* 35 (3): 427–49.

Cunliffe, D., and R. ap Dyfrig. 2013. "The Welsh Language on YouTube: Initial Observations." In *Social Media and Minority Languages: Convergence and the Creative Industries*, ed. E. H. G. Jones and E. Uribe-Jongbloed, 130–45. Bristol: Multilingual Matters.

Czudek, T., and J. Demek. 1970. "Thermokarst in Siberia and Its Influence on the Development of Lowland Relief." *Quaternary Research* 1 (1): 103–20.

D'Andrade, R. G. 1995. *The Development of Cognitive Anthropology.* Cambridge: Cambridge University Press.

Danilova, N. K. 2011. *Traditdionnoe zhilishche naroda Sakha: Prostransvo. Dom. Ritual* [Traditional housing of the Sakha people: Space, home, ritual]. Novosibirsk: Academic Publisher "GEO."

Danilova, N. K. 2013. "Poselenie I tipy zhilishch" [Settlement and types of housing]. In *Yakuty Sakha* [The Yakut Sakha], ed. N. A. Alekseev, E. N. Romanova, and Z. P. Sokolova. Moscow: Nauka.

Dannevig, H., and G. K. Hovelsrud. 2016. "Understanding the Need for Adaptation in a Natural Resource Dependent Community in Northern Norway: Issue Salience, Knowledge and Values." *Climatic Change* 135:261–75. https://doi.org/10.1007/s10 584-015-1557-1.

Dannevig, H., G. K. Hovelsrud, E. A.T. Hermansen, and M. Karlsson. 2020. "Culturally Sensitive Boundary Work: A Framework for Linking Knowledge to Climate Action." *Environmental Science and Policy* 112:405–13.

Danzhalova, E. V., S. N. Bazha, P. D. Gunin, Y. I. Drobyshev, T. I. Kazantseva, A. V. Prischepa, N. N. Slemnev, and E. Ariunbold. 2012. "Indicators of Pasture Digression in Steppe Ecosystems of Mongolia." *Erforschung biologischer Ressourcen der Mongolei*, vol. 12, 298–306. Halle: Martin-Luther-Universität-Halle-Wittenberg.

Da Silva, S. G., and J. J. Tehrani. 2016. "Comparative Phylogenetic Analyses Uncover the Ancient Roots of Indo-European Folktales." *Royal Society Open Science* 3 (1): 150645.

Davis, W. 2014. "Keynote Speech: The Ethnosphere and the Academy." *Explorer in Residence. Nacional Geographic Society.* https://www.wheretherebedragons.com /wp-content/uploads/2014/09/DavisEthnosphereAcademy.pdf.

Demuth, B. 2019. *Floating Coast: An Environmental History of the Bering Strait.* New York: W. W. Norton.

Desiatkin, R. V. 2008. *Pochvoobrazovanie v termokarstovykh kotlovinakh-alasakh kriolitozony* [Soil formation in thermokarst basins-alas of the cryolithozone]. Novosibirsk: Nauka.

D'iachkovskii, F. N., and N. I. Popova. 2014. "Alaas kak kontsept Iakutskoi lingvokul'tury" [*Alaas* as concept of Yakut linguistic culture]. *Uralo-altaickie issledovaniia* 1:12.

Dikov, N. N. 2004. *Early Cultures of Northeastern Asia.* Trans. Richard Bland. U.S. Department of the Interior, National Park Service, Shared Beringian Heritage Program.

Donner, S. D., and S. Webber. 2014. "Obstacles to Climate Change Adaptation Decisions: A Case Study of Sea-Level Rise and Coastal Protection Measures in Kiribati." *Sustainability Science* 9 (3): 331–45.

Dylis, N. V. 1961. *Listvennitsa vostochnoi Sibiri i Dalnego Vostoka* [The larch of eastern Siberia and the Far East]. Moscow: Academy of Sciences of the USSR.

Efimov, A. I., and N. A. Grave. 1940. "Pogrebennye l'dy paiona ozera Abalakh" [Buried ice of the Lake Abalakh region]. *Sotsialisticheskoe stroitel'stvo* 10–11:67–78.

Egeru, A. 2012. "Role of Indigenous Knowledge in Climate Change Adaptation: A Case Study of the Teso Sub-Region, Eastern Uganda." *Indian Journal of Traditional Knowledge* 11 (2): 217–24.

Emel'ianov, N. V., and V. V. Illarionov. 1996. "Epicheskaia traditsiia Iakutov i Olonkho V. O. Karataeva" [The Yakut epic tradition of Olonkho V. O. Karatayev]. In *Iakutskii*

Geroicheskii Epos "Moguchii Er Soghotokh" [Yakut hero epic: *"Moguchii Er Soghotokh"*], ed. G. V. Romenko, 10–41. Novosibirsk: Nauka.

Ergis, G. U. 1974. *Ocherki po Iakutskomu folkloru* [Essays on Yakut folklore]. Moscow: Science Publishers.

Ermolaev, V. 1991. *Uu dolgun kuttaakhtara: Agro-etnograficheskai ocherk* [Phases of Yakut land tenure]. Yakutsk: Sakha Book Publishers.

Escobar, A. 2001. "Culture Sits in Places: Reflections on Globalism and Subaltern Strategies of Localization." *Political Geography* 20 (2): 139–74.

Etzelmüller, B., E. S. F. Heggem, N. Sharkhuu, R. Frauenfelder, A. Kääb, and C. Goulden. 2006. "Mountain Permafrost Distribution Modelling Using a Multi-Criteria Approach in the Hövsgöl Area, Northern Mongolia." *Permafrost and Periglacial Processes* 17 (2): 91–104.

Fedorov, A. N., P. Gavriliev, Y. Konstantinov, T. Hiyama, Y. Iijima, and G. Iwahana. 2014. "Estimating the Water Balance of a Thermokarst Lake in the Middle of the Lena River Basin, Eastern Siberia." *Ecohydrology* 7 (2): 188–96.

Fedorov, A. P. 2009. *Kutana*. Yakutsk: INIT.

Fedorov, A. P. 2012a. *Bihigi Odunu Sirin Ogholorobut* [We are children of Odun land]. Yakutsk: CMIK-Master Poligrafiia.

Fedorov, A. P. 2012b. *Kutana nehiliegin tutuulapa* [Buildings of the Kutana *nehiliek*]. Yakutsk: CMIK-Master Poligrafiia.

Fedorov, S. 2014. "Razvitie skotovodstva v Kutaninskom naslege" [The development of herding in the Kutana village]. 10th grade project paper, Kutana Village.

Fedorova, V. N. 1991. *Bliuda narodov Iakutia* [Food of the people of Yakutia]. Yakutsk: Yakusk Book Publishers.

Fedoseeva, S. A. 1999. *Arkheologiia Yakutii i ee mesto v mirovoi nauke o proiskhozhenii o evoliutsii chelovechestva: Ocherki po dopis'mennoi istorii Yakutii* [Archaeology of Yakutia and its place in the world science of the origin and evolution of mankind: Essays on the prewritten history of Yakutia]. Yakutsk: OOO "Lithorgrapher."

Feldman, G. M., A. S. Tetelbaum, N. I. Shender, R. I. Gavriliev. 1988. *Posobie po prognozy temperaturnogo regima gruntov Iakutii* [Handbook of temperature forecast of the soils in Yakutia]. Yakutsk: SB RAS (Siberian Branch, Russian Academy of Sciences).

Ferguson, J., 2015. "Is It Bad That We Try to Speak Two Languages?: Language Ideologies and Choices among Urban Sakha Bilingual Families." *Sibirica* 14 (1): 1–27.

Filippova, V. V., and N. S. Bagdariin. 2018. "About the Mapping of Toponyms." In *Imia, Iazyk, Etnos: Sbornik materialov vserossiiskoi nauchno-prakticheskoi konferentsii, posviashchennoi 90 letiiu so dnia rozhdeniia M. S. Ivanova-Bagrdaryyn Sülbe* [Name, language, ethnicity: Collection of materials from the All-Russian Scientific Conference honoring the 90th birthday of M. S. Ivanova-Bagrdaryyn Sülbe], 39–42. Yakutsk, November 8, 2018. Yakutsk: Institute of Humanitarian Research Publishers.

Fondahl, G., V. Filippova, A. Savvinova, A. Ivanova, F. Stammler, and G. Hoogensen Gjørv. 2019. "Niches of Agency: Managing State-Region Relations through Law in Russia." *Space and Polity* 23 (1): 49–66.

Ford, J. D., L. Cameron, J. Rubis, M. Maillet, D. Nakashima, A. C. Willox, and T. Pearce. 2016. "Including Indigenous Knowledge and Experience in IPCC Assessment Reports." *Nature Climate Change* 6 (4): 349–53.

Fortier, J. 2009. *Kings of the Forest: The Cultural Resilience of Himalayan Hunter-Gatherers*. Honolulu: University of Hawaii Press.

French, H., and Y. Shur. 2010. "The Principles of Cryostratigraphy." *Earth-Science Reviews* 101 (3–4): 190–206.

Froese, D. G., J. A. Westgate, A. V. Reyes, R. J. Enkin, and S. J. Preece. 2008. "Ancient Permafrost and a Future, Warmer Arctic." *Science* 321 (5896): 1648.

Garibaldi, A., and N. Turner. 2004. "Cultural Keystone Species: Implications for Ecological Conservation and Restoration." *Ecology and Society* 9 (3): 1. http://www.ecologyandsociety.org/vol9/iss3/art1/.

Gartvig, G. 1866. *Priroda i chelovek na Krainem Severe* [Nature and man in the Far North]. Moscow: A. I. Glazunova.

Gearheard, S., M. Pocernich, R. Stewart, J. Sanguya, and H. P. Huntington. 2010. "Linking Inuit Knowledge and Meteorological Station Observations to Understand Changing Wind Patterns at Clyde River, Nunavut." *Climatic Change* 100: 267–94.

Gerasimova, L. P., ed. 2008. *Sakha uonna Alaas* [Sakha and *Alaas*]. Yakutsk: Bichik.

Glick, D. 2004. "The Big Thaw: As the Climate Warms, How Much, and How Quickly, Will Earth's Glaciers Melt?" *National Geographic* 206 (3): 12–33.

Glossary. 2019. Ed. N. M. Weyer. In *IPCC Special Report on the Ocean and Cryosphere in a Changing Climate*, ed. H.-O. Pörtner, D. C. Roberts, V. Masson-Delmotte, P. Zhai, M. Tignor, E. Poloczanska, K. Mintenbeck, A. Alegría, M. Nicolai, A. Okem, J. Petzold, B. Rama, and N. M. Weyer. In Press Annex II, IPCC 2019, 677–702.

Gmelin, J. G. 1747. *Flora Sibirica sive historia plantarum Sibiriae*. Vol. 1. Petropoli: Typographia Academiae Scientiarum.

Gmelin, J. G. 1751. *Puteshestvie po Sibiri* [Travels in Siberia]. *Shorskii sbornik* 1:10–11.

Gogolev, A. I. 1992. "Basic Stages of the Formation of the Yakut People." *Anthropology & Archeology of Eurasia* 31 (2): 63–69.

Gogolev, A. I. 1993. *Iakuti: Problemy etnogeneza i formirovaniia kul'tury* [The Yakut: Problems of ethnogenesis and cultural formation]. Yakutsk: Yakutsk State University Press.

Gogolev, A. I. 1994. *Mifologicheskii mir Iakutov: Bozhestvo i dukhi-pokroviteli* [The mythological world of the Yakut: Gods and spirit-protectors]. Yakutsk: Center of Culture and Art.

Gogolev A. I. 2000. *Istoriya Iakutkiya (obzop istoricheskikh sobytii dol nachala XX v.)* [The history of Yakutia (overview of historical events from the beginning of the 20th century)]. Yakutsk: Yakutsk State University Press.

Gogolev, A. I. 2015a. *Folk Knowledge of Yakut in 17th to Beginning of 20th century*. Yakutsk: Publishing House SVFU.

Gogolev, A. I. 2015b. "The History of Settlement of Sakha in the Central Alaases of Yakutia." In *Alaas: Sakha People's Cradle*, ed. G. N. Savvinov and V. S. Makarov, 64–73. Yakutsk: Bichik.

Goldman, M. J., P. Nadasdy, and M. D. Turner, eds. 2011. *Knowing Nature: Conversations at the Intersection of Political Ecology and Science Studies*. Chicago: University of Chicago Press.

Goldman, M. J., M. D. Turner, and M. Daly. 2018. "A Critical Political Ecology of Human Dimensions of Climate Change: Epistemology, Ontology, and Ethics." *Wiley Interdisciplinary Reviews: Climate Change* 9 (4): e526.

Golovnev, A.V., and G. Osherenko. 1999. *Siberian Survival: The Nenets and Their Story*. Ithaca: Cornell University Press.

Gómez-Baggethun, E., E. Corbera, and V. Reyes-García. 2013. "Traditional Ecological Knowledge and Global Environmental Change: Research Findings and Policy Implications." *Ecology and Society* 18 (4): 72.

Gorokhov, A. N., A. N. Fedorov, D. Skorve, and V. C. Makarov. 2011. "Otsenka antropogennoi izmenchivnosti landshaftov okrestnostei s. Churapcha (Tsentral'naia Yakutiia) na osnove dannykh distantsionnogo zondirovanniia zemli" [Assessment of anthropogenic variability of landscapes in the vicinity of Churapcha village (Central Yakutia) based on remote sensing data]. *Problemy regional'noi ekologii* 4:7–13.

Gould, S. J. 1979. *Ever since Darwin: Reflections in Natural History*. New York: Norton.

Grant, B. 1995. *In the Soviet House of Culture: A Century of Perestroikas*. Princeton: Princeton University Press.

Green, D., J. Billy, and A. Tapim. 2010. "Indigenous Australians' Knowledge of Weather and Climate." *Climatic Change* 100 (2): 337–54. doi:10.1007/s10584-010-9803-z.

Grenoble, L. A., and L. J. Whaley, eds. 1998. *Endangered Languages: Language Loss and Community Response*. Cambridge: Cambridge University Press.

Grigor'ev, A. A. 1927. "Geomorfologicheskii ocherk Iakutii" [Geomorphological Notes of Yakutia]. In *Vittenburg 1927*, 39–90.

Haraway, D. J. 2016. *Staying with the Trouble: Making Kin in the Chthulucene*. Durham: Duke University Press.

Harrison, K. D. 2008. *When Languages Die: The Extinction of the World's Languages and the Erosion of Human Knowledge*. Oxford: Oxford University Press.

Harrison, K. D. 2010. *The Last Speakers: The Quest to Save the World's Most Endangered Languages*. Washington, DC: National Geographic Books.

Harrison, K. D., and E. Raimy. 2007. "Language as an Emergent System." *Soundings: An Interdisciplinary Journal* 90 (1/2): 77–90.

Hiwasaki, L., E. Luna, and J. A. Marçal. 2015. "Local and Indigenous Knowledge on Climate-Related Hazards of Coastal and Small Island Communities in Southeast Asia." *Climatic Change* 128 (1–2): 35–56.

Hoang, L. P., M. T. van Vliet, M. Kummu, H. Lauri, J. Koponen, I. Supit, R. Leemans, P. Kabat, and F. Ludwig. 2019. "The Mekong's Future Flows under Multiple Drivers: How Climate Change, Hydropower Developments and Irrigation Expansions Drive Hydrological Changes." *Science of the Total Environment* 649:601–9.

Hoelscher, S., and D. H. Alderman. 2004. "Memory and Place: Geographies of a Critical Relationship." *Social & Cultural Geography* 5 (3): 347–55.

Holland, D. C., W. Lachicotte Jr., D. Skinner, and C. Cain. 2001. *Identity and Agency in Cultural Worlds.* Cambridge: Harvard University Press.

Holliday, V. T., J. F. Hoffecker, P. Goldberg, R. I. Macphail, S. L. Forman, M. Anikovich, and A. Sinitsyn. 2007. "Geoarchaeology of the Kostenki–Borshchevo Sites, Don River Valley, Russia." *Geoarchaeology: An International Journal* 22 (2): 181–228.

Huntington, H. P. 2000. "Using Traditional Ecological Knowledge in Science: Methods and Applications." *Ecological Applications* 10 (5): 1270–74.

Iakovlev, A. E. 2006. *Iz istorii administrativno-territorial'nogo deleniia Ulusa* [From the history of the administrative-territorial divide of the Ulus]. In *Suntarskii ulus* [The Suntar *ulus*], ed. A. K. Akimov, 48–59. Yakutsk: Bichik.

Ides, E. Ysbrants. 1706. *Three Years Travels from Moscow Over-Land to China: Thro' Great Ustiga, Siriania, Permia, Daour, Great Tartary, &c. to Peking.* London: Printed for W. Freeman, J. Walthoe, T. Newborough, J. Nicholson, and R. Parker.

Ignatieva, V. B. 2014. "Izmeneniye mirovogo klimata: Lokal'nii proektsii v Respublike Sakha (Iakutiia)" [Change in world climate: Local projects in the Sakha Republic (Yakutia)]. In *Etnosotsiologicheskie issledovaniia v Respublike Sakha (Iakutia)* [Ethno-sociological research in the Sakha Republic (Yakutia)], ed. U. S. Borisova, 1:78–98.

Iijima, Y., and A. N. Fedorov. 2019. "Permafrost Forest Dynamics." Chapter 8 in *Water-Carbon Dynamics in Eastern Siberia*, ed. T. Ohta, T. Hiyama, Y. Iijima, A. Kotani, and T. C. Maximov, 175–206. Singapore: Springer.

IPA (International Permafrost Association), Standing Committee on Data Information and Communication, comp. 2003. *Circumpolar Active-Layer Permafrost System (CAPS), Version 1.* Boulder, CO. NSIDC: National Snow and Ice Data Center. doi: https://doi.org/10.7265/N5SF2T3B. Accessed October 14, 2020. Map compiled by Philippe Rekacewicz, UNEP/GRID-Arendal.

IPCC (Intergovernmental Panel on Climate Change). 2001. *Climate Change 2001: Synthesis Report. A Contribution of Working Groups I, II, and III to the Third Assessment Report of the Intergovernmental Panel on Climate Change.* Ed. R. T. Watson and the Core Writing Team. Cambridge: Cambridge University Press.

IPCC. 2014. "Summary for Policymakers." In *Climate Change 2014: Impacts, Adaptation, and Vulnerability. Part A: Global and Sectoral Aspects. Contribution of Working Group II to the Fifth Assessment Report of the Intergovernmental Panel on Climate Change*, ed. C. B. Field, V. R. Barros, D. J. Dokken, K. J. Mach, M. D. Mastrandrea, T. E. Bilir, M. Chatterjee, K. L. Ebi, Y. O. Estrada, R. C. Genova, et al., 1–32. Cambridge: Cambridge University Press.

IPCC. 2018. *Global Warming of 1.5°C: An IPCC Special Report on the Impacts of Global Warming of 1.5°C above Pre-industrial Levels and Related Global Green-*

house Gas Emission Pathways, in the Context of Strengthening the Global Response to the Threat of Climate Change, Sustainable Development, and Efforts to Eradicate Poverty. Ed. V. Masson-Delmotte, P. Zhai, H. O. Pörtner, D. Roberts, J. Skea, P. R. Shukla, A. Pirani, W. Moufouma-Okia, C. Péan, R. Pidcock, et al. Geneva: World Meteorological Organization.

IPCC. 2019. *IPCC Special Report on the Ocean and Cryosphere in a Changing Climate.* Ed. H.-O. Pörtner, D. C. Roberts, V. Masson-Delmotte, P. Zhai, M. Tignor, E. Poloczanska, K. Mintenbeck, A. Alegría, M. Nicolai, A. Okem, et al. Geneva: World Meteorological Organization.

Ishikawa, M., Y. Jamvaljav, A. Dashtseren, N. Sharkhuu, G. Davaa, Y. Iijima, N. Baatarbileg, and K. Yoshikawa. 2018. "Thermal States, Responsiveness and Degradation of Marginal Permafrost in Mongolia." *Permafrost and Periglacial Processes* 29 (4): 271–82.

Ivanov, N. 2017. "*Bekeen Kinaz* and His Progeny." In *Chokhoroonton* [From Chokhoroon], ed. A. N. Mironoff and M. M. Afanaseev, 37–38. Yakutsk: Cmik-Master Publishers.

Jackson, P., and P. Russell. 2009. "Life History Interviewing." Chapter 10 in *The SAGE Handbook of Qualitative Geography*, ed. D. DeLyser, S. Herbert, S. Aitken, M. Crang, and L. McDowell, 172–92. London: Sage.

Jochelson, W. 1895. *Zametki o naselenii Iakutskoi oblasti v istoriko-etnograficheskom otnoshenii* [Notes on the populations of the Yakut region in historical and ethnographic terms]. St. Petersburg: S. I. Khudyakov.

Jochelson, W. 1933. "The Yakut." *Anthropological Papers of the American Museum of Natural History* 33 (2). New York: AMNH.

Jorgenson, A. K., S. Fiske, K. Hubacek, J. Li, T. McGovern, T. Rick, J. B. Schor, W. Solecki, R. York, and A. Zycherman. 2019. "Social Science Perspectives on Drivers of and Responses to Global Climate Change." *Wiley Interdisciplinary Reviews: Climate Change* 10 (1): e554.

Kempton, W. 2001. "Cognitive Anthropology and the Environment." In *New Directions in Anthropology and Environment*, ed. C. L. Crumley, 49–71. Walnut Creek: AltaMira Press, 49–71.

Kerlinger, F. N. 1977. "The Influence of Research on Education Practice." *Educational Researcher* 6 (8): 5–12.

Kimmerer, R. 2013. *Braiding Sweetgrass: Indigenous Wisdom, Scientific Knowledge and the Teachings of Plants.* Minneapolis: Milkweed Editions.

Kirksey, S. E., and S. Helmreich. 2010. "The Emergence of Multispecies Ethnography." *Cultural Anthropology* 25 (4): 545–76.

Klubnikin, K., C. Annett, M. Cherkasova, M. Shishin, and I. Fotieva. 2000. "The Sacred and the Scientific: Traditional Ecological Knowledge in Siberian River Conservation." *Ecological Applications* 10 (5): 1296–1306.

Kondratev, M. 2007: *D'il Bilgete* [Season knowledge]. Yakutsk: Bichik.

Konstantinov, P. Iu., Iu. I. Torgovkin, and A. N. Fedorov. 1996. "Rassmotrena dinamika ekraniruiushchego sloia i razvitie nachal'nykh form termokarstovogo rel'efa"

[The dynamics of the shielding layer and the development of the initial forms of thermokarst relief considered]. In *Vliyanie klimata na mnogoletnemerzlye landshafty Tsentral'noi Yakutii* [Climate influence on permafrost landscapes of Central Yakutia], ed. T. Balobaev, M. K. Gavrilova, and A. N. Federov, 68–85. Yakutsk: Melnikov Permafrost Institute.

Kramer, S., D. A. Miller, and J. Newberger, directors. 2015. *The Anthropologist*. Written by S. Kramer, edited by D. A. Miller. Ironbound Films.

Krupnik, I. 2014. *Arctic Adaptations: Native Whalers and Reindeer Herders of Northern Eurasia*. Lebanon, NH: Dartmouth College Press.

Krupnik, I., and D. Jolly. 2002. *The Earth Is Faster Now: Indigenous Observations of Arctic Environmental Change*. Fairbanks: Arctic Research Consortium of the United States.

Ksenofontov, G. V. 1975. *Elleiada* [About Ellei]. Moscow: Nauk Publishers.

Ksenofontov, G. V. 1992 (1937). *Uraangkhai Sakhalaar* [Points in ancient history of the Yakut (Sakha)]. 2nd ed., vol. 2. Yakutsk: National Publishing House.

Kulakovski, A. E. 1979. *Nauchnye Trudy* [Scientific works]. Yakutsk: Yakutsk Book Publishers.

Kuruppu, N., and D. Liverman. 2011. "Mental Preparation for Climate Adaptation: The Role of Cognition and Culture in Enhancing Adaptive Capacity of Water Management in Kiribati." *Global Environmental Change* 21 (2): 657–69.

Kuzmin, Y. V., and S. K. Krivonogov. 1994. "The *Diring* Paleolithic Site, Eastern Siberia: Review of Geoarchaeological Studies." *Geoarchaeology* 9 (4): 287–300.

Kuzmin, Y. V., and S. K. Krivonogov. 1999. "More about *Diring Iuriakh*: Unsolved Geoarchaeological Problems at a 'Lower' Paleolithic Site in Central Siberia." *Geoarchaeology: An International Journal* 14 (4): 351–59.

Lawrence, R. L., and D. S. Paige. 2016. "What Our Ancestors Knew: Teaching and Learning Through Storytelling." *New Directions for Adult and Continuing Education* 149:63–72.

Larsen, J. N., G. Fondahl, and P. Schweitzer. 2010. *Arctic Social Iindicators: A Follow-up to the Arctic Human Development Report*. Copenhagen: Nordic Council of Ministers.

Larsen, J. N., P. Schweitzer, and A. Petrov, eds. 2015. *Arctic Social Indicators: ASI II: Implementation*. Copenhagen: Nordic Council of Ministers.

Lee, C. 2016. *Multilingualism Online*. New York: Routledge.

Lee, T. M., E. M. Markowitz, P. D. Howe, C. Y. Ko, and A. A. Leiserowitz. 2015. "Predictors of Public Climate Change Awareness and Risk Perception around the World." *Nature Climate Change* 5 (11): 1014–20. doi:10.1038/nclimate2728.

Levin, M. G., and N. N. Cheboksarov. 1955. "Khoziaistvenno-kul'turnye tipy i istoriko-etnograficheskie oblasti" [Economic and cultural types and historical and ethnographic areas]. *Sovietskaia etnografiia* 4:3–17.

Lindgren, A., G. Hugelius, and P. Kuhry. 2018. "Extensive Loss of Past Permafrost Carbon but a Net Accumulation into Present-Day Soils." *Nature* 560 (7717): 219.

Lisitsyna, O. M., and N. N. Romanovskii. 1998. "Dynamics of Permafrost in Northern Eurasia during the Last 20,000 Years." In *Proceedings of the Seventh International Permafrost Conference,* Yellowknife, Canada, June 23–27, 675–81.

Loudon, J. C. 1839. *An Encyclopedia of Cottage, Farm, and Villa Architecture and Furniture: Containing Numerous Designs for Dwellings . . . Each Design Accompanied by Analytical and Critical Remarks.* Vol. 1. London: Longman, Orme, Brown, Green, and Longmans.

Loughry, M., and J. McAdam. 2008. "Kiribati—Relocation and Adaptation." *Forced Migration Review* 31 (2): 51–52.

Maak, R. K. 1994 (1886). *Viliuiskii Okrug* [The Viliui Okrug]. 2nd ed. Moscow: Yana.

MacFarquhar, N. 2019. "Russian Land of Permafrost and Mammoths Is Thawing: Global Warming Is Shrinking the Permanently Frozen Ground across Siberia, Disrupting Everyday Life in One of the Coldest Inhabited Places on Earth." *New York Times,* August 4. https://www.nytimes.com/2019/08/04/world/europe/russia-siberia-yakutia-permafrost-global-warming.html.

Maffi, L. 2007. "Biocultural Diversity and Sustainability." In *Sage Handbook on Environment and Society,* ed. J. Pretty, A. S. Ball, T. Benton, J. S. Guivant, D. R. Lee, D. Orr, M. J. Pfeffer, and H. Ward, 267–77. London: SAGE.

Mainov, I. I. 1927. "Population of Yakutia." In Vittenburg 1927.

Maldonado, J. K. 2018. *Seeking Justice in an Energy Sacrifice Zone: Standing on Vanishing Land in Coastal Louisiana.* New York: Routledge.

Maldonado, J. K., B. Colombi, and R. Pandya. 2016. *Climate Change and Indigenous Peoples in the United States.* Switzerland: Springer International Publishing Switzerland.

Marino, E. 2015. *Fierce Climate, Sacred Ground.* Fairbanks: University of Alaska Press.

Mathews, F. 2019. "Living Cosmos Panpsychism." In *The Routledge Handbook of Panpsychism,* ed. W. Seager, 131–43. New York: Routledge:.

McGhee, R. 2001 [1996]. *Ancient People of the Arctic.* Vancouver: UBC Press.

Melnikov, P. I. 1978. "Closing Remarks." In *USSR Contribution Permafrost Second International Conference Proceedings,* ed. F. Sanger, 892. Washington, DC: National Academy of Sciences.

Melnikov, P. I., and A. I. Efimov. 1953. *Opyt ekspluatatsii podzemnykh vod v oblasti rasprostraneniia vechnoi merzloty Tsentral'noi Iakutii* [Experience of exploitation of groundwater in the permafrost area in Central Yakutia]. Moscow: Academy of Sciences USSR.

Mészáros, C. 2012. "The Alaas: Cattle Economy and Environmental Perception of Sedentary Sakhas in Central Yakutia." *Sibirica* 11:1–34.

Meyer, J. M. 2015. *Engaging the Everyday: Environmental Social Criticism and the Resonance Dilemma.* Boston: MIT Press.

Meyers, S. L. 2019. "China's Voracious Appetite for Timber Stokes Fury in Russia and Beyond." *New York Times,* April 9, 2019. https://www.nytimes.com/2019/04/09/world/asia/chinas-voracious-appetite-for-timber-stokes-fury-in-russia-and-beyond.html.

Middendorf, A. 1868. *Putashestvie na sever i vostok Sibiri* [Travels in the north and east of Siberia]. Part 2. Saint Petersburg: Academy of Sciences.

Mikhaleva-Saia, N. V., A. E. Iakovlev, N. K. Kuz'mina, and N. S. Ctepanova, eds. 2013. *Mikhail Nikolaevich Timofeev-Tereshkin: Na rybezhe dvukh epoch* [Mikhail Nikolaevich Timofeev-Tereshkin: On the eve of two epochs]. Yakutsk: Smik-Master Publishers.

Mironoff, A. N., and M. M. Afanaseev, eds. 2017. *Chokhoroonton* [From Chokhoroon]. Yakutsk: Cmik-Master Publishers.

Mochanov, Y. A. 1969. "Drevneishie etapy zaseleniya Severo-Vostoka Azii I Aliaski" [The earliest stages of settlement in northeast Asia and Alaska]. *Sovietskaia Arkheologiia* 1:79–86.

Mochanov, Y. A. 1977. *Drevneishie etapy zaseleniia chelovekom Severo-Vostoka Azii* [The oldest stages of human settlement in northeast Asia]. Novosibirsk: Nauka.

Mochanov, Y. A., and S. A. Fedoseeva. 2013. *Ocherko dopis'mennoi istorii Yakutii. Epokha kamnya* [Essays on the preliterate history of Yakutia: The stone age]. Vol. 1. Yakutsk: Dani Almas.

Moseley, C. 2009. "UNESCO Interactive Atlas of the World's Languages in Danger." Accessed October 8, 2020. http://www.unesco.org/new/fileadmin/MULTI MEDIA/HQ/CLT/pdf/aboutEndangeredLanguages-WV-EN-1.pdf.

Nadasdy, P. 2011. "Application of Environmental Knowledge: The Politics of Constructing Society/Nature." In *Knowing Nature: Conversations at the Intersection of Political Ecology and Science Studies*, ed. M. J. Goldman, P. Nadasdy, and M. D. Turner, 129–33. Chicago: University of Chicago Press.

Nedokuchaev, N. K. 1927. "Sel'skokhoziaistvennoe delo Iakutii" [Agricultural practices of Yakutia]. In Vittenburg 1927, 494.

Netting, R. M. 1968. *Hill Farmers of Nigeria: Cultural Ecology of the Kofyar of the Jos Plateau*. Seattle: University of Washington Press.

Netting, R. M.1993. *Smallholder, Householders: Farm Families and the Ecology of Intensive, Sustainable Agriculture*. Stanford: Stanford University Press.

Nikitin, S. A. 1930. "Agricultural Methods in the Yakutsk District." In *Materialy po izucheniiu sel'skogo khoziaistva Iakutskogo Okruga po dannym agronomichesogo otriada Iakutskoi ekspeditsii Akademii Hauk SSSR 1926 g.* [Material of the study of agriculture, Yakutsk area, according to the findings of the agronomy sector of USSR Academy of Sciences expedition 1926], ed. S. A. Nikitin, A. N. Skalozubova, K. A. Benua, and V. N. Poriadin, 361–64. Leningrad: Academy of Sciences of the USSR.

Nikolaev, M. E. 2009. "The Inexhaustible Source of the Sakha People's Creative Life." In *Sbornik dokladov i vystuplenii na prezentatsii tre'ego izdaniia slovaria Iakutskogo iazyka E. K. Pekarskogo i iubileiinogo meropriiatiia, posvashchennogo 150 letnym iubileiam E. K. Pekarskogo i V. A. Seroshevskogo* [Collection of reports and presentations of the third edition of E. K. Pekarski's dictionary and the celebratory event, honoring the 150th anniversary of E. K. Pekarski and V. A. Seroshevskii], ed. N. N. Kolodeznikov, 6–11. Moscow: Moscow House of Nationalities.

Nikolaev, S. I. 1961. "Rybnaia pishcha dorevoliutsionnykh Viliuichan" [Fish foods of prerevolutionary Viluchaans]. In *Sbornik: Statei I materialov po etnografii narodov Yakutii, II* [Collection: Articles and materials of Sakha ethnography], 43–46. Yakutsk: Yakutsk Book Publishers.

Nikolaev, S. I. 1970. *Iakuty: Nauchnyi otchet* [The Yakut: Scientific accounts]. Fund 5, Op. 1, delo 501. Yakutsk: Russian Academy of Sciences, Siberian Department.

Nikolaev, S. I. 1976. *Khoziaisvennye aspekty skotovodcheskogo osvoeniia Iakutii* [Economic aspects of cattle breeding development in Yakutia]. Fond 5, Op. 1, Ex 532. Yakutsk: IHRISNA.

Nikolaev, S. I. 1995. *Origins of the Sakha People*. Yakutsk: NIPK Sakha polygrafizdat.

Nikolaev, S. I. 2009a. *Foods of the Yakut*. Yakutsk: Yakutsk Edge.

Nikolaev, S. I. 2009b. *Narod Sakha* [The Sakha people]. Yakutsk: Yakutsk Edge Publishers.

Nikolov, N., and H. Helmisaari. 1992. "Silvics of the Circumpolar Boreal Forest Tree Species." In *A Systems Analysis of the Global Boreal Forest*, ed. H. H. Shugart, R. Leemans, and G. B. Bonan, 13–84. Cambridge: Cambridge University Press.

Noble, A. G. 2007. *Traditional Buildings: A Global Survey of Structural Forms and Cultural Functions*. London: I. B. Tauris.

Nunn, P. D., and N. J. Reid. 2016. "Aboriginal Memories of Inundation of the Australian Coast Dating from More than 7000 Years Ago." *Australian Geographer* 47 (1): 11–47. doi:10.1080/00049182.2015.1077539.

Nyong, A., F. Adesina, and B. O. Elasha. 2007. "The Value of Indigenous Knowledge in Climate Change Mitigation and Adaptation Strategies in the African Sahel." *Mitigation and Adaptation Strategies for Global Change* 12 (5): 787–97.

Oberman, N. G., and A. M. Liygin. 2009. "Predicting Permafrost Degradation: Case Study of North European Russia." *Exploration and Protection of Natural Resources* 7:15–20.

Okladnikov, A. P. 1955. *Iakutiia do prisoedineniia k russkomu gosudarstvu* [Yakutia before its incorporation into the Russian state]. Moscow: Academy of Sciences.

Okladnikov, A. P. 1970. *Yakutia*. Montreal: McGill-Queens.

Oliver-Smith, A. 1999. "Peru's Five-Hundred-Year Earthquake: Vulnerability in Historical Context." In *The Angry Earth: Disaster in Anthropological Perspective*, ed. A. Oliver-Smith and S. M. Hoffman, 74–88. 1st ed. New York: Routledge.

Oliver-Smith, A., and S. M. Hoffman, eds. 2019. *The Angry Earth: Disaster in Anthropological Perspective*. 2nd ed. New York: Routledge.

O'Neill, S. J., and S. Graham. 2016. "(En)visioning Place-Based Adaptation to Sea-Level Rise." *Geo: Geography and Environment* 3 (2): e00028. doi: 10.1002/geo2.28.

Orlove, B., R. Shwom, E. Markowitz, and S. Cheong. 2020. "Climate Decision-Making." *Annual Review of Environment and Resources* 45:1.

Orlove, B. S., J. C. Chiang, and M. A. Cane. 2000. "Forecasting Andean Rainfall and Crop Yield from the Influence of El Niño on Pleiades Visibility." *Nature* 403 (6765): 68.

Orlove, B. S., J. C. Chiang, and M. A. Cane. 2002. "Ethnoclimatology in the Andes: A Cross-Disciplinary Study Uncovers a Scientific Basis for the Scheme Andean

Potato Farmers Traditionally Use to Predict the Coming Rains." *American Scientist* 90 (5): 428–35.

Ostrom, E. 2010. "Polycentric Systems for Coping with Collective Action and Global Environmental Change." *Global Environmental Change* 20 (4): 550–57.

Paerregaard, K. 2013. "Bare Rocks and Fallen Angels: Environmental Change, Climate Perceptions and Ritual Practice in the Peruvian Andes." *Religions* 4 (2): 290–305.

Paine, R. T. 1995. "A Conversation on Refining the Concept of Keystone Species." *Conservation Biology* 9 (4): 962–64.

Pakhomov, I. O. 1999. *Upravlenie zemel'nymi otnosheniiami u Iakutii* [Administration of land relations in Yakutia]. Yakutsk: Sakhapoligrafizdat.

Palsson, G., B. Szerszynski, S. Sörlin, J. Marks, B. Avril, C. Crumley, H. Hackmann, P. Holm, J. Ingram, A. Kirman, and M. P. Buendía. 2013. "Reconceptualizing the 'Anthropos' in the Anthropocene: Integrating the Social Sciences and Humanities in Global Environmental Change Research." *Environmental Science & Policy* 28:3–13.

Pavlov, P., J. I. Svendsen, and S. Indrelid. 2001. "Human Presence in the European Arctic Nearly 40,000 Years Ago." *Nature* 413 (6851): 64–67.

Pavlova, M. N. 2012. *Suntaar Kutanatyn Töröttere: N. I. Ivanov Kuola-Uchuutal* [Suntaar's Kutana ancestors: N. I. Ivanov Kolya-Teacher]. Yakutsk: Dani Almas.

Palova, M. N. 2015. *Suntaar Kutanatyn 100 Alaastara / N. I. Ivanov-Kuola Uchuutal* [Suntaar's Kutana 100 *Alaas* / N. I. Nikolaev—Kolya Teacher]. Yakutsk: Dani-Almas.

Pekarski, E. K. 1958 [1899]. *Slovar Iakutskogo Iazyka* [Dictionary of the Sakha language]. Vol. 1. St. Petersburg: Academy of Sciences.

Pitassio, A., and V. Zaslavsky. 1985. Introduction to *Soviet Peasants*, by Lev Timofeev. New York: Telo Press.

Pitulko V. V., E. Y. Pavlova, and P. A. Nikolskiy. 2017. "Revising the Archaeological Record of the Upper Pleistocene Arctic Siberia: Human Dispersal and Adaptations in MIS 3 and 2." *Quaternary Science Reviews* 165:127–48.

Pitulko, V. V., E. Y. Pavlova, P. A. Nikolskiy, and V. V. Ivanova. 2012. "The Oldest Art of the Eurasian Arctic: Personal Ornaments and Symbolic Objects from Yana RHS, Arctic Siberia." *Antiquity* 86 (333): 642–59.

Pitulko, V. V., A. N. Tikhonov, E. Y. Pavlova, P. A. Nikolskiy, K. E. Kuper, and R. N. Polozov. 2016. "Early Human Presence in the Arctic: Evidence from 45,000-Year-Old Mammoth Remains." *Science* 351 (6270): 260–63.

Platten, S., and T. Henfrey. 2009. "The Cultural Keystone Concept: Insights from Ecological Anthropology." *Human Ecology* 37 (4): 491.

Plows, A., ed. 2018. *Messy Ethnographies in Action*. Wilmington: Vernon Press.

Poriadin, V. I. 1930. "Lugovodstvo v Iakutskom raione" [Meadow farming in the Yakutsk district]. In *Materialy po izucheniiu sel'skogo khoziaistva Iakutskogo Okruga po dannym agronomichesogo otriada Iakutskoi ekspeditsii Akademii Hauk SSSR 1926 g.* [Material of the study of agriculture, Yakutsk area, according to the findings of the agronomy sector of USSR Academy of Sciences expedition 1926], ed. S. A. Nikitin,

A. N. Skalozubova, K. A. Benua, and V. N. Poriadin, 372–76. Leningrad: Academy of Sciences Publishers.

Powell, C. 2016. "Revitalizing the Ethnosphere: Global Society, Ethnodiversity, and the Stakes of Cultural Genocide." *Genocide Studies and Prevention: An International Journal* 10 (1): 44–59.

Pretty, J. 2011. "Interdisciplinary Progress in Approaches to Address Social-Ecological and Ecocultural Systems." *Environmental Conservation* 38 (2): 127–39.

Prokop'eva, A. N. 2015. "Alaas kak element sakral'nogo landshafta v kul'ture sovremennykh Iakutov" [*Alaas* as an element of the sacred landscape in the culture of modern Yakuts]. *Teoriia i praktika obshchestvennogo razvitiia*, 3.

Protopopov, A. V., et al. 2018. *Mamont i drugie drevnie zhivotnye Sibiri* [Mammoth and other ancient animals of Siberia]. Yakutsk: Bichik.

Puri, R. K. 2015. "The Uniqueness of Every Day." Chapter 10 in *Climate Cultures: Anthropological Perspectives on Climate Change*, ed. J. Barnes and M. R. Dove, 249–72. New Haven: Yale University Press.

Putin, V. *Zasedanie Soveta po mezhnatsional'nym otnosheniiam* [Meeting of the Council of Interethnic Relations]. July 20, 2017. http://kremlin.ru/events/presi dent/news/55109.

Rao, M. P., N. K. Davi, R. D'Arrigo, J. Skees, B. Nachin, C. Leland, B. Lyon, S. Y. Wang, and O. Byambasuren. 2015. "Dzuds, Droughts, and Livestock Mortality in Mongolia." *Environmental Research Letters* 10 (7): 074012.

Ray, L. L. 1973. *Permafrost*. Informational leaflet. Denver: U.S. Geological Survey.

Redman, C. L. 1999. *Human Impact on Ancient Environments*. Tucson: University of Arizona Press.

Reyes-García, V. 2010. "The Relevance of Traditional Knowledge Systems for Ethnopharmacological Research: Theoretical and Methodological Contributions." *Journal of Ethnobiology and Ethnomedicine* 6 (1): 32.

Reyes-García, V., P. Benyei, A. B. Junqueira, E. Conde, and T. A. Huanca. "A Complex Matrix: Tsimane' Perceptions of Environmental Change." *Society and Natural Resources*. Under review.

Reyes-García, V., Á. Fernández-Llamazares, M. Guèze, A. Garcés, M. Mallo, M. Vila-Gómez, and M. Vilaseca. 2016. "Local Indicators of Climate Change: The Potential Contribution of Local Knowledge to Climate Research." *Wiley Interdisciplinary Reviews: Climate Change* 7 (1): 109–24.

Ricaut, F. X., A. Fedoseeva, C. Keyser-Tracqui, E. Crubézy, and B. Ludes. 2005. "Ancient DNA Analysis of Human Neolithic Remains Found in Northeastern Siberia." *American Journal of Physical Anthropology* 126 (4): 458–62.

Romanova, E. N. 1987. "Yakutski Praznyk Ysyakh: Traditsii i sovremenost" [The Yakut holiday ysyakh: Traditions and modernity]. Ph.D. dissertation, N. N. Mikhailo-Maklaya Ethnographic Institute, St. Petersburg.

Romanova, E. N. 1997. *Liudi solnechnykh luchei, s povod'iami za spinoi: Simvolika sud'by v kontekste miforitual'noi traditsii iakutov* [People of the sunbeams, with reins on their backs: Symbolism of fate in the context of the Yakut mythological tradition]. Moscow: Academy of Sciences.

Romanova, E. N. 2015. "Lanshaft v kul'ture pamiati" [Landscapes in cultural memory]. *Arctic in the 21st Century Humanitarian Science* 2 (5): 93–98.

Romanova, E. N., and V. B. Ignatieva. 2012. "Anthropology and Permafrost: Landscape and Identity." In *Nature and Culture*, ed. N. S. Pavlova, 61–75. Yakutsk: SVFU Publishing House.

Romanovsky, V. E., A. L. Kholodov, S. S. Marchenko, N. G. Oberman, D. S. Drozdov, G. V. Malkova, N. G. Moskalenko, A. A. Vasiliev, D. O. Sergeev, and M. N. Zheleznyak. 2008. "Thermal State and Fate of Permafrost in Russia: First Results of IPY (Plenary Paper)." In *Proceedings of the Ninth International Conference on Permafrost*, ed. D. L. Kane and K. M. Hinkel, 2:1511–18. Institute of Northern Engineering, University of Alaska, Fairbanks, June 29–July 3.

Roncoli, C., T. Crane, and B. Orlove. 2009. "Fielding Climate Change in Cultural Anthropology." In *Anthropology and Climate Change: From Encounters to Actions*, ed. S. Crate and M. Nuttall, 87–115. Walnut Creek: Left Coast Press.

Rose, D. B., T. van Dooren, M. Chrulew, S. Cooke, M. Kearnes, and E. O'Gorman. 2012. "Thinking Through the Environment, Unsettling the Humanities." *Environmental Humanities* 1(1): 1–5.

Rudiak-Gould, P. 2012. "Promiscuous Corroboration and Climate Change Translation: A Case Study from the Marshall Islands." *Global Environmental Change* 22 (1): 46–54.

Russian Federation. 2016. *Ob osobennostiakh predostavleniia grazhdanam zemel'nykh uchastkov, nakhodiashchikhsia v gosudarstvennoi ili munitsipal'noi sobstvennosti i raspoloz- hennykh na territoriiakh sub'ektov Rossiiskoi Federatsii, vkhodiahshikh v sostav Dal'nevostochnogo federal'nogo okruga, i o vnesenii izmenenii v otdel'nie zakonodatel'nie akty Rossiiskoy Federatsii* [On the specifics of granting to citizens land plots in state or municipal ownership, located in the territories of the constituent entities of the Russian Federation within the Far East Federal District, and on the introduction of changes to individual legal acts of the Russian Federation]. Federal Law no. 199-F3, May 1.

Ruttan, L. M., M. Borgerhoff Mulder, F. Berkes, J. Colding, C. Folke, E. Fratkin, J. G. Galaty, K. Homewood, P. D. Little, E. Ostrom, and H. H. Prins. 1999. "Are East African Pastoralists Truly Conservationists?" *Current Anthropology* 40 (5): 621–52.

Sakha Republic. 2018. *Ob okhrane vechnoi merzloty v Respublike Sakha (Iakutiia) Priniat postanovleniem Gosudarstvennogo Sobraniia (Il Tumen) Respubliki Sakha (Iakutiia) N 2006-3 N 1571-V ЗАКОН, РЕСПУБЛИКИ САХА (ЯКУТИЯ), от 22 мая 2018 года N 2006-3 N 1571-V* [On the preservation of permafrost in the Sakha Republic (Yakutia), accepted into law by the Parliament (Il Tumen) of the Sakha Republic (Yakutia) on May 22, 2018].

Savitskaia, S. V. 2017. "Sopostavitel'noe issledovanie iazykovogo soznaniia russkikh i iakutov (na premere obraza rodiny)" [Comparative study of the language consciousness of Russians and Yakuts (on the example of the image of the Motherland)]. *Questions of Psycholinguistics* 1 (31): 203–16.

Savvin, A. A. 2005. *Pishcha iakutov do razvitiia zemledeliia: Opyt istoriko-etnograficheskoi monografii* [Food of the Yakuts before the development of agriculture: The experience from historical and ethnographic monographs]. Yakutsk: Institute of Humanitarian Research.

Savvinov, G. N., and V. S. Makarov. 2015. *Alaas: Sakha noruotun bihige* [*Alaas*: Sakha people's cradle]. Yakutsk: Bichik.

Schneider, S. H. 2009. *Science as a Contact Sport: Inside the Battle to Save Earth's Climate*. Washington, DC: National Geographic Books.

Scott, C. 1996. "Science for the West, Myth for the Rest." In *Naked Science: Anthropological Inquiry into Boundaries, Power, and Knowledge*, ed. L. Nader, 69–86. New York: Routledge.

Seroshevskii, V. L. 1993 (1896). *Iakuty*. Moscow: ROSSPEN.

Shaffer, L. J. 2018. "Rain Rituals as a Barometer of Vulnerability in an Uncertain Climate." *Journal of Ecological Anthropology* 19 (1): 1–17.

Sheludiakova, V. A. 1961. "Account of the Ancient Land Making of Sakha." In *Sbornik: Statei i materialov po etnografii narodov Iakutii, II* [Collection: Articles and materials of Sakha ethnography]. Yakutsk: Yakutsk Book Publishers.

Shepelev, A. G., E. V. Starostin, A. N. Fedorov, and T. Kh. Maksimov. 2016. "Predvaritel'nyi analiz zapasov organicheskogo ugleroda i azota v porodakh ledovogo kompleksa Tsentral'noi Iakutii." [Preliminary analysis of organic carbon and nitrogen reserves in the rocks of the Central Yakutia ice complex]. *Prirodnye resursy Arktiki I Subarktiki* 2:82.

Shiklomanov, N. I., D. A. Streletskii, T. B. Swales, V. A. Kokorev. 2017. "Climate Change and Stability of Urban Infrastructure in Russian Permafrost Regions: Prognostic Assessment Based on GCM Climate Projections." *Geographical Review* 107 (1): 125–42.

Shimanskii, A. 1886. *Raznye izvestiia: Pishcha Yakutov* [Various news: The food of the Yakut]. Irkutsk: B.I.

Shumskii, P. A. 1952. "Issledovanie iskopaemikh l'dov Tsentral'noi Iakutii" [The study of fossil ice in Central Yakutia]. In *Issledovanie vechnoi merzloti v Iakutskoi respublike* [The study of permafrost in the Yakut republic]. Collection of Scientific Works. M: Academy of Sciences Publishers, issue 3, 142–61.

Shur, Y. L. 1988. *Verkhnii gorizont tolshchi merzlikh porod i termokarst* [The upper horizon thickness of permafrost and thermokarst]. Novosibirsk: Nauka.

Siberian Desk. 2018. "Siberia Activists Urge Government to Keep Mandatory Yakut Lessons." Accessed October 7, 2020. https://www.rferl.org/a/siberia-activists -urge-government-to-keep-mandatory-yakut-lessons/29278777.html.

"Siberia Will Become a Desert! If We Don't Stop the Chinese" [Sibir stanet pustynei! Esli my ne ostanovim Kitaitsev]. 2018. YouTube video. Viewed October 7, 2020. https://www.youtube.com/watch?v=kfTpDWRHUhM.

Silk, J. B. 1980. "Adoption and Kinship in Oceania." *American Anthropologist* 82 (4): 799–820.

Sillitoe, P. 2007. "Local Science vs. Global Science: An Overview." In *Local Science vs. Global Science: Approaches to Indigenous Knowledge in International Development*, ed. P. Sillitoe, 1–22. New York: Berghahn Books.

Sirdik, A. 2006: *Ytyk Kere Sirdere* [Sacred places]. Yakutsk: Bichik.

Sivtsev, D. K. 1996 (1947). *Sakha fol'klora: Khomyyrynn'yk* [Sakha folklore: Collection]. Novosibirsk: Nauka.

Sleptsov, P. A., ed. 1972. *Yakutsko-Russkii slovar* [Yakut-Russian dictionary]. Moscow: "Soviet Encyclopedia" publisher.

Slezkine, Y. 1994. *Arctic Mirrors*. Ithaca: Cornell University Press.

Slimak, L., J. I. Svendsen, J. Mangerud, H. Plisson, H. P. Heggen, A. Brugere, and P. Y. Pavlov. 2011. "Late Mousterian Persistence Near the Arctic Circle." *Science* 332 (6031): 841–45.

Solovyev, P. A. 1959. *Kriolitozona severnoi chasti Leno-Amginskogo mezhdurechiia* [Cyrological zones of the northern part of Lena-Amga inter-river zone]. Moscow: USSR Academy of Sciences.

Solovyev, P. A. 1973. "Thermokarst Phenomena and Landforms Due to Frost Heaving in Central Yakutia." *Periglacial Bulletin* 23:135–55.

Solovyeva, V. 2021. "Climate Change in Oymyakon: Perceptions, Responses and How Local Knowledge May Inform Policy." PhD diss., George Mason University.

Solutions Project, The. 2020. "The Solutions Project." Accessed October 22, 2020. http://www.thesolutionsproject.org/.

Sommer, Doris. 2006. "Wiggle Room." In *Cultural Agency in the Americas*, ed. J. M. Barbero, D. Taylor, and N. G. Canclini, 1–28. Durham: Duke University Press.

Sosin, I. M. 2010. *Kün-D'il Bilgete* [Folk forecasting]. Yakutsk: Bichik.

Steward, J. H. 1955. *Theory of Culture Change*. Urbana: University of Illinois Press.

Suleymanov, A. A. 2018. "'Resursy kholoda' v sisteme pitaniia iakutov: Traditsii i sovremennost'" ["Resources of the cold" in the food supply system of Yakutia: Tradition and modernity]. *Nauchnii dialog* (2): 263–74.

Sumgin, M. I. 1927. *Permafrost Soils in the USSR*. Vladivostok: Academy of Sciences.

Suny, R. G. 1993. *The Revenge of the Past*. Stanford: Stanford University Press.

Svinoboev, A. N., and A. B. Neustroeva. 2017. "Izmenenie klimata i uslovii zhizin na Severe v vospriniatii korennogo naceleniia" [Climate change and living conditions in the North in the perception of the Indigenous population]. *Urbanistika* (4): 28–39.

Takakura, H. 2010. "The Social and Symbolic Construction of Alaas Landscapes in the Siberian Forest." *Acta Slavica Iaponica* (28): 51–69.

Takakura, H. 2015. *Arctic Pastoralist Sakha: Ethnography of Evolution and Microadaptation in Siberia*. Melbourne: Trans Pacific Press.

Tammiksaar, E. 2002. "The Contributions of Karl Ernst von Baer to the Investigation of the Physical Geography of the Arctic in the 1830s–40s." *Polar Record* 38 (205): 121–40.

Tatar, M. 2017. *The Classic Fairy Tales*. 2nd International Student Edition, Norton Critical Editions. New York: W. W. Norton.

Tengö, M., E. S. Brondizio, T. Elmqvist, P. Malmer, and M. Spierenburg. 2014. "Connecting Diverse Knowledge Systems for Enhanced Ecosystem Governance: The Multiple Evidence Base Approach." *Ambio* 43 (5): 579–91.

Tichotsky, J. 2014. *Russia's Diamond Colony: The Republic of Sakha*. New York: Routledge.

Tokarev, S. A., and I. S. Gurich. 1964. "The Yakuts." In *The Peoples of Siberia*, ed. M. G. Levin and L. P. Potapov, 241–304. Chicago: University of Chicago Press.

Trianovski, A., and C. Mooney. 2019. "Radical Warming in Siberia Leaves Millions on Unstable Ground." *Washington Post*, October 3. https://www.washingtonpost .com/graphics/2019/national/climate-environment/climate-change-siberia/.

Troeva, E. I., A. P. Isaev, M. M. Cherosov, and N. S. Karpov, eds. 2010. *The Far North: Plant Biodiversity and Ecology of Yakutia*. Dordrecht: Springer.

Troshanski, V. F. 1902. *Evolutziia chorni veri u Iakutov* [The evolution of the Yakut black belief]. Kazan: Kazan Universitet.

Trotter, J. A., I. S. Williams, A. Nicora, M. Mazza, and M. Rigo. 2015. "Long-Term Cycles of Triassic Climate Change: A New δ18O Record from Conodont Apatite." *Earth and Planetary Science Letters* 415:165–74.

Tschakert, P., K. Dietrich, K. Tamminga, E. Prins, J. Shaffer, E. Liwenga, and A. Asiedu. 2014. "Learning and Envisioning under Climatic Uncertainty: An African Experience." *Environment and Planning A* 46 (5): 1049–68.

Van Everdingen, R. O. 1998. *Multi-Language Glossary of Permafrost and Related Ground-Ice Terms*. International Permafrost Association.

Veland, S., R. Howitt, D. Dominey-Howes, F. Thomalla, and D. Houston. 2013. "Procedural Vulnerability: Understanding Environmental Change in a Remote Indigenous Community." *Global Environmental Change* 23 (1): 314–26.

Vinokurov N. N., A. P. Isaev, N. K. Potapova, and S. N. Nogovitsyna. 2001. "On the Outbreak of Mass Reproduction of the Siberian Silkworm in Central Yakutia in 1999–2000." *Science and Education* 1:65–68.

Vitebsky, P. 2006. Reply. *Natural History* 115:10.

Vittenburg, P. V., ed. 1927. *Iakutia: Sbornik statei* [Yakutia: Collection of articles]. Komissiia po izucheniiu Iakutskoi ASSR, vol 1. Leningrad: Academy of Sciences of the USSR.

Vittenburg, P. V., ed. 2013 [1927]. *Yakutia: Collections of Papers*. Leningrad: Academy of Sciences.

Votiakov, I. N. 1961. *Physical and Mechanical Properties of Permafrost Grounds of Central Yakutia* [Fiziko-mekhanicheskie svoistva mnogoletnemerzlykh gruntov Tsentral'noi Yakutii]. Moscow: USSR Academy of Sciences.

Walshe, R., and A. Argumedo. 2016. "Ayni, Ayllu, Yanantin and Chanincha: The Cultural Values Enabling Adaptation to Climate Change in Communities of the Potato Park, in the Peruvian Andes." *GAIA: Ecological Perspectives for Science and Society* 25 (3): 166–73.

Warner, M. 1995. *From the Beast to the Blonde: On Fairy Tales and Their Tellers*. New York: Farrar, Straus and Giroux.

Waters, M. R., S. L. Forman, and J. M. Pierson. 1997. *"Diring Yuriakh*: A Lower Paleolithic Site in Central Siberia." *Science* 275 (5304): 1281–84.

Yakovlev, A. E. 2006. "Iz istorii administrativno-territorial'nogo deleniia ulusa" [From the history of the administrative-territorial divisions of the *ulus*]. In *Suntarskii ulus* [The Suntar *ulus*], ed. A. K. Akimov, 48–59. Yakutsk: Bichik.

Yakovleva, A. I. 2009. *The Great Nature's Healing Strength*. Yakutsk: Folk Healing Association.

Yletyinen, J., J. M. Tylianakis, C. Stone, and P. O'B. Lyver. 2020. "Cascading Impacts of Environmental Change on Indigenous Culture." *Preprints* 2020, 202005.0475.

Yonova, O. V. 1961. "Plant Food of Sakha." In *Sbornik: Statei i materialov po etnografii narodov Iakutii, II* [Collection: Articles and materials of Sakha ethnography]. Yakutsk: Yakutsk Book Publishers.

Yoshikawa, K. 2017. *Merzlota v nashi vremia* [Permafrost in our time]. Yakutsk: Publishing House SVFU.

Zikov, F. M. 2013. "Hunting." In *Iakuty Sakha* [The Yakut Sakha], ed. N. A. Alekseev, E. N. Romanova, and Z. P. Sokolova, 151–53. Moscow: Nauka.

Zubrilov, V. 1891. *O poleznykh iskopaemykh Iakutskoi oblasti. Pamiatnaia kniga Iakutskoi oblasti na 1891 g* [About minerals in Yakutsk region. The memorial book of the Yakutsk region for 1891]. Yakutsk: Regional Board Printing House.

Index

About the Author

Susan Alexandra Crate is an environmental and cognitive anthropologist who has conducted research in Russia, Canada, Peru, Wales, Kiribati, Mongolia, and Virginia's Chesapeake Bay. She is a professor of anthropology at George Mason University. She served on the American Anthropology Association's Task Force on Climate Change and as lead author on the IPCC Special Report on Oceans and Cryosphere.